Between the Strings

The Secret Lives of Guitars

Between the Strings

The Secret Lives of Guitars

John August Schroeter

*Merry Christmas
2006,
A little Inspiration!
Have Fun!
Love Mike*

John August Music • Colorado Springs, CO

PUBLISHED BY JOHN AUGUST MUSIC

Colorado Springs, CO

Guitar Photography: John August Schroeter

B.B. King Photo: Al Pereira / Star File

Book design by Ed Rother and Carrie Alexander

Visit our website at www.johnaugustmusic.com

ISBN 0-9749737-0-X

Printed in the United States of America

First Edition

Acknowledgements

It is no exaggeration to say that hundreds of people were involved in the making of this book. They include not only the extraordinary artists who kindly shared these personal glimpses of "life with the guitar," but their business managers, publicists, road managers, and friends, whose generous and spontaneous assistance helped connect all the dots. The few I'd like to highlight here are representative of the friends, earth angels, and tireless unsung wizards who pull the strings and push the buttons behind the curtain and somehow make everything work:

Gina Adams, Bruce Adolph, LaReau Anderson, April Arceo, Paul Babin, Jason Bagdade, Sharleen Bazeghi, Pat Berguson, Dick Boak, Lisa Breiner, David Budge, Jim Cosgrove, Sherman Darby, Sharon Devol, Joe Donofrio, Jim Donoughe, Marc Dottore, Holli Noel Dykes, Linda Elfman, Susan Feliciano, Mark Ferjulian, Wendy Foster, Tina France, Ron Garant, Alison de Grassi, Mitch Greenhill, Joyce Hall, Lisa Jenkins, James Jensen, Regina Joskow, Fred Kewley, Meg Lawson, Jared Levine, Suzanne Little, Erin Morris, Dennis McNally, Dave Nichols, Colonel Jack Parber, Milena Parber, Anthony Parber, Chris Parber, Bill Piburn, Lisa Pina, Gail Pollock, Joe Priesnitz, Duane Probes, Eduardo Rother, Tracy Rotkiewicz, David Schenk, Susan Schiffer, Jenna Schroeter, JoBeth Schroeter, Jolene Schroeter, Tom Simonson, Evan Skopp, John Sloan, Aaron Stang, Tiffany Steffens, Paula Szeigis, Maggie Taylor, Jennifer Templeton, Eric Tingstad, Denise Waic, Cathy Williams, Carey Williams, and about a hundred others.

In addition, the vast majority of quotes that appear throughout the book were drawn from the interviews I conducted during my days as publisher and editor of *Fingerstyle Guitar Magazine*. Thanks to *Fingerstyle's* current publisher, MI Media, for the permission to include them here. High praises are also in order for the publishers of *Guitar Player, Frets, Guitar One, Guitar World, Guitar World Acoustic, Acoustic Guitar, Chitarre, Vintage Guitar, 20th Century Guitar, Akustik Gitarre, Guitarra, Performing Songwriter, Guitar Techniques, Flatpicking Guitar*—all fellow celebrators of the guitar life! Thanks also to Mel Bay—he taught us all how to play.

And finally, thanks to you, the musically aware, curious, and searching lover of the guitar:

> May you play well and often; may your strings be bright
> May your calluses not soften, may your harmonies be tight
> May your rhythms be chunky; and your audiences receptive
> May your chords be funky, and your cadences deceptive
> May the 7th and 3rd forever be flatted
> May your music be heard; may your vocals be scatted
> May your solos and blues be played *con amore*
> You cannot lose when the guitar tells the story
> —*John August Schroeter*

To all those who survived their first guitar.

Contents

Introduction

by B.B. King

The first good guitar I ever owned was a Gibson acoustic with a DeArmond pickup that I bought in Memphis with the help of my cousin, Bukka White. It's the guitar I was playing in 1949 at a gig in Twist, Arkansas, about forty-five miles northwest of Memphis. Well, it used to get quite cold in Twist, so they'd take what looked like a big garbage pail and half fill it with kerosene. They'd light that fuel and set it in the middle of the dance floor, and people danced around it. Flames would be coming up out of that thing, and it heated the place right up. Well, one night two guys started to fight, and one knocked the other right over onto this heater. And when that happened, all that flaming kerosene came spilling out onto the floor. Everybody started to run for the front door—including B.B. King! But when I got on the outside, I realized that I had left my guitar behind, so I ran back for it. By that time, the building was burning rapidly and it started to collapse around me. I almost lost my life trying to save my guitar. Two other people weren't so lucky. Well, the next morning we found out that these two guys were fighting about a lady. I never did meet the lady, but I learned that her name was Lucille. I decided to name my guitar Lucille to remind me never to do a thing like that again!

I wish I still had that guitar; I'm playing Lucille the 16th now. But whatever form Lucille has taken over the years, she has always been my friend, my tutor, and my way of life. The guitar has been practically *everything* to me. And though I almost lost my life trying to save my guitar all those years ago, there was one time when the guitar actually saved *my* life. I've been in eighteen automobile accidents in my time, and in one of them, the car rolled over several times. When it came to rest, my guitar was lying on the ground edgewise, holding the car up off of me. It really was!

So I love the guitar. It's still teaching me, and I'm still learning. And knowledge is power. When you learn about anything, it means you know something more than you knew before. So if anyone wants to learn about the guitar, or what we think about the guitar—if anybody wants to learn what it has done for us, and why so many of us still hang on and try to play it today, read this book and you'll learn why.

9

Michael Johnson

GUITARS ARE FROM VENUS—WOMEN ARE TOO

Guitars are alive. They breathe, they break—they even break hearts. "A chattel with a soul," as Segovia put it. Auggie Rassmussen, a luthier from Chicago I met years ago, used to say that you have to build a guitar knowing what the wood is going to do. It's going to shrink, crack, expand in the humidity, dry out, etc. "Nozingk vill stop ze voot," he'd say.

I've had three stolen from me. One, a very expensive designer thing that had no real sound or soul; another was an ancient and beautiful Martin 000-18, and my soul mate was an old Guild Mark IV classical guitar. The top had been damaged, and a guy in a small shop in a subway station in Barcelona had replaced it with an old Fleta top. We drove around the neighborhood looking for that one, trying my ESP on it. You'll try anything. I thought I did feel a couple of pulls a time or two, but no results. Somebody's out there playing *Proud Mary* on it right now. And of course, I drove over one.

It was a friend of ten years or more. The vacation was over. In a Karmann Ghia filled with skis and bags, we were heading home from the airport, just entering the freeway. I was sure the passenger door was latched. It wasn't. I can still hear the sound of that nylon gig bag sliding out the door followed by that muffled thump. Was that a rabbit? It wasn't. I remember opening the case on the highway and seeing the splinters and the broken body and neck. It took Mr. Numb a week to begin to feel the loss, like a death in the fami-

> I can still hear the sound of that nylon gig bag sliding out the door followed by that muffled thump. Was that a rabbit?

11

ly. I took it to Joe, my guitar guru in Nashville where they worked on it for a year, mostly on weekends. There was quite a celebration when I finally got it back. It never did sound the same, though. I had to retire the case, too. It had tire treads on it.

I was in Springfield, Illinois, doing a gig six months before I drove over "Ace." Feeling hypocritical, I went to the Dauphin guitar warehouse in town. It was the largest importer of Kohnos in the country, and I had to have a look. "Just in case," I thought. Well, this one guitar started humming at me when I walked past it, like when you're at the pet store and you see the right puppy and you just know. Anyway, I figured that someday I'd maybe, you know, like, kind of, buy it. They said they'd let me know before they sold it to someone else. They never did. They move stuff pretty quickly there and I figured it was gone. So, after the big crunch, I called them. They looked all over the place and told me that they must have sold it. Mr. Numb said he understood. An hour later they called me back. They said the reason they couldn't find it was that it was in a closet in the back of the shop, covered with dust. My name was taped to the case. They had been holding it for me.

Now there's your miracle.

I have left guitars outside the door of my hotel room on at least three occasions. I've sat paralyzed, watching them slide down a wall and crash to the floor. Once I was so nervous before a show that I strung one up almost completely backwards. That same day I cut the nails on the wrong hand. Later, after we'd flown to the next town, I opened my case to find that it was empty. I had left her lying on a hotel bed a thousand miles away. She made the gig though—they flew her to me, wrapped in a paper bag.

> I've treated guitars worse than I have treated my old girlfriends. I have never driven over an old girlfriend. That's good.

I've treated guitars worse than I have treated my old girlfriends. I have never driven over an old girlfriend. That's good.

My guitars have persevered in spite of my treatment of them. I persevere because I have to make music, and because my guitar is sounding better than ever.

I've heard it said that some guitars are reincarnated into beautiful girls. That would be bad. People stuff cigarettes in between her strings, up by her tuning pegs. They spill drinks on her, which run down her waist and hips; they scar up her back with their belt buckles. They even let others play her, with their acidic and acrid smelling hands. No way to treat a lady. And what if one day an enchanting young thing would walk up, look me in the eye and say, "Hi Michael, remember me?"

And then she'd shoot me. Most of my life I've confused women with art, so it has been second nature to personify guitars as women. Guitars (and cars) perform better when you name them. I've never had a problem determining the gender of a guitar. Like ships, they are usually feminine. Liza and Elizabeth were great friends of mine. Ace was my only boy. Then there was Blue, my first electric guitar, but like a ukulele I once knew, it was neuter.

> Most of my life I've confused women with art, so it has been second nature to personify guitars as women.

I bought a cheap classical one time—it sounded pretty good for a while. It said "Made in Spain" on its fancy label. After it developed a buzz, I decided it was the label rattling, so I tore it out. Underneath it was another label, in Japanese. I called the import company to rage at them. As it turned out, "Sure enough, that label was made in Spain." That's the only time a guitar has ever lied to me.

Otherwise they have all been true. They have mirrored my connection to or separation from myself. So often I'll start to play—a day, or even a week after a show—and there it will be: all the energy of the last moment I spent with her, of the last chord, the tension, the intonation, and of how it all felt at the end.

So, for many reasons, I'm more respectful now. I am a better friend. Women have turned out to be more than art. They are people. This, of course, frightens me. I'm working on that, too.

Visit Michael Johnson at www.mjblue.com

You need to have martyr-like perseverance, because this business is really tough. I've gotten where I am today only because I have persisted against all odds for a long time.
—*Rory Block*

Brooks Williams

THE HUNT FOR RED GUITAR

The red guitar is lost. I've arrived in Dublin, Ireland, but my guitar has not. It's late and I'm the last person in the baggage claim area. I'm stupidly watching the belt go round and round, as if maybe I missed the guitar case on an earlier pass. I drive to the hotel with the airline's assurance that my guitar will be waiting for me in the morning. It is not. I stay at the airport most of the day, watching for my guitar and pestering the airline agents after each new plane arrives. In between I try out every restaurant, café, and shop in the terminal. Besides being over-fed, over-watered, and running out of cash, I've also become an expert on Dublin's airport. Go ahead, ask me anything.

"Give it a few days," the airline representative says. I can tell I am making her nervous and she wishes I would leave. "I have exactly one more day to give it," I say, "before my first concert." In the end, she convinces me that there is little I can do by waiting. "Leave an itinerary and phone numbers and if… when," she corrects, "your guitar arrives, we'll deliver it to you." Reluctantly, I head out into the Dublin twilight. The city center recedes in the rear-view mirror. The gunmetal gray sky that has been spitting all day finally opens up and dumps rain by the bucketful. It's difficult to see for the rain, and even more difficult to navigate the rush hour traffic, but eventually the road opens up and the rain softens as I make my way to tonight's accommodations. Once during the drive, I reach a free hand into the back seat of the car to feel for my guitar case. I forget: there is nothing to put my hand on.

I meet a guy at dinner who spent the last few decades tirelessly traveling to the poorest, most oppressed corners of the world to work for peace and justice. He has, I realize, been to the front lines of human indecency. Though his voice rings with clear hope, I'm guessing the years have taken a toll on him. I think I can see a deep weariness in his eyes. These days he lives a quieter life, directing retreats on Celtic spirituality. The extremes of humanity: from incessant injustice to thunderous silence. As we watch the peat fire burn blue and sip glasses of wine, he asks, "What's your story?"

"The red guitar is lost," I begin.

I tell him how only a few months earlier luthier Brad Nickerson had invited me to his shop. The guitar he had built for me was ready. I remember clearly my awe at seeing the guitar for the first time: the beauty of its shape, smaller than a Dreadnought, larger than an OM, with a high waist, an alluring cutaway, and milky pearl inlay around the soundhole. And, most striking of all, a red sunburst top.

I remember as I played it for the first time, moving my left hand over the neck, exploring the nuances of different octaves. Almost instinctively my fingers fell into an African-like rhythmic riff that traced the ii-iii-I-V triads of the key of C around the third, fifth, and eighth frets. Someone once told me that there is at least one song hidden within every guitar, and I'm thinking this riff is the seed of a new tune. If I've already spotted a shiny little nugget of a song in less than five minutes with this guitar, how many more might be hidden in these frets?

Less than a month later, I was in the studio. There was magic in the notes that danced out of the red guitar. I knew it then and hear it still on the CD that resulted from those sessions. Shortly thereafter I took the guitar to a few gigs—none involved air travel—christened it with a significant scratch, and then packed my bags for this overseas tour. "If it is indeed gone," I conclude to my friend, "its life has been short but sweet."

The fire has nearly burned out. The wine is gone. "Give it a few days" he says. "It may turn up yet."

It's a new day, and I'm driving to a little village along the Southern coast. My directions to the venue (a combination pub, B&B, and music hall) lack detail (to say the least): "Take the road to the sea, stop at the last building on the right." Not much to work with, but surprisingly, they are perfect. Before I know it I am seated at the bar on a sunny Saturday drinking a cup of tea and looking out at a deep green ocean. Word spreads fast. Somehow many of the people here know about my lost guitar. There are apologies, optimistic offerings, and existential comments about travel, possessions, and the modern world. "It may turn up," I am told. Meanwhile, just in case, some helpful local musicians are tracking down a guitar for me to use in tonight's concert.

> If I've already spotted a shiny little nugget of a song in less than five minutes with this guitar, how many more might be hidden in these frets?

Before long, the rays of the sun slide down the wall and into the next room coming to rest on the stage where I will be playing later tonight. The microphones are helter-skelter from last night's performance. I can almost picture where each of

15

the musicians stood or sat. Tonight it will be much simpler: just a man and his guitar; it's a timeless tradition. I'll do the same somewhere else tomorrow night and the night after that, on other borrowed guitars, most likely. If given the opportunity, I am one of those guitarists who will play all the time. It makes no difference that I also play guitar as a job. One might think I'd burn out on it, look for another hobby, but it remains a passion that, if anything, flames brighter. It's like being in love with someone who is also your best friend. It remains, after all the years, a constant thread that connects the chapters, pages, paragraphs, and sentences of my life. Because of this, I think, and because my guitar is lost, I feel like I am not totally "here" yet, as if my full self has not arrived. It is as if my playing, my noodling, gives reality to my being here—or anywhere. I feel like one of those Star Trek characters when they get transported—or beam—from one place to another. I am a glowing body-shaped collection of light particles hovering mid-air. But there is a problem. I'm not fully materializing and Picard and the gang are looking pretty nervous. Only part of me has arrived, the essential parts—body, nerves and senses—but the rest—heart, soul, dreams and history—are delayed. I'm still arriving. It's an ongoing thing. Will all of me arrive eventually? Will all the pieces realign in the correct sequence?

In the meantime, something is missing.

"Awake, my soul! Awake, harp and lyre! I will awaken the dawn," wrote another musician and poet in Psalm 57. These ancient lines resonate with me. When my fingers dance up and down the fretboard it is a call to my distracted soul to wake up and pay attention—even when I feel like a hummingbird that has just drunk a double latte. I'd even go so far as to say that in that place of awareness the notes create the kind of dialogue I think prayer should be. It isn't asking or demanding anything. Rather, it is as if each note, each phrase, simply acknowledges the Divine by saying, "Hey!" Or, to quote an earlier vernacular, "Hark!" No more. No less. Unfortunately, it is difficult for me to reach this place without the guitar. I don't mean playing like when I'm just practicing, but that kind of playing where I truly lose myself in the trance-like zone where melody and harmony take on characteristics akin to water, and I dive beneath the surface.

My boots crunch over the stones as I make my way down the beach. Small waves wash up with a hiss. A tanker passes on the near horizon. A couple is locked lip to lip in golden sunlight. Two dogs chase a thrown ball into the water. Sea birds call and respond, call and respond.

The sun is setting. Back at the pub a new crowd has gathered at the bar to discuss the latest rugby scores and village gossip. Children squeal with delight over melting ice cream. Two men laugh loudly at the punch line to a whispered joke. A young woman speaks on her mobile phone about plans for Sunday dinner. I'm lost in the music of it all, when someone asks if I know a guitar has been delivered for me.

I get off the stool, walk into the other room and up to the stage. There it is, in the half-dark, small and partially hidden. The red guitar! I lay the case flat, unzip the outer bag, and, one by one, snap open the five latches. I hesitate when I come to the last one, unsure of what I will find inside. Splinters? Little stove-sized pieces of red kindling? I take a deep breath and open the lid. Inside I find one hand-built red guitar, shining like a California sunset. Elapsed time from the case to my arms: negligible. I tune up, strum a chord, and pick a riff or two.

Tell Picard and the gang it's going to be okay. I've arrived.

Visit Brooks Williams at www.brookswilliams.com

MAKING ARRANGEMENTS

I try to play in different keys: Ab, Db, or F, for example. Those are the keys in which a lot of other instruments are played. When I first start-ed playing, I learned all the standards and played them in the usual guitar keys: G, E, Am, D. What I found was that nobody plays in those keys except guitar players!
—*Earl Klugh*

When you arrange a traditional tune, you start with a fantastic melody—a timeless melody—which is why it still exists. As a compos-er, you're under much greater pressure because you have to do it all. As inspiration for my original compositions, I spend a lot of time looking at those traditional tunes, taking them apart—seeing *why* they're good.
—*Martin Simpson*

I tend to write detailed accompaniment to my songs. I very often har-monize the vocal with an internal line on the guitar.
—*Paul Simon*

Spencer Bohren

THE PRODIGAL GIBSON

Traveling through Southern Oregon in 1970, one could not help but notice great numbers of rustic, back-to-the-land hippie farmers driving old pickup trucks, living in formerly deserted miners' shacks and farm houses, growing large gardens and long hair. They were determined to change the established order of their parents' society through a philosophy of voluntary simplicity. I was one of those young rural revolutionaries, living in a decrepit but creatively comfortable cabin on a dirt road in the scenic Applegate Valley near the microscopic town of Williams.

I was a professional musician before I moved to Oregon, and have been a professional musician since I left, but for my two years as an Oregonian, participation in that great cultural experiment took precedence over any thought of a musical career. I had some great guitars, though, including an early-fifties Gibson J-45 that I played regularly. One dusty summer day, returning from the weekly trip to the town of Grants Pass, I was bouncing up the rutted dirt road that passed as my driveway when I saw that the cabin's front door was wide open. I got an inkling that something was not right. Going inside, I immediately noticed the guitar case that normally held my beloved Gibson. It was open. And empty. My guitar was simply gone. No damage to the house, and nothing else touched… but the Gibson had vanished.

The local sheriff was not particularly enamored with the hippies, and so he was no help at all. No one in the surprised community had any ideas, either. So after making the rounds of the regional pawnshops and music stores, there was nothing to do but accept the fact that my beautiful J-45 had been stolen.

Fortunately, I had a beat-up old Martin to play, but it was a truck compared to that Gibson. And I truly missed the sound and feel of my all-time favorite guitar. One day, perhaps a year later, I was playing music with some friends on the dilapidated porch of the ol' shack when a sooped-up Mercury—about a 1947 or '48—

rumbled up our funky road. Spotted with gray primer and missing its hood, its three chrome air filters reflected the sun from atop triple carburetors. This fantastic vision finally stopped its rocking and rolling, and out stepped a tall, muscular guy with long sideburns, a duck tail haircut, and rolled-up short sleeves—direct from central casting and a perfect match for the car. He sauntered over, stuck out a big hand and asked if we minded if he listened. He was certainly likable enough, and he loved the Hank Williams and Jimmie Rodgers songs we were playing.

As he sat there, we learned his name was Dean, and that he was a tree topper in the woods. In case you're unfamiliar with the term, a tree topper is the daredevil of the logging industry. He's the guy who climbs way, way up in those giant firs and cedars and fells the top fifty or sixty feet of the tree. When he yells "timber," and that top crashes to the forest floor, the mammoth trunk shakes back and forth like a

> That Gibson J-45 bridged a formidable social gap for all of us, and provided an entree into the local culture that would have been impossible without it.

blade of grass in a hurricane while the topper hangs on for dear life. He's tied to the tree, of course, but it's definitely a job that attracts only the very toughest kind of man. We were impressed. After a while, Dean left for the store in Williams, and rumbled back up our road a few minutes later with a whole trunk full of cold Olympia beer. The music and camaraderie went on for hours, and we'd all become best friends when Dean said in his sleepy Oregon drawl, "That Martin shore sounds good."

"Yeah," I replied, "but not nearly as good as my old Gibson that got stolen."

"Was it one of those big ol' brown sunburst Gibsons?" Dean asked.

"Sure was," I answered.

"Did it have a couple of cigarette burns up by the tuning keys?" Dean wondered.

"Yeah… it did," I said, getting a funny feeling.

"Did it look like someone had scratched it up with a pocketknife down on the bottom part?" he casually asked.

By now, I was downright excited and I cried, "Yes!"

"I'll be right back," he said, and he got in his hot-rodded Mercury and lumbered back down our road. He was back within twenty minutes—and astonishingly, carrying my long lost Gibson guitar. I was stunned. "Where was it?" I had to ask, reaching for my old friend.

At that, Dean sat down on the porch and started crying like a baby. This big, tree-toppin', hard drinkin', chain smokin', tough talkin' logger, just crying and crying! No one could believe it. After several minutes of this, Dean succeeded in shutting off the waterworks and proceeded to tell his story.

"I drove out to Williams a year or so ago," he said, "looking for a hippie gal I ran into at the Pine Tree Tavern in Murphy. They said at the store that some hippies lived up this here road so I come up here and no one was home. The door wasn't locked, so I come on in the house, and I seen that beautiful Gibson a-layin' there in that case. I just took it! I wanted one of those big ol' Gibsons since I was a little boy, and there it was. And I just took it. I never stole nuthin' in my whole life, and I felt so terrible afterwards that I carried it down the road to another tree topper's house and left it there. I've felt so bad about it all this time, but I didn't know what to do about it. I don't even know why I came back up here today, but once I heard that beautiful music you play, and how much you loved that guitar, why, I knew I had to give it back." And with that, he started bawling all over again.

Dean came around quite a bit after that, and introduced me to some of his friends, Gene and Mona, who loved to listen to country music and sing harmony. They came out to my place nearly every weekend for several months. Talk about a cultural experiment! That Gibson J-45 bridged a formidable social gap for all of us, and provided an entree into the local culture that would have been impossible without it.

Since that time, that Gibson guitar has played music all over the world. About ten years or so after Dean returned it to me, it was stolen again after a gig on Mardi Gras Day in New Orleans. I got it back, though. But that's another story…

Visit Spencer Bohren at www.spencerbohren.com

THE BEST YOU CAN DO

A lot of guitar players get caught up in technique and take themselves way too seriously. Let's face it, everybody is trying to do the best they can, whether it's some guy playing third guitar in a country band or Jeff Beck.
—*Steve Lukather*

And I'm okay with the fact that there are a lot of guitar players who are so much better than me. In my opinion, if you're just playing a C chord, and you're doing it well, with technique and passion and conviction, then you're a good guitar player.
—*Wes King*

Jim Kimball

RETURN TO FENDER

In May of 2000, I made a trip from Nashville, Tennessee to my old hometown of Longmeadow, Massachusetts. I was invited to perform at a twenty-year reunion show with my old band, Forest. I hadn't seen some of the guys in nearly as many years, so I was really looking forward to it.

While staying with my folks, I decided to take my sister Wendy up to Northampton for breakfast at a favorite old place called Sylvester's. After eating, we took a little stroll down Pleasant Street, passing by the local music store, Downtown Sounds. Out of the corner of my eye, I caught a flicker of something familiar. I stopped briefly to take a closer look into the window that was now reflecting the full glare of the morning sun. I could just barely make it out. Toward the back of the store, in the last position in a long line of guitars, hung an old sunburst Fender Stratocaster. As we continued on our way, I commented to my sister, "I used to have a Strat just like that one." We took three more steps before I turned around. I felt as though I were being called.

Twenty-six years before, I had taken a trip to New York with one of my band mates. We made our way to Manny's down on 48th Street, and there I found a brand new sunburst Fender Strat with a maple neck. Or maybe it found me. Either way, that was it—true love. I only had $200 of the $280 price tag, so my friend loaned me the other $80. I was so excited to be getting this guitar. The body was swamp ash, and man, was it heavy.

I didn't waste much time making it my own. I replaced the original nut and saddles with brass counterparts and I replaced the original pickups and pickguard with a Schecter unit. It integrated an aluminum pickguard with the pickups, along with series/parallel on-off-on switches instead of the three- or five-way switches that Fender made. The aluminum pickguard was supposed to act like a shield, reducing the amount of 60-cycle hum that was picked up by those single coil pickups. I don't think it did much of anything in that respect, but at the time I really did think that

21

rig sounded better than the original setup.

I also installed an Alembic Stratoblaster—a little switchable preamp that replaced the original output jack. Flipping the switch would effectively double the volume, giving you a much hotter and fatter output to solo with. A very cool unit.

To finish off the hot-rodding, I drove all the way to E.U. Wurlitzer's in the Backbay area of Boston, about two hundred miles roundtrip, just to purchase a pair of Bourne pots—little square, blue volume potentiometers. They were super smooth. You could do all the volume swell tricks using your pinkie with hardly any resistance. With all that customizing, it really felt personalized.

I took the neck off the Strat, and with my rubber bank check stamp, stamped my name onto the heel of the body.

The guitar went with me when I attended the University of Massachusetts in Amherst. I rented a small apartment there and maintained a weekly teaching schedule of about thirty-five students. One day I went to pick up the Strat, and discovered it was gone. My heart sank. I was certain that one of my students had taken it, since these guys were constantly in and out of my apartment. I had narrowed the possible suspects down to one in particular, but I couldn't confront him; I had no hard proof. All I could do was file a police report and just deal with the pain of having it stolen.

It's not surprising to me that guitarists become emotionally connected to their guitars. In the best of situations, the instrument is an extension of the musician. It's the voice through which we express our emotions and communicate with the listener. At times, the connection runs so deep that it's difficult to decipher where the player ends and the instrument takes over. Losing that guitar was like losing a part of myself.

A few weeks later, I went into my closet to pull out what I thought was my nylon string guitar. I opened the case and there was my Strat! It turns out, my sister Susan had been visiting and had put it away for me in the wrong case. I felt so guilty about suspecting my student. It taught me a great lesson about not jumping to conclusions.

That little episode also prompted me to take some extra security measures with my instruments. I took the neck off the Strat, and with my rubber bank check stamp, stamped my name onto the heel of the body.

That guitar served me well for a good while. Eventually, though, like so many things that come and go in one's life, I gave it up. I moved on. I was relocating to Los Angeles and I had picked up some other guitars—a couple of Les Pauls, and a pair of custom guitars that I had commissioned. I just wasn't using the Strat as much anymore; I was always trading up for the next instrument. I guess it was just part of the process of moving forward, trying out new things and saying, "Well, I'd rather have *this* now." I don't remember all the details of my selling it, but I do remember missing it every now and then. Come to think of it, I can't remember selling any guitar that I didn't later regret.

As I looked through that Downtown Sounds music store window, in many ways it looked like a million other Strats I'd seen over the years. But something pulled at me to take a closer look. I got right up on it, looking at it hanging on the wall in front of me, and still I didn't completely recognize it as mine. It had been dinged up; there were a few things that seemed different about it. I took it down, and asked the salesman if he had a Philips screwdriver. I peeled back the Schecter pickguard, and inside I saw those two blue pots. I couldn't contain my excitement.

I didn't think they'd have been too happy with me if I'd taken the neck off, so I settled for taking it to a back room to play it. I plugged it in and BINGO! There was the sound of an old friend. This was my guitar—I was sure of it. I was also sure that I had blown any chance to wheel and deal on the price I was going to pay for it! But that sacrifice seemed small and irrelevant. This was a big moment… my guitar had come back to me.

I bought it back for $500—still a pretty good deal. And believe it or not, being the packrat that I am, I had kept a box of stray parts with me all those years that contained, among other things, all the original 26-year-old Fender parts from that Strat. I knew I could put it back to completely original specs if I wanted to.

When I got home, I took the strings off and tried to determine if any other work had been done on it. Then off came the neck. And when I saw my name stamped there, all the memories came flooding back. This guitar is an old friend. It's a part of my history. And though I moved all around the country, the guitar apparently didn't go too far. It seems it just stayed in the old neighborhood, waiting for me to come back.

And we did that reunion gig… together.

Visit Jim Kimball at www.jimkimball.com

When I hear people who are supposed to be improvising and they play recurring things, they're obviously just pushing a button and these licks come out. I always like to keep it melodically connected.
—*Pat Metheny*

Richie Furay

RETURN OF THE PRODIGAL GUITARIST

In the fall of 1973, I was convinced that Poco was finished; this band was never going to make it. The Eagles had just come along and had their first hit, and here we were, three years into it without any significant success. I had started this band to become a rock and roll star. That was the whole thing for me. Jimmy Messina, Neil Young, Steve Stills, and Randy Meisner—all my bandmates from the Buffalo Springfield—had gone on to greater successes, and that's what was on my mind.

I decided that I needed to start afresh with a new band. And David Geffen would work his magic, just as he did with CSN&Y, Joni Mitchell, Jackson Browne, Linda Ronstadt, and all the others. I got in touch with David, and he suggested that I get together with Chris Hillman and J.D. Souther. He thought that if we put the band together, we'd have another Crosby Stills Nash & Young. I thought, "It's that easy?!" So that's what I set out to do. Chris, J.D., and I got together and formed the Souther-Hillman-Furay Band.

In no time, we were working on our first album, and looking forward to some big things. At one point in the recording process we were doing vocal overdubs on one of Chris' songs. I had driven over to the studio on Ventura Boulevard in my 911, and thought that since we would only be working on vocals, I didn't need to bring the guitar inside. I left it out in the car.

We started at about 2:00 in the afternoon, and I figured we'd be done by 6:00. Well, by 2:00 in the morning, we were still at it, still trying to get it right; that's what great singers we were! When we left the studio that night, stepping out into the night air and trying to shake off the lingering effects of things we shouldn't have been doing, I went out to my car and I thought, "Something's not right here." I was in a surreal frame of mind, but I knew that when I drove in, my windshield wasn't shattered and my side windows weren't smashed in. I looked into the car and I saw that my guitar had been taken. And as I looked a little further, I saw that they had taken the ignition to the car, as well. What they really wanted was the car, but when they couldn't get it hotwired and up and moving, they just took off with the guitar. My heart just dropped. How stupid could I have been to have left my guitar behind in the first place!

That guitar was my most important possession. I didn't play any other instrument; that was the one guitar—a 1962 Martin D-28 that I got when I graduated from high school. Every song I had ever written was done on that instrument. All the songs I wrote before and through Buffalo Springfield, all the songs I wrote with Poco. To me, it was irreplaceable. I had even put a small sticker with my name on it on the headstock. It blended in so well with the look of the guitar that it almost passed as a signature model!

I reported the serial numbers to the police, and shortly thereafter, my wife, Nancy, and I took off for a month-long vacation in Hawaii. When we got home, there was a phone message waiting for me. It was my business manager telling me that my guitar had been found. It was in a little pawn shop out in the east valley, and I should take a look.

We immediately got back into the car and drove out. On the way, Nancy said to me, "I want you to know that the whole time we've been away, I've been praying that your guitar would be found." And I responded, "Yeah, sure. If my guitar is out there and you've been praying that it would be returned, then I'm surly going to consider changing my ways."

We found ourselves in a pretty rough part of town when we pulled up to the shop. I wouldn't let Nancy out of the car; it was that rough. I walked into the cramped little shop and presented the police paperwork identifying the guitar as mine. He looked it over and said, "Follow me." He took me to a back room, and there it was—

> I went out to my car and I thought, "Something's not right here." I was in a surreal frame of mind, but I knew that when I drove in, my windshield wasn't shattered and my side windows weren't smashed in.

my guitar. I couldn't believe it. And sure enough, there was my name emblazoned on the headstock. It was a miracle. You just don't get things like that back. I certainly didn't expect to see it again. That the police found it blows my mind; this isn't the kind of thing they put foot traffic out for. But they did make some calls, and miraculously, turned it up.

I walked back out to the car with my guitar in hand. And of course, once I got it back, I quickly forgot about my promise to change my ways. If I had any thoughts on the way home, it was that I was overjoyed at having recovered my prized possession.

But still, the episode was instrumental in getting me to think about some more important things in life. In the back of my mind was the thought that my wife had been praying for the return of the guitar. It was important enough to her to do that; she knew how important it was to me. The simple innocence of her faith really moved me. A few months later, I did change my ways. In ultimately giving my life to Christ, I also abandoned my vain, shallow dream of rock and roll stardom.

Visit Richie Furay at www.richiefuray.com

THEORETICALLY SPEAKING

I think a personal style comes from first really learning and knowing
your instrument—knowing where all the sounds are. Scales are great
practice. Learning music theory was a tremendous advantage to
me as a player. All of a sudden I understood things that my ears
knew. I understood how I could use that information in my playing.
—*Wanda Vick*

I'd get an inspiration, but I could only take it so far because I just
didn't have the juice. Now that I know more things, I can take it
farther. I can actually see intuitive sparks through to the end.
That's really satisfying. There's really no substitute for
knowing the instrument.
—*Pat Donohue*

Charlie Daniels

LASTING IMPRESSIONS

In 1959, I could finally afford the guitar of my dreams—a custom Gretsch 6120. I ordered it from Paul Marshburn, who ran a grocery store, but also had a small music dealership on the side. I walked into the store, wrote down all the special features I wanted, and ordered it right there. When it came, it was a beautiful blond archtop with sparkly gold purfling, and my name inlaid on the fretboard in mother of pearl.

A few years later, the guitar was inadvertently left in a southern Maryland parking lot after a gig. I had hoped that it might turn up someday, because it did have my name emblazoned across the fretboard; it was a pretty distinctive guitar. But it never did, and eventually, I gave up on it.

Thirty-six years later, my office received a call from a guitar repairman in Maryville, Tennessee, wondering if I had ever owned a Gretsch guitar. Well, the girls at the office didn't know, so they called me, and I said, "Yeah, I sure did. But that was a long time ago."

The repairman, Donnie Barbra, acquired the guitar from the friend of a friend. As it turned out, he had always wanted a Gretsch guitar, and this fixer-upper that he'd just paid $100 for would be the one. It was in pretty rough shape when he got it, but his intention was to get it back into playing condition. In the process of working on it, he had taken off the binding, removed all the electronics and hardware, and had it sanded down to bare wood. It was at this point that he realized that there was something amiss about the neck. Upon closer inspection, he could see that there were *two* fingerboards on it, one stacked right on top of the other.

He used a glue-softening heating iron on the fingerboard to remove it, and the two fingerboards came off in one piece. He puzzled over this, wondering why someone would take the frets off the original fingerboard, sand it flat, glue on a new fingerboard, and then refret it. And the new work was pretty shabby. Turning it over, Donnie saw something even more puzzling. He could almost make out the shadow of a name, but it appeared to be reading backwards. Holding it up to a mir-

27

ror, it suddenly revealed, "CHARLIE DANIELS." Amazingly, the original routing for the fingerboard inlay work left its imprint on the *back* of the fretboard!

Whoever took the guitar all those years ago realized the first thing that he had to do was cover up that name! And once he did, it was just another guitar. If Donnie hadn't pulled it off, he never would have known.

We arranged to meet when I played a gig in East Tennessee a short time later. He brought it out, and sure enough, it was my guitar. It was in pieces, but it was my guitar. I sent it to Wings Guitars in San Jose—they're the Gretsch experts—and had it completely restored. It hangs in my museum in Nashville now, along with a lot of other memorabilia.

How in the world that guitar got from southern Maryland to Maryville, Tennessee, and what hands it had gone through over the years, I may never know. But I'm glad it's back home!

Visit Charlie Daniels at www.charliedaniels.com

HOT FOR TEACHER

I sometimes regret that I didn't take a more formal approach.
But I suppose the flip side is I may have felt that I had to satisfy
somebody else's standard of how the guitar should be played.
—*Alex de Grassi*

Teaching myself made me rely on myself and be more creative.
As a result I ended up being my own guy. Studying traditionally
will get you there a lot quicker technique-wise, but for me, it's always
been my greatest joy to explore and create my own unique thing.
—*Earl Klugh*

You've just spent $30,000 to $50,000 getting through the conservatory,
and what have you got? You look and play just like the guy right next
to you. He hasn't got a job either, and he's possibly better than you are!
—*Dean Kamei*

You can have the greatest inspiration, you can be the most
naturally gifted player, but if you have a music education going
along with that, you can have an unbelievable career.
—*Lee Ritenour*

I had only one teacher, myself, and only one student, myself.
—*Andrés Segovia*

David Carradine

ONLY A GIBSON IS GOOD ENOUGH

During the "Summer of Love"—1967, I think that would be—I was rehearsing a TV special, which meant I'd be unable to attend the Monterey Pop Festival. I thought I'd make up for missing the festival by learning to play guitar, so I bought a Mexican twelve-string at Wallach's Music City for $150, along with a book of Leadbelly songs. A few months later, a holy barbarian of my acquaintance—Peter was his name—convinced me that trying to learn on a guitar with such tough action was probably not the way for me to go. He sold me his guitar, a prewar Southern Jumbo "Banner" Gibson (the "banner" referring to the scroll decal on the headstock that read, *Only a Gibson is Good Enough*). The guitar was all mahogany—the sides, the back, the top, and the neck, with a rosewood fingerboard and bridge. It was finished in sunburst, which, on the mahogany top, was very dark. There was considerable crazing in the finish, pieces of which had flaked off. I thought the thing looked pre-historic. Native American. It felt like a piece pipe. Peter let me have it for $210.

The neck was kind of wide—good for my clumsy beginner's fingers—and I learned to play on it. Later on, I filled in the gaps in the finish with a little lacquer, and lightly sprayed the top to hold the rest of the finish on. I also worked on the action until it played like butter. I've owned many fine guitars since then (sixty-five at last count—fifteen of which I still have), but that old Gibson saw me through a lot.

When I'd had it less than a year, I took it to Harold Hecht's house (mansion) in Stone Canyon to audition for the role of Woody Guthrie in the movie *Bound for Glory*. Harold never made the movie. I kept on playing, though, and I collected other guitars along the way, but the Banner Gibson was the one I took with me everywhere. I carried it without a case, over my shoulder by a heavy strap with German silver inlays. When I took a plane, I'd buy it a seat. In '71 I wrote my first song on it.

I took that guitar with me to Palenque, the Mayan ruins in Chiapas, and played it on the Pyramid Of the Magicians. The pyramid gave it a whack that crushed one of its corners. When I got home, I fixed it as best I could. I had become a tramp repairman of guitars in the interim; many instruments passed by my bench. Once or twice I actually accomplished remarkable restorations. The pyramid repair was not one of my best.

> Many wonderful instruments passed my way, but still, I could feel that old brown guitar in my hands—like the ghost sensations from an amputated limb.

During the *Kung Fu* series, the guitar would lean against the wall of my dressing room every day. I played it in clubs and on tour with several bands I had formed, always with my brother Bobby in the group, playing guitar or his six-string bass.

In 1975, after the series was over, suffering a broken heart and carrying a huge torch, I decided to give up music completely. I gave all my instruments away to friends, strangers, and even an enemy or two, sparing only the custom Mossman I had designed myself (only because it hadn't yet been delivered). The Gibson went to a carpenter who was working on my house.

That summer, Hal Ashby announced that he would be making *Bound for Glory*. I had to borrow the Gibson for the audition. In that first afternoon I spent with Hal, we discovered in one of his reference books a photo of Woody with an identical Gibson Southern Jumbo; the banner on the peg head gave it away. It could have been the same one! So, obviously, we had to use it in the movie. The company offered to rent it from the carpenter, but he happily donated it. I found a similar instrument at Norman's Rare Guitars in the Valley, and they rented that as a backup.

After the filming, I returned the Gibson to the carpenter. A few years later, it managed to find its way into my hands again, but then, in 1982, it disappeared. I missed it every day. Many wonderful instruments passed my way, but still, I could feel that old brown guitar in my hands—like the ghost sensations from an amputated limb. I was always looking around for another like it, with that scroll and that dark mahogany sunburst top.

In 1999, my brother Bobby and I were recording some songs at RCA's Studio B in Nashville. While we were in town, I visited Gruhn's Vintage Guitar Shop. And there it was, hanging on the wall. The scroll decal caught my eye from across the store. I thought, "Naw." But I took it down and turned it over—and there was my funky repair! For sure, it was my old Gibson. They wanted $1,200 for it. Seemed cheap. Bobby had a $1,000 traveler's check in his wallet. I borrowed that from him and came up with the other two hundred, myself.

It was amazing how familiar the neck felt. How my fingers, after a bit of getting used to it again, curled naturally around its wide fretboard. I found myself remembering songs I had forgotten—songs I used to play on it; some I'd written on it, and never thought I'd remember again. One song which I had never finished, I put an ending to. A couple of weeks ago, I had a pickup installed on it so I could play it on stage (no one knows how to mike an acoustic guitar, anymore). I found a pickup that doesn't alter the original guitar at all—no holes to drill in it. Last week I played it on stage in Atlanta. The crowd loved it. It sounds sweeter than ever.

Yeah, only a Gibson is good enough.

Visit David Carradine at www.davidcarradine.org

SOUND ADVICE

There are times when I wonder if I'll ever get the sound I'm looking for. I can't tell you what it is—I wish I could! People praise me for my sound, but it's still not exactly what I'm looking for. I'll go along with it, though.
—*B.B. King*

I don't know that I've really created anything, but I've always felt driven to make my own style, like the guys I love and admire.
—*Jimmie Vaughan*

For anything I have discovered new to play, I'm sure there are countless others who have thought about it even more at some point. For me, it's how you utilize all those thing to create your own identity, your own sound, your own way. There's the magic for me.
—*Earl Klugh*

A lot of young jazz players copied Pat Metheny, and now they sound like bad copies of Pat Metheny. It doesn't work.
—*Lee Ritenour*

When I was younger, I wanted to do so many things on the guitar. I wanted to be Doc Watson, I wanted to be Chet Atkins, I wanted to be Andrés Segovia, I wanted to be Carlos Montoya. But at some point I realized I wasn't going to be anything like any of them. I've come to believe that every artist is supposed to get to the essence of who and what they are, and forget the rest.
—*Don McLean*

Kerry Livgren

THE LONG WAY HOME

In the early days of Kansas, we were touring the southwest, where the dryness around Albuquerque caused the neck of my Gibson SG to warp beyond playability. It got to be a really serious problem. When we got back home, the band bought me a new guitar—a brand new 1969 Les Paul Deluxe Gold Top.

I played that guitar for years, writing dozens, if not scores of songs on it. It was, in fact, the only guitar I played for many years. When Kansas landed their first major recording contract, though, a little more cash began to fill the coffers, and I decided I needed a new guitar. So I traded in that Les Paul for, of all things, a Hagstrom Swede.

It wasn't long before I began to miss that Les Paul. It didn't seem to matter what guitar I played; I always regretted getting rid of it. It's something all guitarists seem to do sooner or later. Like most guitar players, I have a long list of instruments that I wish I had never gotten rid of. I don't know why we do that, but we do.

> Seeing it again after all those years—and ruing the day I let it go—I told him, "Don't even hang it up. Don't even tell me what you want for it. Just sell it to me here and now."

Years went by, and guitars went by, and Kansas achieved its multi-platinum success, and still, I never forgot that Les Paul, even though at that time I could have had any guitar I wanted.

One day in 1991, my wife had gone to visit her parents. Well, I was home alone and it was a beautiful day, so I thought I'd get into my Piper Turbo Arrow and just fly around. We were living in Atlanta at the time, and I got a wild hair to fly off to the northwest. As I continued, I got the crazy

32

idea to fly on to Kansas and drop in on some of my old friends.

I landed in Topeka, rented a car, and drove down to Steam Music, the little music store where we used to hang out. And as I walked in the door, a fellow I had known for years who worked there looked at me as though he had just seen a ghost. At that very moment, he was hanging a guitar up on the wall—my old Les Paul. Somebody had come in that day and traded it in.

He began to tell me the story of that guitar since it left my hands, where it had gone, who had owned it. It ended up being stolen in the southwest somewhere, and was recovered by the police. The guitar somehow found its way back to Kansas, and when it came into the store, he immediately recognized it. And so had I.

I had played that thing so much that I literally sweated off the gold top finish. I eventually stripped it down to bare wood. And I knew that serial number; there was no question that this was my guitar. Seeing it again after all those years—and ruing the day I let it go—I told him, "Don't even hang it up. Don't even tell me what you want for it. Just sell it to me here and now."

I put the guitar in my plane and flew back to Atlanta. I sent it up to Ken Hoover, who refretted it and got it back into shape. But it's not leaving again. I suppose it will go in my coffin when they bury me.

Visit Kerry Livgren at www.numavox.com

A TOUGH AXE TO FOLLOW

A good instrument is really an inspiration. When you have a truly
fine instrument, suddenly even the most simple things sound good.
—*Mason Williams*

A really good instrument will have a tremendous
influence on the design of the song.
—*Bob Taylor*

A good acoustic instrument can help you get a good sound.
However, the guitar is only partially responsible for the sound.
The player must know *how* to get the sound out of the instrument.
—*Roger Hudson*

Uncle Gene's Guitar

By John Schroeter

In 1915 the nations of the world shipped their richest offerings through the inviting portals of San Francisco's Golden Gate, where they would be put on view in celebration of the much anticipated Panama-Pacific International Exposition. And while every state in the Union was also represented, it was *Hawaii*—some forty-four years ahead of its own statehood—that would take the fair by storm.

With such an endearing overture, the American populace was soon swept up in a craze over everything Hawaiian. And further encouraged by traveling Hawaiian troubadours, the exotic and romantic images of the islands would capture hearts and imaginations the world over. In no time, the beauty of its lilting strains would make Hawaiian music the biggest selling genre not only of that time, but well into the 1920s and '30s. Tin Pan Alley and Hawaiian songwriters began to collaborate, as well, blending the Island sounds with jazz and big band swing. The result was a virtual paradise over the airwaves.

Eugene Edward Peck—"Gene"— was one of the rapt listeners. Born on an Indian reservation in Washington State, Gene was raised in South Dakota by his adoptive aunt and uncle in a home seemingly made of music. Like so many in America, young Gene was captivated by the sounds of ukuleles and steel guitars. And dreaming of palm trees and hula dancers lining tropical shores kissed by gentles waves, he longed to rejoin the charm of its calling.

Gene's adopted mother loved the guitar. She played one of the small-bodied parlor models that were so popular at the turn of the century. And having been built by the Martin Guitar Company in 1905—purchased new by the family—it was an instrument made for an age when people were the source of their own entertainment. And in parlors across the land, these instruments reigned right alongside upright pianos, whose hammers struck out the melodious musings of ragtime.

In the early 1930s, the little Martin would find itself in Gene's hands. It was his guitar now, and relaxing its strings to the *Ki ho'alu* slack-key tunings favored by the islanders, he would explore the mysteries of *Taro Patch, Wahine,* and *Mauna Loa.* Immersing himself in the delightful sounds, he stoked the fires of his desire to be near their very source. His opportunity would come in 1939.

Gene joined the Navy, with the specific proviso that he be stationed in Hawaii. His enlistment request granted, he happily reported to the USS Nevada, based in the stunningly beautiful Pearl Harbor, with guitar in hand. And touring the reaches of the Pacific, Gene's guitar playing was a welcome and appreciated source of entertainment aboard the ship.

Back in the harbor, Gene's duties consisted of piloting the small launch boats that ferried officers and crewmembers from ship to ship along Battleship Row. The morning of December 7, 1941, was no different than any of the others. And unaware of the advancing terror, he would leave the Nevada to shuttle sailors across the harbor to the USS Arizona, where he would meet other crewmembers for breakfast and a briefing of the day's assignments.

Only moments into his routine, though, a swarm of incoming airborne fighters suddenly came into view. And curiously descending to an altitude of just thirty feet above the water's surface, the Japanese planes leveled off and rained their torpedoes upon the sleeping fleet. In the opening salvo of an unprecedented disaster, The USS Oklahoma was the first to be struck. As the battleship capsized, its crew abandoned ship and swam in desperation as she rolled and helplessly keeled upward. And while still reeling from the shock of the inexplicable and horrifying spectacle before him, Gene would witness the exploding USS Utah. Chaos ensued.

At 8:10, as the crew aboard the Arizona scrambled to their stations, a direct hit from an armor piercing bomb penetrated its forward magazines, igniting a million pounds of gun powder. Setting off a massive series of explosions, it killed more than a thousand men in that instant. Sadly, Gene was among them.

The Arizona, which had been fully fueled, spread its fire and intense heat across the waters, enveloping those souls hopelessly swimming for safety. Moments later, the great ship would sink into its watery inferno. Most of the bodies remaining aboard would never be recovered.

In the lull between the attacks, and with the sea still boiling, the surviving remnant of the fleet prepared for the second wave. When it came, the US fought back. The USS Nevada, with a gaping hole in her side, was steaming toward the channel. It was one of the few battleships that were moored alone; most of the ships were stacked up side by side against the dock, and had no chance of escape. The Nevada would try.

The Japanese bombers, detecting a strategic opportunity to block the channel with a crippled USS Nevada, rapidly descended upon it, and unleashed the fury of their weaponry. The quick-thinking commander, though, ran his ship aground, where it took on water, but it left the channel clear.

By 10:00 it was all over.

The well-rehearsed surprise attack had caught the Pacific fleet completely unprepared—the devastation in the Harbor was nearly total. The aircraft carriers, though, were spared; Yamamoto failed in that aspect of his mission. The US fleet was crippled, but not dead. Meanwhile, what remained of the USS Arizona continued to burn in the harbor for days afterward.

With the Island communications all but completely cut off, getting word to loved ones stateside in the days after the attack was difficult, if not impossible. The Navy arranged for its personnel to write postcards home, so at least survivors could let their families know that they were alright—or not. Unfortunately for a number of anxious family and friends, many of the cards were belatedly delivered.

When the smoke cleared, the Navy returned to the victims' families what personal effects they could recover. Gene's guitar, though, remained in the watery remains of the Nevada. Most of a year later, a few of Gene's friends retrieved his guitar from the wreckage. Making their way to the crew's quarters they recovered the little Martin. Wet and in pieces, they cleaned it up, and sent it back to his mother.

With the declaration of war came severe consequences for American and Canadian citizens of Japanese descent. In Canada alone, some 22,000 of its citizens were interred at inland camps, supposedly to safeguard the country from potential spies. There were none.

Kiri Ito and her family lived on Vancouver Island's Quathiaski Bay, where the lovely strains of her old piano could be heard on many evenings along the waterfront. But soon the war would impose its will on even the remotest of fishing villages as this. Kiri's husband, like all Japanese males between the ages of fourteen and forty-five living along the coast, would soon be dispatched to labor camps. The fishing boats, homes, and personal property they left behind would be confiscated, looted, and sold, never to be seen again.

In time, Kiri too would join the internees as they stoically boarded the awaiting buses, like so many others who had been swept away by the rising winds of war. Her possessions would be tagged and set out for auctioneers who would claim them in the morning. Yet Kiri's piano would not be among the plundered belongings. The thought of the old upright in strangers' hands was more than she could bear. So Kiri and her daughters rolled that old piano down onto the dock and into the harbor, consigning it forever to the sea.

Fifteen-year old Glenn Eugene Elfman reached under the bed, and clutching the worn handle, pulled the case out from underneath. He had heard about the old guitar that his aunt had kept over the last seventeen years but never played. And when he opened it up, he learned why it had been hushed. The damage to the little guitar inside was extensive, with joints separating, the bridge missing, and the neck severely warped. Taking notice of Glenn's interest in the relic, his aunt offered it to him, reminding him that it had once belonged to his Uncle Eugene.

By this time, the war was but a bad memory. The Hawaiian music craze had faded, all but forgotten in the wake of rock and roll. And with the dawn of the '60s, a great folk revival would sweep the land. As a teenager, Glenn would frequent the Golden Bear—Huntington Beach's legendary folk house. It was there that he met Hoyt Axton and showed him the little guitar, such as it was.

"You'd be surprised," he told Glenn. "Somebody could restore this, and you'd have a really nice guitar." He referred him to Milt Owen, a repairman of some renown. Working from a loft in Wallach's Music City on Sunset & Vine, Milt, in his sixties then, had done work for Axton, as well as Django Reinhart and other luminaries. On Axton's recommendation, he left the guitar with the old man to do what he could.

He kept tabs on the progress of the repair work—a which took most of a year—through his Saturday visits to Milt's shop. The two would become close friends in the months that passed, playing guitar and sharing stories.

When he got word that the work had at last been completed, Glenn, now seventeen, was more than a little apprehensive, anticipating a hefty bill for the services rendered. When asked what he owed, Milt replied, "Nothing. Just promise me you'll take good care of the guitar."

Miraculously, Uncle Gene's guitar would sing again.

Canadian singer-songwriter James Keelaghan's favorite venue is the Pistol River Friendship Hall, an eclectic little place on the southern Oregon coast furnished with old, mismatched chairs and sofas. It was during one of his recent shows there that he performed his deeply stirring song, *Kiri's Piano*. The pathos of the story that unfolded in tune connected in a powerful way with the concert association's president—Glenn Elfman.

Inspired by the performance of this extraordinary song, Glenn showed his special guitar to James, and shared the story of its remarkable journey. And moved by the curious and ironic link between the lives of Gene and Kiri, the two agreed that a circle could be closed if James performed *Kiri's Piano* on Gene's guitar.

"It was one of those moments," James recalls. "It was just incredibly moving.

Maybe in some way, that was the balance of it: a piano goes into the water in British Columbia and a guitar comes out of the water in Hawaii. Kiri's piano will never come up out of that water, but amazingly, Gene's guitar did."

Other performers whose travels have taken them to Pistol River have played the little Martin parlor guitar and shared the story, as well. And the story will continue to be told; Glenn will see to that. It has been his gift to share in a family legacy that reaches back a hundred years. "I'm not the owner of that guitar," he says. "…just a temporary custodian."

And though Gene and more than 2,400 others died that December morning, the music did not.

Visit Glenn Elfman's Pistol River Concert Association at www.pistolriver.com, and James Keelaghan at www.keelaghan.com

DADGAD IT!

The trick for me was to make DADGAD my standard tuning. When you play in an open tuning, the sounds are different. I felt I could have a different approach. I was more connected to what was speaking to me, and I felt I could be good at it. The day I decided to use only DADGAD, I felt completely relieved.
—*Pierre Bensusan*

Seven-hundred years of guitar tuning can't be all wrong! Lots of people have tried in centuries gone by to tune the guitar in different ways. It seems a bit of a curse to inflict on me the invention of DADGAD, which, after all, is very limited in scope. Only Pierre Bensusan has really proved that it is capable of such things as jazz interpretation.
—*Davey Graham*

Johnny Cash

MARTY'S MARTIN

J ust as Marty Stuart has a favorite story about almost everybody in country music, we have our favorite stories about him. Mine, though, is really more about myself. It centers on a guitar he had, a horribly scruffy, beat-up old thing, worse looking than even Willie Nelson's infamous instrument. It was probably a wonderful guitar, one of the best Martins ever made—he certainly treasured it as if it were—but its ugliness was beyond dispute. I took exception to it.

One night on stage somewhere in Minnesota, I stopped in the middle of the show and told the audience, "You know, Marty Stuart started in this business when he was twelve years old. Mr. Lester Flatt hired him and saw that he was a young man who could go far. Marty really appreciated that, so ever since then, at least once a year, he has tried to pick out a twelve- or thirteen-year-old boy and do something nice, the way Lester did for him."

As I said all this, I had my eye on just such a person, a boy sitting in the front row.

I took the plunge. "There's a young man sitting in the front row tonight," I said, "and Marty would like to give that young man his guitar."

Before Marty could do a thing about it, I took that ugly guitar away from him and held it out to the boy in the front row. The boy couldn't believe it. He was so happy. He got up and went over to Marty and hugged him, thanking him repeatedly. Eventually he let go, and I shook his hand before he left the stage. "Learn to pick it, son," I told him. "Learn to pick it like Marty."

I looked over at Marty and his face was scarlet with anger. I thought for a moment he was really going to lose it. I just kept looking at him. I held his eye and started grinning, and then his face broke and he started grinning back.

From Cash: The Autobiography, by John R. Cash, copyright © 1997 by John R. Cash. Used by permission of HarperCollins Publishers Inc.

Every man knows he is a sissy compared to Johnny Cash.
—*Bono*

Adrian Belew

THE BATTERED STRAT

Shortly after I joined Frank Zappa in 1977, we did a two-month tour of the United States. Unfortunately, the Stratocaster I had been playing didn't make the return trip home. Whether it got lost in the world of air travel or someone actually stole it, I'll never know. But I had two weeks to find a new guitar before we headed off to Europe for another two months.

I lived in Nashville at the time, and I went into a music store there where I found a very ugly brown sunburst Stratocaster. It had no case, but that didn't matter; I'd have to get a proper road case for it, anyway. So for $285, I bought that Strat, which was a good deal. But the guitar was *really* ugly.

I flew back to California to begin our rehearsals for the European tour. While I was there, I hooked up with Seymour Duncan, an old friend of mine. He came by, and I showed him the guitar. As he was playing it, I said, "What am I going to do with this guitar? It's so ugly."

He got up from his seat, and holding the guitar said, "I'll show you."

I followed him outside, where he set the guitar up against a tree. At that moment, a neighbor lady was unloading her groceries from her car and looking at these two long-haired guys, wondering what the heck we were doing. Then Seymour went to his car and came back with lighter fluid, which he started squirting on the guitar. Before I could say a word, he lit it. In an instant, that Strat looked like the opening scene of Bonanza, with the flames burning away the title image. Then the celluloid pickguard caught fire, and the thing became a real inferno. We couldn't get the bloody thing out, so we started pouring water and sand on it. By this time the woman next door was ready

> We put twenty-five years of abuse into that guitar in that one afternoon.

to call the police on these two loons, burning a guitar on the front yard.

And then it just lay there, burnt, looking a bit like Hendrix had just had his way with it. We then proceeded, under his direction, to make that guitar look ancient. We dragged it in dirt and rubbed it grass, we gouged it with screwdrivers, and we poured motor oil on it. We put twenty-five years of abuse into that guitar in one afternoon. When we were done with it, it looked like a guitar that had been played forever.

The next day I took it to rehearsals, and Frank looked at it and he said, "If you wanted to make your guitar ugly, why didn't you just loan it to a friend?"

That guitar has since become the Stratocaster that a lot of people associate with me. It shows up in a lot of the early '80s photos of King Crimson, and is also featured on the cover of my first solo record, *Lone Rhino*. Today it hangs proudly in the number one position on my wall of guitars. It's pretty special to me now. It's retired in the sense that I don't take it on tour anymore—I wouldn't want anything *bad* to happen to it!

Visit Adrian Belew at www.adrianbelew.net

WHAT'S COOKIN'?

I like to share, but I'm not going to be a caterer.
I would rather be a chef. I like to share what *I've* got.
—*Michael Hedges*

For some reason we measure musical people by how many records
they sell. We don't measure our chefs by how many meals they cook!
—*Harvey Reid*

When I played classical guitar in restaurants, it was one
of the most enjoyable gigs I ever had. Not only did
I get to play a lot, but I got to *eat*!
—*Steve Morse*

Greg Martin

THE BAPTISM OF "BROWNIE McGEE"

I've always favored a Gibson Les Paul for my work with the Kentucky Headhunters. Ever since seeing John Sebastian play a sunburst Les Paul with The Lovin' Spoonful in 1966, it planted a seed. I also remember the cover of *Super Session* with Mike Bloomfield & Al Kooper, and Eric Clapton on the back of the Bluesbreakers CD. Hearing them, I knew the tone I was after. At one point, though, I picked up a 1957 Strat; it just had a vibe about it. What a tone! And because it had a brown sunburst finish, and my wife's maiden name is McGee, I dubbed it "Brownie McGee." Well, one night in 2000, Brownie took a vacation.

I had been working on my solo gospel project, *The Mighty Jeremiahs with Jimmy Hall*, at a studio here in Glasgow, Kentucky, where I live. I had packed a few guitars, including Brownie, into my van for the session, but only my '58 Les Paul was brought back into the house when we finished. The next morning, I opened the back of the van and noticed that the Les Paul Junior case was unlatched. That was odd—what was I thinking?! So looking around a little further, I also noticed that the Start was missing. Did I leave it at the studio? After backtracking, it became apparent that somebody had broken into my van, and it really began to sink in… *they took Brownie!*

It took a few minutes, but mulling over the scenario, I started putting it all together. That the theives had taken an antiquated Macintosh laptop, a Phillips Discman, and left the other guitar behind told me they were probably after something other than guitars. The Strat was in a tweed gig bag, and could easily have been mistaken for a shotgun or golf clubs. As I later learned, there had been a string of gun thefts in the area. So they took it and left the 1950s Les Paul Junior behind.

The police were on this thing immediately, and for a time, it looked like Mayberry around here. A '57 sunburst Strat is no small potatoes. They can easily go for $15,000. Mine wasn't anywhere near that level when I got it, but since then, they've gone through the roof. So it really killed me to lose that guitar. But what really hurt was that the last solo I laid down at the studio was with that Strat. It had an amazing sound. I wondered if I would ever capture that tone again.

I'm extremely thankful that I took my prize '58 Les Paul in that night. In reality, though, it probably would have been safe, being in a guitar case. Apparently, they didn't want guitars.

Headhunter bass player Anthony Kenney quickly made some posters, and I put them up around the area. I also put the word out on the internet and with dealers. If anyone tried to take it to George Gruhn or another vintage dealer, it was going to pop up. But nobody seemed to know anything about it. I even had several friends around the country praying about the ordeal. But God gave me a real peace about the situation after the first week. I was ready to bend to his will, whatever the outcome was.

One morning before going to Bowling Green to meet some friends for lunch, I got a call from Jeannie C. Riley, the country singer who sang *Harper Valley PTA*. She's a dear friend of the Headhunters and my family, and a very godly woman. We had been talking, so she knew what was going on, and was praying for the recovery of the guitar. She assured me, "Greg, you're going to get your guitar back." Then she gave me a verse—Psalm 41:1—a curious verse having to do with being merciful to the poor. She didn't know why the Lord had given her this particular passage, but she wanted me to read it and ponder it. And when I did read it, it made no sense at all. What that had to do with my guitar, I had no idea.

I came home from Bowling Green that afternoon to a message on my answering machine. It said, "Greg, you don't know me, but I saw your poster at Junior Foods, and I think I might know where your guitar is." The poster I hung at the Junior Foods market was the last I posted, and pretty much as an afterthought when I went in for a cappuccino. Well, this fellow, Mr. Smith, was an ole country boy, a good salt of the earth kind of guy. Evidently, he'd been at a friend's home the night before where they had shown him a guitar they had found. He didn't think anything of it until he saw the poster.

I anxiously called the number several times, but no one answered. Each time I called, my heart sank to new depths of despair. I thought someone must be playing cruel a joke. Since I was preparing to hit the road with The Headhunters that night, my time was tight. I tried one last time, and by the grace of God, I got the fellow on the phone. I only had a couple hours before The Headhunters were to leave; things started moving very quickly at that point. I was also a little wary, so I invited Anthony to come along, and we picked this guy up. Driving out to the house, we pulled up to a dilapidated country shack. Now, I say this respectfully, but if you can picture the Beverly Hillbillies when they were still living back in the hills, you'll be pretty close to what we were looking at. I half expected to find Jed out back, shooting at some food. This place was ready to fall down. And there was this family, sitting and waiting on the shack's rickety wooden front porch. On top the washing machine lay Brownie. Drying out.

"Well," the old man began to explain, "we was out fishing in the creek out back, and snagged this thing. Drug it in. Didn't know what to do with it till this guy just happened to see the poster."

I couldn't believe it. They had fished the guitar out of the creek! And there it was, lying on its tweed bag. And these people were having a rough time, God bless them. They had no idea that the guitar was worth more than their house. I gave him a few hundred dollars for it; it wasn't a lot, but it was something. Then my mind shot back to that verse that Jeannie C. had given me. It all made sense now.

> Of course, the thieves had no idea what they had. They probably took one look at that old Strat and said, "Man, this thing is ugly!"

As I began to piece together a theory, it became clear that my van had been targeted in the recent gun theft spree. When the perps opened the case and found a guitar inside, they must have just tossed it off the bridge over the creek that ran near the family's home. Of course, the thieves had no idea what they had. They probably took one look at that old Strat and said, "Man, this thing is ugly!" And it wasn't extremely clean; it was well-played. But they probably thought the guitar was just a piece of junk, so over the bridge it went. It must have floated downstream, and then got hung up in the underbrush near the shack where this family happened to be fishing.

After retrieving the guitar, we took it to Anthony's house, cleaned it up, and plugged it in. It still worked! On our way to the tour bus, we called the investigating officer. As soon as they got the call, several squad cars converged at the bus. Talk about a scene! The police wanted to know more about these people; wanted to question them further, and see what they could shake out. I told them I didn't think they had a thing to do with it. And even if they did, I wasn't going to press charges. These people were having a hard time. In fact, it wasn't long after, that the county condemned that place and moved the family out. It's since been torn down.

Remarkably, Brownie wasn't too worse for its ordeal, especially considering that it had spent nearly three weeks in the water. I thought it had been ruined, but my wife Ruth looked it over and commented, "It looks as beat up now as it did when you got it!" The headstock was a little discolored, and the tremolo arm was broken—further evidence that it had been tossed. But other than that, it looked fine.

I cleaned up the electronics, going through everything with solvent. I was pretty apprehensive when I plugged it in, but much to my surprise, it sounded great. Those old Strats have a wonderful bell-like tone, and Brownie still had it.

It's truly amazing what those old Fenders can survive; Pete Townsend's and Jimi Hendrix' guitars have nothing on Brownie's three-week swim in a Kentucky creek. But what impresses me more is the spiritual undercurrent that ran through the experience. Jeannie's remarkable faith, the answered prayer, and the lessons I learned about material attachments still encourage me. God taught me some important lessons through this ordeal, and another Bible verse is forever instilled into my heart:

Do not lay up for yourselves treasures on earth, where moth and rust destroy and where thieves break in and steal; but lay up for yourselves treasures in heaven, where neither moth nor rust destroys and where thieves do not break in and steal (Matthew 6:19 & 20).

That Brownie has been baptized is not lost on me, either! Still, I'm very thankful for its return.

Learn more about Greg Martin and the Kentucky Headhunters at www.kentuckyheadhunters.com & www.gregmartin.com

JUST A VAPOR

Until the advent of recording music had a sort of mysticism attached to it—the music was played, and it vanished; you could never capture it. And it is indeed this fact of capture which I find at times almost working against the very nature of musical sound. It shows a sort of greediness on the part of people that they want to conserve something which should vanish. With music, the moment is very important.
—*Julian Bream*

Music is a live form. You go on stage, it happens at that point, and then it's gone. Recording is a very false way of delivering music, because it delivers a fixed and repeatable performance. No performance is repeatable. The whole point of music is you go on stage and communicate with an audience *immediately*— rather than having sat in a studio and sent them a postcard.
—*Adrian Legg*

Pierce Pettis

ST. CECELIA ON GUITARS, FEAR, AND GRACE

I've always played cheap guitars. Yamahas, Takamines—Japanese copies of the American standards like Martin, Guild, and Gibson. There are many reasons for this, not the least of which is expense. Or I should say, my general lack of funds—a condition common to musicians. But there are practical reasons, too. Life on the road is brutal on wooden instruments sensitive to heat, humidity, barometric pressure, and altitude. They invariably get knocked over by stoned sound men ("Soorry, dude"), get beer spilled on them by inquisitive drunks ("Uuurrrph"), and are inevitably mangled and crushed by Satan's minions, otherwise known as airline baggage handlers ("Woof, woof, snort").

> These are the ultimate road guitars—"tough as woodpecker lips," to quote Gamble Rogers.

Therefore, as a solo musician on the road, I knew my guitars had to be tough, tough, tough, and cheap enough to be easily replaced on a moment's notice. Eventually I was able to move up to Ovation guitars—an improvement over the Japanese models I'd been playing, and famous for their hard plastic, lute-shaped backs. These instruments were developed by an aerospace company making the highly flexible but virtually unbreakable plastic used in helicopter blades. These are the ultimate road guitars—"tough as woodpecker lips," to quote Gamble Rogers. So tough, in fact, they have literally been known to stop bullets. Once when touring the Ovation/Kaman factory in Connecticut, I was shown one that had done just that—a Balladeer with a bullet-shaped bulge in its back. The owner claimed it saved his life.

But durable as they are, Ovations still rank among the less-expensive production guitars; the Fords and Chevys of guitars—reliable and lovable, but definitely not a Mercedes or a Jag. Yet for all their ruggedness, they're still not completely indestructible. Years ago, I was proudly displaying my first Ovation to a musician

46

friend at the end of a long, hard night on the five-foot stage of a black-curtained, black-painted club in the "Little Five Points" sub-Bohemia of Atlanta. We were actually trading war stories back and forth, of all the terrible destruction our various guitars had suffered on the road when somehow, suddenly, my new prize slipped from my hand, and crashed down into its half-opened case, cracking the wooden top. Irony is not always pretty. It turns out that, while the backs may be bullet proof, wooden tops are still wooden tops. Since then, the demonic airline baggage handlers have managed to almost completely destroy two of these hardy instruments, smashing tops and slamming one so hard that I found the pre-amp and electronics loose inside the bowl (other non-bulletproof parts of the guitar).

Along the way, I managed to make the acquaintance of the American representative for Lowden and Avalon guitars—exquisite, world class, handmade guitars produced in Ireland. My friend, Miles, a huge and genuinely terrifying-looking Irishman with a shaved head, leather jacket, and heart of gold, kept insisting that I play one of these guitars. Knowing I could never afford such a beauty, I was hesitant at first. But eventually he convinced me to borrow one for use on my album, *State of Grace*.

> Heaven forbid that it should ever be touched by the infernal airport baggage handlers. That would be like handing your teenage daughter over to the Hell's Angels.

I was stunned. At first, the S-25J, a small-bodied cutaway, was a little hard to play with its wide, low-profile neck—very different from the Gibson-style round necks I was used to with my Ovations. This guitar had a neck like an aircraft carrier. But oh, what a sound. There is nothing on earth I've ever heard that sounds like this guitar. If ever an instrument was charmed or blessed, this is the one—a gift from God. Richard Thompson (who also plays a Lowden) once wrote a song about a beloved '53 Vincent motorcycle; that's how I feel about this guitar. Nothing has the soul of a Lowden, and the little S-25J they sent me is angelic. I had heard rumors that the guitars are actually blessed as they leave the factory in Ireland. On a recent visit to the Lowden factory, I was too embarrassed to ask, but something must be going on. Forget harps. I have no doubt the angels are playing Lowdens.

This said, it shouldn't be a surprise that I refused to take this guitar on the road for almost two years. It was strictly for studio and home use. Never would this instrument be thrown in the back of a hot van with amps and mike stands falling all over it, and heaven forbid that it should ever be touched by the infernal airport baggage handlers. That would be like handing your teenage daughter over to the

Hell's Angels. Never, never, never! Well, maybe never.

I recently had the honor of being asked to join Grammy-winning artist, Alison Brown, and her group on a Christmas tour. I'd be doing some of my own songs and lending vocals and guitar to the band. Of course, Alison, besides being an amazing instrumentalist herself, has worked with some of the finest guitarists around—all playing really, really nice guitars. Her standards are pretty high, and clearly she deserved the best sound I could give her. So I was faced with a hard decision. I had to take the Lowden. Only the Lowden would do.

I would also have to install a pick-up in my virgin guitar. Fortunately, though, through Alison's connections, I was able to have a top-of-the-line and non-invasive Fishman pick-up installed, which beautifully reproduced the instrument's sound. I also had a fairly durable guitar case, but still, I would try to bring my instrument onboard the plane whenever possible, knowing that no case is completely safe from the talons of baggage handlers.

> Being a musician, the idea of Cecelia is kind of cool. If anybody could use a patron saint it's probably us traveling musicians—especially if she has any pull with the airlines.

Fortunately, the airline we traveled was musician-friendly that day, and my Lowden fit easily in the overhead. I also brought my Ovation '94 Collector's edition, my main road guitar at that time, which I had to check. The tour went very well, the Lowden sounded great, and on the flight back to Nashville, I was once again allowed to put it in the overhead. Unfortunately, the Ovation, which I was again forced to check, arrived with a large gash in the case. Upon closer inspection it was discovered that my poor guitar had been dropped, kicked, run over, or just smashed so hard that the electronics inside were completely destroyed. The fiendish baggage handlers had done it again, and I simply did not have the hundreds of dollars and several month's time it would take to get it fixed.

So, again I had a tough choice to make. I had a string of dates to play over the next few weeks and my main road guitar was out of commission. Once again I had to do what I had vowed never to do. I had to tour with the Lowden and subject it to all the risks of the road. And so I have to this day. I have carefully loaded it into vans and cars, kept it out of the heat and cold, protected it from curious drunks, and so far kept it out of the hands of the airline's porters from hell. And I have prayed—really prayed—every time I've approached the terminal gate, "Please, oh please don't let them take my guitar away and destroy it." I really don't have any particular fear of flying—in fact, on flights I tend to feel pretty much at peace and in God's hands. But I am absolutely terrified of what the airlines might do to my instrument. I have had to gate-check the instrument a couple of times (which means the guitar is hand-loaded while I watch, and picked up at the gate when I arrive), but I never had to surrender it to the evil baggage handlers (knock on wooden top).

Just a few weeks ago, I had a particularly trying time with the airlines. I had just spent a week at a wonderful artist's retreat in central Washington State, working on new material, doing a small concert, and generally just hanging out with fellow artists: painters, graphic artists, musicians, and writers. While there I met a monk who does wonderful portraits of the saints in contemporary settings and modern dress. I was particularly taken by his portrait of St. Cecilia—patron saint of musicians. So I bought a print for my daughter (who is also a musician) and put it in the bottom of my Lowden case for wrinkle-free transport.

Though many here on the Catholic wing of the church can get pretty wrapped up in the whole saint thing, I tend to ignore the issue as so much ecclesiastical baggage. However, being a musician, the idea of Cecilia is kind of cool. If anybody could use a patron saint it's probably us traveling musicians—especially if she has any pull with the airlines.

So I headed to the Seattle airport, where I ran into some of the most obstinate, pig-headed, mean-spirited airline personnel I've ever encountered. They ignored my pleas, refused to read printed statements from the musician's union and the Transportation Safety Administration (both recommending that musicians be allowed to board with their instruments), tried to take my guitar away, and even threatened to charge me freight on the instrument! Somehow, I managed to get to the gate with it, where it was duly tagged to be gate-checked. But knowing the small-bodied guitar would easily fit in the overhead of this large plane, I approached a kindly-looking flight attendant. She took pity on me and helped me smuggle the guitar aboard, putting it in her coat closet. What a relief to know it had once again escaped the cloven hoofs of baggage handlers. As I was exiting the plane, she smiled and presented me with my undamaged guitar. I looked at her for a moment and then the thought hit. "Thanks for being my saint, Cecilia."

Visit Pierce Pettis at www.piercepettis.com

So many unusual things can happen while touring, all because of a missed ride and lost baggage. Dan Crary put it best when he said, "We do it for the stories we can tell."
—*Muriel Anderson*

John Michael Talbot

BROTHER JUNIPER

I had made the decision early in my career to abandon the musical path I had been traveling. Events in my life converged in such a way that I found myself at a crossroads. I was seeking a quieter, more contemplative way of life, a deeper way of experiencing my faith. I just wasn't satisfied. And the aggressive style of steel-string playing I had become known for was becoming increasingly at odds with where my heart was leading me—a life of simplicity, a life of poverty. And in that, I felt that the Lord was asking me to lay aside my Martin D-35.

It was a very special guitar. I was told that it was originally made for Stephen Stills. He never used it, so it passed to me. I went on to record several of my earlier albums with that guitar: *The Talbot Brothers, The Lord's Supper,* and *The Painter.*

I later found myself out in southern California, working with Keith Green. We got along well, but we also clashed. It was at that time that I felt moved to release the guitar, and so I gave it to Keith as a sort of peace offering for the times we fought. And giving it up became symbolic for me. With it, I was also giving up my past patterns, my aggressions, my violence, my impatience. And in its place, the Lord directed me to play the classical guitar.

Well, I had not played a nylon string guitar since I was ten years old, so this was quite a step of faith for me. I didn't know how to play it. I didn't know how to go about buying one. So I ventured down to the music store, and looked around.

For a spiritual person, the choosing of a guitar can be a very spiritual experience. They're like books—they jump off the shelf and say, "I'm the one for you." The same thing happens, I believe, with guitars. And that's exactly what happened that day in the music store in 1978. It was an Alvarez-Yairi—essentially a very nice, hand-made copy of a Ramirez. And this one was the top of the line. But it was also marked down to $750. As it turned out, it had a minor flaw, and I ended up getting the guitar for $350.

50

By this time, I had also moved into a Franciscan retreat center, where I really began my serious search for a more historical Christianity. This guitar was a great companion there. It's also the guitar that I cut my biggest records with: *Come to the Quiet, Troubadour of the Great King, God of Life,* and the less popular *Light Eternal.* Against all odds, these were all major sellers in the Christian contemporary market of the time.

Billy Ray Hearn was running Sparrow Records in those days. He didn't like my guitar at all. He used to call it the "cigar box." But I loved it, and I traveled with it constantly. And when I traveled by air, it went down below with the rest of the luggage. I didn't even have a flight case for it. It never occurred to me to take more care, to keep it in the cabin where it would be safe from damage. And sure enough, in its travels it got knocked about. Over and over again. The face would get smashed, and I'd have it repaired. The back would split, and I'd have it repaired again. I even had the neck replaced at one point. And every time I repaired that guitar, it got better. Every time it got knocked in, it got looser. And amazingly, the basses got bigger and deeper, and the brights got brighter.

Finally, in 1991, the folks at Westwood Music in Los Angeles told me that this would be the last time they'd repair it. They'd remake it, but that would be it; I'd have to agree to retire it. No more travels anywhere for this one. I acquiesced, and so now it stays at my hermitage.

I developed a love relationship with that guitar. I named it Brother Juniper, after the possibly fictitious, humble, and thoroughly delightful Franciscan of The Little Flowers of St. Francis. Brother Juniper symbolizes to me the essence of Christian life. Like the Franciscan brother, it's simple. It's poor. It doesn't put on airs. It's usable. And it can get hurt over and over and over again, but every time it goes through pain, it comes back better, stronger, and more useful.

> The face would get smashed, and I'd have it repaired. The back would split, and I'd have it repaired again. I even had the neck replaced at one point. And every time I repaired that guitar, it got better.

I also believe that guitars mold to their players. Brother Juniper molded to me in a very special way. There are certain resonances and sympathetic vibrations that result from the way a particular player approaches their instrument. A new instrument hasn't yet been molded. In the case of a used one, it has been molded to someone else's style. And it can take months and sometimes years for that guitar to mold to the new player. And as the player goes through changes in his life, the results of those changes will be transmitted to the instrument. I find a wonderful symbol in that, as we are the instruments of God. The more he plays us, the more we are molded and conformed to his image. But it was time to retire Brother Juniper.

Right at that time, a wonderful woman gave to me a Ramirez Centenario, a special model made for their 100th anniversary. I've played that guitar ever since. It's a beautiful guitar. And technically, it sounds better. But Brother Juniper is always going to have a very special place in my heart.

Coming full circle, after Keith Green died tragically in the airplane accident, his wife, Melody, sent my old Martin D-35 back to me. And for me, that guitar will always be a symbol of when you give something up out of love, that love gift will always come back to you—but in a way that is totally unexpected and cannot be manipulated. God always gives back whatever we give to him, and he usually gives back ten, or even a hundred-fold. And it's always in a way that is beyond what we can expect or imagine.

Visit John Michael Talbot at www.johnmichaeltalbot.com

PLAY IT BY EAR

I do everything by ear. I experiment with the lines. When a line starts to move I try to keep it moving in the same direction for as long as possible. You can find some of the wildest voicings by taking any line in a chord, moving it up or down in half or full steps and see what happens.
—*Howard Morgen*

I learned everything by ear. I think the ear is more reliable than Braille. The ear is always correct; Braille music is not.
—*Jose Feliciano*

My ears are so good now that if I hear someone fart, I can tell you what they had for dinner.
—*D.R. Auten*

John Doan

VISIT TO HEAVEN

Several years ago I often would find myself performing my music in symphony with patron conversations, the clanging of plates, the fizzing of expresso machines in coffee houses, and the gurgling of beer on tap in folk taverns around Salem and Portland, Oregon. I was there to get miles on my fingers, to test out original material on my harp guitar, and to learn to be focused on the music while letting go of the distractions around me. The latter was like a metaphor to me, challenging me to listen for what is beautiful in the midst of a busy world filled with noise.

At one tavern I started promoting my performances with posters prominently displaying the unusual twenty-string harp guitar I play. It has a regular guitar in the middle, with extra strings extending off to either side expanding its range to approach that of the piano. One of its advantages over the piano is that it's a lot easier to carry with you! The owner was willing to have me play on Mondays—his slowest night, figuring that it could only help business given that few people usually found their way there at the beginning of a work week.

As the weeks passed the place began to fill with fans interested in hearing the music. On one such night when I could not play a wrong note and everything fell into place perfectly with extended periods of quiet and standing ovations with pats on the back, the owner pulled me aside to tell me that I could not play there anymore. I thought he was joking but he looked at me in earnest and said that the people who came to hear me weren't buying enough to drink and were shushing some of his regulars who were talking, playing darts, and generally trying to make a move on one another.

I realized then that I needed to look for other settings in which to perform that would focus more on the music and less on consuming stimulates, intoxicating beverages, and partaking in preliminary mating rituals. But before I could throw myself into a concert career I realized that I would need to make a recording, if for nothing else, as a professional statement and publicity tool.

I called a friend of mine who had a studio in his home in Los Angeles to ask advice about recording. I really didn't know what costs would be involved or what equipment or microphones I should be using, among other things. He told me that he would soon have some time open in the spring and would love to have me come down to visit for a week during which time he would record me himself. This was such a generous offer, and in faith I immediately agreed to come not thinking how I was going to free myself from my teaching schedule or how I was going to afford getting myself, with instrument in tow, a thousand miles south.

> I realized then that I needed to look for other settings in which to perform that would focus more on the music and less on consuming stimulates, intoxicating beverages, and partaking in preliminary mating rituals.

After hanging up the phone I realized that Willamette University, where I teach part time, was going to have a spring break, and that could give me the window in time I needed. I then checked into flying down and back but found out that it was fairly expensive, and besides my century old harp guitar didn't have a proper hard case. Air freight cases are costly. It was unclear how I would get it into luggage without it being damaged in transit. I then considered driving the thousand miles each way but realized that my old Kharman Ghia most likely would not be able to complete the journey without various pit stops to replace broken and wearing parts, not to mention what a strain it would be to drive two days each way. Besides, the thought of being broken down in the desert between Fresno and Bakersfield, or chugging thirty miles an hour up Mt. Shasta while trying to avoid becoming a hood ornament for an eighteen-wheeler contributed to my lack of enthusiasm for driving.

So flying was out, driving was out, and obviously walking or thumbing a ride was way out of the question. Then an idea struck me. What about sharing a ride with some students who would be going to Southern California for the Spring break! I began spreading the word among my students that I was looking for a ride. I tried not to think too much about what it could be like in a car crammed shoulder to shoulder with teenagers for eighteen grueling hours of heavy metal blasting from the four inch dash speaker.

One afternoon a knock came at my office door. It was a young unshaven student dressed in jeans, a torn tea shirt, and Harachi sandals. He introduced himself as Paul. He said he heard I was looking for a ride to Los Angeles and that he could get me down there very fast. I asked, "How fast are we talking about." He said, "About eight hours." I said," You mean eigh*teen* hours." He reiterates, "No, eight hours." I laughed and said, "You must be joking, because there was no way that we could travel that distance in that short of time." He then began to tell me about his high school buddy, Pete, who was in the flying club at OSU in Corvallis and that he had reserved a three seat Cessna airplane for the break. They were flying down to Baja, Mexico, and could drop me off anywhere on the way. I would have the back seat to myself and an aerial view of Oregon and California. At that moment I began to imagine how I would be down there refreshed in only eight hours and with even more time to record. All I had to do was share in some gas money. We shook hands, discussed that I would be limited to only one hundred and eighty pounds of weight, and worked out the time we would meet at the Salem Airport.

I was excited that everything was coming together so well and was impressed that with a little faith most anything was possible, especially since this opportunity came along so quickly with schedules open and such fast transportation arranged at a reasonable price. After weighing myself and the harp guitar I calculated that although I would need to travel spartanly, I could at least bring one extra pair of underwear, a tee shirt, and a toothbrush stashed into the cavities of my canvas case.

The big day arrived and I had my wife drop me off at the airport. She gave me a small book to read titled, *The Creative Power of the Tongue* by Charles Capps, telling me that she had just read it and thought that it could be inspirational. I said, "What is this tongue business? Does this have something to do with kissing?" We then kissed and I got out of the car, closed the door and leaned in the window saying, "I'm missing you already." Partly embarrassed, and partly wishing me well and hoping I would take the book, she ignored my making fun of the book's title, smiled, and began to wave as she slowly drove away.

I recognized Paul who was standing next to a small gray aircraft motioning for me to hurry over to the plane so we could get started. He pushed the front seat forward and I got in the back, carefully directing my instrument into the hollow of the tail of the plane which lay directly behind the seat. "What an adventure! What fun this is going to be," I thought to myself as I crawled into this little car with wings. Once I sat down he pushed the front seat back in place, got in, and closed the thin metal door. The engine revved up, and all of a sudden we were taxiing to the runway. I hadn't even had a chance to be introduced to the pilot who was preoccupied with turning dials and looking on his map. Once in place with a clear strip of asphalt before us I tapped our pilot on the shoulders and said, "Hi, I'm John." He turned his head slightly to the right and said, "I'm Pete." Just then he got the go ahead from the tower and we were beginning to move down the runway.

Since it was going to take some time before we got to Los Angeles, I thought that we could engage in a little small talk, so I started by half jokingly asking Pete, "So how long have you had your license?" Pete was concentrating on our lift off, motioned me with his right hand that he would reply momentarily, and just as we left the ground he shouted over his shoulder, "I JUST GOT IT." The little plane vibrated with an all-consuming hum of the engine and what I thought could be idle conversation quickly turned into yelling above the horrendous drone. I shouted, "SO YOU MEAN YOU HAVE BEEN FLYING FOR YEARS AND JUST FORMALLY GOT YOUR LICENSE?" He yells back, "NO, I JUST STARTED TAKING LESSONS A COUPLE MONTHS AGO AND THIS IS MY FIRST TIME OUT WITHOUT AN INSTRUCTOR." And with that ringing in my ears, Paul handed out ear plugs for the rest of the flight.

I tried not to think much about what Pete had just confided in me as I pretended to look interested in the view down below. All the while I was secretly longing to be secure and on the ground again, and envied the people in the little cars and houses that passed beneath us among the green grasses and trees that carpeted the landscape. I found the little book my sweetheart gave me for the trip in my pocket and started looking through it. I first thought it had something to do with the power of positive thinking, but as I continued to read I found that it was more focused on positive speaking and believing. She is forever encouraging me to think deeply, hoping to develop a spiritual side to my earthy nature. In big letters it said, "Say what you want or get what you say." I read on how in order to live fully, "faith filled words will put you over. Fear filled words will defeat you. Words are the most powerful thing in the universe." Wow, that's pretty deep! I tend to need to learn by experience. Often words in a book are, well, words in a book! I guess if God wants me to understand something, he will give me an opportunity to experience it in 3D. So for the moment, I decided I'd just sit back and try to enjoy the ride.

I looked down and saw Albany and Eugene pass by under us as we began to leave the Willamette Valley. There was a different weather system up and into the hills around Cottage Grove that was moist and foggy. Pete quickly turned the plane upward while Paul looked nervously through the front and side windows. Then Paul yelled, "DO YOU SEE IT? THE HOLE OVER THERE. GO FOR THE HOOOOOLE!" Pete responded by maneuvering the plane as if we were in an aerial show and proceeded to dive right into and through the void in the clouds.

I am feeling very frightened and confused. My heart is beating up and into my throat, and I don't know what is going on. For a few seconds I think that I should behave like a faculty member and keep control of myself, but instead I grab Paul around the neck from behind with both hands and begin to shake him while screaming, "WHY ARE WE GOING FOR THE HOOOOLE?" Paul breaks loose of my desperate grip and yells back, "PETE IS ONLY LICENSED FOR VISUAL AND NOT INSTRUMENTS, SO HE HAS TO SEE WHERE WE ARE GOING OR WE WILL CRASH INTO THE SIDE OF SOME MOUNTAIN." He turns around and gets back to intently looking for more holes in the clouds.

After this explanation I'm almost totally petrified. It was then that I looked down and noticed the little book tightly gripped in my hands. It read, "If ye have faith as a grain of mustard seed, ye shall say unto this mountain, Remove hence to yonder place: and it shall remove: and nothing shall be impossible unto you." Well, it occurred to me that this would be a great time to have faith at least the size of a mustard seed, and so I started reading aloud those words from Matthew 17:20, realizing that no one could hear me over the moan of the throttling engine, "Mountain, Remove hence to yonder place!" Somehow it wasn't working as we tossed even more to the left and then up and to the right. Perhaps I needed to say it in my own words as "yonder place" was making me feel a bit like Jed Clampet or some other hill person from over yonder. "Okay mountain, be gone from here. I don't want to be a part of you, mountain." No, I don't think I should focus on being part of the mountain, so I went back to "mountain be gone" saying it over and over.

> Paul kept yelling, "GO FOR THE HOOOLE," while I sought refuge in a prayer plucked out upon the harp guitar. I spoke as I played, "Oh God, there is nothing I can do here. I cannot save myself from what is happening to me and these boys.

The roller coaster ride was making me very sick, so I tapped on Paul's shoulder and let him know of my condition. At the top of his lungs he explains, "I'M A SOPHOMORE IN PSYCHOLOGY AND I JUST FINISHED WRITING A PAPER ON AIR SICKNESS." At this point not knowing whether to laugh or cry I shouted, "AND WHAT DOES THAT HAVE TO DO WITH ANYTHING?" He said, "STUDIES POINT TO PEOPLE BEING ABLE TO AVOID AIR SICKNESS IF YOU BUSY YOURSELF WITH SOMETHING— ANYTHING TO KEEP YOUR MIND OFF OF DYING!"

So here I am, strapped into my seat feeling like I'm home inside my washer and dryer getting an encore presentation of this guy's Psychology 101 term report, all the while feeling like I am at eternity's doorstep. I incredulously shout back, "SO WHAT IN HEAVEN'S NAME COULD I DO TO KEEP MY MIND OFF OF DYING?" He thinks for a second as the plane pitched and yawed. "GET YOUR GUITAR OUT OF THE TAIL OF THE PLANE AND PLAY SOMETHING—ANYTHING!" Without losing a moment I unfastened my seat belt and haunched over the back of the seat and pulled the instrument from its case and to me. Once seated, I fastened the belt around me and the instrument and rested my jaw on the extended bass chamber so that through bone conduction I could hear myself play.

It is hard to describe what happened next. If God could not get my attention by words in a book I thought he sure as hell had my attention now! The plane whined and jerked. Paul kept yelling "GO FOR THE HOOOOLE," while I sought refuge in a prayer plucked out upon the harp guitar. I spoke as I played, "Oh God, there is nothing I can do here. I cannot save myself from what is happening to me and these boys. There is nowhere for me to be but to surrender and place myself in your hands. What will happen from this time forward is completely up to you. I am nothing without you. Hold me. Let me take shelter in your arms. Surround me in your love. Help me to hear your voice, to feel your calm and do this in the name of and remembrance of your Son, Jesus."

As a quiet befell me I whispered, "Jesus, take my hand and walk with me to the Father." And then it seemed as if time and space had taken a quantum shift; the totality of this instant was in slow motion and outside of time. There was no roaring engine that was close to me. No shouting directions that mattered. No buffeting of wind and pounding of rain upon the windows to distract the peace I felt in this moment so near to death yet so close to feeling truly alive. I was riding out the storm in the calm of its eye from what seemed the center of the universe.

Mountain? What mountain?

At one moment in the midst of our struggle I saw the most amazing thing outside the window. With all the misting and the sun's light piercing through from above, I could see against a backdrop of gray clouds the shadow of the plane encircled by a rainbow. I had never seen a rainbow as a complete circle before. Don't they always touch down somewhere and arch up to a high midpoint? This felt like God's promise to Noah that his struggle was past and there would be no more epic floods.

Soon after, we managed to find the Roseburg airport that presented itself as the clouds parted. After landing, Pete had a phone number of an aunt that he called who came and picked us up. We were once again safe and secure on terra firma. I was numb from the experience, and still relishing the distant and calming melody that lingered in my head while we tore through the clouds. I would later record it on my *Departures* CD and title it *Visit to Heaven*.

The next morning the forecasts were for clear skies over Oregon, and so we gathered our things and once again took for the sky. All seemed well except for a weather system ahead around Mt. Shasta. I thought to myself, "Oh no. Not another mountain in our path!" Pete and Paul looked at a map and decided that it would probably be safer to just go inland around the mountain and avoid the clouds altogether. It seemed reasonable to avoid the problem and play it safe by taking more time to go off course and improvise our way back. Besides, by this time I was lost in musing over my new piece while glancing out over the rough terrain.

After some time we made it east of Mt. Shasta, and it was then that Pete and Paul began to become agitated again. Pete grabbed the map out of Paul's hands and shook his head about something. I began to look on while noticing one of the dials on the controls had the needle pointing to the letter "E." I thought, "No, that couldn't mean what I think it means." But sure enough it did not mean things where going to be "E"asy. I was wanting to practice some of the positive speaking and believing I had just started to read about, but the first things that came to mind starting with the letter "E" was "E"gg, when the plane hits the "E"arth. In this language of fear I also imagined "E"vaporate, "E"xecution, "E"xtinction, and so forth. I couldn't allow myself any more of this, as it was too frightening. I remembered a line in the book that said, "Say what you want or get what you say" and "faith filled words will put you over. Fear filled words will defeat you." I sat back and drifted off into a prayer again remembering that I was not in charge of this or most things in my life. We had been in a desperate situation before and made it through, and although a bit rattled, I tried to busy myself with what I was given to do—playing the harp guitar. In this peaceful state of prayer I kept believing that this is not our time to leave this world, and that God will find us a place to land. There was truly nothing else this side of madness to do but to believe that we were going to be alright, in spite of appearances.

With not much gas, they were faced with having to force-land the plane if they could not find an airport. There were no airfields listed on the map in the immediate region. Paul saw off to the right and down below what looked like a runway, but could not understand why it was not on the map. Pete shouts, "WHO CARES IF IT IS ON PAPER OR NOT. ITS THERE!" We waste no time losing altitude making our way down for a landing.

As the engine sputters we coast in and touch down. Pete starts to laugh to release the anxiety of the moment past. Instantly we're all laughing hard, thinking what a comedy of errors this journey has been so far. As the guys start looking around they sober up, trying to figure out what kind of place this is. It wasn't your usual municipal airport; that was for sure. What few buildings dotted the abandoned site were painted the color of the earth, making them hard to distinguish from the barren landscape. They had no markings and were completely shut up. As a tumble weed cartwheeled across the asphalt before us Paul asks, "Now what? Where are we going to get gas?"

Just then several camouflaged vehicles came racing up with soldiers jumping off and surrounding the plane. The officer in charge runs up to the door and shouts, "Get out of the aircraft and keep your hands above your heads." Our jovial mood changed as quickly as its onset. We were interrogated as to who we were and why we had landed here. We were told we had landed in a restricted area that was an ammunition dump for the military. After ascertaining that we were not the enemy but instead were simply stupid and inexperienced aviators, they secured fuel for us and we were on our way once again.

We finally made it to the Santa Monica airport just after midnight some forty hours after leaving Salem the morning before. So much for getting down to Los Angeles in eight relaxing hours! I called my parents who lived nearby and spoke with my dad, apologizing for coming in so late. He knew I was coming and had waited for the call. He assured me that he was glad we made it in safely, and that given the hour it was fine for the guys to stay over for the night. We told our stories in the car and over scrambled eggs and toast into the wee hours of the morning.

The guys were up and off to Baja the next day. I had learned that they were to meet with a group of volunteers who were building houses for families in need. Perhaps their big hearts and spirit of generosity added to our reprieve from harm's way. Little will these people know what it took to have their homes built. It truly is a mystery all the threads that weave together that form the events of our lives.

After dropping them off at the airport my dad took me and my harp guitar to my friend's house where I spent several days making my demo recording. The days passed quickly in front of the microphone. The instrument loomed huge in the headsets washed in reverb, chorus, and delay. Against the background of quiet in the studio the tone of the strings seemed as if they were all that existed for the moment. That reminded me of my time in the storm. While by myself I would go back to the themes I had heard in the clouds, trying to recall the peace I had experienced there.

I was sure that one day while looking back upon this adventure, I would remember this as one of the more foolish things I had ever done. But little did I know I was about to do something even more foolish. At the end of the week, Pete and Paul arrived back in Santa Monica to take on some cargo—namely me, the harp guitar, and a reel of quarter inch tape. I thought since I had already paid my share of the gas, had no proper case for the harp guitar, and hadn't figured out another way to get back home, I resigned myself to the northerly sky with them.

They were all red and sunburned, but in good spirits. The expanse before us was blue and clear. With earplugs in, harp guitar strapped to my chest, and my jaw resting on the upper arm of the instrument, I had the routine down for small aircraft travel. Pete decided to lay over for the evening in Redding as the sun receded its fingers of light to the west. There was an approaching cloud system coming in over Mt. Shasta, and we were hopeful that it would pass by morning. So we found some sleeping bags that had been stowed away and made ourselves at home there on the runway. Lying on my back looking up at the stars I had dreams of being up closer to them in the morning.

As the night sky awoke to gray I could feel the cool wind on my face. The cloud system had not passed yet but in hope of finding a clear patch of blue we got gas and made our way back to the sky. Once up near the clouds that hug about the mountain we could see that there was no opening for us to pass through, so we returned to the field. Within the hour we tried this again and with the same result. Paul said he had a paper due and that he could not hang on indefinitely, so he opted to get a cab to the bus station. Pete had to return the plane to Corvallis and had no choice but to stay with it until the weather cleared. I stayed on with Pete and urged him to try one more time.

Now I was the co-pilot! I got to sit up in the front this time. I strapped myself in and tried to familiarize myself with the maps. We roared up and away like experienced flyboys. It was actually thrilling looking out ahead as we left the valley and approached our nemesis of clouds blanketing across to Mt. Shasta. Pete was about to turn around again when I asked him, "WHY DON'T WE DO WHAT THE BIG PLANES DO AND FLY OVER THE CLOUDS, NOT JUST THROUGH THEM? LET'S PUT THIS MOUNTAIN BEHIND US." He raised his eye brows and thought for a moment and said, "OKAY, LET'S DO IT."

With no doubt in our hearts the little Cessna droned and moaned higher and higher. We had never flown to quite this altitude during the entire trip. Pete kept giving it throttle as it behaved like the little engine that could barely make it up the mountain. We finally broke through the clouds at around 15,000 feet. There was nothing but blue sky, a warm sun in the windows, and a sheet of white cotton just feet beneath us. I was laughing and looking about in wonderment. I called out to Pete, "SO WHY DIDN'T WE DO THIS ALL ALONG?" He slowly turned his head and with concern in his face shouted back, "AT THIS ALTITUDE THERE IS NOT ENOUGH OXYGEN TO BREATH, SO WE CAN'T STAY UP HERE TOO LONG." With that being said I began scouring the carpet of white just below me, and somewhere around Ashland I began shouting, "GO FOR THE HOOOOLE."

Upon returning, after giving my wife a long and extended kiss, she asked how everything went and if I had a chance to look at the book she gave me. I said, "Oh yes, I really learned a lot both inside and out of that little book. It's scary—or I mean to say, remarkable—how so true to life it was."

Visit John Doan at www.johndoan.com

This story excerpted from John Doan's book, *Wayfaring Stranger*, a work in progress.

You get very attached to guitars because they are so personal.
You pretty much almost sleep with them. I do.
—*Adrian Belew*

Robbie Robertson

THE BOOSTED TELE

Before we were The Band, we were the Hawks, playing as Ronnie Hawkins and the Hawks. When we left Ronnie, the Hawks went on to become The Band. At that time in 1964, the Hawks were playing a club in Toronto—The Friars Club—where we had an extended engagement. We'd do our bit each night and just leave our equipment there onstage for the next night. There were never any problems.

Well, we came into the club one night, and I looked up on the stage and my guitar—an early '60s cream colored Telecaster with a maple neck—wasn't there. My first thought was that I had put it away in the back room. I looked, and it wasn't there. All of a sudden it sunk into me that someone had stolen my guitar. And it wasn't like, *oh, I guess I'll just have to use the Gibson tonight*. That Tele was *it*. I only had one guitar. I went into a tailspin.

There wasn't much time before we had to play, and I was getting more and more distraught. I called a couple of people to see if I could borrow a guitar, but I couldn't reach anybody. In despair, I went and sat at the bar, and continued to wrack my brain for some solution to this crisis.

Sitting next to me was a regular we called Downtown Dougie. He was a strange fellow who always wore a trench coat; he made me think of a character out of a Mickey Spillane novel. Well, he could see that I was a little squirrelly, and asked what was going on. "I'm in shock," I told him. "Somebody's stolen my guitar and we've got to start playing before long, and I don't know what I'm going to do!" I was in a real panic. He asked me to describe the guitar, and remembering it he said, "Oh yeah, yeah, yeah. I know what you're talking about." I then excused myself to make a few more phone calls, still without any luck. A few minutes later, Downtown Dougie came walking back into the club, and he says to me, "Did you find it?" I told him I hadn't. And then he said, "Did it look like this one?" He reached under his overcoat and pulled out a cream colored Telecaster—only this one still had the tags hanging off it!

It turns out Downtown Dougie was a booster. And these guys—they called themselves rounders—came in different varieties. There were second-story men, and other kinds of specialty thieves, but this particular guy was a booster; they could steal very specific things for you. If you told him you needed a fur coat in a particular size and color, he'd go out and get it. I looked at that Tele, and thought, "My God, that's exactly like my guitar! Where did you get this?" He gave me a wry little smile that said, "Don't ask stupid questions."

I was nervously tearing the tags off, and looking around thinking I was going to be arrested at any moment. I was in shock again. So I ran to the back room and thought maybe I ought to scuff it up a bit so it doesn't look so shiny and new. I didn't know what to do.

> I looked at that Tele, and thought, "My God, that's exactly like my guitar! Where did you get this?" He gave me a wry little smile that said, "Don't ask stupid questions."

We finally got up and played, and as it turned out, everything was fine. And so I thought, "Well, okay. Maybe what goes around comes around. I don't know." To this day, I still have that guitar. I continued to use it through all the years I was playing with Bob Dylan and The Band. All the paint has worn off now, but I still have it, and it still sounds great.

A few nights after the "replacement incident," Downtown Dougie joined us at the house where we were staying, just hanging out and talking. It got late and I was getting a little drowsy and started to nod off when Dougie said to me, "Don't fall asleep or I'll be compelled to steal your shoes."

For more information about Robbie Robertson, visit
http://theband.hiof.no/band_members/robbie.html

LISTEN UP

The quieter you play, the more people strain to listen.
—*Davey Graham*

I decided that I would become the *quietest* guitarist, rather than the loudest or fastest. I believe this was the right decision for me. And if you believe in what you do, then you are also believable to others.
—*David Qualey*

Peppino D'Agostino

GUITAR PARADISE

I grew up in Turino, the home of Fiat, in the northern part of Italy. As an aspiring guitarist, there couldn't have been a worse place for me to be. There was hardship at home, and as far as making it as a guitarist, I was often misunderstood as an artist. Yet I was determined. Playing the guitar gave me a sense of peace and meaning, and the music became a vehicle for my escape from the darker corners of my young life. As such, playing the guitar was just more important to me than the average kid. Playing was joyful. It gave me an opportunity to make new friends, and it allowed me to be with people in a different way. All of these things served to reinforce my sense of who I was.

In other ways, though, Italy was fertile ground for guitarists—if you happened to be an American guitarist. In my early years, I was exposed to the music of Leo Kottke, Doc Watson, Chet Atkins, Duck Baker, and others who were making regular appearances on stage and on the airwaves in and around Italy. Stefan Grossman

> Italy was fertile ground for guitarists—if you happened to be an American guitarist.

had much to do with that. He was living in Italy at the time, and he created tremendous interest in American blues and roots music through his Kicking Mule label. I was one of the people who bought those records. And what's more, all that vinyl was packaged with the tablature. So not only was it wonderful music, I could learn to play it, too!

When Stefan and his friends toured Italy, they played to audiences of a thousand people or more. English guitarists were welcomed, too: John Renbourn, Bert Jansch, Martin Carthy, Davey Graham, and others. But if you were Italian, forget about it. Italians didn't have much of a taste for the home-grown; they preferred the exotic charm of the foreign visitors. In spite of this, though, I continued to play wherever I could—cafés, small clubs, festivals. Still, the American artists dominated.

I decided then that I needed to see what America was all about. I was curious about this land that produced so many wonderful guitarists. I happened to meet a group of musicians from Maine, and when I made plans to visit, they agreed to receive me. Never mind that I didn't speak a word of English, I figured that in a country populated with the likes of Chet Atkins and Leo Kottke, there was no way I could expect anything, anyway. But I learned that in America, there is a place for everybody. There was actually an audience that would find me and my music attractive.

I ultimately decided to make my home in the states. Oddly enough, when I do return to Italy for visits now, I'm viewed quite differently: I'm the one who succeeded in America. Prior to that, I wasn't worth anyone's attention. It's an interesting thing. This is not to say, though, that there haven't been drawbacks to being in America. For one, Italian ice cream is far better than American ice cream. And, as I was about to find out, it's also far less dangerous.

> So there I was, with one hand driving, and the other hand holding the guitar case outside the car by the handle. I must have driven that way for two blocks before pulling over to settle down.

After one of my performances in downtown San Francisco, I had a craving for some ice cream. I stopped at a grocery store in the Tenderloin district—a fairly seedy area where the streets are lined with porno shops and prostitutes. I had carelessly left my car unlocked, and when I returned, my guitar was gone. I looked around and didn't see anybody, just a group of shady-looking characters loitering nearby. I approached them and asked in my poor English if they had seen anybody break into my car. No response. Nobody said anything.

With that, I got into my car and drove. I drove frantically for several blocks, hoping to spot the person who might be running away with my guitar. I eventually returned to the store, found the same group still there, and I asked them again. This time one of them answered, "Well, it depends." I looked at him and said, "What do you mean, 'it depends?'" He explained under his surly countenance that it depended on how much money I had. "Anything can be bought," he added. By then I understood. I offered him $50, which he accepted. I dug into my pocket and realized I had no money. I left once again to find an ATM. By this time, it was nearly 3:00 AM, and I was really furious. I didn't have that kind of money to blow.

I got the $50 and returned to the scene. He demanded that I give him the money. I told him I'd give him the money when he gave me the guitar. At that, he swore at me and left. Getting back into my car, I caught a glimpse of a man crouching behind a parked car with my guitar in hand. I drove over as close as I could get and told him to give me my guitar. "Give me the money," he screamed. Now I could see that these two characters were working together. If I had given the first guy the money, they would both have disappeared—one with the money and the other with the guitar. So I said, "Let's do it at the same time. But first show me that the guitar is in the case." I lowered my window, stuck out my left hand, and said, "Here's the money—now give me the guitar." He sheepishly came forward, looking left and right, and put the guitar in my right hand. At the same time, with my left hand, I threw the money to the pavement and peeled away. So there I was, with one hand driving, and the other hand holding the guitar case outside the car by the handle. I must have driven that way for two blocks before pulling over to settle down.

In taking my guitar, this punk had taken a part of me. And in getting it back, I was whole again. But I also learned some important lessons. I suppose I was lucky.

And the ice cream? Well, as it turns out it was an Italian immigrant who, in 1903, was the first to file a patent for the ice cream mold. Really! Just one more thing that started in Italy, and yet was transformed on foreign soil.

Visit Peppino D'Agostino at www.peppinodagostino.com

IN MY OWN WORDS

I was more interested in finger pickin' and inventing my own licks. If I played something that sounded like Les Paul or George Barnes or Merle Travis, they would bring it up to me, and I didn't like that. I wanted to be known for my *own* stuff.
—*Chet Atkins*

I hear all these people sit down and say, "This is what Chet did." Well that's good. I heard what Chet did, but he already did that. Things I might play in that style are my interpretation of what Chet or Merle or Jerry might have done. I'm not interested in sounding exactly like them or anybody else.
—*Thom Bresh*

Jimmie Rodgers

GUITAR SCAM

Through various contacts, Jimmie Rodgers learned of jobs with traveling shows, and no sooner did he get the news of one than he was aboard some freight train and headed toward it. Occasionally the information panned out, but more often than not, he was left stranded in some out of the way crossroads or given temporary work in the cookhouse to earn his way to the next stop. When he couldn't manage even that, he fell back on a gambit which he had, by this time, perfected into a minor art. Shined and shaved and dressed in his best—even on the road and down on his luck, he maintained appearances—he'd go into the nearest store where musical instruments were sold, pick out a moderately expensive guitar, and demonstrate his expertise with a song or two, charming the owner or clerk with show business stories and dropping impressive hints about his "current tour." Then he'd casually arrange to buy the instrument on credit. Next stop was a pawnshop, and after that the railroad tracks or highway out of town. Later, traveling through many of these same places after he'd become a star, he'd make a point of looking up the people he'd taken and repaying them, although he admitted that he missed a few because they were no longer in business or he'd forgotten their addresses. As the story got around, hundreds of hock shops all over the country suddenly began discovering and proudly displaying guitars that were "left here by ole Jimmie Rodgers."

From Jimmie Rodgers: The Life and Times of America's Blue Yodeler

---

Most Christian music is deadly boring, because it is made to
be non-threatening Muzak for a gated community. But the rebel
Jesus is alive and well and safe outside those walls.
—David Wilcox

Bruce Carroll

with Jan Northington

AN INSTRUMENT IN GOD'S HANDS

"God, you know my heart, and you know my needs. All I really want to do is please you, to serve you, and to know you deeper, no matter what it costs."

I have often prayed those words in my life, but it was the summer of 1989 when God gave me a unique opportunity to fulfill that desire. I was one of several Christian musicians taking part in the first ever, Soviet-sanctioned Christian music festival, sponsored by Youth for Christ. We were scheduled to perform four concerts in three days in Talin, Estonia.

Taking off from Nashville, I made myself comfortable for the long overseas flight. The roaring jet engine couldn't drown out the still, small voice of God testing my obedience. "Remember, Bruce, I own all that you have. I want you to give away your guitar in the Soviet Union."

My acoustic, six-stringed Takamine guitar was safely stowed with the luggage in the cargo section. At $600, it was the nicest guitar I had ever owned. Everyone who heard it or played it thought it was touched by God. I tried to ignore the voice, but the words kept repeating in my mind as we continued our flight, "I want you to give away your guitar in the Soviet Union."

It seemed a radical request. Why would God want my guitar? Immediately, Luke 11:28 came to mind—"Jesus said, 'Blessed are those who hear the word of the Lord and obey it.'"

"How could this message be from you, Lord?" I asked. "You know I need my guitar for the ministry you called me to." The voice persisted. "I want you to give away your guitar in the Soviet Union." I turned to my wife, Nikki, and said, "Honey, I think I'm supposed to give away my guitar in the Soviet Union."

68

"That would bring honor to the Lord," Nikki replied without hesitation. "It may be God's way of providing an instrument for the people over there to use in worship."

Her matter-of-fact answer confirmed for me that God was speaking to my heart. Still, I was uncomfortable with the idea. How was I supposed to carry it out? I imagined myself walking up to a stranger on a street corner, handing him my guitar, and then running away.

Nikki's voice brought me back. "Bruce, everything you have is on loan from God, anyway. If you can admit that your guitar really never was yours to start with, it should be a lot easier to give back to him."

I knew she was right. But why was it such a struggle? Yes, I had told God I was willing to serve him no matter what the cost. Did I mean it? I needed my precious guitar. Could I trust God to provide for me?

"Okay, God, if you really want me to do this, please give me another sign. Give me a burning bush or at least make it crystal clear to me." I wanted to believe I was willing to give up my guitar. But I'd have felt a lot more confident going into this knowing the specifics.

After we arrived in Finland, we got on a ferry for the three-hour voyage across the Baltic Sea. Standing on the deck of the ferry, we watched Soviet patrol boats cruise by. Still, we had a sense of peace, trusting that God was in control.

The unsettling presence of the KGB at the arena couldn't be dismissed—they sold the tickets and collected them at the door. However, once the concerts began, there was an air of freedom, and the Lord opened many hearts. Seventeen thousand people attended the concerts, Bibles were distributed, and thousands gave their lives to Jesus Christ. I had never before been involved in anything like it. I was humbled that God used me to bring the gospel to another part of the world—to people who spoke another language, and lived another life, yet desired freedom and the right to know God.

After our last concert, the performers, local stage hands, and YFC staff gathered backstage, hugging, crying, and saying our goodbyes. The road master announced we would be leaving in thirty minutes. At that moment, I realized I still had my guitar. "Lord, I know you asked me to give away my guitar. I really do want to be obedient, but you haven't led me to give it away. Perhaps you just wanted to see if I would be obedient?" With a growing sense of relief, I continued, "You know my heart. Are you going to let me keep my guitar because of the obedience you knew I would have shown?"

Just then, an Estonian man—part of the local YFC staff—approached me. In

69

broken English, he said, "I have been wanting to share something with you all day." His next words were the ones I had anticipated. "Your interpreter, Peter, leads praise and worship for his church and he has been praying for five years for an acoustic guitar. I thought you ought to know." As he turned to leave, he added, "Isn't God good? He knows our hearts and all of our needs."

> The words poured out as I handed him the instrument. "This guitar is for you—the case, the strings, the picks, the straps—everything that has to do with this guitar.

My heart pounded. My immediate response was to thank God for his faithfulness, though I still harbored a seed of doubt. Maybe this is just a coincidence, I rationalized as I walked across the stage toward Peter. Maybe this really isn't God; it's just me wanting it to be God.

Suddenly, the Old Testament story of Jonah flashed through my mind—only it was me on the bow of a Baltic ship. I saw myself, clutching my guitar as waves crashed over the sides of the boat, splashing me with salt water. The captain was running frantically around the ship, yelling, "Someone has something he's not supposed to have—*who is it?*" In my vision, I tried to hide my guitar behind me, but the crew pointed and shouted, *"There he is! Throw him overboard!"*

Now it was my time to run—straight to Peter. The words poured out as I handed him the instrument. "This guitar is for you—the case, the strings, the picks, the straps—*everything* that has to do with this guitar. God wants you to have it all!"

I didn't have to say anything more. We both had tears in our eyes, amazed at God's blessings. With a final hug, I hurried off to catch my ride back to the ferry.

Two weeks after I returned home, I reminded God of an upcoming concert. "I know I don't need to tell you, because you already know, but I'm going to need another guitar or some money to buy one." I felt confident God would provide what I needed, although once again, I didn't know how it would happen.

A few days later, the phone rang. An unfamiliar voice asked, "Is this Bruce Carroll, the gospel singer?"

"Yes."

"I'm calling from the Gibson Guitar Company. We'd like to make some inroads into gospel music by way of an endorsement."

"What does that mean?" I asked.

"We'd like to give you a guitar," the man replied.

"Seriously? What kind of guitar do you want to give me?"

"Any one you want."

"Then, I'll take the top of the line!"

"No problem. It's on its way," he replied.

Within the week, the Gibson Guitar Company sent me a black, J200 Gibson guitar valued at $3,000!

One month after receiving this brand-new guitar, an acquaintance called me. "Bruce," he said, "I was leading worship this morning and felt the Lord saying, 'I want you to give your guitar to Bruce Carroll.' It's a Martin D-28 worth about $3,500."

I was stunned, especially since I knew this man didn't know what had happened in Estonia. Then I heard some familiar words as he added, "God told me to give you the case, the strings, the picks, the straps—everything that has to do with that guitar."

"How do you know its God asking you to do this?" I asked.

"I know the Shepherd's voice. When I told God I was going to give you my guitar, an amazing thing happened. A stranger came up to me right after church and gave me his guitar. And it's better than the one I'm giving you."

Since receiving the second guitar, I have been given nine others—most of which I've prayerfully given away. God is good. He knows my heart and all my needs. When he gives, he gives abundantly. God's storehouse is filled with blessings (and guitars) that I never knew existed until I gave back to him what had been on loan to me from the start.

Visit Bruce Carroll at www.brucecarroll.com

I'm not concerned about perfection anymore. I like to hear a
mistake and a little noise on a record. If you get in there, move
things around, clean it up and make it perfect, it's not music to
me anymore. It's like taking a Picasso painting, running it through
a computer, and straightening up the lines; it's not art anymore.
—*Brent Mason*

John Hammond

THE GUITAR SHINES ON

I got my first guitar when I was eighteen—a Gibson J-100. I paid $10 for it in 1960, so as you can imagine, it wasn't in great shape. Actually, it had a hole punched through the top, but it had great action and it sounded good enough. Within a year, I was playing professionally around Greenwich Village and even doing some recording. It all came on me very fast—I guess it was just waiting to happen.

This was at a time when a lot of the originators of blues music were being rediscovered, and there were always great shows at coffee houses, on college campuses, and in theaters. And I got to play with a lot of those blues legends: Bukka White, John Hurt, Reverend Gary Davis, so many of them. And they were all such phenomenal people. But Johnny Shines was one of the greatest guitar players I have ever known. This man toured with Robert Johnson! *Hello!* And Johnny could play and sing as well as anyone I had heard.

The music these men played came from an incredibly deep tradition. It had a sense of timelessness. And you know, a great blues song is never dated. And that's because those songs are about the human condition, and essentially, that never changes. For many of them, life was difficult, to say the least. And so it struck me as such an honest, basic, seminal form of music that just rang my bell. And I've been on the road with it ever since.

Sometime in the mid-1980s I was playing a gig in Tuscon, Arizona—a funky blues joint called Terry & Zeek's Friendly Bar. After my first set, I was approached by a pretty rough looking guy who came backstage. He said to me, "I got somethin' for ya, man." I looked at him and didn't quite know what to make of the situation. He was probably in his late forties, had long hair, and looked like he might have just gotten out of jail. I asked him what he had and he said, "Well, it's out in the car." I was a little nervous now, wondering where this was going. But I followed him out to his car anyway, which was pretty beat up. As he opened the trunk, I started cringing, not knowing what was coming. But when he pulled out a 1932 National Style O guitar, I was taken aback. It was in pretty rotten condition, but even so, you don't see an instrument like that every day. He said to me, "This is for you, man." I told him, "You don't want to give this to me. It's worth some money!" But he wouldn't take no for an answer. Pushing it into my hands, he said again, "This is *yours*."

Now, the problem at that moment was that I was on the road. It was all I could do to take my own two guitars and my suitcases when I traveled. But there it was, in my lap. He just laid it on me and split. So I had to schlep it back home.

> As he opened the trunk, I started cringing, not knowing what was coming. But when he pulled out a 1932 National Style O guitar, I was taken aback.

It was unplayable as it was, and it really needed a lot of work. I brought it to a friend of mine who does work on National guitars, and he started putting it together. It got a new fingerboard, a new resonator cone, and it got cleaned up and set up. By the time it was finished I had put about $600 into it, which at the time for me was no small change.

While the guitar was being repaired, I was on tour, and doing a show with Johnny Shines. He was watching me playing my National, and he came up to me and said, "You know, John, I used to have a guitar like that, but I had to sell it." He went on to tell me how much he admired that guitar as he looked longingly at mine. The seed was sown.

When that old 1932 National was ready to go, I got a case for it and I sent it to Johnny. I told him, "This is for you, man." And he played it up until he died.

Visit John Hammond at www.johnhammond.com

I'm gonna sing some blues of other guys—friends of mine. They're all gone; that's why I'm gonna sing 'em. If I don't who will?
—*Big Bill Broonzy*

Phil Keaggy

FOR WANT OF A GUITAR

Compassion International had invited my wife and I to see the work they were doing in Haiti on behalf of the children there, and to encourage us to be spokespersons for the organization. It was such a powerful and humbling experience that a year or so later, I returned for another visit.

This second trip was in support of a film called *Small World*. Randy Stonehill and Cliff Richard had also come along. We took a small plane to the Haitian island of Lagonave, which was a bit harrowing. Randy Stonehill was keen on having his last will and testament in order before hopping on the small plane which landed us on a beach at low tide!

The island is home to many of Haiti's poorest of the poor. It's very primitive and harsh. There is little fresh water, and no roads to speak of. And with its rocky landscape, it's also prone to famine. Life just doesn't get much harder or depressing than on Lagonave.

It was against this backdrop that we visited a school there, where I sang songs and played guitar for the kids. One of the songs I did is an old standard of mine called *What a Day*. The kids just loved it, and they sang along with me loudly and joyfully. And they taught me some of their songs. We got to know a number of the kids, spending some time with them, and speaking through our interpreter.

Our time came to an end, and so we said our goodbyes. As we walked toward the waiting bus, I could hear the kids in the schoolhouse, singing that chorus again to *What a Day*. Some of the kids followed us out, and as I was stepping up to board the bus, I felt prompted to respond to a little boy who had taken so much interest in my guitar—he had such a smile on his face. He didn't say anything that suggested he wanted the guitar, but he had sure been admiring it. I turned around and said to him, "Here. I want you to have this." And I handed my guitar to him.

This little boy couldn't believe it. He just beamed with joy. It was as though I had given him a house! It wasn't a Ramirez, but it was a fine guitar, and to this little boy, it was a tremendous treasure.

Years later, I learned that the boy grew up to be quite a guitar player, and ended up leading worship in his church community. And for many years, that guitar was used almost every day to bring peace and comfort to hundreds of people in that intensely needy place. And I thought, isn't that fantastic. It reminded me that the first three guitars that I got were given to me! The Lord gives us the tools, and he often provides what we need through other people.

Visit Phil Keaggy at www.philkeaggy.com

YOU CAN'T TUNA FISH

I play almost exclusively in standard tuning; the others are just too limiting. You can't go anywhere with them, they're just too modal. I tend to jump around from key to key, and so standard seems to work best for me.
—*Earl Klugh*

I love to pick up a guitar in a different tuning and play a riff. Because it's in a different tuning, you're hearing it in a different way.
—*David Wilcox*

They allow for some interesting chord voicings that can be difficult, if not impossible, to create in standard tuning.
—*Alex de Grassi*

I was sitting next to this girl who had binoculars and was constantly writing stuff down as she watched Joni [Mitchell] play. When I asked her what she was doing, she told me, "I'm trying to cop Joni's tunings." Tunings! I'd never thought of that. So I started playing around with alternate tunings, and that really opened up my songwriting. It took me out of the simpler folk compositions and into a more sophisticated place.
—*Dan Fogelberg*

I'm famous for some bizarre tunings. I'll not only retune a guitar, but string it backwards, upside down—anything to get a weird sound.
—*Pat Metheny*

Peter Frampton

THE BLACK BEAUTY

In 1969, I was playing with Humble Pie in San Francisco at the Fillmore West, opening for the Grateful Dead. Up until that event, I had been playing a 1960 Gibson SG, which I decided I no longer wanted to play. In those days, though, you had just one guitar—you couldn't get another without first trading or selling the one you had. So I traded in the SG for a Gibson 335. And on this night, I was breaking it in.

We were playing through 100-Watt Marshalls, and every time I'd turn up for my solo, all you'd hear was howling feedback. It was just horrible. The 335 is semi-hollow, which means it's prone to feedback. And as the opening band, our amps were very close to us, which only made matters worse. We did two shows that night and it was a just an awful, awful experience.

Between sets, I was approached by a fellow who introduced himself as Mark Mariana, and he commented, "I see you're having a little trouble with that 335." I said, "Trouble?! Yeah, I should say. All I want is to get my SG back, but it's long gone now."

He nodded in sympathy and told me about the '54 Les Paul that he had just gotten back from Gibson. He had done some work on it and had the factory refinish it for him. Seeing me now in some distress over the 335, he asked me if I'd be interested in playing his guitar. Well, I didn't really care much for Les Pauls; they never really worked for me. But when I thought about playing that 335 again the next night, I said, "What the hell—it can't be worse!"

So Mark met me at the hotel coffee shop the following morning. He opened up the case, and lying there was this absolutely gorgeous guitar. He asked me if I'd like to play it for the night's shows, and I said, "Absolutely! Do you mind?" He said, "No, no. Take it." And so for the two sets we did that night, I don't think my feet touched the ground. This was *my* guitar. It was just everything I had ever *hoped* for in a guitar.

A 1954 Black Beauty, it had to be one of the very first ones made. And it was remarkably light. Mark had rerouted it for three humbuckers; originally it had the two P90s on it. He had always admired the '57 Les Paul Custom with three pickups pictured on the Smokey Robinson & the Miracles album cover, so he set his up that way and had Gibson refinish it. I was actually the first person to play it when it came back from the factory, and it sounded incredible. After the show, I said to Mark, "Well, I guess I'm looking for a Les Paul now."

I asked him if he'd ever think of selling it, and of course, he said no. But I wasn't prepared for what he said next: "I want to *give* it to you." Right there, Mark gave me the guitar! I was just incredulous. I know he saw the enjoyment that it gave me as I played, and he must have thought long and hard about it. That was a strange and wonderful moment, to be sure—and the last thing I expected him to do.

So that guitar started its new life with me, and it served me well through the remaining days of Humble Pie, and into my solo career. That guitar became a part of me—so much so that I couldn't play anything else. It's also the guitar that's featured on the cover of *Frampton Comes Alive*, which went on to become the biggest selling live album ever. That guitar brought me a lot of luck.

I later traveled with my band to South America, where we did a major tour of Brazil, Argentina, Panama, and Venezuela. We had a day off, and so we flew ahead to Panama. It was the only time we flew separately from the gear. When we arrived, my road manager approached me, and somewhat sheepishly. Something wasn't right. I had noticed that all the band were ignoring me, actually running away from me. He obviously had told them something, and finding out more details, came to tell me. The plane that carried all our equipment from Venezuela to Panama had crashed on take-off.

Three people died in that accident, which immediately put a proper perspective on the loss of the equipment. It was tragic, but we did lose the complete stage, all the gear, and thirteen of my guitars—including the Black Beauty. I was devastated.

> It was tragic, but we did lose the complete stage, all the gear, and thirteen of my guitars—including the Black Beauty.

I owned that guitar for ten years, and clearly, it was meant to be mine for that period of time. I still mourn the loss of it. I really couldn't play anything else; every Les Paul I picked up after that just didn't feel right. All the Les Pauls were made of mahogany, but those made in the fifties and a few of those from the sixties used the lighter Honduras mahogany. All the others are much heavier, but the old '54 Black Beauty was almost as light as a Strat. So I stopped playing Les Pauls altogether, and went with Schecter Strats set up with humbuckers in an effort to at least approximate the sound and feel of the old Black Beauty. But it never really did.

I later moved to Nashville, and that's when the people from Gibson suggested that it was time to build a replacement. I was doubtful that anything could replace that guitar, but I thought it would be worth a try. We first worked on making it as light as the original. Gibson's approach was to route sound chambers into the body. That didn't thrill me, because I thought it would alter the tone, but what it did was make the guitar sound and feel just like my original. And when that vintage tone and resonance came through in that prototype, it was almost like having my old guitar back in my hands again. The new model is very reminiscent of the old Black Beauty, but this one has my name on it. It's got my own neck, my own fretboard, my own electronics—everything. It's such a delight to have that all together again.

So to go from not having a guitar at all to having a special signature model is a great thrill. And a long, winding, and tragic story had a happy ending after all.

Visit Peter Frampton at www.peterframpton.com

LESS IS MORE

I've always loved the one good note. More and more, my approach to music has been to slow things down a bit and get the absolute most out of every single note I possibly can.
—*Ed Gerhard*

It can be easy to add too much to an arrangement. My rule of thumb is less is more. It's okay to put every idea down, but then you have to start weeding them out. That's the way it is with my gardening. You plant too much, and as things begin to grow, you start pulling things back and allowing space in there.
—*Eric Tingstad*

It's good to play within limits; there is real power in restraint.
—*Andy Summers*

William Ackerman

UNCOMMON GOOD

I left Stanford University with five units to go. I had always been able to write about anything with complete ease but suddenly there I was, in the spring of my senior year, suddenly dramatically wordless. I took it as a sign, and literally headed for the hills; in this case the foothills of the Sierra Nevada where I got a job pounding nails for a wonderful Norwegian boat builder turned California general contractor.

House building was child's play for Ozzie, and he took me under his wing, soon sending me off to Mendocino to build a rather nice house on a cliff overlooking the Pacific Ocean. With me came my greatest friend from the Stanford University days, Otis Wollan.

Otis and I saw things more or less the same way. More politicized than I, Otis had been more active in resistance to the Viet Nam War, but we shared the same dreams of living in the country and building eco-friendly homes. Mendocino in 1972 was just about heaven. Hippies ruled the place and anarchy pretty much reigned. Every house, bar, and restaurant was the site of an ongoing jam session fueled by smoke and cheap wine. Otis and I had made the jam sessions mobile.

We'd bought two Ford half ton 4x4s in Sacramento; their serial numbers were sequential. Otis' truck was white, mine green. We built redwood cabins on the backs of the trucks, which roughly equaled the weight of a full grown male rhinoceros. These would be our homes while building the house in Mendocino. Both trucks had alternator power take-offs that allowed us to plug in for electricity. Ostensibly, these were for our power tools. But at night, we plugged in Otis' keyboard and my guitar and played out into the night air of the Casper, California graveyard, where we parked our trucks for the night: a fine home for a couple of HippieCraft musician/builders. The towering Douglas fir trees dripped a misty rain from the coastal fog on most nights that threatened to electrocute us, but we didn't seem to care.

At Stanford I had started by playing my acoustic guitar in the stairwells of the student dorms. A bit like singing in the shower, the stairwells were natural reverb chambers and made for a wonderful place to practice. Sometimes I'd look up after being lost in a trance and find four or five people who had gathered to listen. I remember loving that my music was something they wanted to be around. On Saturday nights I might look up and find fifty people there. It got to be like a coffee house without the coffee.

There were other guitarists who were in the area who shared a lot of the same musical influences with me, the Bert Jansch, John Renborne, Leo Kottke, John Fahey, and, for me, Robbie Basho. We had no idea that we were going to be adding to this legacy, but really that's what was happening. My cousin Alex de Grassi was already a remarkable guitarist, and somewhere on the periphery of all this was a pianist/guitarist named George Winston who was soaking up the same vibe and heading independently in much the same direction. Soon the size of the impromptu audiences forced us to move out of stairwells to other "reverberative" spaces around Stanford. We found a permanent home in the tall, vaulted, masonry arches near the old student union. Here the numbers of people often exceeded two hundred as we played late into the night. Musicians always talk about the clubs and coffee houses where they learned their craft. For me it was this one dead end archway where I played just for the love of it.

> Soon the size of the impromptu audiences forced us to move out of stairwells to other "reverberative" spaces around Stanford.

Musicians never mention ego as a factor in their playing. I'm done with this omission and want it corrected. I started playing guitar when I was twelve primarily to win the heart of Mary Jo Porter. Mary Jo had shown a disturbing fondness for some kid with a guitar. It never occurred to me at the time that her attraction to him might have been more complex than the guitar alone. It could have been because he was handsome. It could have been because he was a foot taller than me. I don't remember exactly, but maybe his ears didn't stick out from his head at a perfect 90 degrees as mine did. And he was an older man; fifteen. All I saw was the guitar and I was determined to get one.

My first guitar was one of those nylon-stringed monsters with the action about an inch from the fretboard; playing was both impossible and painful. It didn't matter. I played for hours. We were just coming out of the folk revival, so my first songs were from the Kingston Trio and Peter, Paul and Mary. Then The Beatles arrived and swept all this away. I bought a Gibson electric, a red starburst beauty.

My parents didn't seem to recognize the invasive potential of this lurking threat to their serenity, and supported all of this enthusiastically… until I bought the amplifier. Then they understood why it was called an *electric* guitar. Most of my musical musings for the next four years were on this Gibson. Then in the spring of my senior year two things happened that changed my life: I won a 12-string Epiphone guitar in a bet, and my friend Jim Baldwin taught me a piece called *Mole's Moan* in open-D modal tuning—my introduction to the freedom and joyful anarchy of the world of open tunings. I never looked back, and that was it for the electric guitar and EADGBE.

I arrived in Mendocino with my Guild D 25, a beautiful mahogany guitar. I'd gone through rack after rack in every guitar shop from San Francisco to San Jose playing every D 25 I could get my hands on. I finally bought one from Gil Draper at Draper's Music on California Avenue in Palo Alto. Maybe the happiest day of my life. The guitar and I were inseparable. Except for the cheap wine and the occasional hope that I might get lucky with some girl, there was nothing else to occupy my attention. It amazes me that I was actually in college during this period, as it doesn't seem to have made any impression on my memory at all. What I do remember is that guitar and my music; that was my world.

> My parents didn't seem to recognize the invasive potential of this lurking threat to their serenity, and supported all of this enthusiastically.

I don't remember her name, but she was a waitress at The Uncommon Good Restaurant in Mendocino, and she was beautiful. Long dark hair, big smile, and the soft voice of an angel. Just to get a good look at her, Otis and I ate at the Uncommon Good every night and stayed way too late, drinking better wine than in our college days, and showing a fondness for the Burgundy Cherry ice cream. Eventually, though, you kind of had to give up the seat and move on—unless, of course, you were one of the guys playing music. So Otis and I played music at The Uncommon Good and drank the decent wine till 2:00 AM or so night after night.

Even young men get tired. One morning I woke up to yet another painful hangover in the Casper Graveyard (which was beginning to feel more and more like an appropriate place to be) and went to grab my guitar. No guitar next to the bed. The guitar was always by my side, and this felt like waking up in a house with all your furniture removed overnight. Panic hadn't set in yet and logic prevailed. Hop out the back of the redwood camper and peer into the front seat of the truck. No guitar. Mild panic. Run to Otis's truck and look on the front seat. No guitar. Panic stirring. Yell at Otis to wake him up. Otis opens the door with glowing red eyes. No guitar. Complete panic just millimeters away. Take refuge in logic. Reconstruct your steps. The waitress, the wine, the Burgundy Cherry ice cream, the music. It's 2:00 AM and you walk out into the cold, wet night of fog. You put the guitar on the roof of the truck and unlock the door. You start the truck and reach to turn on the heater full blast. You drive off. The guitar on the roof. This is beyond panic; it's some fatalistic certainty that you've entered a personal hell.

> My ego whispers to me that maybe the waitress has the guitar and is guarding it for me, because secretly, she really wants us to get closer. This is pathetically easy for logic and self-realization to refute.

Otis and I rushed to my truck and drove off to Mendocino where we were sure we'd find the guitar at The Uncommon Good where the early shift was baking bread. Einstein postulated that everything is relative, and this was demonstrated conclusively in the fact that a ten minute drive now seemed to take about seven hours. The baking crew at the Uncommon Good didn't have the guitar, and there was no note from the night crew. Somewhere hope screams out to you that it's locked safely away in an upstairs room, but you know that's a lie. My ego whispers to me that maybe the waitress has the guitar and is guarding it for me, because secretly, she really wants us to get closer. This is pathetically easy for logic and self-realization to refute. Then the physics test began. The first question is, "how long can a guitar case stay on the roof of a truck when partially glued to that surface by a layer of ocean fog?"

As we drove through the town of Mendocino, we were looking at the roadsides with deep and considerable interest in the hopes of answering that very question. By the time we'd made it to Route 1, the coastal highway, the investigation of physics changed focus. Having not found the guitar along the quaint streets of Mendocino where one drives at a leisurely twenty to twenty-five miles per hour, a second question was posed, namely, "at what speed does the friction of wind blow a loaded guitar case off a truck roof covered by a layer of ocean fog?" We never did find out the answer to that one, either. No guitar, no guitar case, no pile of suspicious splinters on the roadside. Just gone.

According to the song, sometimes you have to go through hell to get to heaven. I called my friends in Palo Alto with my story. I'd be down that way in a couple of weeks to see what I could buy in the way of a guitar with what was left of my nail-pounding income, diminished by the nightly purchases of decent wine and Burgundy cherry ice cream. I spent two lonely weeks without a guitar and finally went down to the Bay Area. My friends were waiting for me. Somehow they'd found all those people who came by to hear me play in the arches, and one by one, told them the story of my loss. Everyone had dug down into largely threadbare pockets and managed to scrape out some change and a few bills here and there. It was enough. I was handed a new Guild D 50, the next step up the ladder from the D 25 I'd always played.

There have been a lot of blessings to come my way though this miracle of music, but this act of kindness on the part of so many people will remain particularly beautiful in my memory. To all those people, and all the people who have listened to my music since, my deepest thanks. I marvel at the relationship between those of us who play music and those who listen. I don't think we could survive without each other. I also wonder if the waitress is still playing my D 25.

Visit William Ackerman at www.williamackerman.com

When I first saw Will Ackerman play, I was struck by how
accessible he was to his audience; he was connecting with them
both as a guitar player and an entertainer. I had never seen that
before. It was his delivery, how his music went straight to the heart.
—*Eric Tingstad*

Randy Bachman

WANTED: ORANGE GRETSCH 6120

In 1958, as a teenager growing up in Winnipeg, Canada, Duane Eddy and Chet Atkins got my attention in a big way. Rock and roll guitar had arrived, and with it, the time to trade in my $35 black Sears Silvertone catalog special.

I had seen Lenny Breau playing an orange Gretsch 6120, and so it instantly went to the top of my wish list. That orange Gretsch became my dream guitar. I mowed lawns, baby sat, washed cars, and did all sorts of odd jobs to earn the $400 to buy a used one. And it was a really great guitar. It had an incredible twang—a real Duane Eddy twang. And that guitar would become my main axe for many years to come. It's the guitar I played on *Shakin' All Over, Taking Care of Business, These Eyes*—so many of the Guess Who and BTO hits. This guitar was my left hand, the one I really worked for.

In later years, I also acquired a Les Paul and a Strat, but that Gretsch always came along; it had a tone like nothing else. I kept it in a white case with beautiful tooled leather binding, and I wouldn't ever let it out of my sight. When I'd go to a hotel room, I'd chain the guitar case through the handle and around the body twice, and then I would chain it around the base of the toilet and lock it up with a padlock. I did that in every hotel I stayed in. If someone wanted to take my guitar, he'd have to rip the whole toilet out of the floor to get it.

In 1976, we had a recording date in Toronto. I was just finishing the mixes when my roadie, who was loading the van, offered to take the Gretsch along with everything else back to the hotel so he could finish packing up and check out. I told him no. When he promised that he wouldn't let it out of his sight, I reluctantly agreed. Well, he took it back to the Holiday Inn, put it in the room, and went to pay at the desk. So yes, he did let it out of his sight. When he returned to the room, it was empty; the guitar was gone.

When I got the news, it was like your childhood dog being run over, or your first girlfriend telling you to hit the road. I was just totally heartbroken. I couldn't sleep or eat for days and days. I called the Mounties—the RCMP—and reported it stolen. I put the word out to all the pawn shops that if this guitar came in, I'd pay the going price. I didn't want anyone to go to jail; I just wanted the guitar back. Well, the word went out that I'd pay anything for this guitar, which wasn't quite true. I said I'd pay the going street price for the pawn shop guy.

I then got a call from Chuck Young, who was writing the *Random Notes* column for *Rolling Stone*. He called to confirm a story he'd heard, thinking it was a little insane that I'd pay up to $10,000 for the return of my orange Gretsch 6120. I told him no, that was grossly exaggerated. For ten grand, I could buy twenty 6120s! At the time it was not a high-priced, highly sought-after guitar. So Chuck got the story straight and ran the notice in his column.

A few months later, I was staying at my farm in the states with my son and daughter, and we were building a tree house. Now, if there are any fathers out there who have built a tree house, you realize that a kid can only hand you the odd nail and a hammer; they can't do much else, let alone help you lift a heavy sheet of plywood. So there I was, with one end of a 4x8 sheet of plywood awkwardly propped in the crook of the tree, and the other end resting on my head. At that convenient moment, the phone rang. I asked my daughter to run in and answer it. She returned, telling me it was Chad, and that it was very important that he speak with me. Chad Allen was at one point the lead singer in the Guess Who; he sang on *Shakin' All Over*. Well, I couldn't drop the plywood just then, so I told her to tell him I'd call him back. She did and hung up the phone. She walked halfway back across the patio and the phone rang again. Getting it again, she came back saying it's not Chad Allen, but a guy named Ned. Ned used to do our T-shirts—he was our merchandise guy. And again, I asked her to tell him I'd call back, and "…please come out here and help me!" The phone rang again, and by this time, I was pretty angry. My daughter told me I needed to come to the phone, and that it was about the stolen Gretsch guitar. "It's not Chad," she says. "It's not Ned. I can't understand his name. He's sounds kinda funny." So at that, I laid down the plywood, went into the house and pick up the phone. The voice on the other end says, "Howdy. This is *Chet*."

> If someone wanted to take my guitar, he'd have to rip the whole toilet out of the floor to get it.

My daughter, who was only five years old at the time, had never heard the name Chet. Add to that his Nashville accent and she couldn't understand him. And I was falling all over myself, like Jackie Gleason. Chet Atkins. My idol. He said he had read about my Gretsch being stolen. He had had one, too, but over the years had lost it and was trying to find another. He really sympathized with my loss. Then he said, "What's your address? I'm going to send you something." So I gave him my address and a few days later a prototype of the Gretsch Super Chet arrived. It was the transparent charcoal black one with a phaser and flanger onboard, and a few other bells and whistles. I was absolutely stunned. I had never seen this as a prototype, and he had only three of them made—a left-handed one he gave to Paul McCartney, the one he sent me, and the one he kept. He explained that he had done a few modifications on mine, and hoped I wouldn't mind. I thought, "Wow—a mod done by Chet Atkins, himself!"

A month later he was playing with the Vancouver Symphony, and so I went, and then had him present the guitar to me again and had photos taken. And he signed the pickguard. Now this really fired me up and started me on a crazed, absolutely insane midlife crisis to find my missing orange Gretsch. I bought every used Gretsch I could find, and called every store in the yellow pages in every town in every city and every state. I'd call and leave messages, saying, "I'm Randy Bachman from the Guess Who and BTO. I'm trying to find an orange Gretsch 6120. Here's the serial number. Please call me." And they'd call back and say, "We don't have an orange one, but we have a silver sparkle." Another would have a white one, or some other type. And I ended up buying them all anyway. I now have the world's largest Gretsch collection, thanks to the roadie who left mine in a hotel room to be stolen. I've still not recovered that guitar, but I have twenty-eight 6120s in all the different varieties of headstocks and trim—the horseshoe, the longhorn, the black markings with the engravings, the neoclassic, the thumbnail edge—I have every single one possible. I even found one that is very much like my original; the serial number is only a few digits away. And it's a wonderful guitar. It's like having a new girlfriend that looks a lot like your old girlfriend. It's kind of nice and it's kind of different, but it's just not the original.

> He explained that he had done a few modifications on mine, and hoped I wouldn't mind. I thought, "Wow—a mod done by Chet Atkins, himself!"

From time to time, I get new leads. A fellow came up to me at a show and told me he knew where my guitar was. "It's three blocks from here," he says. "The guy works for a carpet company. Here's his number. Call him." So I'd have to track that down, and there'd be nothing to it. I also heard the Thompson Twins had it, and had actually used it in their video for *Doctor, Doctor*. I watched it, and yeah, there's one of the Thompson twins playing this Gretsch that looks exactly like mine. And right by at the cutaway where the master control is located is what appears to be a blemish. Mine had a light orange finish, and in that spot is a darker orange splotch. Those Gretsches were made of plywood, and on mine was a darkened knot—it's actually a beautiful part of the grain. It's a pretty distinctive feature.

Six months later, the Thompson twins were playing in Vancouver—and my roadie was doing the back stage work for the concert! So I told him, "When the Thompson Twins do their soundcheck, go and see if the orange Gretsch is there. I'll be waiting outside with a Mountie. I've got my stolen property report from 1976, and I've got my original insurance policy with the serial number on it. And I have the original police report from Ontario. All I want is to have the guitar back." So the roadie waited while the Thompson Twins did their soundcheck, watching for the appearance of the orange Gretsch. When it didn't show, he approached him and said, "You know, I saw your *Doctor, Doctor* video, and you had a beautiful orange Gretsch. I'm just wondering if you're going to pull that out for the soundcheck." And he answered, "Oh, I would never take that out on the road. It's too valuable. Someone might steal it!"

I'll have to follow that one up.

Visit Randy Bachman at www.randybachman.com

> I now have the world's largest Gretsch collection, thanks to the roadie who left mine in a hotel room to be stolen.

I JUST WANT TO BE UNIQUE—LIKE EVERYBODY ELSE

It occurred to me that I had been involved in playing the guitar in two different ways, and if I combined my experience playing jazz with my experience playing classical guitar, then I would have something unique. And something unique in the music business is quite a good thing!
—*Charlie Byrd*

While the record companies may not be out looking for unique music, the public certainly is.
—*Earl Klugh*

Don McLean

A MAN AND HIS GUITAR

A long, long time ago, in the days of black and white, a person could fall in love with their instrument. And because there was first a longing, a yearning, and a deep hunger, an enchanted relationship was cultivated. And it grew. Little was taken for granted in those days—certainly a good guitar was not. They were expensive and they were hard to come by. To own one called for sacrifice of both time and treasure. And when the dream of ownership at last gave way to reality, that union of guitar and player was duly celebrated. But also like the days of black and white, that era has sadly come to a close.

As I survey the current spate of performers calling the tune in popular culture, I doubt that they have much at all to do with their instruments in that relational sense. For the most part, their guitars are just props, playing a supporting role in a play that is more about attitude and less about music. The guitars that are pressed into this lonely service have been relegated to mere accoutrement. They come, they go, they change. When one is lost, it's replaced with no more thought than the changing of a flat tire. They've become commodities, where any number of makers has stepped in to satisfy the demands of a fickle and capricious market. "Tools," they call them.

When I began to play the acoustic guitar, things were quite different—and simpler. At that time, there were essentially two kinds of players in the world: Gibson players and Martin players. And those two camps were thoroughly entrenched, with little understanding between the two, really. Their styles were clearly delineated, and there was never any mistaking one for the other. The shape of the Gibson and its appointments, and the shape of the Martin and its appointments were very specific to those particular brands. And that was it.

And regardless of which instrument one chose, the unmistakable identification a musician had with his instrument produced an indelible image. Who can forget the Everly Brothers playing their Gibson guitars? And Gibson guitars are precisely what they should have had. Can you imagine the Everly Brothers playing Martins?

No way! It would have been wrong! But if you saw Josh White or Lester Flatt or Elvis Presley or Ricky Nelson, it was always a Martin guitar strapped around their necks. The guitar formed a part of who they were.

In the electric world, it was the Fender guitars that knocked you out. Can you envision Buddy Holly separate from his Tele? It was all so natural. It was all so exciting. And it also stimulated the imagination.

In those days, there were no instructional videos or collections of guitar tablature. Oh, you could pick up a Mel Bay book and learn to play *Paddlin' Madeline Home*, but that had nothing to do with playing *If I Had a Hammer* or *Walk Don't Run*. If you wanted to learn *those* songs, you had to learn them from other people. You had to learn them from fleeting glimpses on a small, black and white television screen, where you saw something being done that you heard on a record a million times, but couldn't figure out *how* it was done. All this contributed to a tremendous amount of imagination, and that imagination is what yielded the relationship. And when that relationship came to fruition, when you were finally able to afford that castle in the sky guitar, it was a magical moment.

I experienced that magical moment when I was just twelve years old. I grew up in New Rochelle, New York, where the only music store in town was the House of Music. You never saw a Martin guitar in New Rochelle—no one could afford one; Martins were strictly for professionals. But one day I happened to be walking by, and that's when I saw it in the window: a 000-18, 14-fret orchestra model. And then I saw the headstock—that venerable, squared-off headstock bearing that Holy Grail of nameplates. I'll never forget that moment. I had to have it. Now, $150 was a heck of a lot of money in 1958—especially for a kid. You'd get fifty cents to mow a lawn. But that's where it began.

By 1964, I was finally able to afford a Martin D-28—one of the best guitars I ever owned, and the one I had been working up to. With its Brazilian rosewood back and sides, it was absolutely gorgeous. I was married to that instrument. That guitar meant more to me than any woman, more than any physical thing in the world.

Elvis had a D-28—a leather-covered one. I'm sure you've seen it in pictures; it's so strongly identified with him. That guitar was his jet engine, his way of getting traction on stage, and moving out of this life and into another world. And he'd take the audience with him. That was magic. That was an extraordinary relationship, and unfortunately, I don't think it exists anymore. People are sadly deprived for want of that imagination, the hoping, and the belief in the instrument and what it could do—and where it could take you.

> That guitar was his jet engine, his way of getting traction on stage, and moving out of this life and into another world.

The guitar certainly took me out of my comfort zone. As a kid, I had never really been away from home. I wasn't a terribly adventurous person—I didn't need to see the world. I liked my room, and that was where I played my guitar. In my senior year at Iona Catholic High School, though, I decided it was time to step out. At that time, only a few of my friends knew that I played and sang—I had been keeping that under wraps—when I decided to enter the school talent contest. And the experience was right out of a Ron Howard movie. The entire student body was there in the auditorium, and I got up in front of those people and I played.

> It wasn't just dented, it was *destroyed*. It looked as though it had been run through with a forklift! I'm very superstitious about things, and I thought to myself, "That could be me!"

By then, I had a few things under my fingers. I played a stinging arrangement of Josh White's *Well, Well, Well* in a dropped D tuning, a banjo breakdown, and a couple of tunes that I had written. And the place went absolutely crazy. The kids hollered and cheered and threw things into the air. It was bedlam! And that's when my relationship with the guitar, which had been under wraps for all those years, just exploded. The next thing I knew, I was being managed by Howard Levanthal, who worked with the Weavers. I was only seventeen, and he had me out playing clubs in the Village, and with Pete Seeger on a sailing sloop. It was amazing. And the guitar had brought me there. Before I knew it, I was on a plane, and going someplace else with my guitar. I went and I went and I went. And I'm still going!

That D-28 was my constant companion throughout those years. But sadly, our association came to an end. In the summer of 1969, I was performing with Pete Seeger at the Newport Folk Festival. I had left the guitar backstage for a moment, and someone, seizing that moment, quietly walked away with it. Needless to say, it was a terrible time for me. I never found another guitar that could completely take its place. I found others that were just as good, but I never got over that loss. I had lost something that had become a part of *me*.

My prized D-28, though, wasn't the only guitar I lost. At one point in the 1980s, Washburn asked me to play their guitars. And against my better judgment, I agreed to try one out. I took it on a fly date, and when it emerged from baggage claim, it was completely smashed. It wasn't just dented, it was *destroyed*. It looked as though it had been run through with a forklift! I'm very superstitious about things, and I thought to myself, "That could be me!" Lesson learned: "Your Martin guitar… don't leave home without it." And I never did again! And yet, maintaining that ethic could be just as difficult. The Martin D-41 that I had been traveling with in the '80s and

90

the '90s was mistakenly routed by the airline to New York, instead of my destination, which was Philadelphia. That wasn't good. Fortunately, though, I had brought along a second guitar, and I was able to do the concert. But when the D-41 didn't show, I became convinced that someone had stolen it. It was one of my favorite instruments, and I hated losing it.

Six weeks later, I received a tip through a phone call that the guitar had been found. It had been stolen, alright. Baggage claim tickets weren't checked at the New York airport, and so an unclaimed guitar was an easy mark. A fellow had bought it off the street in front of Manny's Music in New York for $300. He knew it was hot and probably stolen for drug money. When he got home with it, he opened the case, and inside found picks with my name printed on them, along with some other things that suggested that the guitar was mine. He wondered if it might be a signature guitar, and so he called Martin to inquire. At that time, though, I didn't have a signature model. He then managed to track me down through my record company, and ultimately he returned the guitar. I paid him the $300, and got it back.

I retired the D-41 from the road after that episode. It had served me well. I did many world tours with that guitar. It must have had ten cracks in the top, repaired with biscuit joints, and glued together in many places. But its hard knocks notwithstanding, it was a terrific stage partner. I knew exactly what that instrument could do, and it always responded to my touch.

There is a certain sense of confidence that you have in your instrument when you spend that much time together. You go through date after date after date, and it always does exactly what it's supposed to do. No surprises. You set it up, you work on it, you stretch its limits, and you know what that instrument can do—what it can do *for* you.

And that's what it comes down to, really: a man and his guitar. Roy Orbison once said that he was one of those people who got a hold of a guitar and never let it go. And when you hang on, you just can't imagine where it will take you.

In those days, you could be alone in the world with your instrument, bolstered by an Emersonian sense of self-reliance. There is a purity that comes forth from that simplicity. It's honest, innocent, and uncorrupted by excess or trappings of any kind. And when the two of you work out your dance in the form of a song, the result is a wonderfully deep sense of satisfaction. Every player should know it.

Visit Don McLean at www.americanpie.com

Nothing is more beautiful than a guitar, save perhaps two!
—*Frederic Chopin*

Janis Ian

OF GUITARS AND RIGHTEOUS MEN

*"There are men who steal silver, and men who steal gold
But the worst kind of thief is the man who steals your soul"*

It started with my father, who made the transition from chicken farmer to music teacher when I was around three. Actually, it started with his membership in various socialist organizations, since he needed a guitar to take to the meetings when he led them in singing. No, I guess it started before that, when he bought "The Guitar."

He bought it in 1948 from the widow of a farmer who'd had it laying around in her attic for years. When she asked what he thought it was worth, he replied "I dunno, twenty-five bucks?" He brought it home three years before I was born, and began learning to play. It was rural New Jersey; there weren't exactly a lot of other guitarists around. He got a Pete Seeger book with chord diagrams, subscribed to *Sing Out!*, and he was on his way.

I grew up with that guitar. It was miles too big for me, a colorful, beat-up window into another world. My small fingers could barely get around the neck. As I began learning chords, I discovered new ways of fingering them to compensate for my size. To this day, I play a D chord wrong, but it works for me. The Guitar went everywhere—to summer camp, where my father obtained eight-week stays for us by teaching music for nothing; to my grandparent's, where we went every weekend to pick up groceries from my grandfather the bagger. It went with Dad to work, it went with us to play.

> The guitar you grow up with, the guitar you learn on, is a special thing. It doesn't matter whether it's expensive, pretty, even playable—it trains you.

The guitar you grow up with, the guitar you learn on, is a special thing. It doesn't matter whether it's expensive, pretty, even playable—it trains you. I wrote my first song on that guitar in my twelfth year, and played it to a captive audience from the back seat of our car. I remember my mother turning and staring at me, wondering what had happened to the child she thought she was raising. I learned to write a lead sheet with it, sent the song in to *Broadside Magazine*, was invited to play at the Village Gate. The Guitar and I got a standing ovation; we were on our way.

One day another performer mentioned that it was a Martin D-18; when I got home I said "Dad! Dad! This is a Martin!" He shrugged. "Yep, honey, it's a guitar. I knew that."

We did everything wrong. I faithfully polished it with cheap lemon oil once a month—everywhere. Fretboard, pickguard—if you were attached to my guitar you got polished. When it buzzed, I'd fold over a cardboard match-cover and stick it under the string, right up at the nut; that always worked. I took apart the tuning machines and cleaned them periodically, squirting them with WD-40 to keep them moving. When a waitress dropped a tray on it in 1967, we had no idea where to go for repairs. A violin maker in Newark rebuilt the top, re-glued the braces, and installed a larger, heavier bridge plate. Having no idea how to take care of a valuable instrument, I went on instinct and *Mechanic's Weekly*. In return, The Guitar played, and played, and played.

> It was an extraordinary instrument, a 1937 D-18 that somehow, through a combination of wood, break-in, temperature, humidity, and just plain love, wound up being the best acoustic guitar any of them had ever heard.

It became My Guitar when Dad gave it to me for my 16th birthday. By then we'd met Leonard Bernstein, recorded two albums, been on The Tonight Show, and done concerts from coast to coast. We'd lived through *Society's Child* together, getting spit on and booed off the stage by crowds chanting "Nigger lover!" We'd survived being called a has-been shortly after, and written *Jesse* two years later. One of us, at least, had remained universally admired. Artists like Jimi Hendrix would greet me and say, "How's The Guitar doing, man? What a sweetheart!" Vinnie Bell, legendary New York studio musician, offered me $5,000 for it—in 1966!

It was an extraordinary instrument, a 1937 D-18 that somehow, through a combination of wood, break-in, temperature, humidity, and just plain love, wound up being the best acoustic guitar any of them had ever heard. Reverend Gary Davis would beg for it at folk festivals; other artists kept offering me money. Why? It has the best bass tone I've ever heard on a guitar, bar none. And unusual in a guitar from that era, it sounds as good finger-picked as strummed, flat-picked as frailed.

I moved to Los Angeles in 1972 and took her with me (somehow over the years she'd become "her"— my closest confidante, dearest companion), in large part hoping the more temperate climate would be good for my aging friend. One day I came back from a morning at the beach to find my apartment burglarized. Although clothing had been flung from the drawers, credit cards and jewelry were left alone. The only things missing were a rented television, and my two guitars. Ironically, I'd bought a Gallagher just months earlier, having decided the road was too dangerous for my Martin.

I called the police; they were pessimistic, saying a large ring specializing in stolen guitars had been operating in LA for months. I called Martin, and registered it as stolen. I canvassed the apartment complex. I telephoned every pawn shop in the area, offering a reward for any scrap of information. Then I sat, dulled by fatigue and pain, waiting and hoping.

> I hoped someone kind had bought her, someone who played her frequently and treated her well. I hoped they bought her not knowing she was stolen. I hoped she wasn't living overseas. I hoped.

The phone rang two days later; a young man had pawned my Gallagher, demanding exactly what it was worth, "like he knew what he was doing." He'd used his draft card for ID. A few days later the police picked him up.

I went to court and testified that I hadn't given him permission to borrow my guitar. The detectives (knowing he already had a thirteen-page rap sheet) threatened him, trying to break the ring. Although told it was illegal, I desperately offered him a $2000 reward if he'd just bring it back, no questions asked. In the end he chose to do three to five years of hard time rather than reveal anything.

That was the end of that. I mourned for years—twenty-six of them, to be exact. Nothing in my life—not breakups, not the death of beloved friends and family, not the loss of every dime I had in 1986—nothing affected me more deeply. You may think that's crazy, but then again, maybe you've never owned a guitar like this one.

Somewhere in the back of my head, though, a small part of me clung to hope. "If she ever comes back…" I would think, "everything will be all right." When I began recording again, I put a note on every album cover: "Missing since 1972, Martin D-18 serial #67053. Reward for return; no questions asked." I meant it. I hoped someone kind had bought her, someone who played her frequently and treated her well. I hoped they bought her not knowing she was stolen. I hoped she wasn't living overseas. I hoped.

One day I was scanning my e-mail and noticed something from a stranger. Now, I get e-mail from strangers all the time, but most of it does not have "RE: YOUR D-18" in the header. I read on with growing excitement. Eric Schoenberg, owner of a guitar shop in Tiburon, CA, was telling me he had a client who had my guitar. Did I want the client's phone number?

I wrote back immediately, saying "Yes," then gave full reign to paranoia. Could someone have replaced the serial number, hoping to claim a reward? For that matter, how much of a reward would they want? What were my rights under the law, and what were my ethical and moral obligations?

I contacted everyone I knew, from Stanley Jay of Mandolin Brothers to Preston Reed. Do you know this guy Schoenberg? I asked. Is he reputable? Would he lie to me, or participate in a coverup? And Geoff Grace, the fellow who says he has my guitar, does anyone know him? The answers flew back. Eric Schoenberg was highly respected by one and all, with an impeccable reputation. It was impossible to replace an old Martin serial number. And legally, since I'd filed a police report, the stolen property was mine. All I would owe Geoff was whatever he'd spent on maintenance and repairs.

A day later, heart in mouth, I called Geoff Grace. *He's not home, this is his mother.* Ah, he had a mother. That was already good. She lived with him, or spent time there—even better. She didn't sound like a con artist; she knew about the guitar. I left word, then sat in an agony, waiting. Hours later I was still waiting, having completely forgotten the time difference between East and West Coasts. My partner Pat joined me in the waiting, and suddenly tears began pouring down my face. I couldn't speak, couldn't explain myself. It was as though a 26-year-old dam had burst, throwing the debris of all those hopeless years out of my heart and into the open air. When I finally became capable of speech, I spoke through my hiccups. "If it is her... if it is my Martin... then I've come full circle, finally... I'll get back the only material thing that ever mattered to me. All those years of waiting will finally be over. I can be myself again, if she comes back."

Make no mistake—I am not a fetishist. I don't cling to objects for luck, or believe my life is over without them. Yet when my Martin was stolen, it left a hole in me that nothing could replace—a big, dead spot where no life grew.

The phone rang, and I met Geoff. He'd bought the guitar in 1972 from a shop in Berkeley. It was pretty beat-up; someone had done a bad lacquer job on the back, so the price was only $650. He'd had the neck reset and a couple of other things fixed, but never touched the body or frets. Oddly enough, the same guitar was stolen from his home in Sausalito in 1976, which is why he'd memorized the serial number. The guitar had been with him all this time; although he bought and sold instruments regularly, he'd hung onto her because "It's the best D-18 I've ever heard."

He'd read an interview with me in *Vintage Guitar Magazine* by Steve Stone, praising my playing and mentioning at the end that I was still looking for my Martin. "It took me fifteen seconds to realize that was my Martin you were looking for," he told me. And amazingly enough, he immediately decided to give it back. "Then," he continued, "I called two friends in the Bay Area with big mouths and told them, just to keep myself honest. I figured after that, there'd be no turning back." He called Eric Schoenberg, knowing Eric could contact me through e-mail. The rest was history.

Now, the moment of truth. What did he want? What, in his estimation, was the guitar worth? I won't say we fenced; he quoted a figure I couldn't afford, then he thought about it and said that figure was for insurance purposes—the real value was half that. Even half was too much for me. *Well, since I did file a police report, isn't it mine anyway?* I asked. He thought about that and said yes, he supposed so. He thought some more, then said "Hell, I don't want to keep someone else's guitar! Just tell me where to ship it—it's yours." I couldn't do that—this man had loved my Martin as long as I had, even longer. I suggested we try a trade—he could ship it to me at my expense, and I would ship him my two small Martins, a turn-of-the-century 0-28 and a 1924 0-42. He could have whichever he liked, and the Mark Leaf case. Geoff agreed.

I arrived home two days later and raced to the package. I pulled it out and began to cry again. It was her, just as I remembered. I stroked the fretboard, afraid to play her. What if she didn't sound the same? The lost fish is always biggest in memory. What if she wasn't special, wasn't extraordinary? What if I'd spent the last twenty-six years mourning nothing more than an imaginary ideal?

I hit the first chord; she sounded just like herself. I tuned the E down to a low D and hit a second chord. It rang forever. I pressed my ear against her side to hear the aftertones, the subtones, all the little nuances I remembered. Everything was there. Everything was stunning. Everything was beautiful. We were finally home.

Geoff ended up taking the small Martin I preferred, but as Pat said, "If he hadn't taken the one you liked best, what kind of sacrifice would it have been on your part? You can't get something for nothing, you know." And when I finally met Geoff and Eric a few months ago, I found myself speechless. How do you thank someone for giving back your dreams? How do you thank someone for filling a hole in your heart?

The bottom line is you can't. You can only hope he understands a small part of the gift he's given you—how it made up for every petty moment in your life; how it erased all the bad memories and left only the good. How you know now, in every fiber of your being, that in this world righteous men still walk, and you're fortunate enough to have encountered one.

Visit Janis Ian at www.janisian.com

PEDDLING HARD

I never thought of chops on an instrument as playing a whole bunch of notes—not without reason. That was never musical to me. It has always been my goal to play tastefully through chord changes.
—*Earl Klugh*

When you listen to your stereo, you don't have to pedal hard to make it sound good; you just sit back and listen to it. That's how I approach the guitar. I want it to sound stunningly good. I'm not invested in how my fingers are on the fretboard. I just want it to sound good.
—*David Wilcox*

I consider technical difficulty to be an unimportant aspect of music. I would rather hear one note played well than any amount of fancy licks, harmonizations, or so-called hot guitar played for the sake of complexity or athleticism.
—*Martin Simpson*

A lot of guitarists are so involved in the acrobatics of playing that not much music comes through. I believe that your technique should be so good that the audience doesn't even notice that you are doing difficult things. If they do, then they've missed the music!
—*David Qualey*

Almost every steel-string player I encounter has hands that are far more advanced than his or her head. That is, musicianship is lagging far behind technique. Our musical minds know everything they have ever heard, while our hands know only what we've trained them to do.
—*Chris Proctor*

Playing has been advanced *technically* very much over the years. However, I don't think it has advanced *musically* to any great extent.
—*Carlos Montoya*

David Wilcox

THE HEART OF THE MATTER

The guitar was the first thing that made my heart feel right. And I didn't know a heart could feel that good. That set a whole new standard for the rest of my life. If it hadn't been for guitar, I guess I would have assumed that that knot in your stomach was just the way stomachs were. But the guitar gave me this little oasis of joy. And I knew it wasn't just the sound that came from this little wooden box with strings on it. It was more like a compass—it lined itself up somehow with something that I couldn't feel directly, but could navigate my life by.

It seems to me that just getting the music to sound as good as it can has been a way to navigate my life. And big decisions become easy. You bring the guitar along when you're looking for a house. You play the guitar in the house, and if it feels good, you buy the house. If not, you don't. You play a new song for someone that you're dating, and do they get it, or not? The guitar chooses your life partner; the guitar chooses where you live. Obviously I'm kidding a little, but in a way I'm getting at something that's really true. It's the thing that really makes my heart sing. It knows something about me that I don't know. It knows not just who I am, but who I *could* be.

I've often joked that there should be a little pamphlet inside every guitar case that says, "Congratulations on the purchase of your new guitar; please see warning." And the first page says, "If you like playing along with your favorite artists and pretending that you're a music star, you will get many hours of enjoyment from your new purchase. Please see warning." You turn the page and it says, "However, if you feel great joy when you hear the sound of a guitar and you don't know why, you may be in danger of having your life changed forever."

I really think that many people come into this with their heart somehow already knowing the language of this particular kind of music—but without the conscious understanding of where it's taking them. It's going to take you places that if you knew at the start, you would walk with fear and trembling, because there is much at stake. For me, I knew that the world didn't need another song; I didn't think the world needed another guitar player. But I knew that my heart understood this language that seemed to be coming from much further away than just this empty little wooden box. It was a language of *possibility*.

At first nothing feels as good as a good song. And you think, "Well, that's as good as my heart is going to feel." But little by little, you start to realize that it's asking you to put the rest of your life in order so that it also *sounds* that good. In order for the music to feel good and sound good, I have to have strong fingernails. And if I'm going to have strong fingernails, that means I'm going to have to eat right. So for the sake of the music, you say, "Well, no. I'm going to have *this* instead of *that*." And you eat right.

And then you think to yourself, "What I really want is to have people come to hear my music who are really listening and really are able to get it." And so you decide that maybe you don't want to play a particular gig if it has a lot of background noise, or doesn't have good focus. And you turn down gigs, which gives you the opportunity to have more time and focus on what you want out of music. For me, I had to be very clear with myself. When I first started, I was playing music on the street and in a little health food restaurant for tips. At the end of the day I would leave the tips for the waitress, because I really didn't want to confuse my livelihood with the almost mystical lesson I was getting from the music. I felt I needed to make it clear that what I wanted from music was not just to grab what comes. It's like the difference between sustainable agriculture and chemical farming. The chemical farmer just says, "Okay, let's grab this year's harvest and make a profit." But if you're thinking of making the soil better year after year after year for your children and their children, then it's a very different decision making process.

And so for me, the music always feels new. It feels surprising and it feels like it's teaching me that my life can feel as good as the music. It's teaching me to sing my life, live my music, and not see a difference between the two.

I've actually been really blessed in that I have not been churning out pop hits. There are some performers who become famous for a song, and then night after night they're sort of doing an imitation of themselves. For me, it's never been that way. I've been really lucky in that when people come to hear me, they want to hear about what I've been up to, how life has been, what the new songs are. So it's like a conversation with a friend, and not just replaying old stuff you've talked about before. It's about what matters to you now, where you've been, where you get your joy, where you get your hope.

Music has always been my teacher, not just something that I do. It's like the headlights in the car that reach out into the night way beyond where I am. I used to think I wanted to catch up, but now I'm grateful that I hope I never do. I hope music stays that place where it is the frontier of my life. The things that I'm singing about are not the things I know, but what I'm learning. Each time I'm writing a new song, the process of writing it teaches me the lesson of what this mysterious feeling in my heart is, or what this dream felt like when I dared to imagine my heart finding a place that felt like home.

When I come to the guitar, I have a strange little ritual that I do: I will put my hands on the latches of the case, but I won't let myself open it until I can think of a particular thing that I really want to play—a song or a riff or a something that I just can't wait to hear. And then when I pick up the guitar, what I'm expecting is this oasis of joy.

I've talked to guitar builders about this, too. There are many people who will buy a beautiful acoustic guitar, not only for its aesthetic beauty, but because it is an oasis of perfection. It is the one thing in their life that is just the absolute best. They might be playing a guitar that is worth twice as much as the car they drive! But it's this one little place in their lives where they can enjoy the best that humans can do. And it can be afforded somehow in most any life. You can have that pearl of great price. It's that one material thing in your life that you can come to, and be lined up with the magnetic north, which you can't feel by yourself, but a guitar somehow does. I swear it's true!

> If you're blind to the heights of the ambitions of your heart, you might be satisfied with a life of less yearning and less struggle. But the guitar won't let you stay asleep!

If your heart happens to have this kind of sound as its native tongue, which my heart does, then this particular sound is something to trust, something to navigate by. It knows where your life is headed, what it's going to feel like when you find the person that you truly love, what it's going to feel like when you find the work that satisfies your heart and mind, what it's going to feel like when you find a community that feels like home. You can remember the feeling that you got in the song, and then when that thing comes around, you can recognize it. You can say, "Aha! I know you—you're from that song!"

If you're blind to the heights of the ambitions of your heart, you might be satisfied with a life of less yearning and less struggle. But the guitar won't let you stay asleep! The guitar wakes you up to the deeper yearning, and the possibilities of what your heart can feel. And because of that, you have to set out on the hero's journey, as Joseph Campbell would say. You have to risk everything, you have to be willing to sacrifice everything else and say, "Okay, I will buy my freedom with the money I don't spend so that I can afford to work at what I love. I will give up the societal acceptance of the picket fence in order to have this home which is made of music—a home that is made of *possibility*."

If you're half way through the hero's journey, it feels like, "What have you gotten me into?" You look at the guitar, and say, "If it hadn't been for you, I would have been happy!" But the guitar is saying, "Keep on. You're not through yet. There is more, there is more, there is more." The suspicious person would say, "What—more to give up?! I want comfort, I want safety." And the guitar says, "No you don't. You want *life*. Life has got great risks, and great gains, and there is more and we must persevere." And if you're willing to trust it, it will bring you home, I swear. But it does require that kind of commitment. So obviously what I'm talking about is much beyond a little wooden box with strings on it. I'm talking about this whole journey of faith. And it doesn't have to have any sort of dogmatic language to it, because even if you haven't heard any of those ancient stories, if you follow the language that your heart most deeply understands, it will lead you and it will guide you. For me, that language happens to be music. That was the start of this secret, this treasure map, and there was a treasure that desired to be found. And it would sing to me somehow. It was saying, "Your heart will feel this good!"

At first, you just don't believe it. You think it's some kind of drug or something that is bad for you. You wonder if you'll end up shaking a cup on the corner and mumbling to strangers, "There was this song... I don't know what happened, but all of a sudden I couldn't keep a job." You just don't know if this is something to be trusted; the logical mind can't get it. But if your heart knows this language to be true, then little by little, you learn how to calm your mind by saying, "If I can find a place that feels better, then I'll move on. But so far, this is the best that I have found, and so I will follow it." But your mind rails against it. It says, "Come on! It's nothing! It's just a song. There is no substance to it. It's just vibration in the air and it dissipates and it's gone." But your heart says, "No, that's not true!" It's teaching you that this is not something to hang on to; it's not the thing, itself. It's not the song. It's not the guitar. You can't hold it; you can't grab it in your fist. But it is whispering something to you. It tugs at something mysterious. When you watch a field of wheat give way to the wind and give the wind away, you can see something invisible moving in that field. In just that same way, when a song strikes a chord in a listener's heart, you see them move at the hand of this invisible, mysterious, and disappearing sound. That's when you're certain that this is not just a little wooden box with strings on it. It is somehow an oracle that comes from far away and can whisper to your heart, "There is more. Don't give up. Don't be satisfied with anesthesia. Don't be satisfied with distraction. There is more. There is home. There may be a mountain to cross, but carry on."

There is always going to be something that your heart is absolutely cracked open to. Whatever it is, I say trust it. It won't hurt you.

Visit David Wilcox at www.davidwilcox.com

THE DANGEROUS GAME

Music did bring me to the gutter. It brought me to sleep on the levee
of the Mississippi River, on the cobblestones, broke and hungry.
—*W.C. Handy*

Music should never be harmless.
—*Robbie Robertson*

Badi Assad

WHILE MY GUITAR GENTLY SINGS

"**B**ring me the guitar!" cried Isabel, the heroine of Melville's novel, *Pierre*. "Now listen to the guitar; and the guitar shall sing to thee the sequel of my story; for not in words can it be spoken." And so begins the marvelous passage describing Pierre's encounter with the ever mysterious and seductive Isabel.

The old guitar had found its way into Isabel's young, lithe hands by way of a peddler. As femininity is so often defined through attachment, Isabel formed an immediate bond with the instrument. As she began to pluck its strings, the guitar began to speak. "The dear guitar was singing to me," she said. "Murmuring and singing to me. Then I sang and murmured to it with a still different modulation, and once more it answered me from a different string. So listen to the guitar." As she began to play now for the rapt Pierre, "...the room was populous with sounds of melodiousness, and mournfulness, and wonderfulness; the room swarmed with unintelligible but delicious sounds. They hung pendulous like glittering icicles from the corners of the room; and fell upon Pierre with a ringing silveryness." And among the "droppings and swarmings of the sounds," Pierre began to discern Isabel voice singing the song of her own mystery.

In a subsequent encounter, Isabel's mystical interplay with the guitar returns to give voice once again to her story. As Isabel drew the instrument from beneath her "dark tent of hair," her playing rendered Pierre "almost deprived of consciousness by the spell flung over him." Isabel now revealed some of the guitar's story. She believed its original owner was the mother she never knew. And as a convincing demonstration for Pierre, she longingly breathed into the instrument's soundhole the words, "*mother, mother, mother.*" And the guitar, untouched, "responded with a quick spark of melody that long vibrated and subsidingly tingled in the room."

Such magic—the mysterious, mystical, and marvelous counterpoint between a player and her instrument! And a magic I have been blessed to know.

My guitar was not owned by my mother, but by my brother. I was fourteen years old when it passed to my hands. In his mind, my brother Odair had merely loaned me the instrument. But like Isabel, I formed a most certain and immediate attachment. In the years previous to the gift of the guitar, my brothers had been away, and during the period while we were apart, my father taught me to play.

My father played the *bandolim*—a kind of Brazilian mandolin—a solo instrument. As such, it needed guitar accompaniment. That's where I came in. He taught all of the kids in our family the chord changes to all the Brazilian music he played. But he also taught us how to interpret the music, how to play with dynamics and passion.

By the time my brothers returned for a visit, I had learned much of the traditional Brazilian *chorinho* repertoire. So surprised and impressed was Odair that he immediately put his own guitar—a very fine Fisher—in my hands, replacing the cheap one I had been playing. And though I was too young to realize it at the time, Odair's guitar bore his very personal imprint, as well.

I've only just come to realize this, but when Odair practices, he has the habit of resting his bearded chin on the side of the upper bout. I noticed on my guitar—the one he gave me all those years ago—that in that same spot is a mark; the wood is much darker in that place. The guitar may be with me now, but at one time, it was his, and their relationship was also a very strong one. In time, though, it would take on an imprint of my own.

Odair recently played that guitar, and commented that its sound had changed. To his ear, it was rounder, softer, more... feminine. He sensed a very different energy surrounding the instrument now. And I shouldn't be surprised—wood is a very responsive material, and very much alive! It absorbs and reflects the energies of its player. And when we play, we *embrace* the instrument. We hold it close. There is an intimacy. There is a special connection to the instrument in both a physical and a spiritual sense. When I play, the guitar and I become one, and naturally, there is an infusion of the feminine element. It responds to my touch. When my fingers stroke its strings, all the aspects of being a woman come forth in its sound: the fluidity, the sensuality, the softness, the intense and deep emotions played even in subtle ways. We somehow enter into each other's nature with mutual sympathy. And like Isabel's guitar, it sings my song.

Visit Badi Assad at www.badiassad.com

Bob Weir

with John Schroeter

A GUITAR IN THE FAMILY

If he ever felt like he needed a belt of Scotch, it was now. He'd do this alone, though, without any "help." As he began to punch the numbers on the phone, the only comfort he drew was from the decision to make the call at all. Writing was his first thought, but he knew the old man could just crumple up the letter and throw it away. That wouldn't do. Showing up unannounced was also out of the question; he imagined the old man clutching his chest and collapsing to the floor in the doorway before him. No, phoning was the way to go. And now was the time to do it.

"Hello, Colonel Jack Parber?" Once he got him on the phone, he figured he had a twenty-second window—just enough time to drop the bomb before the old man hung up on him. "My name is Robert Weir. I live in Mill Valley, and I've been doing a little research."

He had rehearsed this little soliloquy countless times in the past few years, playing it over and over in his mind, and with dread anticipation of this day. But there would be no more putting it off. "I turned up some information that might be of considerable interest to you," he continued, half expecting the dial tone at any moment. "But first I need to ask you a couple of questions pertaining to a certain event that transpired in Tucson in early 1947."

The first question was the only one he needed to ask, and he delivered it point-blank: "Were you perhaps romantically involved with a young lady by the name of Phyllis?" He held his breath in the uncomfortable silence that followed. Relieved by the Colonel's positive, if extremely wary response, he said, "Well sir, I don't know how many children you have, but there is a strong likelihood that you have one more than you know."

Long silence.

104

In 1946, the war was over, and airman Jack Parber returned home. During the conflict he had been a pilot, flying B-26 bombers. At nineteen, he was already the captain of his own crew, but his group wouldn't see any action on the other side of either ocean; the war ended before they could be deployed. Once back home, Jack enrolled at the University of Arizona in Tucson, where he met and fell in love with Phyllis Inskeep. Less than a year into their romance, Phyllis discovered she was pregnant.

Complicating her situation was the fact that her recent divorce had not yet been made final, a detail she had kept from Jack. And facing a custody battle for the two-year old daughter that the marriage produced, her condition would surely seal the issue in favor of her former husband's family. Desperate to keep her daughter, she took flight to San Francisco, where a secret adoption had been arranged for her unborn child. She told no one—Jack included—about her state or her plans.

To Jack and the others she left behind, Phyllis simply disappeared.

The healthy baby boy was born in October of 1947 in Atherton, a quiet community on the San Francisco peninsula. He left the hospital in the loving arms of Fredrick and Eleanor Weir, "Bobby's" joyful adoptive new parents. Nearly 900 miles away in Tucson, though, an utterly uninformed new father was going about his studies and, having not seen Phyllis in almost a year, was dating a new love.

Jack and Milena married in 1949 and raised four sons, while Jack resumed his military career with the Air Force. He'd go on to serve with distinction in Korea and Viet Nam, more than making up for the action he missed in Europe and Japan. In time, he rose to the rank of Colonel, and found himself Director of Operations at Hamilton Air Force Base in Novato.

Meanwhile, young Bobby stoked and fanned the flames of his emerging musical passions. And while bluffing his way through school on account of his undiagnosed dyslexia, he plugged into the burgeoning Bay Area folk scene, where he connected with the likes of Jorma Kaukonen, David Nelson, and Jerry Garcia. The series of bands he'd formed and co-founded in the intervening years would eventually yield a lineup called the Grateful Dead. Ultimately, he dropped out of school altogether and ran off with The Dead.

The four Parber sons—James, Anthony, Jonathan, and Christopher—loved the Grateful Dead. James brought his girlfriend to one of their concerts, where she took notice of the band's rhythm guitarist and teased, "That Bobby is good enough looking to be a Parber boy!"

James had a band of his own then, and in fact, had begun to enjoy some renown as a guitarist by the time he joined Lawrence Hammond & the Whiplash Band.

Playing a fusion of progressive southern rock and bluegrass, they were signed to Takoma Records, and were beginning to make a mark when James, at age 27, developed spinal cancer. He endured a painful final tour before hanging up the guitar, and with it, his dreams.

Phyllis had clandestinely spied the name in the file lying on her doctor's desk. The identities of prospective adoptive parents were to be legally sealed, yet she knew. And armed with this vital information, Phyllis would keep track of young Bobby, and follow his budding career—but at a distance; she faithfully abided by her agreement to not contact the family while they were living.

The door would open, though, in 1972 when Bobby's adoptive parents passed away. They died within a month of each other—and on each other's birthdays—prompting Bobby to initiate a search for his biological parents. His efforts, though, would be thwarted as he continually ran into dead ends. Whoever they were, they had covered their tracks well; even the mother's name on his birth certificate proved to be fictitious.

It would be ten years before Phyllis would muster the courage to contact her son, proving her identity by confirming the name on the birth certificate. Bobby was satisfied, and agreed to a meeting. During the course of their initial encounter, Phyllis explained the difficult circumstances of Bobby's birth, the desperately painful decisions she was forced to make, and told of the bumpy path her life had taken upon her return to Tucson and her eventual return to the Bay Area. But more importantly, she told him the name of his father.

"Will you call me back in a few minutes?" the Colonel asked. "It's not every day you get a call like this."

Bobby had gathered just enough courage and conviction to make the call. And now he wasn't sure whether his mission had simply been momentarily interrupted or aborted altogether. He wondered if he could do it again. Of course he would. He'd opened Pandora's Box and there was no turning back. Moments later, he was on the phone again, resuming the thorny conversation.

"The only Robert Weir I know of," asserted the Colonel, "plays guitar with the Grateful Dead."

"Well, sir," Bobby answered, "that would be me."

After another long silence, the sparring defused and the two would continue to talk, cautiously feeling each other out, and filling in the gaps in their respective histories. When they decided to meet over lunch the next day, the Colonel would be astonished at their physical similarities and shared mannerisms. Bobby was likewise impressed, later agreeing that there would be no need for a DNA test.

As for the Parber sons, whom he'd later meet, they were equally impressed as surprised that their straight-laced Air Force Colonel—the model of discipline and sobriety—had illicitly fathered a heretofore unknown son—and a rock star, at that. But recalling James' girlfriend's remark many years earlier about Bobby's strong family resemblance, their doubts were wholly assuaged; Bobby was, indeed, their brother.

Milena, on the other hand, wasn't as quick to appreciate the deeper significance of the sudden extension of her family. She had been in Houston visiting friends when the Colonel called with the news. In time, though, the shock would abate, the anger would subside, and she'd welcome Bobby into their lives, becoming his de facto "current reining mom."

The Telecaster had its original cream finish when James got it in 1969, but he'd stripped the heavy swamp ash body down to bare wood, and replaced the tuning machines and pickups in the bargain. It was a real working man's guitar—the one he'd been waiting for. And the custom touches he contributed would make it his own.

The guitar came into James' hands via the long and winding path typical of such workhorses; since its manufacture in 1956 it had been bought, sold, and traded many times along the way. James got it in exchange for a commensurately beat-up piano. But the guitar was silent now. It stood perched upright, secure on its stand against a wall in his bedroom, while he lay somewhat less securely in his own bed. Twelve years earlier, he was told his condition was terminal, yet he defied his doctors' prognosis of only weeks to live.

The Colonel remained by his side, having retired from military service, in order to help Milena care for their dying son. But this was one battle the decorated war veteran would not win. "The night has been unruly," Shakespeare wrote. "Where we lay, our chimneys were blown down." In an eerie echoing, James died, and in that moment, his much-loved guitar inexplicably fell from its stand.

Ironically, Bobby, the Colonel, and Phyllis lived within a few miles of each other, yet in all the years, their paths never crossed. Now, though, a brief, if not reluctant, fifty-year reunion would be arranged, allowing the circle to be fully closed at last. It would be their final meeting, as Phyllis passed away only a month later.

Bobby, his wife Natascha, and their two young daughters, though, continued to bond with the Parbers, making a tradition of visiting "the grandparents" on weekends, and often for the night. When they did, Bobby and Natascha always stayed in James' old room, where Milena had kept his old guitar. The shabby case had variously been stashed in the closet, stood in a corner, or stowed beneath the bed. Curiosity got the best of Bobby, and rising to the bait, he unlatched the case and opened it up: before him lay the road-worn '56 Tele. With broken knobs and a pickup sprung from its moorings, it still bore the scars it incurred when it fell to the floor that heartrending day in '91. As he lifted it from its case, he wondered what it might have to say.

Bobby called Milena to the room and asked her if he might be allowed to fix the guitar and possibly play it. "I thought you'd never ask," she said. And so, with her blessing he delivered the guitar to AJ, his roadie and guitar tech, who got the guitar back into playing shape in no time. Coincidentally, The Dead had been preparing for their summer '03 tour. At their next rehearsal, Bobby plugged the old Tele into his rig, and with its first biting notes it unequivocally claimed its place in the mix.

Being a large group, Bobby had struggled with his sound; the fatter tone of his Modulous just couldn't cut through to his satisfaction. Between the two keyboards, lead guitar, and bass, his guitar was fighting for its life in the overcrowded midrange. But James' Tele, a characteristically thin sounding guitar, poked right through the mix and spoke right up. The cutting quality of each note, line, and chord defined its own space within the flux of the music. And when it did, all the previous sonic frustrations evaporated. At once Bobby began to imagine the possibilities this newfound clarity would lend to his rhythmic and harmonic explorations within the band's sound.

So excited were the band that Bobby invited the Colonel and Milena to their studios, only a couple miles from their home, to hear it for themselves. And when they did, the Tele's sparkling tone drew a satisfied smile from the Colonel and tears from Milena's eyes. They knew its voice well; each attack of the strings invoking a long-silent spirit.

The ensuing tour would take the band—and James' guitar—across the country, performing with Willie Nelson and Bob Dylan along the way—two musicians James had most admired.

James never got to meet his older brother, but somehow they commune. "Needless to say," reflects Bobby, "I feel a deep and mysterious bond with the brother I never met; I can't help but wonder if he could see me coming from where he is now, if perhaps he even helped guide my steps toward my newfound family. One thing is for sure, though: the voice of his old guitar has changed my whole approach to how I play." Fate, it seems, mercifully intervened and made up for its cruel twists.

Visit Bob Weir at www.dead.net and www.rat-dog.com

Band of Brothers

Johnathan Parber, with John Schroeter

T he dull black Corvette—a mid six-ties roadster—looked as though it had been sitting out in the elements too long, neglected for many years. But now it was sitting at the curb in front of the house. I had flown out from Colorado Springs to my parent's home in Novato for this arranged meeting, and I was more than a bit on edge.

He got out of the Vette, wearing the look you see on kids' faces when they're about to jump off a high-dive for the first time. It never occurred to me that he'd be even more nervous than me. "What the hell," I said to myself. "It's time to break this ice." I walked out across the lawn with outstretched arms and cried, "Bob, long time, man! You never write!" I gave him a big hug, for which he braced and stiff-ened—he clearly wasn't used to this kind of thing—and said, "I'm Jonathan, your brother."

From the time I was a kid in junior high, I looked up to Bob Weir. In the early days of the Dead, we'd see them all the time. I especially liked watching Bob—he was the cool one. I loved the way he played guitar, the funky little rhythmic accents that he'd work into the fabric of the sound, always just underneath the surface of the song. Oh, I liked Jerry, too—how could you not like Jerry? But I was a "Bob guy."

We were all fans, my three brothers and me. Jim, though, was the one who pulled us into the whole experience of the '60s. He was the one who, when we were still living in Merced, was listening to the San Francisco radio stations. He intro-duced us to Hendrix before anyone really knew who he was. He was our connec-tion to the music of the Doors, Jefferson Airplane, and the Grateful Dead.

All four of us played guitar, too. But Jim, who always took the music a little more seriously, was the one who'd stay up all night practicing. (Music seems to run in our family; my grandfather met his future wife when he gave her guitar

109

lessons at fourteen!)

Jim went through a lot of guitars in those days, trading all the time, keeping them for a week or two, then moving on, looking for the right one. There had been a Strat, a Gibson or two—just a string of guitars that passed through in quick succession. The '56 Tele, though, is the one that survived—the one that stuck. And it was a beautiful guitar; I loved the feel of the neck. But Jim had that delicate touch; he played it so well.

Later, when Jim got sick, he'd sit in his bed and play that Tele. No matter how sick he was, he could still work his fingers and play some guitar. He had been in the hospital, where they did all they could to treat him—chemo, radiation, everything else—but it all failed. The doctors had given him only two weeks to live. At that point Mom took him out of the hospital and got him into experimental alternative treatment. And eight months later, the cancer was in remission. Jim lived another twelve years—some years better than others—but the damage done to his system by the radiation eventually caught up with him. He died on November 4, 1991 at thirty-nine.

Losing our dear brother was devastating. Even now not a day goes by that we don't think about him and miss him; he was an amazing guy. We were really just starting to get over our grief when Bob came along. And his presence proved to be a healing force, especially for my parents. All of a sudden their lives opened up again. It was a very good thing for everybody.

We thought it was a bit odd, though, that Bobby seemed to avoid the subject of Jim; whatever his reasons, he just wasn't comfortable talking about him. But then, none of us really knew how to act. We were delighted that he had come into our lives, but the deeper connections came slowly and cautiously. At times, we sort of awkwardly danced around each other as our lives began to become more and more intertwined.

Bobby and Natascha stayed in Jim's old room when they came to visit, and though Jim's guitar was always in the room, Bob never opened the case. But then again, none of us, probably out of deference, touched the Tele after Jim died; it just stayed in his room. I'm sure Bobby sensed that it might have been put out for him, quietly and subtly inviting him to pick it up. And eventually he did. In some ways I think it was easier for him; it would have been hard for me to play that guitar.

At the same time, though, when Bob did start to play it, I was surprised at my mixed feelings. On one hand it was a wondrous thing, but on the other, there were some conflicting, if not confused, emotions. Call it sibling rivalry, but when Bob came along, a lot of energy and attention was poured in his direction—and naturally so! But I felt that I had lost some of my identity within the family. It wasn't easy for Bobby, either. It was an adjustment for everybody, really. We were an established family, and Bobby—a guy you'd never think of as having to prove any-thing—had to somehow prove himself, and establish himself as part of this family. And though we were very grateful—in many ways we took an unmitigated delight in his sudden appearance—it took years to effect that familial settling in. And despite our efforts, there was no short-circuiting the process. Interestingly enough, though, Jim—through the vehicle of his guitar—would be the final conciliator.

About an hour's drive from my home, Red Rocks Amphitheatre is a true natural wonder. Nestled in the foothills of the Rocky Mountains, it's a geologically formed open-air venue surrounded by majestic 300-foot sandstone monoliths that form acoustically fabulous walls. Tonight, it would play host to the Grateful Dead on the Denver leg of their 2003 tour.

I knew that Bobby was using Jim's guitar on this tour. I'd even seen photographs on the internet. And though I was deeply moved to see those pictures, I thought I was prepared to see him playing it live. But when he brought that guitar out onstage for the first time that night, it hit me. There it was, projected on the big screen. For a brief moment I could see Jim. In that moment, I was overcome with a wave of emotions that ran the gamut from laughter to tears. I wondered, what would my brother think if he could see this, if he knew what was happening? He didn't know about Bobby—he had died only a few years before he came to light as our brother. I looked around at the faces in the crowd. And people were enjoying the beauty of the sound. Bobby had a rack of guitars—beautiful, exquisite custom guitars in gorgeous colors—and yet, here he was, playing this beat up old Tele with the paint stripped off. People noticed and wondered.

Something happened when he played that guitar. Everyone could see it—and hear it. Throughout the history of the Dead, Bob's guitar always seemed to be buried in the mix. He was very much a part of the sound, but his guitar never really cut through in an obvious way. But when he played that Tele, I suddenly realized just how good a player he is. Jerry had always told him to "stay underneath." And to this day, I hear Bob say that Jerry's just over his shoulder. He comes off stage and says, "I overplayed. Jerry was right there telling me. And he was right. I overplayed." Yet when he plays the Tele, somehow the shackles fall off.

> In that moment, I was overcome with a wave of emotions that ran the gamut from laughter to tears. I wondered, what would my brother think if he could see this, if he knew what was happening?

Backstage, he pulled me aside to a quiet corner of the room. And with his intense, focused eyes he looked at me and told me with the zeal of an evangelist about how that guitar had changed his life. I thanked him, and said, "Bobby, you don't know what that did for *me* to see you play that guitar."

Just when you think you know how things work…

OPPORTUNITIES IN WORK CLOTHES

Figuring out solutions to the problems is part of the fun. And there
are always problems. It's not that any of the stuff comes that easily.
There are very few pieces of which I can say, "I wrote that in an hour."
—*Laurence Juber*

Playing guitar is and endless process of running out of fingers.
—*Harvey Reid*

Alicia Adams

FOR LOVE OF THE TREES

VIVA FUI IN SILVIS
SUM DURA OCCISA
SECURI DUM VIXI TACUI
MORTUA DULCE CANO

I was alive in the forest
I was cut by the cruel axe
In life I was silent
In death I sweetly sing

Those words from the inscription on an Elizabethan lute have come to resonate in me in a deeply meaningful way, although my understanding of the trees' position on the matter has changed! For four years I worked with wood from five old growth redwood trees, manufacturing musical instrument soundboards. During that time, I was blessed with a reawakening of my childhood ability to enter into relationships with individual trees. As a child, I spent much time in the tops of tall elms and maples on our northern Ohio farm. Although I originally climbed them in an attempt to reach a place of light that I called "Home," I soon discovered that there was nurture and comfort that flowed from the trees themselves. I learned to be open to "tree language," which was not spoken but was very clear to me. The trees taught me a great deal: for example, that one must grow strong roots in this world if one is to be strong and tall, reaching toward the light. In crucial ways, I was raised by the trees I climbed.

When luthiers commented on my "love of wood," because of my passion for finding the right musical instrument home for the soundboards I'd cut, it didn't ring quite true. What I revered was not so much the wood as it was the trees from which the wood was taken. I gave each log a name, for example, and the soundboards were marked with letters designating this name. It was then that my awareness of my unique relationship with trees—individual trees—awoke.

"Love" implies a relationship: intimate and reciprocal. It has been much misused and thus misunderstood. If I "love trees," it is in this context: my relationship with individual trees.

> It wasn't until we started looking for possible soundboard wood in odd billets of old growth redwood that we began to develop an appreciation for the unique characteristics of each tree; thus our relationship with individual redwood trees began.

Luthiers and musicians may understand this need for relationship in a different context. My former husband, Craig Carter, was a classical guitarist and would-be luthier. I entered the world of guitars, guitar music, luthiers, and finally, musical instrument soundboard manufacture as my husband's side-kick. Craig understood very well that in order to play music that truly sang he had to be in a reciprocal relationship with his instruments. He had several guitars during our marriage: a Fleta, two Hausers, and a de la Chica. Earlier, he'd had a number of guitars built by American luthiers. Craig spoke articulately about the differences between each instrument and demonstrated that difference to me and his musician and luthier friends by playing the same music on different instruments. He knew how to showcase the strengths of each instrument and minimize its weaker characteristics. He was always searching for the "perfect guitar" but he admitted he'd probably never find one that answered all his musical needs. This was impossible, because the strengths in one instrument automatically limited its range or sensitivity in other aspects. It was best, he thought, to have different instruments for different musical requirements.

He approached guitar wood from the same perspective. For twenty-five years, he collected sets of backs, sides, and soundboards for the building of classical guitars that he planned as his main focus in his later years. I learned his standards for wood by osmosis by helping him sort through many piles of guitar wood sets, and by his discussion of the points to look for in each type of wood. It wasn't until we started looking for possible soundboard wood in odd billets of old growth redwood that we began to develop an appreciation for the unique characteristics of each tree;

thus our relationship with individual redwood trees began.

Craig cut into billets or fallen logs from over a hundred redwood trees, by his estimate, before he found one that satisfied all his criteria for classical guitar soundboards. By that time, we had hiked over many miles of logged redwood forest, looking for pieces large enough for guitar soundboards. Craig discovered that the redwood "snags"— the butt end of redwood trees—standing or fallen, did not make good soundboards. He discussed this at length with other luthiers, especially Brian Burns, who tested many of Craig's potential soundboard finds. Their supposition was that the compression of the wood, from the weight of the tree, resulted in denser wood that did not transmit sound freely. Mostly, these snags and rotten logs were all that were left of what had been vast redwood forests in both Mendocino and Humboldt Counties of Northern California. It was very disappointing.

Craig and I visited the local office of CalTrans, (California Transportation Department) which governs freeway right-of-ways in California. From this office, he received maps of the freeways in Humboldt County, where we had moved in 1992. He also received verbal permission to harvest guitar wood, on a small scale, from fallen logs—provided we used discretion and hand tools and did not disturb the surrounding area. The log that Craig found ideal for his purposes was one that fell when the freeway was constructed, about thirty years previously. The tree grew in a dense forest, so it grew straight up, without any twist to the wood. It was on sloping ground that was undercut by the freeway construction; it fell down the slope and across a dip in the ground. Thus it was supported at both ends but suspended in the air for much of its middle length—perfect conditions for air-drying its wood. This is the "LS" log that has become rather famous in luthier circles. Craig originally gave it these initials to designate it was the "Log Splitter" because of its uniquely straight splitting characteristics. Luthier Jeffery Elliot, of Portland, Oregon, decided that this log needed a more appropriate name, and dubbed it the "Lucky Strike" log.

I had begun to have a relationship with the redwood forest by the time we discovered the LS log because of our many hours spent walking in both cut-over forests and in the nearby Humboldt Redwoods State Park. The forest was, for me, a living entity comprised of all the plant and animal lives it supported. In the cut areas, it was more than dead, it was desecrated. Working on retrieving wood from the LS log was the first opportunity I had, though, to begin to tune-in to a particular tree. Perhaps because this tree fell naturally, rather than being cut by man, I felt its essence, which was much more than the character of its wood. I revered the tree even more as I worked with its wood. Trees like this, I thought, should be declared national treasures; they are now so rare as to be almost extinct.

Removing wood from the LS log was arduous work. We'd been warned that we must be "discrete" because the officials at CalTrans did not want wholesale destruction along the freeways by drivers who saw opportunities to gather wood for fence posts or split products. We therefore went to great lengths to slip into the area unnoticed, and to make sure that the surrounding bushy growth was undisturbed. Craig hand-cut half rounds in the log with a five-foot-long hand saw: half-rounds, because the lower half of the log was needed to support its length, initially. He then split out billets with special wedges, called "checkers," handmade by blacksmiths in the last century, and a mallet. I marked the ends of the billets for guitar-sized sections: vertical growth at least 8" wide, across the grain. We left a wedge of wood to one side, where the wood went out of vertical, in order to screw the billet into a carriage for Craig's band saw. (Brian Burns hand built the carriage for Craig.) The billets were cut at 26" length in order to make sets around unseen flaws. We hand carried each billet through the forest to where we could load them into Craig's 1966 230 Mercedes sedan. It is amazing what that sedan held in its trunk and, with the back seat removed, in the back seat area, piled to the roof. This faithful car made many trips over winding, rough roads to our home in Petrolia, about an hour's drive from where it was loaded.

In eight months of harvesting this log, Craig only collected enough wood for about a hundred soundboards. His original idea had been to collect the wood for his own building. However, failure of our investigative/legal business in 1993 resulted in the lack of income. Craig began marketing his LS soundboards to luthiers in Spring, 1994.

In July 1994, Craig was diagnosed with two blood disorders that were said to be fatal. He was given six weeks to live. There had never been a successful treatment by our medical system for the combination of these two disorders. Instead, Craig and I went to India for thirteen months so that he could receive Ayurvedic treatment. Craig's friends and family, including his bike racing, musician and luthier friends, supported us the entire time. Our neighbors took care of our home, animals, and financial affairs. Craig lived two and a half years past his medically-projected death, but he died at home in December, 1996.

That is how I became the owner of Craig's woodworking equipment and the inheritor of his passion for fine guitar wood. With much assistance from my neighbors, I continued Craig's guitar soundboard business.

Until this time, the only relationship with Craig's woodworking tools that I had developed was with Craig's 1900 12" jointer. Craig had shown me how to joint the base of billets to prepare them for cutting on his large band saw. After we returned from India, his strength was much diminished; he had to allow his friend, Ed Gilda, to help him harvest the LS billets. I did the jointer work while Craig cut sets. I enjoyed my work and developed respect for the intricacies of the jointer—my introduction to the reciprocal relationship that a woodworker must develop with his or her tools. Later, I developed a reciprocal relationship with the band saw, after initial fear of it, and much confusion as to how it worked and what it needed. Finally, I realized that I didn't have the strength to use the carriage Craig and Brian had designed. I had a power carriage designed and built for my usage.

When I began to market sets from trees other than the LS one, I discovered that luthiers and musicians wanted a particular cosmetic look to their soundboards— one very rare in redwood trees, but common in cedar and Spruce. Mostly, the other trees I harvested did not have this look: a light, even coloration. Most luthiers and musicians would only accept redwood soundboards that looked like cedar. Unusually, many of the LS soundboards looked almost like Spruce in their coloration.

> I'd "promised the trees" that, in taking their wood, I'd "give them a voice," that they'd sing.

A local logger, Lloyd Partee, who'd cut both cedar and redwood, explained the difference between the two types of trees to Craig and me. In his forty years of experience, he'd found that nine out of ten cedar trees were alike; they grew straight and split straight, with little or no color variation. In contrast, EVERY redwood tree was unique, in coloration and other wood characteristics, and only about one out of ten was a "splitter"— one that split straight with the grain. Of these, most had a great deal of color variation.

All the trees whose wood I worked were "splitter" redwoods, and thus were rare for this type. Of the five, only the LS and the inner section of the "Truly Awesome" (TA) logs were of even coloration.

Color variation in soundboards was not acceptable to most luthiers, I discovered. It hadn't been to Craig, either, with his high standards for classical guitar soundboards. But I came to this work with a different perspective: I'd "promised the trees" that, in taking their wood, I'd "give them a voice," that they'd sing. That, to me, meant I was committed to finding luthiers who would use every usable piece of musical instrument quality wood that I harvested. This proved to be impossible for me, with no capital or income and limited strength and working facilities.

Of the five logs, the "Fine Art" (FA) log was so old and battered, with most of it rotten or cracked, that I couldn't really sense the essence of "tree" any more. My relationship with it was with the wood, which was fine-grained, very dark and sometimes striped, and very hard. Some luthiers bought sets because the wood, colored over many years from minerals in the soil, was so uniquely beautiful.

The TA, the "Tono Basso (TB) and FA logs came later, after I was no longer able to harvest wood from the road easement. My ability to take wood from the LS log was limited by the help I could get; I couldn't cut it with a hand saw and could barely lift Craig's chain saw. I could split the billets but only for a short time; the mallet was too heavy for me. But I did become good at trimming the billets with a froe. Two neighbors helped me harvest some billets by taking turns cutting them out with the hand saw, but they could only do this infrequently. It was more than disappointing to discover, when we returned to the LS log after an absence of several weeks, that my hidden hand tools had been found and stolen, along with a large section of the log—probably for fence posts. One of the original friends who'd helped me, and an engineer who was over 6'3" in height and built to match, helped harvest the rest of the log. The engineer used Craig's chain saw while my other friend, who was tough, but like me, small in stature, hand split and carried the billets. I made these billets into sets and sold them to a national guitar company, a luthier supply company, and to individual luthiers. I was then out of wood—and out of income.

> I stood on the log about sixty feet from the cut and was amazed to hear and feel the whole log ring like a tuning fork! It was very exciting for me to think of the instruments that could be made with a musical log whose tones could be heard above the roar of a chain saw.

I went back to the easement to look for another log. I discovered another fallen log in the vicinity of the LS log, uphill from it in a more inaccessible location. This tree had fallen across the slope; it needed to be supported by wedges of wood on the down slope side while it was cut and split. The portion of the log lying on the ground was not usable, due to splits and rot. Billets that we took out of the upper surface showed wood of bright, warm colors—striped. I hoped that luthiers would find it as beautiful as I did. But it was certainly not in the classical tradition!

Neighbors and friends cut the log into rounds with Craig's chainsaw. No one wanted to hand saw it, and besides, my hand saw had been stolen. Bill Smith, a tool collector and friend of Grass Valley luthier Michael Lewis, heard of this theft and restored two beautiful old hand saws, which he gave me. Unfortunately, neither was long enough to cut across the LS log.

I marked-out the billets on the end grain of the cuts and the men hand-split it. Together we carried each billet through the dripping forest, down steep muddy slopes to a pull off on the highway where it could be collected later. By the time each day's work was finished we were drenched through and covered with mud.

I called this tree the "Singing Tree" (ST). When it was being cut into rounds with the chainsaw, I stood on the log about sixty feet from the cut and was amazed to hear and feel the whole log ring like a tuning fork! It was very exciting for me to think of the instruments that could be made with a musical log whose tones could be heard above the roar of a chain saw.

It was this chain saw noise and the engineering friend's jury-rigged system to slide logs over a high wire downhill, to save all that carrying, that proved to be our undoing. I was not present the day that my friends were ticketed for taking wood out of a state park; I'd injured my back, and had to rest it. It seemed that there had been a long power struggle between the park and the highway department as to who had the right to say what became of the trees that fell in the freeway easement. Though we were clearly within the easement and had verbal permission to take wood, my friends' usage of a chain saw was not "discrete." A new reason for "discretion" unfolded, during our lengthy court hearings: it was one authority against another, and the fate of the trees, the fine musical instrument wood that they represented, was irrelevant. Finally my friends were acquitted, on the promise that we would no longer harvest wood from the road easements.

This shut down my operations for quite a while and almost cost me my home as I couldn't pay the mortgage payments or support myself. Then a neighbor stepped in to support a cottage industry, as he said, and bought three logs. The FA log was first: it was left over from a logging operation of forty years ago. Unfortunately, it proved to be very low in soundboard yield, and that yield highly colored. The "Truly Awesome" (TA) and "Tono Basso" (TB) logs were each seventeen feet long and five feet wide: it was an enormous project to split out billets on the ranch where they'd fallen, after having the logs cut into rounds by a hired chain saw operator, and transport all back to Petrolia in our small vehicles. There, we marked each billet as to type of instrument usage and number of sets, gave them letter and number designations and sealed the ends with paraffin. The ranch mill foreman estimated that we had 26,000 pounds of billets, all transported and lifted, over and over, to be stacked carefully under tarps in my yard.

> The question is, are luthiers willing to take their understanding of the reciprocal nature of their relationship with their tools and their instruments one step further: to develop the same type of relationship with this soundboard wood?

My neighbor and I cut sets and hung them to dry in my small, dehumidified drying shed. To our disappointment, the sets from both logs were too "green" to immediately yield marketable soundboard sets. When these sets were perfectly dry, they were streaked in coloration, and when tapped, they lacked the clear tonal quality of cured soundboards. Soundboards from both logs promised to yield high quality sets of distinct tonal and structural characteristics, eventually. We cut a few excellent soundboards, from each log, from inner wood that was cured in the tree. However, that "eventually" was too much for me. I had no funds to keep the business going, let alone my home and myself. I left my home in Petrolia in December, 1999, to seek work in Santa Rosa. Though I returned, with my new partner, Daniel Richards, to cut soundboards for George Lowden the following March, my soundboard manufacturing business was essentially over.

> I couldn't realize my promise to the trees, but luthiers can do so if they can pass their inspiration on to the musicians that purchase their instruments.

The problem now was what to do with all this wood? The billets were moved—three times—by Dan as our plans changed. They finally ended up back in the dirt floor garage where I'd once housed my jointer. My property was bought by Ed Gilda, my neighbor, one of Craig's best friends and my main support initially in retrieving LS billets after Craig's death. Ed rented the property but allowed my billets to remain in storage there. Recently Hank Mauel, a luthier from Auburn, has undertaken to find luthier homes for both my left-over soundboards and these billets. Thanks to Dan, Ed, and Hank, some of this fine wood is still available to luthiers.

The question is, are luthiers willing to take their understanding of the reciprocal nature of their relationship with their tools and their instruments one step further: to develop the same type of relationship with this soundboard wood? Craig's idea, which I continued, was that working with wood from one known source, one log, would allow a luthier to experiment with construction techniques to improve his or her instrument with the soundboard qualities known, consistent. This was what he planned to do with the LS wood. It was also my thinking when I marked each set with both the log name and a billet number. To make several instruments from not just the same log, but even the same location in the log—one billet—should allow luthiers to "come into relationship" with the soundboard aspect of their building in ways not usually possible.

To do this with redwood, though, one needs to have a relationship with these ancient trees that is more powerful than current cosmetic standards for soundboards. Redwood doesn't look or act like cedar or spruce. Also, one cannot generalize about the characteristics of redwood; each tree is unique. Each tree is also a musical instrument treasure, never to be duplicated and, therefore, irreplaceable. My hope is that luthiers will honor these magnificent trees by giving them a voice:

by helping them to sing their songs through many varied instruments. I couldn't realize my promise to the trees, but luthiers can do so if they can pass their inspiration on to the musicians that purchase their instruments.

Musicians who are interested in ways to give unique flavor to their music are finding that instruments made from redwood soundboards broaden their tonal and musical range. Many types of stringed instruments have been made from wood of these five trees, including different types of guitars as well as mandolins, dulcimers, and some exotic folk instruments. Every step of turning the flesh of trees into musical instruments, and thus to the purpose of making music, can be performed in an attitude of reverence and relationship. When this happens, the making and playing of hand built wooden instruments will truly be an act of love.

As for the trees? Well, as I alluded earlier, they've enlightened me with a message of their own: "We don't need you to give us a voice," the trees now sing to me. "Don't you remember? We sing our songs with our *lives*. Our deaths and decay, or the usage of our wood by humans—*all* are part of our songs. Have you grown so many roots in this world, grown so dense in consciousness, that you don't hear the songs any more?"

ON THE ROAD AGAIN

The best measure of my success as a musician is the amount of hotel soap I have at home. If I get to the point where I have to buy a regular-sized bar out of necessity, I'm simply not working enough!
—*Bob Bennett*

People think it's exciting, but you just think about getting back home. The best time you have is that two hours you spend on stage. That's where all the fun is. It's not the coming and going—that wears your butt out. But it is better than hauling gravel.
—*Paul Yandell*

Performing is the best thing for a musician; it keeps you from becoming stagnant. I'll never be able to stop working on the road, I'm sure. Let's face it, I'm a showoff!
—*Peter Frampton*

I'm a musician; I have to drive!
—*Adrian Legg*

George Lowden

REDWOOD

I arrived in Eureka on a plane from San Francisco, rented a car, and drove for a few hours southward over the dry rolling hills. From the map there appeared to be only three small towns between myself and my destination, Petrolia. The first had a distinctly English flavor, rather like what I might have expected to see in BC—beautifully painted wood frame houses, the stuff of picture postcards. Then nothing for miles and miles and miles. I continued on, up and down, up and down over the endless hills running more or less perpendicular to the blue-gray Pacific. I was looking for Cape Town, the next dot on the map. Eventually I came upon a house and one disused school building with a piece of driftwood nailed to a post, heralding that I was, in fact, in Cape Town! It was a scene right out of the Wild West. I've heard of one horse towns, but I still can't figure out how this one justified the ink on the map.

My trip was a quest to source redwood guitar tops—a tonewood I had never used in my twenty-six years as a guitar maker. As always, I was excited at the prospect of rummaging through the many tops I anticipated seeing, but even more so this time, because redwood was something new and fresh for me.

Eventually I arrived at Alicia Adam's shop and home, a humble group of stick-built buildings on the bank of the Mattole River. First we talked. I was anxious to learn the ins and outs of retrieval of fallen redwood trees and logging in the area. A friend of Alicia's dropped in during the evening. His conversation led us to conservation issues, trees, steelhead, plant and animal life. I was impressed that here was a fellow who actually chose to work and live in this remote area—and in a very simple way—so he could do his bit to protect the environment. Here was the genuine article: a real life tree hugger! Then Alicia told me the story of how, since her husband (also a guitar maker) had died, she had been struggling to eke out a living splitting the redwood billets up in the forest and then cutting them up into guitar tops by herself.

I followed her to the shop, where she showed me many such billets and tops. The wood frame building was crammed so full to the roof with billets of redwood that the only available light came through the open door. For me as a guitar maker, even though I am used to seeing "mountains" of wood, there's something special about seeing large quantities of *split* billets; somehow they retain the feeling of being part of a tree so much more than sawn planks.

Much of the wood was beautiful; some displayed color variations, while others were a more even reddish brown. But the best had great tap tone, and I loved it. I had the impression that its stiffness and weight ratio would voice it somewhere between Sitka spruce and cedar. That idea appealed to me, and I decided then I'd use it for the Millennium Twins limited edition guitars I was planning.

Some time before this I had been offered a large quantity of very special Claro Walnut (also from northern California), all from the one tree! I was so struck by this wood—the figure and color and texture—that I decided it might be a nice idea to design twin guitars as a celebration of year 2000. My idea was to build a limited edition of about thirty "guitar twins," each being made with adjacent sets of Claro walnut back and sides, and matching redwood tops (also from adjacent tops cut from Alicia's billets). So the wood for each guitar would exactly the same, but one twin would be the larger O model and one would be the small body S model—identical twins except for the size and shape! Some of these redwood trees are so old it seemed fitting to celebrate the dawn of the next millennium with their legacy.

In fact, my first experience with using redwood for guitar tops came through these "Millenium Twins." I used figured maple bindings to compliment both the redwood and the Claro walnut, and the subtle blend of wood textures and colors was very alluring in the end. I finished these guitars with my usual sense of excitement and anticipation... will they be bright? Have I got the voicing right? Will they be too quiet, will they be clear enough, will they have enough bass, and will the trebles be full and rich, or will they be a little thin? I should have known that the majestic redwood would not let me down. They were indeed warm and yet clear and defined; they were loud and yet capable of great subtlety—they seemed to have everything to my ears.

> Some of these redwood trees are so old it seemed fitting to celebrate the dawn of the next millennium with their legacy.

I left Alicia's shop that day with a lighter heart. The time spent in this rather remote part of California fellowshipping with unpretentious folk who shared with me a deep sense of respect towards nature and the Grand Design was a truly uplifting, and yet leveling experience. Another joyous landmark in my guitar making journey.

Visit George Lowden at www.georgelowden.com

Chris Martin IV

ALL IN THE FAMILY

I thank God that I wasn't born into the world's most famous accordion family! And though I run the Martin Guitar Company today, I didn't actually grow up in the business. When I was young, though, I'd go out to the factory in the summer time, and spend time with Grandfather Martin. I'd get to do odd jobs like packing strings or pushing the neck blank falloffs into the bin as they passed through the bandsaw—things that OSHA would never allow today!

One Christmas, when I was about ten or so, I got my first guitar, a nylon string 5-18 Terz guitar. My teacher, learning who I was, tried to steer me into a more formal method. He had me sitting with my foot on a pedestal and my thumb properly placed behind the neck in the classical position, and playing scales. I just wanted to learn some chords and go right into Beatles tunes—it was really very frustrating for me. But later I got the electric guitar—one of the old archtop GT models with the f-holes—and a Fender Twin Reverb, and I could finally make some noise. And of course, the Twin Reverb has become much more valuable than that electric Martin will ever will be!

I never did become much of a guitar player—or builder, for that matter. One year at camp, the shop class instructor told me it was time for me to move beyond Popsicle sticks and build a more significant project. So I contacted my dad and my grandfather and told them that I wanted to build a guitar, and asked them to send me a guitar kit. And they said, "What do you mean, a guitar kit?" I said, "You know, just put all the pieces in a box and send them to me." At that time, guitar kits as such didn't really exist. Fortunately, though, my request came at a time when the company had been doing some research and development on some unusual body shapes. So what they ended up sending me were the parts and a blueprint for a trapezoidal-shaped guitar. The body wasn't quite square, but trapezoidal, where the upper bout is narrower than the lower bout, but the sides are straight. They figured I wouldn't be able to bend the sides, so they'd send me this thing that they kind of threw together.

So with the guidance of the camp counselor, this project became my first attempt at building a guitar. And we were really on our own. There was no book, no instructions, just a bunch of parts and a big blueprint thrown into a box.

Now, not having grown up in the business, and not having spent a lot of time in the shop, I didn't realize that you had to assemble the rim first. So I cut the top and back to what I thought was the appropriate dimension, and then tried to build the sides around it. What a nightmare—that's *not* how you build an acoustic guitar! You build the rim first, and *then* you glue on an oversize back and top, and trim it. When it was all said and done, there was an awful lot of wood filler that had to go where there should have been a nice joint with the wood. And then that whole thing of fitting a dovetail neck to the body was something that not even my counselor knew how to do.

> The guitar I built was really an embarrassment. The closer you got to it—oh my God!

It's an amazing thing that the guitar got built, but it did, and I still have it. I took it to a luthier's convention several years ago, where I told the story and played it. People find it quite charming. Thank goodness it's a nylon string guitar; the action isn't as critical. And because it is trapezoidal, it's very much like an Ovation in that it keeps sliding off your leg.

Back in the '60s, the company did make a few production units of that design. Of course, those were well-made! The guitar I built was really an embarrassment. The closer you got to it—oh my God! It was apparent that this kid didn't know what he was doing. But it gave me a taste. And it really taught me that if I was going to get involved in this business, I'd better do my homework.

One year, I went to Nazareth for the entire summer. And it was at that point that I sat down with my grandfather and told him that I wanted to build a *real* guitar. He suggested a 12-fret Dreadnought, "Because," he said, "if you want the best sounding guitar, that's what you should build."

So there I was, out in the plant with all the parts and specs, and ready to build my first real Martin guitar. But what happened was I would get to a particular workstation and the individual doing that job would take my part, and demonstrate on that part how the job was done. And it was done perfectly. And then he would give me some reject D-18 parts and say, "Okay, now you try it." And I'd screw them up. And then I would take my perfect part to the next workstation, where that person would demonstrate the operation on my part, and give it back to me and let me practice on reject material. When it was done, the stinking guitar was perfect. But I did very little of the work. I watched them assemble it, too, because none of the craftspeople wanted to be the one who passed bad work onto the next person, knowing that I would be the one who had done the bad work. It was pretty hilarious. It was not the guitar I built, but rather, the guitar I *watched* being built. But I really did learn quite a lot from that experience. My brother has that guitar now. In fact, he learned to play on that guitar.

In the fall of that year, I went out to UCLA, where I didn't do particularly well; I really didn't like it out there. I called my mom to tell her I was coming home. When she asked about my plans, I told her I was going to work in the guitar factory. And she said, "You're gonna *what*?! You're not going to go back to college?" I said, "Not right now. I'm going to work in the guitar factory."

So I went out in the plant and worked on the bench. And I could put ribbon on with the best of them. But when it came to fitting necks, I'll be the first to admit that I never really quite got it. And hand-bending sides, I never quite got that, either. But some of those simpler tasks I could do. And through that experience, I learned to speak the guitar maker's language. And it gave me an understanding of what it's like to work in a shop with people who have said to themselves, "I'm willing to do this for a living, knowing that I'm never going to build a whole guitar. But I also know that I'm working for a company that really prides itself on its quality." And the more I did that, the more I said to myself, "I'm going to *run* this business, not work on a bench." So I ended up going back to college, to Boston University, and I got a degree in management. When I came back, not only could I talk about guitar construction, I could talk about business.

My grandfather was more of a guitar builder than my father. My grandfather played, and he knew and could talk guitar construction. My father was more of a businessman. If you were to sit down with my dad and talk X bracing, he would very quickly just glaze over and space out. But running a business and growing it and maintaining the quality—*that* he understood. So it was a good thing that they were both here at the same time. They represented the best of both worlds to me. I learned everything about guitars from my grandfather, and what I learned from my father was, "This is a business. We have to treat it like a business. It's not a hobby; it has to make money. And if it doesn't make money in a sustainable manner, someday it will go away."

Unfortunately, I also got to see my father make some pretty significant mistakes; there were some bad acquisitions along the way. When he bought the Darco String Company, he should have quit right there. That was a brilliant move. But then he bought Fibes Drums, Vega Banjos, and Levin, a Swedish guitar company. We had to divest ourselves of all three after horrific losses. But Darco remains our second-most important product line. The nice thing about strings is they need to be replaced. And while people may eventually buy more than one guitar, they're going to be buying strings for the rest of their lives.

And so now, the company is moving into a new generation, and a new millennium, and with that, we face new concerns—especially as guitar makers. But I just can't imagine being anywhere else. What better product for a liberal Democrat to be intimately involved with than the guitar! I so identify with Woody Guthrie. I don't know what I would have done had my family's name had been Winchester or Beretta! And the characters that I've met and worked with over the years are just precious. It's an industry full of characters. And it's not always about the money. The money helps, but this is an industry where the money is almost always secondary to the more personal and emotional attachments for the people who play, make, and sell the guitar. That's really what's behind it all.

Visit Chris Martin IV and Martin Guitars at: www.martinguitar.com

DON'T QUIT YOUR DAY JOB

My father tried for a year to talk me out of being a musician, but I wasn't afraid. You know, if you're not afraid, you got nothing to lose. And you can't lose anyway; losing's just a lesson.
—*John Hammond*

Studiously avoiding the phrase, "Would you like fries with that?" I've been writing, singing, and playing since my sheltered childhood."
—*Bob Bennett*

This business will weed you out. If you're not cut out for it, you'll be miserable.
—*Brooks Williams*

It's very hard. As a business, it's frightening. But I have never done anything nearly as rewarding as working hard on a creation, then presenting it to people and have them appreciate it. Sometimes it is the most wonderful job on earth, but it's different, and only a small group of people keep it alive. As a solo guitarist, it's hard to make a living. Every other guitar player I talk with seems to agree with me that we love it, but it's got a small audience. It's special. It's different.
—*Preston Reed*

127

Paul McGill

STILL HERE

I t was fall and getting colder. If Wisconsin is known for anything outside the Green Bay Packers and cheese, it's the brutally unforgiving winters. Ordinarily the pending change in the weather wouldn't have been a major concern, but I was virtually homeless at the time, living in the upper floor of a garage. I kept a small workbench up there, where I did what few guitar repairs I could, but business was slow. With little money, I meted out $3.00 a day to an all-you-can-eat salad bar in a pizza joint for my daily sustenance.

A friend later invited me to set up in the back of his shop where he had some extra space. I was eager to find the room to build guitars, and took him up on his offer. I made a small-bodied archtop there, and got started on a classical guitar for my thirteen year-old niece who wanted to learn to play. The full arrival of winter, though, would drive me from the place. I "flew south" to Florida, where I stayed with family until I could pull together enough resources to get a place of my own.

I returned in December, and finished the classical I had begun. It came to be known as #43. As I was playing it in my new digs, something told me that I should hang on to this one; I could build another guitar for my niece later.

More difficult years would follow during my seven years in the north land. I ended up living in a storefront with no facilities but a sink and toilet before I decided to answer an ad for a job in Nashville.

The position was for a guitar repairman/restorer at Gruhn's. It got my attention, because I remembered an article I'd read earlier about George Gruhn, in which he said, "…as long as the repairmen are good, I couldn't care less if they worked at 3:00 in the morning in their underwear." I thought I had a good chance of fitting in. I was invited to send down a guitar so they cold evaluate my work, the result of which was an invitation to come down and work for a week in the shop on a trial basis. I got the job.

Nashville guitar dealer Jerry Roberts was familiar with my work, and he rented an apartment to me in an old building on Broadway. It had a closed-in porch area where I set up my workbench, as I was still filing orders I had taken in Wisconsin. I ended up selling #43 to Jerry after I repaired it from abuse by a client to whom I had loaned it. The guitar developed a large crack in its back—the result of its being kept in a house constantly heated at 90 degrees.

Jerry eventually sold the guitar to Muriel Anderson, a fine classical guitarist from the Chicago area. She saw the guitar on a visit to Jerry's shop, and later that day, while she was waiting at the airport for her flight out, she called Jerry. She decided then that she had to have it! Jerry drove out to the airport and ran down the concourse—guitar in hand—while they held the plane long enough for him to make the hand-off. He waved, and told her, "Tell me what you think." That was the extent of their sales contract. Since that time, #43 has been her primary guitar.

In the summer of '87, I bought a small house in Nashville, and worked there for a little more than a year. After battling a neighbor over zoning issues, and ultimately having them resolved in my favor, someone torched the house, taking with it not only my home, but my work, my shop, and my wood stocks. I was devastated.

During the time I was pulling myself back together, I learned that Earl Klugh had purchased a classical I built in that little back porch room in my apartment on Broadway. I later learned that he used that guitar when he recorded his phenomenal *Solo Guitar* album. And then in the fall of that year, old #43 won the National Fingerpicking Championship in Muriel's hands. Things were finally looking up, and I began to imagine the possibility that I might soon crest above the poverty line!

In time, Earl and I would become close friends, and I would go on to build quite a number of guitars for him. One day he asked me to build a resonator guitar—something along the lines of the Brazilian del Vecchios, a fairly exotic instrument with a hauntingly beautiful cry. I was a bit hesitant at first, but I agreed to try. As it turned out, it was no small task; it took me weeks to unravel the mysteries of spinning the aluminum resonator cones. I was at my wit's end when the phone rang. It was Chet Atkins, calling to check up on my progress. He knew I was attempting to reinvent the wheel in building a resonator, and so he generously loaned me one of his del Vecchios so that I could study it.

> It became increasingly apparent that someone was looking out for me. And while things were still difficult, every bad turn gave way to something wonderful.

It became increasingly apparent that someone was looking out for me. And while things were still difficult, every bad turn gave way to something wonderful. And every time I was tempted to quit, something would encourage me to persevere.

And now, as I page through Chet Atkins' coffee table book, *Me and my Guitars*, I come across a photograph of the resonator I built for him. And I just shake my head in amazement. I think of the many astonishing experiences I've enjoyed over the years with Muriel, Earl, and another dear friend, Nato Lima. In more recent years, I consider the guitars that have landed in the hands of Peter White and Marc Antoine, and again, I shake my head. And then I remember: There was a cold winter. I was homeless. I was burned out—quite literally and figuratively. But I'm still here. I think it's going to be all right.

Visit Paul McGill at www.mcgillguitars.com

HELLHOUND ON MY TRAIL

Sold blood to buy guitar strings. The blues spoke to me, and I didn't
have any choice about it.
—*John Campbell*

Now take a knife. How many things can you do with a knife? You can
cut fish, you can cut your toenails, I seen guys shave with it, you can
eat beans with it, you can kill a man. There. You name five things you
can do with a knife, you got five verses. You got yourself a blues.
—*Big Bill Broonzy*

I never thought I would be a blues singer. I wanted to be a
gospel singer. But when I played and sang gospel songs on the
street corners, people would always pat me on the head, but
they'd never put anything in the hat. But when people asked
for *blues*, they'd always put something in the hat. And that's
the reason I'm a blues singer and guitarist today.
—*B.B. King*

130

James Olson

GOING FORWARD

It was the last straw—the one that broke the camel's back. I won't say it precipitated a nervous breakdown, but I was probably just this side of it as I stood in the shower and cried. Only moments before, I had finished a guitar for a customer in England—a high-end guitar with a few custom touches that made it really special. It was strung up and ready to ship when I noticed a tiny spot on the top near the bridge that I'd missed when buffing. It was no big deal, but being a perfectionist, I took it back to the buffing wheel.

The buffer spins at an extremely high rate of speed, and for dust collection and safety's sake, the wheel is partially covered by a shroud. So with the guitar in one hand, I grabbed a lemon-sized piece of buffing compound with the other, and held it against the buffing wheel. Inexplicably, it tore out of my hand and shot around that shroud like a baseball thrown from a pitching machine, smashing the face of the guitar. The top was shattered into splinters before I could react.

It was late, I was tired, and I was completely overwhelmed by a backlog of 160 guitars. I was already working seventy hours or more a week as it was. How was I going to find time to start another guitar to replace this one? How was I going to explain to the customer that the guitar he had been waiting on for over two years would not be shipping tomorrow as promised? Overwhelmed, I made my way to the shower.

I had always been a player, but by the mid seventies, I decided I wanted to build a guitar. I was a fairly accomplished woodworker, and so, despite the dearth of instructional materials of any kind, I thought I might be able to do it. The one resource I was eventually able to get my hands on was the now-classic book on guitar construction by Irving Sloan. Building those first few instruments was such a wonderful experience that by 1977, I made the decision to quit my day job and go

131

full time into making guitars. The only problem was that I couldn't sell them. I couldn't *give* them away! Those first few guitars ended up going to friends for two hundred bucks or so.

I thought my prospects brightened when I was approached by a distributor who promised to buy everything I could make. So I killed myself over the next two and a half years building seventy-eight guitars under the arrangement we made. At a list price of $895, I would get half of that. The stores and distributor would split the other half. They didn't sell well at all, and ended up being closed out at cost. The entire venture netted me a profit of $5,300. People just weren't interested in guitars without name recognition.

Fortunately, my wife worked full time as a schoolteacher, and she essentially supported me as I tried to build a business. Nearly every penny I made, though, got plowed back into the shop as I bought more wood and tools. On the bright side, I did gain a lot of experience, but by the end of this period, I was broke.

I had been sharing a building with a harpsichord maker who also made dulcimers and ran a small music store. But unable to afford the rent, I moved into a building purchased by an inner city church my wife and I attended. They had just acquired a large property—a once glorious, but now old, mostly gutted, dilapidated brick building. The previous tenant had beds of dirt inside and had actually been raising worms there. In exchange for rent, my job was to help rehabilitate the building. When the rehab was complete, my position changed to full time janitor and building mainte- nance. In other words, I cleaned toilets and scrubbed floors. That was the downside. On the upside, there was plenty of room there for my shop. In my off hours I man- aged to do guitar repairs and make about a dozen or so guitars a year.

Coincidentally, though, it was also the dawn of the disco era, and with its rise, came the fall of everything acoustic. Once again, I could hardly give a guitar away. I sold most of what I made to church members and friends just to buy more wood. I was addicted; giving up never crossed my mind.

In 1984 I had the good fortune to meet Phil Keaggy. I was blown away when I first heard him. Amazingly, he liked my guitars and started playing them. The first guitar I built for him was a spruce top, but he requested a cedar top version to replace the Mark Whitebook he had been playing. It was the first cedar top guitar I ever made. Over the course of the next year, as Phil began touring with that guitar, I began to get calls. More orders began to follow, and things started to pick up—so much so that I now had to juggle my guitar building with my janitorial duties. It was a real struggle to find the time to complete the orders and still see my family.

In 1989, my business would receive a huge boost when James Taylor began to play my guitars. It was an unbelievable turn of events! The orders began to pile up and with them came deposits. It was great! It enabled my wife, Susan, to quit work and stay home to raise our three young sons. Before I knew it, I found myself with a backlog of 160 guitar orders. With that deposit money in the bank, I finally felt secure in my chosen vocation. I moved out of the church and bought a ten-acre property with a large shop building close to the house. It was just a tin "pole" building that needed the interior to be finished. That meant sheetrock, heating, electrical, etc., but it was mine! The house needed some work also, but things were looking pretty good. With some hard work and help from friends, before long I was set and ready to go.

Managing the backlog, though, was more difficult than I had anticipated. It seemed that everyone with a guitar on order would call to "chat" or check on its progress. Spending an hour with each of the 160 customers was equal to four weeks worth of forty-hour weeks! That, along with visitors and prospective customers, left me with less time for production. Even with my wife answering the phone, people still wanted to talk to me. I thought an apprentice might help matters. I've had several over the years, but I usually found that I ended up spending so much time teaching them and repairing mistakes that I preferred working by myself.

Also at that time, I was switching over to a UV finish process. Although eventually it would be beneficial, the initial changeover was wrought with problems. I was also trying to get up to speed on a Fadal CNC machining center I had acquired. Someone jokingly told Steve McCreary at Collings Guitars that I had gotten a Fadal, and that last year without it I had made sixty guitars. The person said, "How many do you suppose he will make this year?" Steve answered, "About twenty." And that was the truth! You don't just throw wood into these things and have them spit out parts. Creating the computer drawings and setting up the fixturing for that machine was no small task. I spent every waking hour learning how to get it up and running. In the meantime, the work was piling up, and my first real wakeup call was just around the corner.

> I've had a whole guitar ripped from my hands as it caught the edge of the spinning wheel and bounce across the floor and come to rest demolished!

I was pushing some stock through the table saw, cutting a neck blank. The blade caught the tail end of the piece and kicked it back with such force that it embedded it into the eighteen foot-high ceiling—but not before it blew past my head on its way up. I realized in that moment that had it hit my head, I'd be a vegetable. My wife would have to either learn how to make guitars really fast, or skip the country. All of a sudden, I realized that maybe I wasn't doing so great after all; with all those orders booked with deposits, the fact is, I had a tremendous liability on my hands.

And then I smashed that guitar at the buffing wheel.

This wasn't the first time I'd lost a guitar buffing. I've had a whole guitar ripped from my hands as it caught the edge of the spinning wheel and bounce across the floor and come to rest demolished! Almost every guitar maker has witnessed that nightmare scenario. But this was something new. Something I hadn't ever anticipated. A perfect guitar set to go, destroyed in a second by what appeared to be a cannon ball shot from the mouth of "Beelzebub," my buffing machine!

In no time, what seemed a great blessing morphed into a nightmare. Working as a one-man shop, I was overwhelmed and exhausted. And staring at years of grossly overcommitted work before me, I began to slip into despair. The only certainty at that point was that I wouldn't be taking any new orders.

Over the next year I made some headway and managed to work through a good bit of the backlog. In the meantime, though, demand for my guitars continued to rise; the market for them had gone incredibly high, selling for considerably more than the prices at which I had originally booked them. I'd deliver a guitar to a customer only to see it show up on eBay for twice the price. But that's the American system. I was happy when I took their orders, but it still stung when things like that happened. Just the same, I was determined to deliver everything that I promised and at the price it was promised, and I'm proud of that. But once I got through that backlog, I was able to make some adjustments.

It can be difficult to maintain perspective at times—even when you have success. Sometimes people look at what I have, and seeing the pictures on my wall say, "You must be *so* happy." I am very blessed to have enjoyed success as a guitar maker and I am relatively happy. Yet whether it was in the early days of my building or now, my happiness has remained fairly constant. But I never want to go backward. Happiness is dependent upon going forward. It's those day to day triumphs. Those are the moments that make us happy. There is no plateau where suddenly everything has accumulated and you've "arrived," and happiness remains. You can never stop going forward. There is always a new challenge, a new idea, a new jig, a new song—always something new to conquer.

I'm more thrilled now than ever to be making guitars; there are so many more possibilities. And the bar has been raised so incredibly high. There are so many people doing astoundingly beautiful work today. I'm always amazed at what I see at the guitar shows; the guitars look great, and there's no doubt they all sound good, too. These people are really nailing it. The guitar buying public is going to have a hard time choosing an instrument; there are so many good choices. But it's also going to be hard for the newer makers to distinguish themselves. That's just the nature of life and business.

It doesn't really matter, though. It's no different than being a player: you get into making music because you can't stop. You've just got to do it. You've got to learn the next song. And even if you can't get a job playing, you do it because it's something you just have to do. That's how it is with guitar makers. You start on one, and before you're finished, you have to make another because you have learned so much and have new ideas. You don't care that it's hard.

The fact is there isn't a guitar maker on the planet that hasn't gone through hardships and heartbreak. My story is certainly not unique. But when you're working on a guitar, you know you're doing what you were destined to do. It feels that good. You're excited to see your ideas come to fruition; you're excited to see how quickly and efficiently and perfectly it can be done. For me, there's just nothing better.

Visit Jim Olson at www.olsonguitars.com

EMO RULES

I've never consciously tried to be a flash. Emotion rules everything I do.
—Jeff Beck

Good music is good music, as long as it feels right emotionally. I think
that is much more important than being technically correct.
—Richie Blackmore

I'll rearrange things. I'm not worried if I don't play it exactly
the way it was written, as long as I play it with feeling.
—Jose Feliciano

Take Joseph Spence. His guitar was out of tune half the time
and he was pretty sloppy. But the *music* was so exciting.
He enjoyed it so much, even to the point of grunting and
groaning along with it in an almost self-hypnotic state. When
the emotion is there, you can really move an audience.
—Peter Lang

The reason I liked Charley Patton and those other delta singers so
much was because they were angry: Their music is ominous. Patton
had a rheumatic heart and he knew that he was going to die young,
which he did. In Skip James you hear a lot of sorrow, but also
a lot of anger. In Son House you hear a lot of fear. When I first
heard these guys I couldn't identify the emotions, because
I didn't acknowledge that I had them myself.
—John Fahey

Kevin Ryan

IN THE SHADE OF THE TREE OF LIFE

There are very few loves that a man takes with him all through his life. One of those loves for many men is baseball. We cannot remember a time before we loved baseball and we will surely love it when we are too old to play it. I suspect that for a great many of us the love of guitar is very like that, too.

The guitar had been with me from almost the very start, and it has affected nearly every turn in my journey through this unexpected life. I remember my brother and me as little boys getting lessons on guitar and banjo because my parents were crazy for the Kingston Trio. I remember camping with the family back in the '60s. We would bring our musical instruments along, thinking they were just the coolest girl-magnets (which boys are apt to think about anything they happen to be doing with girls as the intended but disdainful audience!).

From the very first time an older kid at a campground showed us how to play the nifty guitar part from *Suzy Q* to this very day as I build guitars for a living, the guitar has always been there. It gave me my first sense of accomplishment, playing before the whole school in a talent show. It ushered me into a world of music and creativity. Almost the first thing I wanted to do was to write my own music. It introduced me to friends that I still have today, thirty years later. It has consoled me through loneliness, much reflection, and many times added to the inexplicable joy of life. I have used it to worship the Lord of Heaven—alone and in church. It gave me my first sense of vocation and my first job. In the '70s and early '80s I played in a band that traveled and played at hundreds of coffeehouses as far west as Indiana, as far east as Buffalo, but mostly in Ohio where I grew up. It introduced me to the love of my life and best friend Barbara, whom I luckily married out of high school twenty-five years ago—the romance began as a promise to teach her to play the guitar! And now guitars have become my career as I am in my sixteenth year of building acoustic guitars professionally. I think I must be the luckiest man alive to be allowed to do something I love.

Of course, it was not lost on me that the guitar had been somehow involved in many pivotal moments. But what really became apparent is the sheer pervasiveness of this musical instrument in my life and almost all of my life's provinces. Take away the guitar and the landscape of my entire life would be unrecognizable.

I wonder what it is about the guitar that it can provoke the attachment and devotion it does. I suppose that many kinds of musical instruments can elicit similar devotion in the folks who love and attempt to master them. But with guitar it seems different—somehow there is a more instinctive or emotional attachment. I think only the violin family has the capacity to evoke a similar range of emotion and musical beauty as the guitar does. And it is not an accident, I believe, that both the guitar and the violin are so intimately held, even caressed. No other instruments are quite like that. Perhaps the piano can begin to rival these stringed instruments in expressiveness, but finally, it does not become a part of us in the same way, its voice and tone not as dependent upon the hands playing it. Among the great artists (of both guitar and violin) it is hard to tell where the musician ends and the instrument begins.

> Take away the guitar and the landscape of my entire life would be unrecognizable.

Also, considered as a pure object of art, the guitar is a wonder. There are curves to a well-designed instrument that are sensuous and breathtaking. The three-dimensional landscapes of a guitar can evoke appreciation that borders on adoration. And men, being the little boys we are, are fascinated with engineered and mechanical things. A fine guitar can be an unparalleled marriage of art and engineering; of high, meticulous craftsmanship and the homeliness of simple wood. Though we pretend to, we really don't understand guitars. At the end of the day, any truthful luthier will confess that the guitars he builds with his own hands are still a mystery to him. When I am making a guitar, I always have the sense I am in uncharted waters.

But when the dust settles, guitars exist to make music. I take the love of music very seriously. Many years ago I read in Professor Allan Bloom's book *The Closing of the American Mind* that Plato and Aristotle both taught that music was the centerpiece of all classical education, music being the indispensable liaison between rational man and visceral man. And C.S. Lewis of Oxford once remarked in a letter to a friend that he thought the rapture we can experience in music was the closest we could get in this life to a direct, emotional experience of God.

In some way, all these things work their enchantment on us when we fall under the spell of the guitar. The beauty of form and music; the fascination with created and engineered things; the need to touch the earth and her elements to make something clever. And lastly, the haunting call most ordinary humans feel for a lost Paradise. Guitars and the music they make can ignite these passions and longings which they can almost, but never quite, satisfy.

Naturally, others will have their own story, and the threads it contains will be very different. But the point is that there is a story in the first place. Behind the randomness and capriciousness of much of our lives, there is a story unfolding. Therefore, there must be a Storyteller. I think of a man in a gallery staring intently at a small patch of colors on a wall. He sees no pattern, no design and, more importantly—for our man desperately wants to see one—no apparent purpose. But if he would only step back twenty paces he would see a large and masterful mosaic. Our lives are sometimes like that. Considered individually, the events can seem so random and without apparent purpose, being filled with so much that is tragic and sorrowful or just simply routine. But perhaps from a higher perspective there is an order and meaning to all the disparate events and happenings. Sometimes we think we can see a compelling meaning (if we so choose perhaps) and sometimes we cannot. My conviction is that there is an inexorable purpose to our lives. I suppose we can thwart that purpose or else collaborate in it (or, what is most obviously the case, do a little bit of both). But if there is such a path and purpose I think it not unreasonable to expect small signposts along the way, hinting at the destination for which we were made. For me, those signposts have been accompanied by guitar music. And, in a master-touch, there is something of a wonder and astonishment to the fact that our Lord almost certainly was a woodworker (as his earthly father had been). The beauty of wood and the honor and nobility of woodworking was forever hallowed in that far-away and long-ago workshop.

Visit Kevin Ryan at www.ryanguitars.com

KEN HOOVER, ZION GUITARS

It was another day at the shop and the phone rang as it had done many times before. I answered, eager to help the caller with whatever guitar request he might have. The caller was serious about having an electric guitar made to his specifications. The form it should take was most unusual. This guy played in barrooms for a living and wore an artificial leg. He had the idea that we could make an electric guitar that would double as his prosthesis. In his performance, at just the right moment, he'd take off his leg, play a blues tune, and "make the ladies cry."

Visit Ken Hoover at www.zionguitars.com

Pat Kirtley

THE OLD MARTIN AND ME

"The smell of old guitars," someone once wrote, "is the smell of history." I'll never forget that.

Almost every guitar I've ever owned has meant something beyond just being a musical tool. They have hearts and souls. I'll always remember my first "real guitar," a $25 Stella purchased by my parents from the paint and hardware supply store in Bardstown. And the svelte red Silvertone three-pickup electric that was my first performance-level guitar—the first one that would make me some money. It cost $210, and I was proud to know I paid off the bank loan myself giving lessons and playing band gigs. And there was the 1965 Fender Jaguar, which had lured me with its sensuous curves—all promise and no performance. But the guitar that meant the most, and brings the sweetest memories, is the mahogany Martin.

Bardstown, Kentucky, 1964: My first real job as a teenager was working as a stage hand in a local outdoor drama *The Stephen Foster Story* during summers. The pay was low, but the work wasn't that hard, and I had a taste of "stage life"—working at night, with summer days free to mess around. It was also my first contact with theatrical performers, and I hung out with the cast at every opportunity. The show had hired a singer-guitarist, John, and it was cool because I knew a lot more guitar than he did, and ended up going to his apartment to give him lessons. One day we were hanging out there and I noticed an old guitar on top of a clothes cabinet. I took it down and beheld an instrument in pathetic shape.

First and most obvious, it had been painted black, brush-slapped with poor-

> One couldn't tell how the guitar might sound, because the bridge was almost completely lifted away from the body, with two orphan strings still tensioned up, trying to finish the job.

quality paint. I learned that the guitar had originally been used in the outdoor show—some long-ago stage manager ordered the paint job to kill an annoying glare from the lights. At a later time, layers of now-yellowing varnish were added over the black, in well-meaning reparation for the schlocky paint job. One couldn't tell how the guitar might sound, because the bridge was almost completely lifted away from the body, with two orphan strings still tensioned up, trying to finish the job.

Running my hands across the back of the neck, even a novice like me could tell it was a quality instrument. The neck shape was sleek, worlds apart from the crude contours of the old Stella. The tuning machines betrayed a decent manufacture too, which is why I began chipping at the old paint at the top of the headstock with the edge of a quarter. The squared-off, businesslike shape of the headstock didn't tell me who made it, but I knew there had to be a nameplate. Carefully scraping away while John sat hunched over his guitar, asking about fingerings, flat-fives, and major-sevenths, I began to uncover the edge of a gold-tinted decal. After a few more scratches I gulped at the prestigious "C.F. Martin" script, with its reassuring "Est. 1883."

By then my curiosity was scarcely veiled, and John said, "Why don't you take it with you and see if you can make it play again." He assured me that it had been cast aside by at least one generation of cast and management before—they had thrown it out and he had saved it from the dumpster. "I don't have time to fool with it—it could be a good guitar for you with some work." Some work? I had no idea.

I took it home, and carefully finished scraping the headstock, just to make very sure. Inside the body, visible through the soundhole, was the model, "00-17," but who could tell what that meant? And then under the dust I saw the C.F. Martin brand stamped across one of the back braces, and a six-digit serial number. Oh yes, this was the genuine article. I released the bridge from its tenuous mooring and put it aside.

Soon the guitar was oddly but satisfyingly naked.

I saved the two bridge-pins, looking like yellowed teeth from a dead witch, and knew I'd have to come up with four more somehow. I carefully removed the six tuning machines and sealed them in a bag with the twelve tiny mounting screws. The pickguard was warped like a potato chip, and I knew it had to come off, too. Soon the guitar was oddly but satisfyingly naked.

I had no idea how to remove the finish without wrecking the guitar. My mom suggested furniture stripper (she was excited at the time about the prospect of finding cast-off furniture items, refinishing them and saving scads of money). But this wasn't furniture. Something told me that it would take time and some finesse to properly reveal the undoubtedly beautiful wood beneath. I read in a book that guitar makers sometimes use scrapers. I found a paint scraper with a razor-edged blade and gave it a try. Though my fifteen year-old hands were competent with guitars and confident with hand tools, I could tell that this approach wasn't going to work for the major finish removal. It was just too tedious—with a little too much force or the wrong angle, you might bite into wood. I sensed the solution would be some chemical substance, but not the take-no-prisoners concoctions my mom was fond of slathering on old wash stands and night tables.

I became an excellent sales prospect for the paint experts down at Shelton's Furniture and Home Center, and did most of my research through their informative brochures, inscriptions, and warnings on the backs of product cans. I had long discussions with the salesmen, who indulged me, knowing the ultimate sales receipt would be in single digits. With due diligence, I got a second opinion from the folks at Grigsby's Hardware, and a third from Settles' Home Supply, where the Stella was purchased for my tenth birthday. I listened closely, because the guys at Settles' obviously knew something about guitars.

The purchase order was awarded to Shelton's because my parents had an account there, and my mom said they had quality stuff. So I came home with a can of Porter Paints' best finish remover, guaranteed not to damage even the finest of woods. It became a messy job, with rags, gloves, and lots of newspaper. Because of the intense vapors, I had to build a rig out in the yard with two sawhorses and an arrangement of clamps to keep the guitar in the right position for every angle I had to turn it. I found that the work was best done in the shade of the afternoon, because the summer sun tended to evaporate the remover before you could remove the remover.

The work on the body itself went smoothly, as long as I took care not to let anything drip down inside to stain the bare wood there. The neck was going to be a problem, because I couldn't risk getting anything on the fretboard or headstock, where I knew the remover would obliterate the Martin decal in nothing flat. It turned out that the best way was to apply a little remover and then take it off with a scraper, carefully working on a small section at a time. Within a week or so, the job was done, and I could now see and appreciate the grain and color of an all-mahogany guitar. My mom, being smarter than I would have imagined, had identified the wood species for me. "I believe it's Honduras mahogany," she said, and I went to the library to learn more about this open grained, tropical wood.

It was time to consider putting on a finish, and it scared me to think how bad it might turn out. I had held several fine guitars in my hands, including my uncle's 1957 Telecaster, and my other uncle's late '40s Gibson archtop. I knew that a good guitar finish was thin, hard, and very shiny. I had no idea what it took to achieve that, though I'd heard the term "lacquer" used in talk about guitars. The eyes of the salesmen at Shelton's lit up when I went in asking about lacquer, because they also sold paint spraying compressors, and knew I was talking my way toward a sale in the three-digit range, courtesy of my parent's charge account. But I knew that I knew nothing about spray finishing, so I kept on looking.

I also knew that all the other finishes available at the stores in town wouldn't be right for the Martin. The most popular finish for re-doing furniture and the like was generic "varnish," and it always turned out soft, uneven, and dull. And you had to put it on with a brush, which I already knew from experience was the wrong thing to use on a guitar. It was during one of my treasured "music store expeditions" into the big city of Louisville that I found the answer.

My brother and I, accompanied by fledgling band-member friends, often rode the Greyhound bus from Bardstown to Louisville on Saturday morning and spent the whole day haunting the music stores downtown on Fourth and Fifth streets. We knew that this was where the big boys did their business, and though we had no money to spend on anything beyond guitar picks or a Beatles song book, it was our duty as burgeoning consumers to check out the guitars, and collect bountiful arm-fuls of handout literature from Fender, Gibson, Gretsch, Guild, and the others. At Shackleton's (who had Gretsches a Chet Atkins fan would die for in a temperature-controlled vault downstairs) and Durlauf's (where a kind and friendly salesman with a big mustache named Ralph Lampton showed us Fender amps and guitars, knowing that someday each kid would grow up to be a real customer), we'd spend hours trying out all the new gear, in relatively unimpeded bliss.

But down a few blocks over on Fifth Street was Music Center—a welcoming name for such a forbidding place. There, amid displays of Guild Copicat echo machines, futuristic Mosrite guitars, and the Guild Zal Yanovsky signature guitar, was a most inscrutable gentleman, an immigrant from Germany named R. A. Emberger, proprietor and resident curmudgeon. Mr. Emberger had no time to think about kids growing up to become future bank-note signing, check-writing customers. He seemed happiest when we bought our picks, then grabbed our brochures and got the hell out. All of us were afraid to ask him to hand us a guitar or turn on an amplifier. We knew the store must have customers, but we were sure they weren't us. Then one day, out of my frustration over completing the Martin, I asked Mr. Emberger if he knew anything about refinishing a guitar, and behind his thick glasses, his eyes lit up. He almost smiled, and said with a wave of his finger "Come, I show you something."

As my brother and friends registered open-mouth astonishment, I, alone, fol-lowed Mr. Emberger behind the rear counter and into the area where he did repairs. It was a different world back there, and Mr. Emberger seemed to transform into a kinder, gentler person when he entered that space, for in this domain he found his passion—repairing violins and other fine stringed instruments for the likes of the Louisville Orchestra. The shiny guitars and amps out front were just a mere show of commerce.

I told him about the guitar and what I had done so far. He seemed respectful of the diligence I'd shown, and said, "It's a fine guitar and deserves a good finish." He produced a small bottle with a hand-lettered paper label in German. The fluid inside looked like honey, but darker, the color of fine Kentucky Bourbon. As he held it up to the light, I didn't know if he wanted me to buy it or just admire it. It was a small bottle, only a few ounces, and it was twenty dollars. "This is violin varnish," he said, "the best." I was afraid to ask, but needed to know how four ounces of this stuff could do a whole guitar. For the first time in my experience, he actually smiled. "This is enough for *twenty* guitars!" and he proceeded to unscrew the top and show me how to use it. "You put a little on the end of your finger, and you rub it into the wood"—he demonstrated on a scrap of spruce from the workbench.

I felt trapped. Maybe it works for some old craftsman in the Black Forest on something the size of a violin, but I couldn't see spending the rest of my summer massaging the grain of the old Martin this way. "You will do this maybe seven times, with light sanding between each coat," (he said "vil" and "zanding"). Yes, and I could push a peanut to San Francisco vit my nose if I wanted to. Yet, in a state somewhere between unconditional faith and utter panic, I went back into the store and obtained loans from my brother and friends adding up to twenty bucks for the magical fluid. He put the bottle into a small paper bag and smiled again. "Let me know how it turns out!"

It seemed poetically fitting to use a special glaze from Germany to refinish a guitar that Mr. Martin, who came from Germany, built. The whole rest of the summer I rubbed the oily fluid into the grain of the wood. I knew nothing of grain fillers or sealers, which would have made the job much easier. The first application revealed the luster and depth of the formerly dull wood, and I knew my patience and faith would be rewarded. I hated sanding between the coats, because it removed some of the carefully applied finish, but I knew it was necessary for smoothness, and for the next coat to adhere properly. When I had built up seven coats and the surface was acceptably smooth and even, I used a rubbing compound for the final

> Mr. Emberger had no time to think about kids growing up to become future bank-note signing, check-writing customers. He seemed happiest when we bought our picks, then grabbed our brochures and got the hell out.

polish. It looked, and smelled, like a quality guitar. I had glued the bridge in place before applying the finish, reinstalled the tuners, bought some new strings and bridge pins in Louisville, and finally it was complete.

I played it morning and night, and it was my entry to the joy of acoustic guitar. Though I still played electric guitar in bands, and would continue doing so for years, this guitar represented my passion. When I recorded my first album some years later in 1974, it was the only guitar I used. I've thought about the guitar's history and how it was originally used to perform the songs of Stephen Foster in the show. It surely knows the chords to *My Old Kentucky Home*—and all the rest of those tunes—down in its wood fibers. I regret that I never took the guitar back to show it to Mr. Emberger, who is now long departed. I once took it to a Martin dealer who looked up the serial number, told me it was made before 1952, and shot me an offer. Sell this guitar? I'd just as soon push a peanut to San Francisco with my nose.

Visit Pat Kirtley at www.win.net/mainstring

TRUTH BE TOLD

Playing the guitar is like telling the truth—you never have to worry
about repeating the same thing if you told the truth.
—*B.B. King*

The blues—there's no black and white—it's the truth.
—*Van Morrison*

What Muddy Waters did for us is what we should do for others.
It's the old thing, what you want written on your tombstone
as a musician: HE PASSED IT ON.
—*Keith Richards*

Andy Griffith

FREE GUITAR IN THE MORNING

I began my film career in Elia Kazan's *A Face in the Crowd*, which was released in 1957. My character, Lonesome Rhodes, a hard-drinking, backwoods drifter, and bit of a philosopher, finds himself in a southern jail cell with a few others of his kind. It's there that he's discovered by Marcia, played by Patricia Neal. Marcia is a radio producer in search of "common man" stories to air on her program. And in Lonesome, she meets her match. In no time, Marcia promotes Lonesome to national stardom, his Will Rogers-like appeal being irresistible to the masses. But there is a dark side to Lonesome's character that eventually brings him down.

In that early scene in the jail, Marcia asks Lonesome to play a song for her. Still waking from a drunken stupor, he reaches for his old Stella and belts out his impromptu *Free Man in the Morning*, which of course, he expected to be!

When we rehearsed that scene, I told Gadg—that's what everybody called Kazan—that I didn't think I could play what he wanted to hear. He asked me what I thought we should do, and I told him that he ought to hire a fine blues guitar player to do the part, and I would synch his playing while he sat off camera. When he asked if I had anyone in mind, I said, "Brownie McGhee."

Brownie McGhee was one of the greatest players of the Piedmont style of blues. He skillfully blended gospel, rhythm and blues, and other styles in his playing, and had a longtime partnership with harmonica player Sonny Terry. Well, at the time we were filming, Brownie and Sonny happened to be performing in *Cat on a Hot Tin Roof* just backstage from where we were shooting, and so I was able to recruit him for the part.

When we shot the scene, Brownie was sitting off camera with a microphone in front of his guitar, and I was faking his playing onscreen. It was all done live. It took a bit of practice to get it right; I had to hit that down stroke at just the right time.

When Gadg saw how excited I was to be playing with Brownie, he hired him to come by and just sit and play guitar with me. And he came by three days a week—every Monday, Wednesday, and Friday. So for weeks during the course of making the film, we played together. I can't begin to tell you how much I enjoyed that.

Now, as Lonesome's character rose to prominence, there were also noticeable improvements in his clothing *and* his guitars. Elia's company, New Town Productions, bought a new Martin D-18. The prop department got a hold of that guitar, painted it black, and glued spangles and sequins onto its face, spelling out "Lonesome" and "Momma"—a reference to another one of Lonesome's songs, *A Momma Guitar Beats a Woman Every Time*. Lonesome never actually played that guitar in the film, but it did make a brief appearance.

> The prop department got a hold of that guitar, painted it black, and glued spangles and sequins onto its face, spelling out "Lonesome" and "Momma"

When the picture was over, I was asked to go out and promote it. And the publicity people had me take that black Martin out and play *Free Man in the Morning* at all these appearances. And after each one, I'd return the guitar. I'd take it out to do another promotion, give it back, take it out, give it back. It went on like this until one day I decided I wasn't going to give it back anymore. They said they'd like to have it, and I said, "Nah, I'm keepin' it." And I did.

Over the next two years or so, I kept a rented house in Rye, New York, and I traveled between there and my home in North Carolina. And I always took that guitar with me. In 1959, while I was on Broadway in a play called *Destry*, I decided I'd do a little work on the guitar. I got some paint remover and sandpaper and I cleaned that guitar down to bare wood, removing all the sequins, the pickguard, and even the Martin scroll logo in the process. It took me nine days to get it done. I knew I wouldn't be able to put a nice finish on it, though, so I found a guitar shop on New York's lower east side, and asked the man there if he could refinish it for me. It turns out that the proprietor was none other than John D'Angelico, the legendary archtop guitar maker.

John congratulated me for not destroying the guitar, even though I had thinned it down a bit with all the sanding. Who knows… I might have improved it! It did have a beautiful tone. John refinished it, and restored that D-18 to its original luster, but at my request, without the pickguard. I don't use a flatpick when I play; I generally pick with my thumb and three fingers. And if it's a fast tune, I'll just pick with my thumb and middle finger. It may not be great technique, but it works alright for me. You can catch a bit of that on the Andy Griffith Show episodes where I played guitar. I used that guitar on the show. You'll notice there's no pick-guard on it. There was another guitar on the set that I played once in a while, but mostly I played the original.

That old Martin has gone through a lot of changes in its life. It developed some cracks over the years, which I've had repaired. And at one point, I had a pickguard put on it, but I hated that. There's a clear pickguard on it now.

The Martin Guitar Company recently gave this guitar a special honor when they created the Andy Griffith D-18AG Signature Edition Model, based on my original. And it is a magnificent instrument.

I didn't have any history with Martins prior to making *A Face in the Crowd*; I had a Gibson at that time. But I became a Martin convert. In fact, when the filming was completed, I bought a D-18 for Brownie.

I kept in touch with him over the years, although he passed away in 1996. He made a special appearance in a 1989 episode of Matlock, playing himself. Brownie also inspired an unfilmed episode of the Andy Griffith Show called *The Wandering Minstrel*, and he also worked on my 1959 album, *Shouts the Blues and Old Timey Songs*. I had a great admiration for Brownie, and I'm a better man—and guitar player—for having known him.

IN GOOD COMPANY

That's the trademark of a good accompanist: making the one you're accompanying sound *better*.
—*Lee Ritenour*

Patti and I decided a long time ago that we wanted to get to what the origin of accompaniment was. In Latin it means *to be with*. It's not to be back in the background. It's a partnership, and we're supporting each other.
—*Tuck Andress*

The important thing is to play *behind* the singer. One cannot antici-pate. The singer is improvising, so the guitar must follow.
—*Carlos Montoya*

Rick Derringer

THE FLYING EXPLORER

At a very young age, something in me knew I wanted to be a guitar player. In 1956, anticipating my ninth birthday, I asked my parents for a guitar. Happily, they consented, and bought me an electric guitar and amplifier. And playing came really quickly. Within a few weeks of having the guitar, I landed a gig playing with my uncle. We passed the hat around that night, and I pocketed $43.

Later that year, my folks thought it would be fun to take a family trip to Kalamazoo, Michigan to visit the Gibson guitar factory. In those days, when you entered the Gibson building there was a large showcase on one wall where they exhibited the new and experimental models. On this particular occasion, there were two prototype guitars displayed in the showcase: a Flying V and an Explorer. These were ultra-modern guitars at that time, and just out of this world.

As I looked them over, it occurred to me that the headstocks on each model should have been reversed; the V headstock was on the Explorer, and what has come to be known as the banana headstock was on the Flying V—just opposite from what my already well-honed sense of guitar aesthetics thought they should be! I mentioned this to my dad, and we continued with the tour, never really giving those guitars another thought.

Several years later, in 1962, my brother and I formed a garage band, and we called ourselves The McCoys, after a favorite Ventures song. By this time, I was well on the path to becoming a professional musician. My folks, though, doubted that I would be able to make a living playing guitar, and encouraged me to think about getting a "real job." So following their advice, I made plans to enter the Dayton Art Institute, where I would study to become either a commercial artist or an architect. But those plans got permanently interrupted, because during the summer following my high school graduation, we recorded *Hang On Sloopy*. I was just seventeen when it was released and it became an instant hit.

148

The band began to tour, and we suddenly found ourselves with a lot more money on our hands. I started investing in guitars, and by the time I was in my early twenties, I decided I wanted a Gibson Explorer. I checked around and discovered that they were no longer in production; if I wanted an Explorer, I'd have to find an old one. I called Gruhn Guitars in Nashville and spoke with George. He said he had one he could send, but he wasn't very sure about it and doubted that I'd be happy with it. "It's not like the other Explorers," he explained. I had him send it anyway; I was curious.

When it arrived, it was indeed different. It had a V-shaped headstock. I decided to keep it and I played it for a while. I happened to mention this new acquisition to my dad, and he opened up my brain and said, "Hey, don't you remember we saw an Explorer with a V headstock in the showcase at Gibson when you were just a kid?" I had completely forgotten about that. And as I began to recall more details, I remembered that the Explorer at the factory had a Bigsby on it, as well. I looked at my guitar, and sure enough, there were holes that had been filled where a Bigsby would have been attached. Still unsure as to the authenticity of my guitar, though, I contacted Gibson. They suggested I look to see if the area under the pickguard had been hand-routed. It was. With that, Gibson told me that it might very well be the very first Explorer they made. Their original plans did, in fact, call for the V headstock on the Explorer—and only one was made. I then realized that this guitar—*my guitar*—was the very same guitar that I saw as a kid displayed in that Gibson showcase. George Gruhn had no idea. He sold it to me for $1,500.

> I then realized that this guitar—my guitar—was the very same guitar that I saw as a kid displayed in that Gibson showcase.

I eventually sold the guitar, because I wasn't playing it anymore. And I'm not a collector. I believe that if you're not playing a guitar, you should give it up. So it went to a prominent collector in New Jersey for the sum of $15,000. I thought that was a nice profit until he told me his appraisal came in at $150,000. Who knew?!

Visit Rick Derringer at www.rickderringer.com

If I weren't playing guitar, I'd be a doctor, but not as rich.
—*Chet Atkins*

Eric Johnson

HAPPY TO PLAY THE BLUES

W hen I was growing up, my dad worked as an anesthesiologist at St. David's Hospital in Austin, Texas. One day, he tapped one of the hospital's technicians, Morris Young, to install some electrical outlets outside the house so my dad could light a landscape garden.

Morris had his own way of testing the circuitry. Most people would just screw in a few light bulbs, but Morris brought his guitar along. He plugged his little amp into one of the outlets and just started jamming away. Old blues stuff: Elmore James, Jimmy Reed, a little bottleneck with an old piece of pipe.

I was just a young boy at the time, and it was my first experience hearing a guitar. And the first thing I heard coming out of it was this fantastically distorted blues. It just sounded awesome. Morris was just playing for fun, and I know he saw me jumping around to the music, and having a great time. I just flipped out. I'm sure it made him feel good.

The memory of that day has always been with me. Morris planted that seed. He was the spark that set it all off for me.

By the time I was eleven, my dad brought home a Fender Music Master. He wasn't quite ready to commit to it, though; the guitar was on loan from the store for a one-week trial period. At the time, I was taking classical piano lessons, and my parents really wanted me to stick with that; they weren't terribly enamored with the idea of my dropping piano to play Rolling Stones and Ventures music!

But a happy accident changed all that. I had the guitar sitting on my bed when it fell off and hit the floor hard. Put a big scratch in the bottom of it. Dad looked it over and said, "Well, I guess we have to buy it now." That scratch was a blessing.

Many years later, I learned that Morris had passed away. And though I didn't keep in touch with him, his wife, Lillie Mae, had followed my career. When Morris died, she gave me his guitar. And when it arrived, a very special circle had been closed. This was the first guitar I had ever heard—a 1958 Gibson 225 big-bodied

150

archtop with a two-tone sunburst finish and a single P-90 pickup—and that old piece of pipe that he used as a slide was still in the case. Morris' guitar. And now it was mine.

Whenever I pick it up and play it, there seems to be a bit of a vibe to it—a bit of Morris in it. The magic of the music he made all those years ago still comes through.

Visit Eric Johnson at www.ericjohnson.com

THE MAIN THING IS
TO KEEP THE MAIN THING
THE MAIN THING

You can never be good at anything by changing all the time. You have to get on one thing and ride it out. If you want to be a stylist you have to make up your mind what you want to do.
—*Paul Yandell*

It's like the sculptor who sees in the stone a form, but he can only realize the vision when he chips away everything that is not absolutely necessary. For me, that means recognizing that I am a singer and I am a songwriter. And finally, the guitar is to serve those priorities. I've had to let everything else go.
—*Don McLean*

I've got to stick with my own thing; it's what I do best.
—*Christopher Parkening*

Liona Boyd

A GUITAR IN THE WINDOW

The summer holidays had come to an end. The next day we would leave my grandparent's home in Spain, and jump on the rickety-rackety train to the French border, catch the night train to Paris, and then the ferry back across the Channel to England.

Our bags were packed, but I heard my mother pestering my father about a classical guitar she had spotted that afternoon in a shop window as we strolled for the first time through the back streets of Bilbao and up the Gran Via. "What does Mummy want a guitar for?" my six-year old mind wondered.

"Oh, let's buy it! It's so cheap and it would look lovely on the sideboard" she pleaded.

"Too late, darling. The shop is closed and it's impossible for me to carry a guitar along with these over-packed cases," my father stated matter-of-factly.

Next morning as we prepared for our departure my persistent mother was still trying to persuade my father to buy the guitar. Finally he capitulated and together they dashed around the winding streets in search of the music shop.

My mother returned breathless but triumphant! My father stuffed the delicate instrument with its canvas cover into his rucksack so he could carry it to England on his back.

The guitar was an attractive addition to our sparsely furnished living room and a constant reminder of our holiday in Spain. Occasionally, while my baby brother slept, my mother placed it on her lap to pluck a single tune she had taught herself. Its simple notes delighted my six-year old sensibilities as I listened with fascination to the familiar melody.

A year later when my family emigrated to Canada, the guitar was once again shoved into the old rucksack. It found a place on a ledge over a heating vent in our new Toronto home until one night a shattering noise woke us as the bridge and taut strings had flown off, cracking the guitar's wooden body. The hot, dry air had

152

almost proven fatal for the instrument. Fortunately my art teacher father was able to use his skills to glue the guitar together and repair the damage.

After three years we packed up our belongings again and headed back to England. This time the guitar seemed too cumbersome, so my mother was reluctantly persuaded to give it to a friend who owned a summer camp in northern Ontario. Sadly, she let it go after being reassured that it would have a new life; strumming would be the accompaniment to children's songs around the campfire.

Unexpectedly after a year we returned again to Canada and who should show up to welcome us back but the friend with guitar in hand. "Here, you must have your guitar back" she insisted, thrusting it into my mother's hands against her protests. Back it went to resume its decorative role in our new living room.

> It found a place on a ledge over a heating vent in our new Toronto home until one night a shattering noise woke us as the bridge and taut strings had flown off, cracking the guitar's wooden body.

"Liona, what would you like for Christmas?" my parents asked me a year later. At a loss for a reply, my eyes alighted on the guitar, and with little thought I responded, "I guess you could give me that old guitar and some lessons so I can learn to play it."

Thus the die was cast. My long love affair with the guitar was about to begin. Call it what you will—fate, destiny, chance, or fortune—but that patient instrument was waiting for me, biding its time until I was ready. It had entered my life because of a last minute whim. It survived ocean crossings, the dryness of the Canadian winters, and the silence of the years. It had been abandoned, given away, and tossed from hand to hand around a campfire. But amazingly the little guitar returned to inspire me, to start me on my life's calling, fulfilling my destiny as a performing artist and composer, and sharing my classical music with the world.

Visit Liona Boyd at www.classicalguitar.com

I started listening to other musicians—sax and trumpet players—who would play simple lines, and yet they would say so much more to me.
—*Jimmie Vaughan*

Grant Geissman

MAD ABOUT GUITAR

Some older kids in my San Jose, California neighborhood had a surf band called The Adiabatics, and seeing them play made me realize just how cool guitars were. I used to run home after school to watch them practice. The lead guitar player had a sunburst Fender Jaguar; I remember the sun glistening off its chrome. I was mesmerized. But when I saw the Beatles play on the Ed Sullivan Show, that was it.

I started relentlessly badgering my parents to get me a guitar. This went on for at least six months, and I'm sure they were stalling, thinking that I would soon outgrow this youthful obsession. I didn't. So finally, under the tree on the morning of December 25th, 1964 were three identical black and red sunburst Stella acoustic guitars. My Grandfather had bought them at Sears for $25 each: one for me, one for my cousin Katie, and one for himself. (He already played a Beacon Silver Bell banjo, so this wasn't that much of a leap for him.) It was magical. I was eleven years old.

I took private lessons right away, which was enormously helpful, as I didn't have to try to completely reinvent the wheel. I would sit and play for hours, trying to play along with songs on the radio, or to records. (Remember records? Remember the wonderfully satisfying "whoomph" sound when you put the needle down into the groove, or the endlessly spinning white noise at the record's conclusion—an invitation to sit and contemplate what you just heard?)

The big controversy in sixth grade (well, with regard to music, anyway) was which camp you were in: The Beatles or The Beach Boys. Somewhat courageously, I announced that I still liked both groups, and that I saw no reason to pick one over the other. The 1960s were an incredible time for music. Imagine this: on the same radio station you could hear The Beatles, The Rolling Stones, The Beach Boys, Motown, Burt Bacharach, Jimi Hendrix, and even Frank Sinatra. I took this musical diversity to heart, which actually benefited me great-

154

ly in later years doing studio work, where you never know going in exactly what style you will be asked to play.

In high school and college I played and studied both pop music and jazz. Trying to mix the two seemed like a perfectly natural thing to do, and always with a guitar; it was always about the guitar.

Incredible-but-true-fact: in recent years, armed with a guitar I have played on albums by Ringo Starr, and through my friend Van Dyke Parks, Brian Wilson. Like sound, life has echoes.

It occurs to me that my life has been guitar-shaped—informed, shaped, and molded around a wooden instrument with six strings stretched across it. And a lot of good fortune has come my way through strumming across those six strings. I have

> Remember records? Remember the wonderfully satisfying "whoomph" sound when you put the needle down into the groove, or the endlessly spinning white noise at the record's conclusion—an invitation to sit and contemplate what you just heard?

traveled the world, made records, appeared on TV, performed before thousands and thousands of people, and written music that other people seem to like to hear. This is all quite amazing to me. My old Stella is long gone, traded up for a better guitar, and that one for a better one, and on and on. But I now have the one my Grandfather had, and my cousin Katie's, too, and each time I pop open those guitar cases, I am transported back to that magical Christmas morning in 1964. And I remember how I would run home to watch the surf band rehearse around the corner, and how the light glistened off the chrome of that Fender Jaguar—a time when the world was filled with wonder and mystery. I had a real, palpable sense that anything was possible.

Visit Grant Geissman at www.grantgeissman.com

I think the main thing in composing is getting away from distractions, seeking to have a little repose, and letting the music take you somewhere. You stop growing on the guitar when you quit exploring.
—*Phil Keaggy*

Ranger Doug

OF MONTGOMERY WARDS AND STROMBERGS

As I began to open the case, I wondered if I might be surprised to find an old pearly Martin inside. The anticipation and excitement built as the sunlight once again danced off its contents for the first time in perhaps many years. It wasn't a Martin, but something far more valuable— a 1937 Montgomery Ward. Yes, Sears had the Silvertone, but Montgomery Ward was not to be outdone. With a finely pressed plywood archtop, round soundhole, and a tiger-striped finish, we're talking a $15 guitar new—*at least*. And it tuned right up and played! Just as it did all those years ago when I first took it down off the wall in Uncle Hank's cabin in the jack pine woods of northern Michigan when I was eleven.

> He took his mustering out pay in Boston and went straight to Elmer Stromberg's shop and ordered the best guitar he could get. And he got it—a blond Master 400.

Uncle Hank had followed my career with Riders in the Sky over the years, and decided that I should have his old guitar. At 88, he didn't play it anymore. He passed away last year, and so it means even more to me now. It's the first guitar I played.

In those summers by the lake, our family sang the songs they learned off the old national barn dances. I started banging on that guitar, learned a handful of chords, and eventually joined right in, playing songs like *Red River Valley*. Playing guitar in that remote little place was just part of the experience of being there. And having that guitar now is a real link to that long lost past.

I keep that old Montgomery Ward in my vault where it keeps company with

156

my Strombergs. Ah, the Strombergs. Not to change the subject, but I'll tell you, there's nothing like a Stromberg. They just move so much air! I got into them when I worked at Gruhns in the early '70s. At one time, a Deluxe came through the shop, and at $800, there was no way I could afford it. But before long, they were $8000. Now, of course, they are approaching $80,000! Even then, as primitive as my ears were, I could tell that it was the best archtop guitar I'd ever heard—by far. I finally managed to corral a few of them over the years.

One of the Strombergs—#574—has a wonderful history. I managed to track down the original owner, who is still alive. He bought it when he came out of the Navy in September 1946. He took his mustering out pay in Boston and went straight to Elmer Stromberg's shop and ordered the best guitar he could get. And he got it—a blond Master 400. He ended up playing with the Larry Clinton Orchestra and several other big bands before he moved to Houston and enjoyed some renown as a teacher. When I got it, I wrote to him and sent some pictures. He wrote me back with the sweetest note, and said, "I think Elmer made that guitar for me *and* for you. It's in the right hands." He was 83, and so happy that his old guitar belonged to somebody who cared about it—not a collector, but somebody who would play it and love it. And I do play it.

When we're on the road—driving, never flying—I take a Stromberg and keep it by my side at all times. I figure that I have these wonderful things, and life is only so long—I'm 57 now—so I might as well be enjoying what I'm playing every minute. And I must say, alongside those Strombergs, the old Montgomery Ward is in pretty tall cotton. But even so, it still means more to me than anything else.

Visit Ranger Doug and Riders in the Sky at www.ridersinthesky.com

---

Back in the late '40s I thought, hell, I'm not gonna make a living playing the guitar. Nobody cared for what I was doing—or at least I didn't think they did. If there was somebody out there listening, I didn't know about it.
—*Chet Atkins*

Chet Atkins, C.G.P.

with John Schroeter

MR. GUITAR

As Paul Yandell demonstrates a hot new cross-string lick, an attentive Pat Berguson looks on and says, "You have to teach me that one." "Fifty cents," comes Yandell's response. In the hall, Johnny Johnson warms up his bass, while road manager George Lunn talks over some final technical details with the stage crew. By now, the auditorium is full of fans and anticipation. As Chet emerges from his dressing room, buttoning up a fresh shirt, Yandell stops him to ask about some tricky *Happy Again* fingerings. "Right there," he says as puts his finger on the designated fret. No sooner than the tuner and play list are dug out from beneath a pile of coats and guitar cases, it's show time.

Yes, it's another sold-out performance of Chet Atkins' traveling road show. "I don't know why all these shows are sold out," teases Atkins. "I'm not a big star, you know—just a dim bulb in the marquee of show business."

That dim bulb, it should be noted, has earned thirteen Grammies—more than any country artist—has been named Country Music Association's Instrumentalist of the Year for nine years, received numerous lifetime achievement awards, and was inducted into the Country Music Hall of Fame. It goes without saying that he is an icon of American music, but to the self-deprecating Atkins, it's all in a day's work.

Over the years, the cumulative effect of his days at work has produced nearly eighty albums with unit sales nearing the 40-million mark. In addition to defining the "Nashville sound," Atkins' recordings have inspired and influenced generations of guitar players the world over. They still do. Sure, his seventy years have grayed his hair and slowed his steps, but they haven't begun to diminish the dexterity of his fingers, nor his love of music or the adoration of his fans.

It seems incredible, but in today's world, where an endless stream of instructional videos, books, and CDs are on tap for any aspiring guitarist, Chet Atkins,

158

growing up in relative poverty and isolation on his father's Georgia farm, had to invent the music he played. "We were a mile from the main road back in the sticks," he explains with a certain "I beat the odds" pride. "There weren't any fingerpickers around anywhere—none playing solos anyway."

Atkins did enjoy one advantage, though: he was brought up in a very musical family. His father taught music and traveled as an evangelical singer. His older brother Jim performed in a trio with Les Paul. As such, Atkins' musical seeds were sewn at a very early age. He acquired his first guitar at the age of five—actually, a broken ukulele strung with wire from the screen porch door. He also developed an interest in the violin, an instrument he still plays. As a youngster, Atkins would read about the successful violinists of the day in his father's music magazines. It seemed, though, that all of them had started playing when they were seven years old. He decided that at eleven years of age, he was too old to be a violinist, so he became a guitar player instead. The rest, as they say, is history.

Atkins spent many of his childhood hours with his ear glued to his neighbor's radio, or the crystal set he later built. It was there that he first heard the legendary Merle Travis. "I didn't know what the heck he was doing," Atkins recalls, "but I got bitten by that bug."

Atkins went on to play with the thumb and two or three fingers, because, as he thought, "That's how Travis did it." In reality, though, as Atkins would later learn, Travis' approach was quite different. "I guess Travis could play with two or three fingers," he says, "but mostly, to get the sound he had, I think he had to get his hand in a position to where he was almost compelled to use his first finger only. He picked down on the strings and got a big sound. He also played on two bass strings instead of one."

Atkins' clean alternating bass style was probably influenced to a greater extent by the stride piano players of the day. "I loved that sound that Travis got, but I never tried to emulate him. I wanted to be different and play my own way."

Later, it was Atkins' guitar work that would mesmerize and mystify struggling guitarists listening by their radios. It was during his radio days that he really began to expand his approach and technique for solo playing. "I had to play a new tune almost every day," he recalls, "so I would sit around and figure out different ways to play the melody. I learned to play it in thirds and sixths—everything you can think of—and it's helped."

> It was just a whole lifetime of searching and seeing what I could find. And I was pretty good at it. I came up with some pretty good things, I think."

One of his challenges was working out ways to extend a 90-second tune to the radio's requisite three minutes. "I'd change the chords a little bit, using substitution chords here and there, and I'd try to play the melody in different ways to make it interesting. I'd play it on the bass strings, on the treble strings, with harmonics, or with harmony, octaves, whatever. It was just a whole lifetime of searching and seeing what I could find. And I was pretty good at it. I came up with some pretty good things, I think."

> They weren't technically or musically perfect like they are now, but they sounded pretty good. Even the mistakes got so that they sounded right after a while!"

Atkins was also pretty good at creating hit records in his role as A&R boss for RCA Nashville. The legendary Studio B, located in the heart of what would become known as Nashville's Music Row, opened in 1957 with Atkins at the helm. It was there that he pioneered the commercial use of reverb, tremolo, wah-wah, and multi-track recording. He produced hit after hit with such artists as Charley Pride, Jerry Reed, Waylon Jennings, Gary Burton, Dolly Parton, Willie Nelson, and many others. Between work on his own albums, he also found time to play on many of the Everly Brothers recordings, not to mention his sessions with Elvis (that's Chet's rhythm guitar on *Heartbreak Hotel* and *Hound Dog*).

Was there a secret to his consistent successes? "I've always been kind of square," he answers. "If I like a song, the public will usually like it, too. That was a great advantage. If I had been a jazz player who detested everything but jazz, I'd have been a flop. When you hear something and think, "That's clever; I wish I had written that," that means it's good. I never second-guessed things. Today, they'll work and work on songs and albums for so many months that they get tired of it and lose all conception of what's good and what isn't. That's the way they make records nowadays—they take forever. We used to make an album in two or three days. In about three or four sessions, we'd get twelve sides and ship it out and that was it. They weren't technically or musically perfect like they are now, but they sounded pretty good. Even the mistakes got so that they sounded right after a while!"

As for his secrets to his enduring longevity in the ever-changing music business, Atkins says, "I try to stay alert and not become too predictable. That's helped me a lot. Plus, I've never really been a big star. I think the public gets sick of you if you start rises too high—they don't want to hear you again in their lifetime! I've never experienced that. Unlike Elvis, I've never had to beat the girls off with a stick!" He admits, though, that he is well enough to known to find himself in a crossword puzzle now and then. "Baker or Atkins," the clues read.

Although Atkins is happier with the sound of his music today, he believes he was at his best in his late twenties and early thirties. It was in 1950 that he introduced such trademark techniques as right hand harmonics picked with the thumb and forefinger, alternating with pure tones picked with the ring finger, creating a shimmering cascade of sound. "It was my most productive time," he says. "I was ignorant, but I played with a lot of authority and energy. Today, though, I know a lot more about music and taste. I don't play with as much confidence as I used to; I can't get out there anymore and play a difficult arrangement like I once did. I can get through it, but I'll screw it up somewhere. And that has shaken my confidence, somewhat. I think musically, though, I'm better. I know more harmony, I know more chords, I know more about musical subtleties, and how to arrange music to make it more interesting.

Reflecting on his earlier days, Atkins recalls a time in 1954 when a "hot shot producer" came to Nashville to film the music makers there. "I look at those old films now, and I think I was kind of ahead of my time. I played it all pretty good, considering the time—1954. Of course, now people have learned so much and have passed me by, but for that time, I was pretty good. And I could play with confidence. I see that now and think how did I do that? Look at those young fingers! Look at that tight skin! What happened?! But I didn't realize it at the time. I remember thinking that I was so bad—if I could only play like Django Reinhardt or Les Paul. But here I am. I'm still doing it, and I'll continue to play shows as long as people will come and listen."

And they keep coming! Atkins' shows feature his guitar prominently against a tight ensemble backdrop. His performances are a thoroughly entertaining event, full of great music and peppered with stories—and even some stand-up comedy: "I'm not going to bore you with a lot of talent," he deadpans. "Every once in a while, I'm going to sing for you." Putting down the electric classical, he reaches for his Country Gentleman. "This is an electric guitar. It's a lot better than the gas guitar."

Flanked by guitarist Paul Yandell, his sideman of more than twenty years, and newcomer Pat Berguson, his music

> I remember thinking that I was so bad—if I could only play like Django Reinhardt or Les Paul.

is taking some new turns. Atkins particularly enjoys the energy Berguson brings to his music. "He can improvise almost anything," he says. Pat is an excellent jazz player, and a tasty player, too. He plays with a rare straight-pick technique. He has a way of *pulling* the notes up with the edge of the pick. It's strange. I guess that's what attracted me when I first heard him on a record. He gets such a great sound. And he writes some nice things, too. But Paul knows everything I've ever played backwards and forwards. He knows all the intros and endings. Paul used to work at the Post Office, you know. He picked up a few licks down there. He'll come into my office with licks and say, 'Hey Chet, I figured out a good one,' and I can take it and make a tune out of it, usually. And Berguson is always showing me licks. I absorb one once in a while."

> "This is an electric guitar. It's a lot better than the gas guitar."

Atkins adds the constant stream of ideas to his already impressive arsenal of improvisational tools. Still, he wishes he were able to execute his ideas better at faster tempos. "I've always tried to improvise, and I can do it fairly well at a tempo that suits me. If I'm not too embarrassed to hum and play what I hum, I can improvise fairly well. I think when you're a fingerpicker, that's your thing, really. You can't do too many styles and do them well. I know very few people who can do that. I've never been like Brent Mason who can just play all kinds of good notes at a terrific tempo. Fortunately, in this life, it's not important. It's important on stage, and it's important to other musicians, but on records, fast picking doesn't mean a thing. People want to hear melody and nice harmony. So I've worked with my limitations, and everybody is limited in some way or another. Maybe if you are very fast technical player, you didn't have the heart. If you don't have the facility, maybe you've got more heart. I think that's true in my playing; I think I play with a lot of heart. I know there's something there that conveys it to the listener, otherwise, I wouldn't have put out seventy or eighty albums. I wouldn't be on a record label when I'm seventy years old! But I don't try to analyze it, I just go on and play like I play and hope the public will continue to like it."

Over the course of his career, Atkins has traversed many disciplines: artist, studio engineer, record producer, business executive. Despite his rapid rise to become RCA's VP of Operations, he seems characteristically unimpressed. In fact, he sometimes regrets the time he spent away from his true love: playing the guitar. "Everything I do besides play guitar," he says, "is half-assed." I'm a half-assed engineer, always have been. I built radios when I was a kid, but I had to follow a diagram. I couldn't build you a crystal set right now without a diagram. I've become a pretty good businessman, only because I've had people I can trust. Overall, I've done pretty well, but I've made some bad investments, too. So the only thing that I do pretty well is play the guitar."

For all his years of playing, though, Atkins says he's still trying to get it right. Over the past twenty years," he says, "I've learned some new positions that helped me play fingerstyle melody and rhythm. Lenny Breau showed me some chords, like some major sevenths and other things in different positions where it's such a help if you're playing alternating bass and melody. And Jerry Reed came up with a lot of rolls and things that I play that have helped so very much when I improvise. I played golf with Jerry the other day, and told him that if it weren't for him, I don't think I could play anymore; I use so much of the stuff that he's shown me and written for me. He and Lenny helped me so very much to improve, but I was always intimidated by them, they were so good. I'd hear them and I wouldn't want to play! Fortunately, they were good influences. They made me work and try harder—but it sure was intimidating."

Today, Atkins is trying to relax his busy schedule to make more time for writing. He continually records solos at his home studio in Nashville. "I've worked up so many tunes in my life, but I didn't record them. Unfortunately, I can't remember the arrangements anymore, so now I've started putting them on tape as I work them up. Eventually, I'd like to put out an album of solos. I think that's really the best way to be remembered—through your music and your compositions. And I'd like to leave some good tunes."

More than a few of Atkins' good tunes can be heard on his recent recording projects. His 1994 landmark album, *Read My Licks* features collaborations with Goerge Benson, Mark Knopfler, Eric Johnson, and Steve Wariner in a recording that mixes jazz and fusion with Atkins' country roots. The result is an extraordinary collection of sparkling arrangements, all produced with Atkins' trademark taste. It's definitely a "90s" Chet Atkins. The album's opening cut, *Young Thing*, won a Grammy for best country instrumental. Atkins' finely-honed accompaniment skills are readily evident on *Simpatico*, recorded with Suzy Bogguss. His 1992 release with Jerry Reed, *Sneakin' Around*, features that magic Atkins-Reed chemistry on new compositions and classic Reed tunes like *The Claw*. An historical retrospective on his recordings is summarized in the box set, Chet Atkins, The RCA Years, featuring the cream of his work from 1947 to 1981—work that Atkins describes as "squeezed in between trying to run a record label."

On advice to other players, Atkins offers, "I think all solo instrumentalists have a bad habit of practicing, making a mistake, then stopping and correcting it. On the stage, you can't do that—you can't go back and correct a mistake. You've got to keep on going or embarrass yourself. One thing that's helped me a lot—and I don't do it enough—is when I rehearse, I try to play a tune all the way through without stopping. I don't go back and correct any mistakes. That's helped me tremendous-

> I think that's really the best way to be remembered—through your music and your compositions. And I'd like to leave some good tunes.

ly when performing on television and on stage. You've just got to plow through it. It's tough, but it makes a better man out of you, and a better performer."

A seasoned and veteran performer, there is still one thing that unsettles Atkins' stage nerves. "If there's a guitarist in the audience that I admire," he says, "I'll tighten up a little bit. Johnny Smith will be here Friday night, and every note I play, I'll think Johnny Smith is watching—one of the greatest musicians that ever lived. He's one of the greatest guitarists of all time. So I won't play as well Friday night, but I'll struggle through it. Sometimes someone will come back and say so and so is in the audience, and I'll think, *damn*, why did you tell me that! I don't want to know that! I think most players are that way." Even if you're Chet Atkins? "Even if you're Chet Atkins," he answers. "If you're Chet Atkins, it makes it even worse, because you've got this reputation that you have to live up to. People say you're the greatest guitar player, and I always tell them I'm not! There are so many players that play much better than I do." But, as Atkins likes to point out, he got there first. "I'm one of the best known—I'll admit to that, and I'm proud of that," he says. "I've worked hard for that. I've fulfilled my goals. I never wanted to be anything but a famous guitar player. I wish I had other ambitions, but I guess I didn't set my sights that high. I just wanted to be a famous guitarist. And I did it. I'll settle for that."

Postscript:

This piece was written in 1995, six years before Chet Atkins' passing on June 30, 2001. On my way home from the evening we spent together that spring in '95, I found my thoughts returning to something he had said to me. I had asked him, "Chet, looking down from your tier of seventy years, is there anything you wish you had done differently, anything you wish you had done, but didn't?" Without a moment's hesitation he answered, "Yes, there is. I wish I would have helped more people."

In subsequent conversations with countless guitarists over the years, I would hear time and time again about how Chet had helped them—often sacrificially. Stories about how he had given them a break, arranged for their housing, gotten them through detox, recorded one of their songs, signed them to a record deal, or just offered an encouraging word at a critical juncture. Another told of how he was kicked out of Chet's band so that he could get on with his solo career. Like the fledgling bird evicted from its nest. The stories could fill volumes. And yet what he regretted most was that he hadn't helped more. I am blessed to count myself among the many hundreds the he did.

164

In the last year of his life, anticipating his end, he sat down and wrote these poignant words:

> *Now that I've retired from performing, I don't practice much anymore, but I still like to sit and hold my guitar. It's a familiar comfort to cradle it. When I pluck the strings and feel the vibrations against my chest, I know the life I feel buzzing inside is really my own. For all the success I've had doing the thing I most loved to do, I count myself as one of the luckiest men ever born. Every night I thank the Lord for the many blessings I've enjoyed. I pray for the safety of my family and friends, for a good night's sleep, and that I'll wake up the next morning in good health. Beyond that, it's all in the Lord's hands because I know I've done the best I could.*
>
> *And now it's about time to wrap up my story. We wish it could go on and on but I've reached the point where it has to end. Years from now after I'm gone, someone will listen to what I've done and know I was here. They may not know or care who I was, but they'll hear my guitars speaking for me and maybe they'll understand something. That's the way it's supposed to be. The players come and go, but the music lives on, and eternity will take care of the rest.*

DEAD END JOB

The guitar's all right for a hobby, John, but you'll
never make a living at it.
—*Aunt Mimi to a young John Lennon*

Well, I never heard of anybody paying money
to hear a guitar player.
—*Elvis to his cellmate in Jailhouse Rock*

Paul Burlison

IF IT SOUNDS GOOD, DO IT

Credited with creating the distorted guitar sound that would become the quintessential hallmark of rock and roll, Paul Burlison, of The Rock'n Roll Trio, turned the guitar world on its head—quite by accident. "Yeah," he says in his southern drawl. "I've been accused of that."

The prototypical rock trio had been working out their particular brand of country-blues-swing fusion when Elvis came along. "And when that happened," Burlison adds, "well, everybody just got on the bandwagon."

Still, the little band was determined to chart its own path. "We just did anything we could to sound a little different," he says. "If something sounded good, we just used it. And it was a little wild in those days. I'd lie on my back and play guitar, get down on my knees, and chewed gum all the time. Yeah, I guess it was a little wild—for that time, anyway!"

But the introduction of the sound in 1956 that would alter the course of rock music forever was somewhat less deliberate. "I dropped my amplifier," he deadpans.

> I didn't know it was going to create a big stir until engineers started calling me, asking what I was doing on this thing!

"It happened as an accident. We were playing in Philadelphia, and I was walking down the hallway to the stage, and the strap on my amplifier broke. When that happened, the amplifier fell to the floor. I picked it up, put it under my arm, and carried it out to the stage. And I plugged it in, not knowing what had happened to it. There was no time to check it out. The announcer introduced us and the curtain opened, and we started playing."

Upon hearing the sonic surprise that followed, band mate Johnny Burnette immediately turned around. "The guitar sounded fuzzy," says Burlison. "Johnny looked at me, I looked back at him, and we just smiled at each other. I shrugged

166

my shoulders and kept on playing. After the show was over, we went back stage and I took the back off the amplifier. I looked it over, examined the wires. I thought maybe my speaker was busted, but it wasn't. But what did happen is one of the tubes had dropped down and was acting like a dimmer switch; it was delaying the sound going through there, and that created the fuzz tone. So I pushed the tube back up and it worked fine."

Burlison had all but forgotten the incident when several weeks later the band went to Nashville to record a new album. "We were fixin' to do *Train Kept A-Rollin'* when I remembered the fuzz tone. So I went in and pulled that tube down. And the Fender Deluxe amplifier was the only one you could do that on. It was the third tube from the back, and you had to wiggle it to get it just right. And that recording session was the last time I pulled it down. I liked it, but I didn't know it was going to create a big stir until engineers started calling me, asking what I was doing on this thing! A lot of people had taken razor blades and sliced their speakers, and stuff like that trying to get that sound."

The way I look at it, I have a bag of stuff that I do. It's more flash than cash, but I do it well. If I step outside of it, I usually fall flat. Occasionally I'll have a little moment of brilliance, and then I'll fall flat if I try to get any further outside.
—*Scott Dente*

Scotty Moore

with John Schroeter

THE GUITAR THAT CHANGED THE WORLD

When Elvis Presley strolled into Sam Phillip's Memphis studio to make a recording for his mother's birthday, the only thing that impressed Phillips was the $3.98 the 19-year old was willing to pay for the two-sided acetate. Secretary Marion Keisker, though, somewhat more impressed, kept the young balladeer's number on file.

Meanwhile, a 22-year old Scotty Moore, fresh from a four-year stint with the Navy, was angling for work at Sam's Sun Records studio. And Sam, always fishing for fresh talent, was open to new ideas. Recalling the vanity session months earlier, Marion dug out Elvis' number, and suggested they call. Scotty got the assignment.

When the pimple-faced and duck-tailed Elvis showed up at Scotty's home for an informal audition, he was wearing a lacy shirt, pink pants, and white buck shoes. Scotty's wife announced his arrival with, "That guy's here."

Somewhat underwhelmed by their initial musical meeting, but anxious to get something going, Scotty assured Phillips that a tape audition in the studio would not be wasted. And long into the session that night in the unbearable Memphis heat, the trio, made up of Elvis, Scotty, and bassist Bill Black, foundered in mediocrity until they hit upon an upbeat rendition of *That's All Right, Mama*. Suddenly Sam's internal hit meter was pegged. Two weeks later, the 1954 release, with *Blue Moon of Kentucky* on the B side, would rocket-launch a movement.

Scotty Moore remembers those times, and how they worked their magic in the studio. "Elvis played a Martin D-28 back in the early days, and he'd beat the strings off of it through half a song. But when he played, he had terrific rhythm; his timing was impeccable. And he had that same kind of timing in his singing; I was always amazed at his phrasing. So we'd build the house around that, and just try to stay out of the way."

When asked if they were even aware that they were laying the very bedrock of rock and roll, he answers, "No. The only way I can describe what we were doing in those days is that we were just trying to play something that fit the song. Elvis would pick a song for the session, and we would all learn it together as he sang through it. We all worked on it together. And other than having us speed it up or slow it down so that he could find his groove, Elvis never told us what to do."

Scotty recalls one session in particular. "The song was *Too Much*. And the only key that Elvis could sing it comfortably in was A-flat—not exactly a great guitar key. But that's what we were working with. We went through it several times, got our parts worked out, and then I would go off into my solo. On this particular cut, I went absolutely blank. And back then, you didn't stop. You just kept on going, because you might be able to splice a cut or two together and salvage the thing if everything else failed. Somehow, though, I came out of it exactly where I was supposed to, but it was a train wreck as far as what I had been trying to do."

When the song was over, Elvis raised his hand, signaling the engineer for the playback. "He walked over and leaned on the speaker," Scotty remembers, "a big RCA floor speaker, with his head down, and hands on top of it. He liked to listen that way, with the sound hitting him full. The song was going along, and when it came to that solo, he cocked his head a little. Then he looked over at me with a nasty little grin, and I knew I'd been had. 'That's the one,' he said. 'That's the one. It felt good.' He knew I was in quicksand up to my neck, and he was going to make me live with it. To this day, I can't duplicate that solo; it doesn't make any sense to me. It sounds alright, I guess. Sounds like jazz; that's the only way I can describe it. But Elvis liked it. To each his own!"

> The song was going along, and when it came to that solo, he cocked his head a little. Then he looked over at me with a nasty little grin, and I knew I'd been had.

His apparent success notwithstanding, Scotty's days with Elvis would be numbered. Contract, pay, and management issues would plague him to the point that he'd finally just throw in the towel. Ironically, he could no longer afford to work for "The King."

While Elvis served his stint in the Army, Scotty took advantage of the time to start his own studio. "I had always been interested in the engineering side of things," he says. "And we actually had a hit. But then we spent all the money we made building a bigger studio. Things just never came together, so I bailed out and left it to my partner. Sam offered me a job as the production manager for the new studio that he'd just built, and so I joined him. At that time it was state of the art."

For some quite time, Scotty had wanted to cut some instrumentals of his own. "I wanted to see if we could have any luck with them," he says. "The other big Memphis studio, Stax Records, was having great success with Booker T. & the MGs, and I had some ideas. But Sam would never commit to it, which was a great frustration."

But when Billy Sherrill, a producer for Epic, approached Scotty with an idea for an instrumental album, Scotty jumped at the opportunity. The result was 1964's *The Guitar that Changed the World*, a collection of instrumental covers of Elvis' hits. Scotty remembers, "I guess they thought the thing would get out there on its own legs and move up the charts without any promotion—which it didn't; they didn't, and I didn't. Sam learned about it and fired me."

"I guess they thought the thing would get out there on its own legs and move up the charts without any promotion—which it didn't; they didn't, and I didn't. Sam learned about it and fired me."

With that, Scotty moved to Nashville, where he built a new studio, Music City Recorders. By that time, though, the industry had grown up a bit, and the session scene had changed. "With Elvis," he explains, "we had an unlimited amount of time in the studio. And now everything ran on a union clock. I just didn't care to do sessions. And none of us in the early days could read music. Well, I couldn't—not enough to hurt my playing anyway, as Chet Atkins used to say!" And while he continued to do sporadic session work—including some for Elvis—he contented himself with working on the other side of the glass.

In 1968, long after abandoning any ideas of performing again, he got a call from his old friend. NBC had just contracted Elvis for a television special—an intimate, back to his roots concert in the round. Scotty agreed to participate, but with some reservation; he hadn't performed live with Elvis since 1961!

For Scotty, the reunion was, indeed, just like old times. Once onstage, they hit the ground running with *That's All Right, Mama*. Elvis looked great, sounded great, and was at the top of his game. And the music, coming through as lean and as powerfully as it did fourteen years earlier, brought back all the magic of happier times.

At one point in the performance, Elvis, apparently envious of Scotty's Super 400, unstrapped his Gibson J-200 and said while reaching for Scotty's guitar, "Let's swap axes." A horrified drummer D.J. Fontana remembers, "Scotty wasn't very happy about that. Elvis was a flogger and I knew he was afraid he'd scar up the guitar. It worked out okay, but oh boy, he doesn't like anyone to touch that guitar."

Like many outings with Elvis, the experience ended up costing him money. "That TV special," Scotty says, "was the last thing that I did with him."

Scotty enjoyed a reunion of a different sort with his original Gibson L5 when its present owner invited him to play it at a recent event. "I don't have any of the guitars I played back then," he laments. "I wish I would have kept that L5, though—it was a good one. It belongs to a guy in Memphis now—Robert Johnson, of all names. It's on display at the Rock and Soul Museum in Memphis. It's still in good shape." Scotty had traded it in on a blond Super 400 sometime in 1959. "I wish I hadn't, because the L5 was a better guitar. But the Super 400 was good; in fact, it's the guitar that Chips Moman ended up with. And Reggie Young used it on several cuts with Elvis, including *Suspicious Minds*. That guitar sold at Christies in London a few years back for $108,000."

Following the highly praised '68 TV special, Scotty, D.J., and the Jordanaires were invited to do a two-week engagement, backing Elvis in Las Vegas. And once again, the terms were insultingly unacceptable. Declining the offer, Scotty hung up his guitar, and wouldn't touch it for the next twenty-four years. When asked why, Scotty, who always managed to put a positive spin on even the worst of situations, would answer, "Well, I'm an engineer now. I'm playing the whole band!"

Ironically, it took a little encouragement from the Rolling Stones for Scotty to bring his guitar out of retirement. "Keith Richards had called and invited me up to St. Louis to their show during their *Steel Wheels* tour. I wasn't a huge fan—I knew some of their music and had seen them on TV a time or two—but I agreed to go. And that night, I became a fan. Those boys worked. They played for two hours and forty minutes. We never did more than forty-five or fifty minutes with Elvis! I was thinking that somebody's going to pass out here any time. And they're still working that hard. After the show, we had dinner, and went up to Ron Wood's room. There were a couple of guitars there, and Keith wanted me to show him how to play *Mystery Train*. So we sat down, each with a guitar in hand, and we went on trading licks and stories till five in the morning. With two hour's sleep, I flew back to Nashville hurtin'."

Upon his return, Carl Perkins, a fellow Sun Records alumni, coaxed some more playing out of Scotty for the sessions that culminated in their album, *706 ReUnion: A Sentimental Journey*, recorded in the original Sun Studio. Scotty hadn't been inside those walls for nearly thirty years. But it wasn't until the Jordanaires—Elvis' backup singers—convinced Scotty to join them for a series of performances in England that things really began to turn around. Jamming with the Stones in a hotel room, or doing sessions with an old friend was one thing, but live performance was quite another. But he agreed to do it, thinking it a safe setting. If they didn't remember or like him in England, at least it wouldn't at home. But when he walked out on the stage, the audience just exploded. They remembered him, alright. Scotty was back.

Happily resigned to playing the music the audiences love best, he's still on the road with mates D.J. Fontana, the Jordanaires, and others in an ensemble that brings back to life the amazing sound—and guitar—that was.

Learn more about Scotty Moore at www.scottymoore.net

Keith Richards on Scotty Moore

I grew up just outside of London. The only radio station that played at night—the BBC shut down real early—was an English station out of Luxemburg. But the reception was terrible. You'd be carrying your radio all around the room, and it would be going in and out. One night they played *Heartbreak Hotel*. That's how I met Scotty Moore. It's as simple as that. And he keeps fading out on me, and I'm running around the room trying to hang on.

Scotty was the one who turned me on to the whole thing. That's when I suddenly realized what I wanted to do. I can't imagine what it's like to go through life not doing what you want to do. I got lucky. And Scotty is one of the cats that made me lucky.

His was the greatest rock and roll band in the world. There wouldn't be any others without him. Give thanks. Give praises.

My very first guitar was a Stella—a little red guitar. It cost me
$15, and at that time I was only making $15 a month. So I got
my boss to buy it for me. He took out half my salary the first
month, and the second month he took out the other half.
That meant more to me than I know how to tell.
—*B.B. King*

Andy Summers

ROLLIN' AND TUMBLIN'

Rob slumped over his desk and stared at his computer screen. The figures on the monitor stared back. Little green characters floating in a sea of black, they were now beginning to weigh heavily on his soul. He sat at this desk five days week and ran numbers for the Harvey Group, an investment house in central London. It had been alright in the beginning—the job came with an aristocratic style, a large paycheck, and the promise of an upwardly mobile career. But it was eating him alive; this was not the life he had aspired to.

So far, this had all been about his mother. She had used him as a marker of respectability—a thin plot to veil a troubled past. And the refined profile of the Harvey Group completed the picture, allowing her to maintain the illusion of a sober middle class family, unruffled by the shadow of past events.

The truth, though, lay elsewhere. And day by day, the task of maintaining the illusion became increasingly difficult. But young and under his mother's dominance, he submitted to her wishes, and conformed to the vision. But like a moth drawn to a flame, something bigger was at work in Rob. Something was pulling him onto a very different path—one that was in direct opposition to his mother's notion of a nice, respectable career.

The other brokers in the firm were okay, but they seemed different to Rob. Some of them had been to public school or came from upper middle class backgrounds. They spoke with posh voices, drank Claret, and had girlfriends with names like Prudence or Clarissa. Rob had assimilated himself smoothly enough into the group by carefully guarding his background, modulating his diction, and giving them a story about being raised in India by his father who had an overseas government posting. Even in post-millennium London, the class system still prevailed. With his gift for numbers and a sufficient knack for acting, he had slipped through the net and entered the elite world of a boutique investment group. By all appearances, his future was set. Deceptively propped up as it were,

173

his mother was happy.

In some ways it had all seemed too easy, but with his innate ability, he would be well regarded here as long as he kept up the act; he was, in fact, a natural for the investment game.   As he looked blankly into the glowing phosphor of his computer screen, he felt the sudden conviction. "I'm a liar," he thought. A line from an old Robert Johnson song taunted him still more: "I'm standing at the crossroads." The words strobed through his mind like a garish neon sign. He fingered his mouse and stared past the line of computer screens to the grey London sky, where the sun was only present as an ambient yellowing in the cloudbank to the east.

Thirty-five years earlier, Rob's dad had emerged from the East End as a bottle-neck blues guitar player of some renown; he had risen to fame as a true working class hero. When he and Rob's mum met in the late sixties, he was, by every measure, a star guitarist on the thriving London scene, complete with rabid following and women falling over themselves to be near him.

Despite their dissimilar social backgrounds, they moved in together, caught up in the headiness of the times. They married a couple of years later when Rob was born. As the euphoria of the sixties faded, the marriage began to grind. In time, it became something to be endured only for the sake of the child. The guitarist's downward spiral was accelerated with London's emerging punk scene. The change in the musical guard combined with heavy drinking to finish off his career. Blues music was out, the band broke up, and that was that.

> The change in the musical guard combined with heavy drinking to finish off his career.

"Right then," he begrudged, "if you weren't punk you weren't nothin'. It was over. No one was interested in Leadbelly or Robert Johnson. I was dead in the water. Couldn't get a record out, couldn't get a gig. It was over."

Alcoholic and looking much older than his forty-five years suggested, he stopped playing altogether. And when the last of the royalties dried up, he signed on for unemployment. Whatever love Rob's mum held for the old man now faded as she realized that the handsome young blues guitarist she had dared to marry was in fact a fragile being who couldn't relate to the world without a guitar in his hands.

The tension between them came to a head when he returned from the pub one night, drunk and wearing a brass bottleneck on his finger. They got into a row, prompting Rob to crawl beneath the kitchen table, holding his hands over his ears. The ensuing struggle ended with the old man bringing his bottlenecked hand down across the woman's forehead, leaving a deep and bloody gash.

The police were dispatched. They took the old man away, sobbing pathetically, and swearing he'd never do it again. Rob slept in his mother's bed that night and cried himself to sleep. As for his mother, the old man had gone too far. Furious, and with all capacity for forgiveness evaporated, she saw to it that the former blues legend would spend the next two years in prison for grievous bodily assault. The marriage, such as it was, was quietly dissolved while he was still inside.

He left the prison thin and shuffling like a broken rabbit. He never returned to the house, but went to work in the scrap yards of the East End. He found a flat somewhere over there. There was a brief contact between Rob's parents, and an establishing of an odd, formal relationship with an exchange of addresses. Rob saw his dad only twice in the ensuing years. He had made an effort at reconciliation when he showed up with a birthday present—a small toy gun, at which his mother sneered. The three of them sat together in a stiff strangeness until his father, without speaking, suddenly got up and left. The second time he arrived on Christmas Eve smelling of alcohol. Rob's mother simply shut the door in his face.

> It moved him as nothing he had heard before—the animal sounds, the cry in the voice, the razor scream of the bottleneck as it snarled up and down the strings answering the singer's moans.

At ten years of age, Rob clung to his mother as he suffered through jeers and taunts at the hands of school children. The trauma of "the incident" combined with the stigma of his father being a convict caused the boy to become withdrawn. Concerned for his emotional health, his mother put him through several years of therapy with a child psychiatrist.

It was the therapist who suggested that young Rob might be well served to take up music. At fourteen, he began to teach himself the guitar. It came to him naturally, and the seeds for a passion had been sown. But haunted by the memory of his father, he followed his mother's advice to keep his playing on a strictly amateur basis. It also became apparent at this time that Rob had a gift for mathematics. His mother wasted no time in seizing upon this emerging talent, and steered his thinking in the direction of a career he could rely on.

The city below the office floor throbbed like an anthill, full of life and sound—reminding him of everything that his life was not. Trapped in an office, consigned to running numbers all day like a robot, he thought of his mother, incarcerated in her own prison of rigid middleclass respectability, and his dad, an ex-con living miserably on his own. With a sigh, he turned off the PC, got up, and left the office.

Riding the underground train back to Ealing and staring at the gray English faces opposite, the old Hendrix phrase "white collar conservative" ran through his brain like ticker tape. Rob imagined himself a fifty-year old with a lawn, a car, and a house in the suburbs, returning each night on this train to end up stuck in front of the TV watching a sitcom. He felt sick inside.

His thoughts then turned to something he remembered from the seemingly endless therapy sessions: "Bring out what is inside you, and it will save you. If you do not bring it out, it will kill you."

"Of course!" he thought. "Music! Music would be the way out." The strains of *Hellhound on My Trail* chased the thought he thought as his eyes settled on an ad posted on the train, an idyllic picture of a sun-drenched Majorca—the reward, the carrot at the end of the stick for all those who slaved like ants at their desks day in and day out.

Mother would not be pleased. But he had stood by her, done everything she asked of him. But now there was no denying the more powerful forces that rose up from a place deep inside. And wasn't it the point of all those therapy sessions to bring out the beast?!

A few months earlier, he had been poking about in the attic and came upon a roll of posters and a couple of LPs by Delta Blue, his dad's blues band. He hung the posters on his bedroom wall, scrounged an old turntable, and listened to his dad's great blues slide playing. Mesmerized by the sounds, Rob choked up realizing how much he loved and missed his father. His mum, hearing the slide guitar screaming out of the speakers, opened his door. Seeing the posters on the wall and looking back at Rob, she immediately recognized the father in the son. A tidal wave of bitter emotion overcame her, welling up, but then receded with her quiet resignation.

The more he listened, the more the music got under his skin. He began searching out the old blues albums that had inspired his father. In time, he amassed a respectable collection of the old masters—the recordings of Tampa Red, Son House, Charlie Patton, Elmore James, and Muddy Waters. Hunched over the old record player, he spent endless hours lifting the licks that called to him like a siren from some far off misty delta. Looming large and looking down upon him was his father's face, depicted on the posters from the Manor House and the Ricky Tick club in Windsor. It must have been great then, his Dad young and handsome, whipping that slide up and down the neck of his guitar. There was no question—he played the most authentic blues in London.

But what began as an effort to get closer to his dad had mutated into an intense desire for the blues, itself. He had fallen under the spell cast in the grooves of those old records. In his imagination, the blues were alive in the house, crawling like a king snake through the floral wallpaper. It moved him as nothing he had heard before—the animal sounds, the cry in the voice, the razor scream of the bottleneck as it snarled up and down the strings answering the singer's moans. The music filled

176

him with a powerful urge. His one desire now was to front a blues band of his own—just like his old man before him. He understood now.

Suddenly the Harvey Group and all its trappings seemed a million miles away as he imagined himself on stage shouting into a mike and playing a deep blues on his slide guitar. Maybe there was room now in today's electronica music world—a world that was so plastic and predictable—for something raw and real. Maybe it could work. Maybe. But to play the blues with real feeling—from the inside out—somehow eluded him. Maybe you really did have to be born into it to get the depth, the stinging vibrato, the wailing sound of pain and loss, the woman cry, the African wail.

He wondered how the old man did it. He sat transfixed on the floor, staring at the pile of black vinyl stacked there. His father truly was a great blues player. If anyone could teach him, surely he could. On the heels of that thought, though, came a surge of fear. There was a deep estrangement, a pain to confront, the open wound of the chasm between his parents. But already drawn like an arrow with its target in sight, his passion for the music propelled him forward. The voice of his therapist rang loud in his ears.

He rifled his mother's room for her phone book. He found it in the drawer of the night table, with the name Bill scrawled on the back page in blue biro. He picked up the phone.

The voice that answered was gruff. Still finding his courage, Rob announced himself with some hesitation. "This is Rob, your son." After a brief, tense silence came a terse, "Oh, what do you want then." Steeling himself once more, Rob explained to the old man that he wanted to play the blues. And he needed help. "No," came his father's reply. "I ain't doin' that again. Gave it up, din' I? No one wants that stuff now; you'll never get on *Top of the Pops* with that crap. Anyway, I've forgotten how to do it."

They gradually eased into a conversation, and with a few more exchanges, Rob got the old man to agree. He'd meet with him the next day.

Rob had trouble sleeping that night, as he anticipated meeting with his father and delving into this strange and powerful world of the blues. Its watchwords turned and churned and became twisted in his dreams. In the morning he called in to his office and told them he was sick. Putting the phone down, he thought to himself, "Yeah, I got blues fever." Clutching the National steel that he had brought on the internet, he crossed London in a black cab and made his way to the East End, churning with apprehension and excitement at what lay ahead. He got out in an area that looked as if it was still recovering from World War II. Following his father's directions, he walked a couple of streets until he came upon a large brick high rise that stood alone. With laundry hanging from various windows, damaged brickwork, and an entrance covered in graffiti, it looked shabby and worn.

He climbed the stairs, experiencing a potent mix of fear at seeing his father again and shame that he had been brought to this. "God, this is sad," he thought to himself. Fragments of TV noise, the screams of children, and upraised voices echoed through the stairwell as he came to the landing outside his father's flat. He looked at the battered door and felt a wave of nausea. He could make out the sounds of a soccer match on the television inside as he knocked nervously. The door opened, and standing there with a bottle in his hand and holding the stance of a wary animal was his dad.

> As he opened the case a musty smell from another world wafted out and across the room. "The stink of the blues," he said chuckling.

"Alright, come in," he growled. They looked at one another like strangers. "Alright?" said the old man. "Alright," Rob answered. "Well sit down then. Whatchya got there? National? Let's 'ave a look at it then." Rob timidly pulled the guitar from his case and handed it over. "Ain't touched it in years," he said. "Why don't you gimme a tune." He handed the guitar back to Rob. "No, I don't really know," he coughed. "Alright, give it 'ere." Rob handed the guitar back, and the old man stroked a few chords. A grunt rose from the back of his throat as the exotic silvery sound filled the room. "Hmm… this one's alright. It's a beaut. Boy, it's got it. Don't see many like this anymore—not that I'd know." Handing the guitar back to Rob, he said, "'ere you are. Go on then, play something."

Rob slid the bottleneck onto his finger, and zipped it up the first string to the twelfth fret and attempted a vibrato at the end of his glissando. It came out flat and without the singing sound. He sheepishly looked up at his father, whose eyes narrowed and seemed to look right through him. "Yeah, try again," he said, and took a slug from his bottle. "By the way," he added, "just in case you're wondering, this is non-alcoholic. Swore off the brew years ago. Alright, go on. Make it sing." Rob made an attempt at the *Dust My Broom* riff at the twelfth fret, but it again, it came out flat and tuneless.

"No!" His dad leaned foreward, reaching for the guitar. "Here, gimme that thing. Look, you've got to get it more into the *arm*. That's where the power is. Wait a minute. You don't even have this in an open tuning." Rob returned a blank look. "Bottle neck is always done in open—open G for the Johnson stuff, open E if you want go the Chicago route. Now sort it out." And he handing the guitar back to Rob, he returned to the TV. The sound of cheering soccer fans filled the room as Rob half heartedly twisted the tuning pegs, miserably wondering what an open tuning was. "E bloody major," his dad shouted over the raucous sound of Chelsea scoring against Arsenal. "Don't know much, do ya?" He turned and took the guitar, and absentmindedly tuned the guitar to an E chord while watching the match. "Gimme that slide," he said. "A bit rusty." He whipped the bottle neck up the to twelfth fret in a dead on imitation of Elmore James. "That's more like it," he said. "'ere, you 'ave a go."

Rob took the slide back and fitted it onto his the little finger of his left hand and then slid it up to the twelfth fret, and attempted a vibrato by waggling the bottle neck vigorously with a result just as unconvincing and out of tune as the previous tries. "No," said Bill as he rose from his chair to fetch his own guitar. "Listen. Hang on a minute." As he opened the case a musty smell from another world wafted out and across the room. "The stink of the blues," he said chuckling. "I 'aven't opened this in years. What a pong! Gawd, look at this!" He pulled a beer bottle from the case, and then lifted a beautiful National steel guitar out into the flickering light of the television where it gleamed like a mediaeval shield. "Look at this. This one is from the twenties—a real National, not one of those bloody Dobro things they made later. This was made in Los Angeles, California, and here it is now in bloody East London. Marvellous, innit?"

He reached into the case again and found a piece of brass tubing about an inch and a half long. "Feel that," he said as he handed it over to his son. Rob weighed it in his hand. "God, that's heavy, Dad!" And as he said it—the word "Dad"—something broke in the room. A boundary had just been crossed. It was as if two strangers had arrived at a crossroads together and recognised each other. But they avoided eye contact, their attention being diverted to the TV as Chelsea scored a half time goal.

"Okay, give it 'ere." The old man reached out and slipped the bottleneck back onto his finger and then said, "Right. Listen a minute." He tuned the guitar to open G and played the riff to *Rollin' and Tumblin'*. After a while, he began to sing along softly with his guitar. Rob sat spellbound. It was magic. The sound and intonation were perfect. He felt the electricity in his spine replacing the tension he had brought into the small dank room. His gut began to unwind. His Dad was great—really great .

He finished playing and looked over at his son. Bill stared at the floor for a moment and said, "I didn't think I would be able to do that. I guess it didn't leave after all." He looked back up at Rob and said, "Okay. C'mon, son. We'll do it together."

Visit Andy Summers at www.andysummers.com

Phil Madeira

METAL AND ME

Although I started out as a drummer, I'd always loved the guitar, and I even played a little in college. For ten bucks, I bought an old Gibson archtop with "Gibson" painted in scroll lettering on the headstock. My friend Tom had refinished it for me one summer. I guess we both know better now.

During college, I played drums and piano with a couple of bands. One day a guy asked me if I would want to buy his aunt's old metal guitar. He called it a "dobro," but it said "National" on the headstock. It was a roundback that was set up for dobro playing, but it just seemed "broken" to the seller and to me. It was impossible to fret, and I thought my friend David Wessner might want it. David played pedal steel in one of the bands. So, I bought it for him for $15. Again, I know better now.

At some point, I bought a very plain Airline lap steel guitar. I knew some open tunings, and I liked playing that guitar. I didn't see the writing on the wall, but I look back and wonder if I was some sort of a magnet for steel bars and metal guitars.

As fate would have it, I wound up playing keyboards in The Phil Keaggy Band. Given that Phil was such a magnificent guitarist I felt it was only fair to put all my energy into keyboards, so I rarely played my old lap steel or my Gibson. I probably quit because Phil's playing was so highly developed that I couldn't imagine becoming even moderately proficient.

After my stint with Phil, I got married. My wife Elinor and I eventually moved to Nashville. I started writing songs for people, and started falling back in love with guitars. I had long since sold the old Airline lap steel, but once in a while I'd play my acoustic on my lap with a bar.

Enter Kenny Meeks. Kenny is a real unsung hero—a great singer and a great guitar player. He's also written some beautiful songs in his time. Like me, Kenny is

180

happy to oblige anyone with three chords: I, IV and V. One day, he showed up at our little log cabin on Nebraska Avenue. He had a beat up National Guitar, a style "O" with a small hole in the back that made me think it might have sat in a puddle for a few years.

Kenny said, "I'm giving this to you, but you can't sell it. If you want to get rid of it, you have to give it back to me." I thought about it, and called him up. "Kenny, that's a great gesture, but deals like this always seem to wind up wrecking friendships. What if I traded you something for that guitar, and that way I won't feel caged in?" He said that was okay, and he took a Mesa Boogie amp which I'd paid $100 for.

I tried playing the National on my lap, but I knew that I really had to take the bull by the horns and learn to play it like a slide player or I'd never be satisfied. My wife gave me a little Coricidan bottle and I was ready to go.

> Jerry McPherson, a great Nashville guitarist, has said that my guitar is "haunted." He might be right. Or maybe there's just a screw loose that's rattling away deep inside that humming piece of metal.

Eventually, I settled in on bottleneck guitar, and reached the point where whatever I was doing "worked" for certain people, and I would get asked to play on records, along with my Hammond B-3, which is what I've mainly gotten called for. As time went by, I started buying other guitars, and I probably have fifteen that I use regularly, including a National Reso-Phonic Baritone Tricone.

I have several guitars that I don't think I'll ever be able to part with. They include a Gibson L1 and a Gretsch 6120 Setzer model—my main electric. My early Lowden that I got in England back in 1995 is the one that has coaxed more tunes out of me than any other instrument. My 2002 Eric Clapton model Martin was a Christmas gift from my wife; everyone needs a Martin! The Clapton model is a perfect instrument.

Over the years, I've bought several lap steels, including the requisite Rickenbacker, Gibson, and mother of toilet seat Fender (with a fantastic Telecaster pickup). The Fender has been my ticket into a few great recording sessions from Brooks Williams to (believe it or not) a lap steel solo on a Vanessa Williams single.

But that old National has found a unique voice in my life and in my heart. Jerry McPherson, a great Nashville guitarist, has said that my guitar is "haunted." He might be right. Or maybe there's just a screw loose that's rattling away deep inside that humming piece of metal. I like playing it in open tuning and trying to see if the ghost in the machine might be Son House.

One late night, while an engineer and a producer were chasing their tails, Gordon Kennedy, Tommy Sims, and I sat in a room and started strumming, and fell into a version of *Just a Closer Walk* that we still play eight years later. We felt young and ancient all at once.

I don't know about it's former owners, but I've been fortunate enough to have played the National on records by artists including The Neville Brothers, Toby Keith, Amy Grant, Keb' Mo', Kenny Loggins, and my ole boss, Phil Keaggy.

Truth be told, I just do what I do, and it's a wonder that I've found a voice that someone wants on a record. That old guitar keeps reminding how little I really know, but it doesn't seem to mind being played.

Visit Phil Madeira at www.philmadeira.com

NAME THAT TUNE

It's important to other musicians, but on records,
fast picking doesn't mean a thing. People want to
hear melody and nice harmony.
—*Chet Atkins*

I have always been a big believer that a great melody is a great
melody is a great melody. You can write the most interesting piece,
but if it doesn't have a strong melody, it doesn't get very far.
—*Lee Ritenour*

There are three basic elements to good music: rhythm, harmony,
and melody. If you fail to use any one of these, then don't call
what you do music; call it something else.
—*Jorge Morel*

George Thorogood

BLUES TO THE BONE

Growing up in the sixties, it seemed to me that the price of guitars tripled after everybody saw the Ed Sullivan show in 1964. After that, every kid got a guitar, just like they got a baseball glove; it became the standard American thing to get. Rock and roll brought the guitar out to the front of the stage. Before that, it was pretty much a backup instrument in the big band era, in the days of Benny Goodman. With the exception of a few people like Charlie Christian, guitar players sat in the background and strummed rhythms. But guys like Chuck Berry and Eddie Cochran and Buddy Holly changed all that.

Oh sure, the guitar was right there all along in the blues world, but at that time, the blues wasn't exposed to young white middle class America. That didn't happen until people like Bo Diddley and B.B. King really brought the instrument home. And then in the '60s, with the help of Keith Richards, Clapton, Beck, and Hendrix, the guitar really ruled as king in the rock and roll world. And I wanted to play one like everybody else.

> There is a lot of power in the blues—a lot of passion. I could apply that to just one or two chords and really make a statement.

One Christmas my parents bought me an electric guitar. I had it for about a month before I traded it in for a Framus bass—the kind Bill Wyman played in the Rolling Stones. I fiddled around with that for a while, but I wasn't real comfortable with it, either. Later on I got an acoustic Harmony guitar, but I still didn't think of myself as much of a guitar player; I really just hadn't found my thing.

I got out of high school, and a couple of years went by, and I said to myself, "George, if you're going to make your move in the music business, you'd better get on it now before you get too old." I thought if I worked real hard at it, I might be

183

able to play slide guitar and get on top of this blues thing. Like John Lee Hooker. I thought I might pull that off. I thought I might make a living with it. It was kind of a last ditch effort to put something together, and I got a little faith in myself and went for it.

What drew me to the blues in the first place was its very nature. The blues was basic and primitive. It was spawned and made famous by people who didn't have a lot of musical education. Hell, they didn't have a lot of grade school education! So the music itself was very primitive. It was difficult to play but it was not complicated. So I, being an unschooled musician, was naturally attracted to it. There is a lot of power in the blues—a lot of passion. I could apply that to just one or two chords and really make a statement. Plus, it was just so wonderful to listen to; the lyrics were funny, and the guitar playing was wild and crazy. And it was obscure. That appealed to me, too. It gave me an advantage in that nobody would know if I was playing it right or wrong! So the blues was a wonderful little world to dive into—a tiny world of the hip.

I found my heroes in people like Paul Butterfield, Elvin Bishop, Taj Mahal, and John Hammond. These people were totally dedicated to the craft, and I really respected that. So I thought that's the road I wanted to go—get a hold of something and go all out and see if I could make a go of it.

So naturally, the guitar became the instrument of choice, almost out of design. And I've been stuck with it ever since. I'm not saying I've mastered it, but it's done all right by me.

Visit George Thorogood at www.georgethorogood.com

ROBBIE ROBERTSON

The guitar obsession started for me at a very young age—before I could even wrap my hand around the neck. But I knew that's what I wanted to do. My cousins and uncles on the Six Nations Indian Reservation started showing me chords here and there. And like anything else in your life, you find out you have a little knack for something, and so you carry on. You put one foot in front of the other. Before long, it became evident that I had a particular passion for this, and it was just around the time that rock and roll began. So there I was, reaching puberty, rock and roll was born, and I was standing there at the crossroads with a guitar in my hand. It was a set up, really.

Catfish Keith

THE BLUES DON'T FLOAT

Searching for the roots of it all, I finally discovered it in the cutout bin at the record store. Son House. *Father of the Folk Blues*. His *Death Letter* both riveted me and left me disturbed. The doomed conviction and drunken tone of his propulsive, crying slide just kept calling me back.

As a teenager in the mid '70s, I couldn't have cared less about rock and heavy metal—all the music my friends listened to. I wanted to hear Blind Willie Johnson, Charlie Patton, Fred MacDowell, Bukka White, Barbecue Bob, Little Hat Jones, Tampa Red, Sol Hoopii, Lonnie Johnson, Bo Carter. When I listened to that music, whole new worlds opened up for me. When I was eighteen, I mail-ordered a shiny, chrome-plated 1930 National Style O. Angels sang when I opened the case the first time.

After leaving high school in late 1979, I started to travel around and played some music—in general, just seeing what was out there. For a time I lived in my rusty Oldsmobile, traveling through the east, south, mid-west, the old west, and California. With my National guitar, I was a happy man.

In January of 1982 I bid farewell to my folks in Iowa; I'd bought a one-way ticket to the Virgin Islands. It was thirty below zero at home with two feet of snow on the ground. My thoughts turned to a fellow I had met at a party in Cedar Rapids who told me, "If you ever come to the Islands, look me up. You could crew on my sailboat." Seemed like a good enough excuse for me to bolt! My Dad, wrapped up like Nanook, took me, shivering, to the Greyhound station with my duffel bag and my National.

> Angels sang when I opened the case the first time.

Stepping off the plane in St. Thomas, I was immediately struck by the bright sun, heat, humidity, and fresh salty Caribbean air. I had on my keep-from-freezing-to-death long john union suit and sweaters, which with great celebratory flair, I

185

chucked wholesale into an airport garbage can. "I'm never going back there again," I thought to myself. Before me was the kind of paradise I'd dreamed of but never experienced. Shunning taxis, I ran with my gear right to the water's edge, and jumped into clear blue water warm as a bath.

Following my inaugural dip in the sea, I proceeded across the Island into Charlotte Amalie, where I jammed with a dreadlocked sax player from New York for awhile. I then learned that to find my captain, I'd have to taxi to Red Hook, then ferry to Tortolla (in the British Virgin Islands), and look for him in the little bay where the ferry docks. It was dusk by the time I arrived; the ferry and all the people were gone. The captain's name was Curly, so I called out a few times to a handful of boats, "Currr-leeee! Cuuurrr-leeee!" My voice echoed across the bay without reply. It was getting darker, and I was starting to get a little nervous. Again, "Currr-leeeeeee" and finally, "Yeah, waddaya want?"

> In the bright moonlight, I could see my National, floating along in its wooden case, just out of reach. Then moments later, it keeled up like the Titanic and plummeted to the bottom.

Well, Curly was terrific, a kind of merry pirate, and true to his word, he took me on as "crew." I hoisted the mast mizzen, scraped barnacles off the hull, caught big tunas and lobsters, played his Gibson, and slept in the fo'csle—the little forward area of the boat below deck. Since I was only nineteen, sleeping at a right angle was no problem; I was made of rubber then.

I was overjoyed with my new island life, sailing around... man, what a life! One calm moonlit night Curly and I took the dingy ashore to a little restaurant & bar off the Island of Tortolla. I brought my National along and played a few tunes. Curly and I had a few rum drinks, which were followed by a few more rum drinks. As the evening turned to morning, the staff bid us farewell (kicked us out), and, aglow with good cheer, we got back into the dingy and shoved off. When we got to the edge of the yacht, Curly stood up, but suddenly stumbled sideways. "Oh, no!" he yelled. "The dingy's sinking!"

Down went the dingy, down went the captain, down went the National, and down went me. Curly was flailing in the water, trying to save the outboard motor, swallowing gasoline and seawater in the process. In the bright moonlight, I could see my National, floating along in its wooden case, just out of reach. Then moments later, it keeled up like the Titanic and plummeted to the bottom. Instinctively, in a sort of drunken adrenaline rush, I dove down, grabbed the guitar, and heaved it up onto the deck of the boat. Curly, helplessly watching the dingy and outboard go down, was aboard too now. After purging himself of gasoline, seawater, and rum, he was okay.

The next morning, saltier but wiser, we assessed the previous night's damage. The dingy is found, right under the sailboat; the engine needs some work. Guitar and case are hosed down with fresh water; it still has good tone. We both require pain relief. Entropy and oxidation ensue.

My adventures on Curly's boat continued for another few weeks. When a group of Curly's friends came to charter the boat, there wasn't room for me anymore. I said my farewells and moved onto the island of St. John, where I happily lived in a tent on the beach. I did gigs all over the island with my trusty, rusting steel-body until springtime came and the island got real quiet. With my pocket full of gig money I bought another one-way ticket back home to Iowa, brown as a nut, and sun-bleached hair down to my shoulders.

That old National guitar, though rustier over the years, has served me well. I continued to use it on thousands of gigs and on my first five albums. I put it in semi-retirement in 1998; the guitar just kept rusting until it came to resemble the blown-out bumper of my 1973 Oldsmobile. It was one of the first Style O guitars made in 1930, with a body made of steel, not brass, as they later were. When I'd give it a good strum, little chips of rusty dust would crumble onto the floor. It's now in the hands of Don Young and McGregor Gaines at National Reso-Phonic Guitars, being lovingly restored to its original, salt-free condition.

Looking back, I miss those cocky, carefree days. But a fellow eventually learns about danger, heartbreak, and gravity (the one law you really can't break). Hopefully, you live through it, ebullience intact. All those things I was so damn sure about then don't seem so clear to me now. Dreams can get bent when confronted with years of hard-bitten reality. The dope don't work no more.

But the songs and the music go deeper. What you have left has more meaning. Velocity gives way to space and authority. You ain't the kid no more. It's time to pass it on, and listen to that Son House sound inside, that for good reason, still scares me to death.

Visit Catfish Keith at www.catfishkeith.com

Don't fall prey to 'playing-overly-difficult-and-needlessly-
convoluted-polyphony-while-obscuring-natural-
musicality-and-beauty-of-guitar-sound' syndrome.
—*Tim Sparks*

Taj Mahal

THE WORLD INSIDE MY GUITAR

The trouble with rock and roll is it forgot to go back to its black roots. If the players had done that—*even periodically*—the music would have stayed alive. But instead, they exploited it for the moment, and made their money until it ran out of juice.

And then the British invasion came along. The English would never have come if these guys hadn't sold out to the Elvis factor. Now, Elvis was great, but what he was really telling everybody was, "You gotta go to the source, and come out from there." And that's exactly what the English did. They jumped right over Elvis and went straight to Elmore James and straight to Buddy Guy and straight to Albert Collins and straight to Albert King and straight to B.B. King and straight to Freddy King. They went right to the door. And they didn't settle for some derivative version. It took the British to point out our own roots music to the general populace! It's pretty obvious, but who knows why they didn't really get it. All the Americans could do was play catch-up.

> People tend to chew the sugar out of the gum of whatever it is they're doing. Well, pay attention, because there is always some sweetness coming from somewhere when it comes to guitar music!

People tend to chew the sugar out of the gum of whatever it is they're doing. Well, pay attention, because there is always some sweetness coming from somewhere when it comes to guitar music! I'm lucky I got to taste some of that sweetness early on.

Quite a lot of people in the post-war days migrated out of the Deep South for the jobs up north, and for and better schools and the opportunity to buy a decent house. My mother was from South Carolina. She was a gospel singer with aspirations to sing like Mahalia Jackson. And of course, she also sang in church. And because of her southern Baptist tradition, there was always a tremendous amount of gospel music in the house. But it was a couple of transplanted rural southern families who lived in my Springfield, Massachusetts neighborhood that really turned my head around. There was one fellow about my age who played country blues guitar. I drove him crazy getting him to teach me that stuff. And it always amazed him that somebody who was born up north would be so interested in that music. So he and some other cats from Mississippi turned me on to all that old stuff, listening to records by John Lee Hooker, Muddy Waters, and Robert Johnson. But hearing it played live and in front of me was an entirely different experience. You could study your scales and read what's put in front of you, but *this*—this music was their own experience coming out through the instrument, their own *cultural* experience. And it just captured me.

> There were always a lot of good, flashy players around, but they didn't get into the inside body rhythm like these cats could.

There were always a lot of good, flashy players around, but they didn't get into the inside body rhythm like these cats could. It was something that you could really feel. There was never any thought that you were listening to the "Devil's music"—I just heard it as the music from the culture. But it didn't end there. In fact, that was just the beginning.

My father was from the Caribbean, and he brought the musical culture of that area into the house. He was also a jazz musician. He gave up his dreams for the business, though, to start a family, and have a more secure livelihood. Back in those days, a black man playing music could have a big name, but he'd never have any money, and he'd be gone most of the time. So thankfully for me, he opted not to have that kind of life. But boy, did he bring music into the house!

We also had a shortwave radio that I used to play with, and I could tune into different places around the world. I could punch into Havana, Moscow, Prague, Sydney—anywhere. One night I punched into Honolulu and got the shock of my life. It was some of the most beautiful music I had ever heard. It was so soulful and so deep. I was just transfixed. All I could remember was my consciousness; I could not feel my body. That's how powerful that music was to this young kid. When I hear a guitar sing like it's supposed to sing, I don't care who's playing it or what culture it's coming from, I'll listen.

I'm lucky that my home was such a cultural melting pot: the music from the south, the music from the Caribbean, and the music from all over the world through my radio—all of it merging with the European classical traditions that were common in the Northeast. I came out of that with a much more positive look at my own culture, and American culture in a broader sense. I could see where I was a part of that, and not only that, where I was a part of the world.

I never saw myself in that typecast image of a bluesman from Mississippi. To quote Guy Davis, who also grew up in the Northeast, "…the only cotton I picked was my BVDs up off the floor!" I never identified with the stereotype depicted in the romantic imagery that surrounds southern black bluesmen who say, "I don't know nothin' past picking cotton and pickin' guitar. I ain't had much edumacation in my life; I just knows how to pick this here guitar." But I absorbed it. I soaked it all in. That's a valid colloquial dialect that creates the very sound and essence of the music. That music comes from deep down inside that experience and from deep down inside that culture. So the best you can do is to take a picture of the music that day, and somehow work it into the way we live the music today. And there's a world of it.

Visit Taj Mahal at www.tajblues.com

THE BRITISH ARE COMING

If it wasn't for the British musicians, a lot of us black musicians in America would still be catchin' the hell that we caught long before. So thanks to them, thanks to all you guys. You opened the doors that I don't think would have been opened in my lifetime. When white America started paying attention to the blues, it started opening a lot of doors that had been closed to us.
—*B.B. King*

Oh, it's seven chord, you know. You hit the blue note. Listen, all we're doin' is copyin' the Rolling Stones, and all they're doin' is copying Bo Diddley, Muddy Waters, Jimmy Reed, T-Bone Walker, and Albert King, Albert Collins, B.B. King, and Freddie King. That's it.
—*Billy Gibbons*

The Funk Brothers

JOE MESSINA, EDDIE WILLIS, AND ROBERT WHITE

with John Schroeter

From swing to shuffle, rumba to rock, blues to bossa, musical genres are defined more by their rhythm than any other single attribute. It was no less the case when Barry Gordy set up shop in a converted house in Detroit, Michigan, better know as the home of Motown.

The richly varied sounds of Motown artists ranged from Smokey Robinson's falsettoed leads to Marvin Gaye's soulful grit; from Dianna Ross' sweet clarity to the Temptations' choreographed harmonies. With such a diversity of styles—all bearing the Motown moniker—one must look behind the front men and women to see just what transcended the personalities of the "stars" to deliver that consistently "Motown" sound.

It all started in 1959 when Barry Gordy, a black entrepreneur who saw a market for contemporary black music among white audiences, founded Motown Records. It would become the largest, and most successful African-American-owned corporation in American—and it delivered on its promise to bring black music into the American pop mainstream. It was there that the likes of Stevie Wonder, The Four Tops, The Jackson Five, Gladys Knight & The Pips, Martha Reeves & the Vandellas, and The Spinners literally cranked out hit after hit. In fact, it wasn't unusual for Motown singles to occupy as many as five of the top ten slots on Billboard's charts at any one time!

First headquartered in a patched-up and painted two-story shingle-roofed house with a large front porch, Gordy dubbed the operation "Hitsville, USA." Located at 2648 West Grand Boulevard, the upstairs bedrooms were converted into offices. The studio, which was originally located in the garage, was subsequently moved to a basement, or as it was known, "The Snake Pit." This was where they laid it down; those legendary, locked-in-the-pocket grooves that would turn the music world upside down.

It is said that art imitates life, and Motown was very much a product of its times. As the baby-boomers among us will recall, LBJ was waging war on poverty, Mississippi was burning crosses, and Cassius Clay was in the ring. Integration, civil disobedience, and Vietnam were the watch words of the evening news. It was against this tumultuous cultural backdrop that Barry Gordy's small independent record label was making a certain social history of its own. Theirs was an odd juxtaposition of peace and love and all-out war—*Dancing in the Street* was all too often heard amidst the rioting in the streets.

> Soupy used to break me up. His line to me was, "Joe, if you keep picking that thing it will never heal."

But back to the music. Original Motown drummer Benny Benjamin, along with bassist James Jamerson, guitarist Robert White, and keyboardist/bandleader Earl Van Dyke, launched the Motown sound, a quartet so tight they became known as the Funk Brothers. Others would enter and leave the brotherhood, but whatever the lineup, they took the Motown Beat to Main Street. The innovative and gritty grooves they laid down in the Snake Pit hit—some 350 tunes—in Motown's Golden Era included such classics as *I Heard In Through The Grapevine, My Girl, My Guy, The Way You Do the Things You Do, I'm Losing You, For Once In My Life, I Second That Emotion, Baby Love, Heat Wave, Uptight, Higher And Higher.*

As much as their work defined the Motown sound, their unique contribution also found its way into the very lifeblood of funk, R&B, and indeed, contemporary pop music at large. You want roots? These guys invented it!

The Funk Brothers didn't play in rotation, though, simply being drawn from the pool of available Motown musicians; they played together—that is, *simultaneously.* They were a team. That was a key ingredient to "the sound"—the magic that was Motown.

In the late 1950s, Joe Messina was a jazz guitarist and band leader with Soupy Sales' *Night Show*—a live televised variety program that featured prominent jazz artists of the day, including Charlie Parker, Stan Getz, Dizzy Gillespie, and Ella Fitzgerald. "I had some good times on the show," remembers Messina. "And Soupy used to break me up. His line to me was, 'Joe, if you keep picking that thing it will never heal.'"

When he wasn't working the show, Messina could be found at the Twenty Grand—a black club, where he, being white, mixed quite comfortably with his black band mates. Considering the often pitched racial tensions of the time, for Messina, it had no meaning at all. "It was the music," he says. "I was driven to play jazz; I didn't care who I played with or where it was happening. It just happened to be mostly with the black people."

One night Barry Gordy came into the club. He knew of Messina from his television work, and he also knew where he could find him after hours. He was determined to recruit the best musicians he could find for his fledgling enterprise. "That night he approached me," Messina recalls, "and asked if I'd be willing to do some recording for him. I told him I'd love to. Of course, I had no idea what he was about to do!"

> We'd have a number one hit and not even know it! "So what," we'd say. As soon as we left the studio we put our jazz programs on.

Messina's first session at Hitsville was almost as memorable as the music the followed. "The place was just a garage with cinderblock walls," he says. "You entered from the back and came into this room with a dirt floor where this beautiful baby grand sat on a large sheet of plywood. It was pretty amazing. I came in and set up my amplifier and sat on it for the recording. You couldn't believe what it came to, though. Before long, the place had gotten quite sophisticated. They added three isolated recording rooms to the building, and when it was all fixed up, it was pretty nice. It's a museum now."

Amazingly, the guitar section comprised of Messina, Eddie "Chank" Willis, and Robert White—with eighteen strings between the three of them—never ran into each other. Finding their respective voices in the mix, White's easy yet solid approach laid the foundation for Messina's razor-sharp backbeats and Willis' funky fills. Willis, originally from Mississippi, brought his early country blues influence to White's and Messina's more jazz oriented sensibilities. When funneled together into the context of pop music, they wrote a whole new chapter.

"The key," Messina offers, "was that we all really listened to each other. Many times I would just double the bass line, or if there was a high back beat—like what you hear on *Ain't to Proud to Beg*—I'd take that. Sometimes, the writers, Holland and Dozier, would come in and sing the parts they wanted us to play. And then we'd run it down, and do the little fills that we thought would go well with the chord changes—not even knowing the melody. They were smart enough to keep a lot of that in!"

Often times, the band didn't even know who would be singing to the tracks they laid down. "But it didn't matter," Messina adds. "We still didn't know the song. We generally didn't record live with the vocalists. We just put down our tracks, and moved on to the next song."

With Messina seated between White and Willis, the trio unavoidably came to be dubbed the Oreo Guitar Section. "I was just known as the white guy at Motown," laughs Messina. "A lot of people coming in and out of there didn't even know my name. Some of them called me Mancini, which I didn't mind!"

But the guitarists did mind that they were often relegated to the background in the final analysis. "I always thought we weren't featured enough," says Messina. "No one really got a chance to stretch out. I always expected to play more when I got there, but there wasn't much happening solo-wise."

Lack of spotlight notwithstanding, the three would make certain that their grooves in the studio made it into the grooves on the vinyl. And Messina's axe of choice was a Telecaster fitted with a JazzMaster neck he'd bolted on; its sharp attack always found its way to the top of the frequency spectrum. White favored the warmer, fatter-sounding Gibson ES 335 and L-5 archtops, his distinctive tone coming by way of an unusual upstroke of the thumbnail. That's his intro on the archetypical Motown classic *My Girl*. Willis' trademark sound came courtesy of his early '60s Firebird, ideal for the fills that rounded out the ensemble.

> The fact is we were so good we could take a chicken and squeeze his neck on two and four and get a hit record.

And were they even aware that they were on to something big? "We had no idea," Messina says. "All of us, except for Eddie—he was the blues guy in the band—were jazz musicians. We played pop music during the day, but at night, we'd go blow it out jamming in the clubs. We never listened to pop radio. We'd have a number one hit and not even know it! 'So what,' we'd say. As soon as we left the studio we put our jazz programs on. But a lot of other people were listening, thank God!"

In no time, like Sun and Stax before them, Motown grew from a regional sound into a national phenomenon. "If I had to explain how that happened," says Messina, "I would say we were just lucky. Of course, once you get one hit and go with basically the same sound again, you're bound to hit it again. That's not always the case, but it did happen."

But greater rewards for the unsung house band did not necessarily follow the label's tremendous success. Messina explains, "When Barry hired me he wanted to give me $5 per song. That's what he said the other guys were getting, and that they recorded four or five songs in an hour. I knew they couldn't do that; I knew better.

So he upped it to $10 per song. I said to him, 'I'll tell you what, Barry. Give me $10 an hour. And if we do ten songs in that hour, the nine other songs will be on me.' So we did that for a while, and I actually got paid over scale, which was $28 for a three hour session; I was getting $30. After a while Barry had to let me go—he couldn't afford me any more! But he called me a week later when they went union."

Jack Ashford, whose definitive vibes and tambourine work are every bit as much a Motown signature adds, "We were paid weekly—very weakly!" Overtime pay went into a so-called black box. "The trick," Ashford says, "was to find the black box! The fact is we were so good we could take a chicken and squeeze his neck on two and four and get a hit record. And when a chicken lays a golden egg, do you feed him grain, or just give him scraps? You take care of that chicken so he keeps pumping out those golden eggs. He's no unsung hero—he's a good chicken!"

Despite the chickens in the Snake Pit, the Funk brothers would go on to do more for a great many artists' careers than any one group of musicians in the history of commercial music. And while they would receive the equivalent of $8 or $10 for their work on *Baby Love*, recognition would, indeed, come. Alan Slutsky's *Standing in the Shadows* documentary film and recordings would net Grammy Awards for the Funks in 2000 for Best Soundtrack and Best Traditional R&B Performance with Chaka Khan for Marvin Gaye's *What's Goin' On*—one of the few songs for which the Funk Brothers actually received musician credits! In 2004 they were recognized with the Recording Academy's Lifetime Achievement Award.

Too little too late? Not according to Ashford. "We're not bitter," he says. The story is bitter, but we are not."

I can't remember when I didn't play the guitar. And I can't remember when playing the guitar didn't lift me up to seventh heaven. Sleeping and eating were never nearly as important to me, and up to the time I was twelve, there wasn't a pretty girl within a hundred miles who looked half as good as my old guitar.
—*Chet Atkins*

Alex de Grassi

ONE WAY TICKET

I bought my first really good guitar in 1971 at a pawn shop in Oakland, California for three hundred bucks—a Martin D-18, mahogany back and sides, in pretty good shape, with case. I'd heard stories about people getting amazing deals from pawn brokers who didn't know what they had, but this guy knew exactly what he had and wasn't willing to bargain.

I played that guitar a lot. I took it to Colorado where the finish got cracked in the cold, dry mountain air. I took it to Mexico and played it on the beach where it was subjected to tropical heat and moisture. I played that guitar in coffeehouses in Santa Barbara while pretending to go to university for six months. I also acquired a banjo and a Yamaha with high action that I used to play slide, but I mostly played the D-18.

In the spring of 1973 I dropped out of college and drove a huge car from Santa Barbara, California to Red Hook, New York. In exchange for delivering the car to its owner, I received gas money, a free ride coast to coast, and a bus ticket to the airport. Somewhere in the desert near the Arizona line, I picked up a hitchhiker who claimed to have been a truck driver. We took turns driving while the other slept in the back seat, and two and a half days later we were in Baltimore. The next day I delivered the car to its owner in Red Hook and caught the bus to JFK. After a night sleeping on a bench in the terminal, I boarded a plane and flew to Stockholm. From there I caught a train that took me through Denmark and all the way across Germany and into Austria to the tiny village of Braz where my friend Nick was living with his girlfriend. Not the quickest or most direct route, but the only one I could afford at the time.

Nick and I spent the next three weeks writing, arranging, and rehearsing. We played guitar constantly and managed to land a couple of gigs in southern Germany. But after a month, I was restless and decided to hitchhike to London. A day later I was there. I stayed in a B&B for a few nights, and when my money was gone, I decided that I would try my luck playing in the streets.

196

I had seen street musicians, or "buskers," in the London Underground so I headed down to Marble Arch Station at the corner of Hyde Park and waited my turn to play. I hadn't come to London with a particular plan. I had a vague notion that I might be able to survive playing music, but I hadn't really thought it through and now I found myself suspended between two worlds. I was about to cross some invisible line between being a tourist and a street person. I didn't know anyone in London, I had no money, and no place to stay. There didn't seem to be an option.

The first moments playing for the steady stream of passersby were intimidating. Somewhat shy, and uncertain about what I was doing, I found it challenging to stand behind an open guitar case expecting people to throw money into it. It was at once terrifying and liberating; terrifying to realize that I was now living on the street, and liberating to have broken with some lingering convention I had about what I could or couldn't do. I was embarking on an entirely new journey.

> It was at once terrifying and liberating; terrifying to realize that I was now living on the street, and liberating to have broken with some lingering convention I had about what I could or couldn't do.

The first few nights were a bit rough. I met some fairly down and out people who showed me where I could crash. These were somewhat desperate places, and I slept on floors with my head on my wallet and my arm around my guitar. But after a few days, I met some street performers from South Africa who invited me to the house where they were staying. Due to the peculiarities of the English housing laws, they had been able to rent a house marked for restoration (and deemed "unrentable") for next to nothing. It was funky, and there was no furniture, but it was really cheap and I felt an instant camaraderie with my new friends. I ended up renting the attic space for one pound, ten shillings (a little more than $2) a week. There was a skylight, a mattress, and an odd geometry of bare walls where the angles of the roof met. It was a perfect place to hide out and let the imagination wander.

With a steady place to stay, I could now devote all my time to playing music. I spent most of my days underground in the maze of subway stations commonly referred to as "the tube." The long cylindrical passageways lined with tiles amplify the sound acoustically and serve as a P.A. system complete with a long echoing reverb. You can hear performers from the moment you step off the train till you leave the station. It made the music sound big. The air gets stale down there, especially in the really deep stations that require a lift to get to the surface. That made the return to street level for fish and chips or a tea break all the more rewarding.

There was a system to busking in the Underground. You had to book your "pitches," those places where you were going to play. This meant stopping off at a few different stations and reserving a time slot. Every slot was an hour long beginning on the hour. To book a pitch you had to wait for the performer to finish their song and then ask what times were available. It was the responsibility of the current busker to relay the schedule to anyone else who showed up. In this manner, you would attempt to piece together a schedule that would allow you to get from one station to another in time for your next pitch. It took some planning to maximize the number of pitches you could book and still show up on time. If you were late, you might lose your place. Nothing was written down; it was all by word of mouth, and it worked amazingly well. I got the hang of it pretty quickly, and for the price of a single subway ticket, I could play five or six gigs a day.

The whole world was passing through London and you never thought much about who you were playing for. Responses ranged from indifference or outright disdain, to mild enthusiasm. Mainly, people were in a hurry to get somewhere else and didn't stop even if they tossed a coin as they sped by. Occasionally people would drop an apple or half a sandwich in your case, or even a can of beer. Even rarer were those occasions when someone would actually stop to listen to a complete song. I got to know musicians from all over the world as well as the panhandlers and assorted street people. "Spare a few bob for an old seaman," soon became a familiar phrase uttered by some of the old-timers who wandered the Underground. When they were having an especially hard time, they'd come by and offer you their very finest "hard-ups" (half-smoked cigarettes) that they'd scrounged off the ground. In exchange for this generous offer, they hoped to get a few coins from your open guitar case. As unappetizing as it may seem to me now, I confess that on occasion I smoked them.

One day, my friend Nick showed up. I was busking at Marble Arch and looked up to see him walking down the steps. He had just driven his VW bus from Austria, parked the car near Hyde Park, and walked down the steps only to find me in midsong. As simple as that. He hadn't been in London and out of the car for five minutes and he'd found me.

From then on we mostly worked as a duo playing arrangements of Dylan, Simon & Garfunkel, Stevie Wonder, the odd Beatles song, and of course our own songs and instrumentals. In the evenings we would make the rounds to audition at folk clubs, hoping that they would invite us back to be one of the featured acts. And sometimes we were. We picked up a couple of regular gigs playing in restaurants, which covered our meals, a drink, and a couple of quid. Other nights we cooked at the house in a *tagine* that Nick had picked up in Morocco. This was a welcome change from the steady diet of fish and chips I had gotten used to. A diet which came to a sudden and violent end one night when some tainted fish brought the entire contents of my stomach up and onto the walls of my little refuge in the attic.

Nick slept in his VW bus, which he parked in front of our house. Every morning he would wake to see a little old lady peering disdainfully through the curtains of his bus trying to ascertain what kind of creature lay within. He got to be known in the neighborhood as that American with the wild hair who slept in his car. His bedroom on the street ruffled a few feathers, but there was never an official complaint.

Our summer in London culminated in a gig in the crypt of the church of St. Martin-in-the-Fields. We had already been paid to play sets in a couple of tiny folk clubs, but this was an actual concert. Somehow we had managed to convince the folks there that people would actually pay to see us. We even managed to get our names on a poster and drew a decent crowd.

By then we had a fairly polished act and the gig went well—well enough that we had started to dream about getting an agent and a record deal. But other factors were intervening. Nick was missing his girlfriend back in Austria, and my girlfriend in California had written to say that she would be arriving in Paris soon. I had agreed to meet her there. Nick and I debated returning to London after a break, but once we were in the VW bus heading for Paris, it became clear that our summer in London was over—it was time to move on.

We picked up Jane in Paris, and the three of us spent a couple of days at the house of some friends in a village nearby. Nick headed for Austria and Jane and I returned to Paris. I tried busking there once but it wasn't the same. The French police were busting street musicians in the Metro and there were only a handful of places to play on the streets in front of the big cafés. After a week of camping out in an impossibly small studio space, we decided to take a train to Greece.

But there was one catch: we had enough money for only one ticket. It was a painful and difficult decision but I knew what I had to do. I headed down to Place Pigalle and hit the music shops. I found a place that sold Maccaferri guitars—the model played by the great gypsy guitarist Django Reinhardt—and for a moment I imagined trading in my D-18 for one, adopting a new persona, and trying to make a go of it in France. But in the end, I sold it.

I felt bad and a little desperate selling that guitar. It had been my means of survival for the past few months, and in the two years it was mine, I had undergone a transformation from amateur player to seasoned street performer. I had played that guitar all summer, from the time I got up till the time I went to bed. Now summer was over and I was trading it in for a one way train ticket. Being a Martin, it was perhaps worth a little more in France than in the States, and I sold it for almost the exact same price I had paid two years earlier in that Oakland pawn shop. Looking back, it was a pretty fair deal—I got my money back and a whole lot more.

Visit Alex de Grassi at www.degrassi.com

Arthur "Arturo" Carnrick

ST. PETER'S BY THE LAKE

I was delighted when a minister of music from the swanky part of town called just before Thanksgiving about a Christmas pageant to be held at the local Episcopal Church. I gave what I considered a competitive (cheap) bid. She agreed, and asked me to contact her after the holidays for confirmation.

Right away I set to practicing, and got reacquainted with the sounds of the season through my favorite book of Christmas songs, *Carols for Guitarists with Day Jobs and Fumbly Fingers*. This would be a piece of cake—fruit cake being in season this time of year.

With Thanksgiving now quite literally under my belt, I called to confirm the date, but was met with a bit of hemming and hawing. "Oh, uh, well," she stammered. "We need to think about a few things; let me call you." Hopes dashed as they were, I decided to leave my calendar open anyway, but heard nothing.

On the eve of Christmas Eve, a rather anxious music minister phoned me at work, apologetically explaining that she had lost my home number, and asked if there were any chance that I could still perform for the program. I could, of course, and so over the phone, we agreed on a few solos and all the accompaniment I could say grace over: the *Bach Prelude in C*, *Away in a Manger*, and *Oh Little Town of Bethlehem*. The one glitch was that she wanted the last two songs played in the key of F, which is rather gauche for me; using a capo is against my religion. But then again, they call me *Arturo*—a man of honor who sneers at Eb, chuckles at G#, and who can be "gig ready" in two days. She then added *What Child is This* in Em (I play it in Dm) and *Silent Night* in any singable key. We agreed to rehearse at 5:30—just before show time, as we were both "pros." How pride cometh before the fall.

Christmas Eve arrived, and I felt like a child, full of anticipation, and reminiscing over days of Christmas past. Back in the early 1950s, long before I can remember, our family converted from Catholicism to Southern Baptist. We later converted to water skiing. As a youngster, I remember Barney Gallagher, our neighbor friend who was still Catholic, because he fasted on Christmas Eve. One year he forgot about the fast and ate some fudge. All of us kids were afraid they weren't going to let him into heaven.

On this eve, I would not only get to attend a service of a similar order, but would also be an invited guest. We Baptists have notions about Episcopals being a little loose, but my mom told me that way back in history, they used to be Catholics, too—just like us. My family was also invited, and so we arrived with me wearing my expensive "ruffly" shirt, crushed velvet bow tie, and classical guitar at the beautiful church set placidly beside a lake. The music minister soon arrived, unlocked the door, and led us inside a glassed-in mini-cathedral with acoustics rivaling that of the Mormon Tabernacle.

> I happily set my digital echo to halfway between "angelic glory" and "new age rapture."

She was a petite blond, dressed in a short, black skirt, and sporting hair just as short. She introduced herself as Ethel. She brought along her seven-year-old son, who reminded me a little of Barney Gallagher. She told him to sit in a pew and mind his coloring books. She had a take-charge personality, advising me that I probably wouldn't need my amp, as the acoustics in the sanctuary were excellent. My wife piped in just then, "But he needs his amp to get the 'Arturo' sound!" Ethel consented and let me plug in. I happily set my digital echo to halfway between "angelic glory" and "new age rapture."

As we worked out the music, I began to realize that Ethel was one of those gifted professionals who can really become irritating. In no time, it was clear that she was practically perfect in every way. Her performance on the keyboard was without flaw. And she was an intimidatingly quick study, as well. She set the MIDI keyboard to a flute patch, and mentally transposed the Bach *Prelude in G* to my key of C, because she could do that faster than figure out how the keyboard's key modulator switch worked. Within eight bars of accompaniment, she was playing it like she had done it all her life.

Oh Little Town of Bethlehem went without a hitch, but during *Away in a Manger*, I discovered that Episcopalians are a little confused about the tune; they play some old Civil War melody instead. I tried to correct her, but sure enough, she was playing page 327 in the hymnal, correctly and as written. So I began to fumble with a few chords to fill in.

Next we went to *What Child is This*, only we disagreed on whether the V-chord is major or minor, and if you went to major or minor on the chorus. This caused a little fuss. It also helped me understand how Holy Wars begin. So we compromised: one time her way, one time my way, and one time God's way.

Silent Night would be a solo, and so I debated as to whether I should play it with natural harmonics or even attempt a tremolo, since everyone would be singing along. I did make sure, though, that the fermata—that note sustained beyond the written value—was sufficiently long and emotional on the first "sleep in heavenly pe-e-eace." Usually a Baptist minister of music will raise his hand at this point, and won't let it down until it's time to breath, or the organist has turned the page.

Rehearsal was over, and now I needed a place to warm up and practice a bit more. Ethel pointed to the back and said, "In there." It was the cry room... a fine place for colicky babies and frantic musicians. Five minutes before the start of the program, Ethel escorted me, her son, and his crayons to the front of the sanctuary.

Soon the Bach prelude began, and the program commenced. This would be the only and final confidence-building event of the evening.

The attendance was more than had been expected, which prompted Ethel to abandon the MIDI keyboard in favor of the grand piano. It had been sitting in a cold room all day, and was now slowly warming up, but still in what I affection-ately refer to as "rest home" tune. And I was sitting within striking distance of each dissonant note. This was not good.

Meanwhile, the priest and white robed followers processed, bearing candles and banners. The scripture readings that followed were as inspiring as they were beau-tiful. Ethel elbowed me, and whispered that they would be having an open com-munion. If I wished to join, I was to hold out my hands for the bread and guide in the wine goblet. Otherwise I was to cross my arms over my chest. Well, I wanted to show that I was a good Christian, so I joined in. When the priest placed the bread in my hands, I ate it. "That was odd," I thought. It wasn't the unleavened kind that we Baptists generally eat. "Gee, I wonder what else is different," as the priest raised the wine goblet toward me.

Now, I was wearing my only clean white ruffly shirt, for which I had paid $25 some twenty-five years ago during the Arab Oil Embargo. So I was trying to be very careful to guide the goblet of red "fruit of the vine" properly as the priest began to tip the cup. Suddenly he slipped, and pushed the cup down to his right. So that the wine would not spill all over me, I turned my head and opened wide, catching a major gulp, which I chased with a slurp before anything could spill on my shirt.

Guess what... this was not fresh fruit of the vine in the Baptist sense; it was very fermented and aged fruit of the vine, and it warmed its way down. I'm not much of a drinker, and I try not to have any more than Paul or Timothy would approve of, but at this very moment, I had definitely consumed more than a medicinal amount trying to save my shirt. I found my way back to my seat, and tried to com-pose myself.

My thoughts shifted to the play list, as I couldn't remember which song was next. "Now let's see," I thought. "Okay, an F on the 5th fret is kind of like a C chord... Amazing how this stuff relaxes you." Soon I had tuned up to play, and was ready for the new version of *Away in a Manager*, which I did indeed play like a Civil War tune. Later, my wife would remind me that the Civil War tune was *Flow Gently Sweet Afton*, not *Suwannee River*. Next, *What Child is This* could have been called *What Song is This*, as the wine was beginning to confuse me as to which part was my way with the minor and which was Ethel's with the major. Finally, it was time for *Silent Night*—my big solo—and then with singing by the church members.

It was then that I learned Episcopals, unlike Baptists, believe in breathing while singing, and generally ignore fermatas. So when I came to the big, emotional moment, I was really getting into it when I discovered that everyone else had finished the chorus and was already on to the next verse.

With that, the concert was over, and I, Arturo, unplugged, grabbed my check, and packed up for home having experienced firsthand that liturgical Christmas Eve I had never experienced as a child. Someone once said there are two major disappointments in life: One is never having fulfilled your greatest dreams, and the other is having fulfilled your greatest dreams. As I tell you this story now, I realize that it really wasn't so bad after all. In fact, it was kind of funny how things turned out. But I did learn a thing or two. In the future, I don't think I should take myself so seriously. And maybe next time I should do like Barney Gallagher or Ethel's son... just plan to eat some fudge, bring my crayons, and praise God.

When I was a little kid, my brother cut my finger off
with an axe. That's why I'm not a piano player.
—*Jerry Garcia*

Doc Watson

FINE GUITARS AND ANGEL DUST

Dad finished his cup of coffee and leaned back in his chair at the breakfast table and said son, "I put in with a little ole guitar. If you'll learn to play a tune on that thing by the time I get back from work, then we'll go to town on Saturday and find you a guitar of your own."

I was really looking forward to that. A guitar is what I wanted most. My first instrument was a banjo that my dad made for me. It was a fairly crude one with a fretless maple neck and friction tuners. But what made it really special was the head. My grandmother had a cat, a very old cat. I never knew the animal, but it was old and decrepit. Well, Dad persuaded my brother to put it out of its misery, which he did, and that cat skin made the best banjo head you ever heard! But a guitar—now that's what I really wanted.

When my dad came home from work that evening, I was ready for him. I could play and sing *When the Roses Bloom in Dixieland*. And to that he said, "Well, I guess I'll have to keep my word, won't I?" Little did he know, though, that my school friend, Paul Montgomery, had taught me a few chords only days before!

That Saturday we went into town to Rhodes & Day's Furniture Store in North Wilkesboro, and he bought me a little Stella guitar for twelve and a half dollars. I had a little money in my piggy bank—three or four dollars—and he finished it out. That was my first guitar. And as far as I was concerned, it might as well have come from the king's treasury. It was a wonderful little ole guitar. Now I might have a different opinion today if I had to compare it with my Gallagher, but at that time it was the most wonderful thing I ever owned.

I was thirteen then, but I was in love with the guitar before I even knew what a guitar was. When I was six, my dad got one of those little wind-up Grammaphones that played the old 78 records. And I listened to all the records that came into the house—Gene Austin, the Skillet Lickers, the Carter family, and of course, Jimmie Rodgers. Those early recordings really hit my ear hard. I loved that slam strum lick that he had when he backed up his blue yodels; I had to learn how to do that. Luckily, when I got my first guitar my hands were big enough so that I could play it.

I learned everything I know on the guitar by ear—every bit of it. I learned a little theory as I went along, listening and talking to other musicians, but I never took a lesson in my life. It's not that I have a great ear, but I do think there's something to it. I believe when one comes into this world, a little angel walks up and hands you a box filled with talents. There might be five or six in there that will work with whatever plight you might have in your life. Music must have been mine because of my particular handicap, blindness. And the talent you're born with is the reason you jump into a thing and learn it. You have to do it. You're compelled to do it. It's a gentle persuasion, but you are compelled to do it. And I love the guitar and I love music.

> I believe when one comes into this world, a little angel walks up and hands you a box filled with talents.

But then, I think everyone should learn to play by ear. That way when you do learn to read, you'll know what you're reading. And it's pretty easy to do. You can learn what a chord sounds like. When you train your ear, you can recognize major, minor, seventh, ninth, diminished or augmented chords. You know what it is when you hear it. My ears were my eyes—like good radar.

As my knowledge of music progressed, other guitars came into my life, and each one was a dear friend. But eventually you find one that's a little better, and so you retire or trade in the other one.

My second guitar I worked out on the end of a crosscut saw. My younger brother David and I cut pulp wood out of the old chestnut saplings for the tannery extract, and we sold it to the tannery in North Wilkesboro. They ground it up and extracted the tannin from it to use in tanning the leather. We cut two truckloads, which bought David a suit of clothes and a Sears Roebuck Silvertone guitar for me. It wasn't much of a guitar, but I was proud of it—a step up from the Stella. It cost a little more, too; I paid $16 for it—one load of wood. And David, well, was as proud as a peacock in his new duds.

By then I was playing with some other young fellows, and we did a few shows at the local schoolhouses. But my first big opportunity was a talent contest. Arthur Smith had a TV show in Charolotte in those days, and every year he would host a talent contest. By that time I had been playing the guitar a good long time. I had a good ole Martin D-28 that I had bought the summer before. And I decided I'd enter as a guitar player and singer. Amateurs and professionals could participate, so when they asked me which category I wanted to enter I told them, "I'll take the professional side so I can get beat like a man."

My name was called, and I played *I Am a Pilgrim* and *Nine Pound Hammer* Travis style. And I won it! The contest was judged by the strength of the applause, and mine was the loudest. And the $25 prize, well, that was money in 1941!

By the way, that would make that D-28 of mine a pre-war Dreadnought. I sure wish I still had that guitar!

Learn more about Doc Watson at www.folkloreproductions.com

MY OWN THING

Sometimes I feel like whatever style I have is basically the
inability to do something else. It's like, "Well, I can't do this,
but I'm a musician and I'm going to do something."
—*Bill Frisell*

Hang on to your eccentricities, because they will give you a style.
—*John Scofield*

You play a couple of notes and say, "That sounds like Eric Clapton"
or "That sounds like George Benson." But then you play two or three
notes and say, "Man, that's me." And you concentrate on those ones."
—*Carlos Santana*

My own thing is in my head. I hear sounds,
and if I don't get them together nobody else will.
—*Jimi Hendrix*

Jose Feliciano

MY DELIVERANCE

Life began for me in the peacefully idyllic hills of a Caribbean island where the weather was kind-hearted and the air always smelled of sweet things like sugar cane, and coconut trees, and especially, of orange blossoms. There, in my little world, was my mother and dad, my grandmother and my older brother. Though our possessions were few (I know this now), our days and nights were filled with family and friends and food to nourish not only my body but the soul of a little boy who (I found this out later, too) was born blind. I didn't realize it at the time, because I knew who loved me and where I could find them almost all of the time. I knew where the river was, where my mother would wash her clothes; I knew where the fire pit was located, because it was there where she prepared our meals. I would follow a familiar path down to where our neighbors lived, where music would fill the air and beckon me with an invitation to become a part of it.

By the time I was three I was joining in with my uncle who played the *cuatro*, the beloved stringed instrument of Puerto Rico. I would tap on the bottom of a tin cracker can, fully immersed in the delightful sounds of his instrument's singing strings and my percussive accompaniments. I was whole, at peace, and completely unaware of the harsh realities of a world beyond us.

That was to abruptly change in less than two years when my parents brought my two brothers and me on what I was told was an airplane, where we flew all night to a place called Florida. The next day we continued on this trek only to be swallowed into the gigantic thunder of a place called New York City. It was here that I would learn—and learn fast—what it meant to be poor and blind. I learned what it meant to be foreigners, unfamiliar with the language or the culture of the life of those who had come here before us in the hope of building a better life for themselves. It was awful. It was cold. It smelled bad a lot of the time and most of all, it was lonely.

207

Early on, it was music that was to become my best friend. Even as I slowly began to become accustomed to the pace of this new life which was so far away from everything I had ever known, it was the music that wove a familiar thread throughout my day, making it tolerable amidst the poverty and prejudice of Harlem in the early 1950's. In school, I struggled to learn Braille and keep up with classmates who looked down on a kid from the ghetto. I tried to keep up in class with other kids who had help at home from parents who understood the language and were able to offer them their support.

> Little did I realize at the time that it was that answered prayer of redemption—that reprieve from a life sentence of loneliness and despair. It was a guitar.

I managed, somehow, to get by, but my head and heart was always somewhere else, thinking of a song I'd heard in the car on the way to school or on our radio at home. I spent a lot of time with my mother in the kitchen, listening to the radio as she prepared our family meals. She would sing along as the boleros of the day were played on the only Spanish station on the air in New York at that time. Her seemingly carefree song would lighten my heart, calling to mind an easier day, back in Puerto Rico when life asked of me no questions and required no answers.

By the time I was nine, I was one of eight boys; two having died before my older brother was born in Puerto Rico, another having passed away in New York, and then my three younger brothers and myself. Our apartment on the Eastside was very small and getting smaller with the addition of each new arrival.

The stresses of raising a family were great for my parents and the added concern of a blind child added to their anxieties. I could hear them at night, after I'd gone to bed, discussing the problem at length with questions like, "What are we going to do?" "What will happen to him?" "How are we going to manage?" The same questions went through my head over and over too, as I wondered, "Why was I the one to be born blind? What *will* I be?" School was really tough. I didn't fit in, and everywhere I turned there was the reminder of what I *couldn't* do—always of what I *couldn't* do.

Then, I remember one night, I had a dream about a beautiful lady. She was young and very sweet and made me feel at ease. She lovingly brought me down a long corridor, into a room where she sat me down. She put her hand on my forehead and said that she knew that I was troubled about my blindness. She said that she understood what I was going through, but that it was going to be alright and to not be troubled anymore. Though I've never been what you might call a very religious man, I am spiritual, and I know now, years later, that it was the Blessed

Mother, Mary, who came to me that night because—and I tell you the truth—from that point on, not only was I was able to cope with my situation, but the answer of my salvation was close at hand.

Shortly afterwards, on one very cold winter day, a friend of my father, a fellow by the name of Tomas Pastorisa, came to our apartment with a brown paper bag tucked under his arm. He came in and said he had a gift for me. Little did I realize at the time that it was that answered prayer of redemption—that reprieve from a life sentence of loneliness and despair. It was a guitar.

Later, I would know that he had gotten it from a pawn shop with my dad, and that it was a small Stella worth about $10.00. No matter, for to me, it was beautiful! And, it was mine! It took me some time to learn how to tune it, and being a steel string guitar, my fingers would bleed in my attempt to make it sound the way I heard it play in my head. But slowly, after the hours upon hours had turned into days and the days had turned into weeks and the weeks into months, my guitar became the answer to my question, "What will I be?" I will be a *musician!*

The guitar, from that point on, truly and absolutely became my better half, my consoler and my best friend. I remember that I would come home from school eager to practice and literally, wouldn't stop until I'd fall asleep. On many occasions, my mother would find me with my guitar in my arms, having played it well into the night, until I'd lose consciousness. There were many times, especially during the summer, where I would practice for fourteen hours a day!

Soon enough, I brought my guitar to school and played during lunchtime, then after school and all weekend long. I was invited to play at the school assemblies, then at birthday parties and family gatherings of all kinds. I finally felt as though I had something to offer, something that defined who I was… a musician!

This little Stella showed me that I was, after all, a bone fide musician—a guitarist! And because of it, I saw a way out of the loneliness of being blind, and the isolation of never having fit in as a child. But if I had been asked at that time what I thought was going to happen to me, I don't think I would have imagined that a simple piece of wood would ultimately lead me to do all of the miraculous things that I have done over the years. I often say that the guitar has been my passport to travel the world to see places and people that I never could have, otherwise. It truly has been my personal miracle; my deliverance and a dream come true.

Visit Jose Feliciano at www.josefeliciano.com

Rick Foster

THE FAITHFUL GUITAR

The music of Chet Atkins and Andrés Segovia was the spark that ignited an uncontrollable desire in me to play fingerstyle guitar. It was this drive that eventually led to the purchase of a guitar that came to be known as *Excellent*—a misnomer if there ever was one.

I acquired Excellent slightly used in about 1966 from Ontario Music in Ontario, California, where I had taken my first teaching job several years earlier. Since enrolling that year as one of the first two guitar majors at Cal State Fullerton, I'd been borrowing a classical guitar from the school, which had to be one of the worst guitars I've ever played. I had to suffer through several performances on it before purchasing Excellent. About that time I ordered a José Oribé classical, which arrived in May of 1968.

Prior to that time I'd been playing an old Gibson Les Paul, a Fender Jaguar, and a Gibson ES355. I recall with some embarrassment attempting to play a Fernando Sor study on an electric for my audition as a classical guitar major. I used a thumb pick, which seemed to amuse the faculty all the more. Needless to say, this kind of music was not well suited to steel strings, so Excellent was purchased in hopes of learning to play like Segovia.

After the Oribé guitar arrived, Excellent was demoted to the position of practice guitar. And since I do more practicing than performing, I've probably put more hours in on Excellent than all of my other guitars combined. Most of my original arrangements were worked out on Excellent, including *Jesu, Joy of Man's Desiring*

> I recall with some embarrassment attempting to play a Fernando Sor study on an electric for my audition as a classical guitar major. I used a thumb pick, which seemed to amuse the faculty all the more.

210

and three others that were eventually recorded by Christopher Parkening.

After teaching for several years, I decided to visit my cousin in New Haven, Connecticut. Since a Honda 450 was my only means of transportation at the time, I strapped a sleeping bag, tent, raincoat, and Excellent to various parts of the frame and headed across the country. How either of us survived the trip I'll never know. Poor Excellent was subjected to everything from intense desert heat to rough roads to downpours that soaked right through the case and left her drenched. The glue under the bridge came loose during that trip, probably because the wood under it warped so much, but the bridge held thanks to two screws that ran through the bridge and into the guitar. When I got to Connecticut, I ended up staying for two years, teaching the kids of Yale University professors how to play *Stairway to Heaven*. I also played in a musical production of *Man of La Mancha* given by the Yale drama department—my first experience in an orchestra pit. Since I needed a good guitar for the job, my folks shipped the Oribé guitar from California, and Excellent was once again demoted to practice guitar.

> I thought about giving her a fret job, but the grooves remind me of thousands of hours of finger exercises and thousands of hours on the road. They tell a story that new frets would erase forever.

It was so cold in New Haven that I used to put a hot plate under the chair as I practiced in my third floor room. Excellent tolerated this well, but the Oribé couldn't withstand the dry air and cracked along the top, necessitating a bus and subway ride into the heart of New York City to have the crack repaired. (I remember climbing a rickety flight of stairs, passing barred windows, and waiting for the owner of the shop to open the barred door.)

During our two years in New Haven I would frequently strap Excellent to the motorcycle and head for the beach, where we spent many hours together on the tar covered sand looking out over the Atlantic at all the ships coming from and going to who knows where.

Whenever Christopher Parkening was in the area for concerts, we would make a point of getting together. Often I would pick him up from the airport. We spent many hours together driving to concerts all over New England. Occasionally he would pick up Excellent and make her sound like a million bucks. Over the years Excellent has been played by other great players, but none could make her sing like Christopher.

On one of his trips to Connecticut, Chris introduced me by phone to John Sutherlin from Sutherlin's House of Guitars in Atlanta, Georgia. John offered me a teaching position, so I sold my 450 Honda, bought a car, and headed for Georgia. It was in Georgia that I began playing in restaurants including "Dante's Down the Hatch" in underground Atlanta and "The Abbey" where all the waiters dressed like monks.

From Atlanta, Excellent and I traveled to Colorado where we lived for two years in ski resorts. I played dinner music for two summers at the Casa Che restaurant in Snowmass at Aspen and one winter at the Crested Butte Lodge just over the hill from Aspen. We once again found ourselves living in hotel rooms, so for the sake of peace and quiet—Excellent is not a loud guitar—and to avoid wearing out the strings on my performing guitar, Excellent took the brunt of the six or so hours that I played each day. From there we lived for several months in the Hilton Hotel in Columbia, Missouri, and the Chase Park Plaza Hotel in St. Louis before embarking for Santa Barbara where we stayed for several years and met my wife Wendy.

By now Excellent was beginning to really show some wear. Her frets were very deeply grooved, especially frets one through eight on the treble side, which makes me wonder if guitarists play more on the treble strings or if the trebles by nature cause more wear than the basses. I thought about giving her a fret job, but the grooves remind me of thousands of hours of finger exercises and thousands of hours on the road. They tell a story that new frets would erase forever.

Since Wendy and I have been married we've spent close to 2,000 hours traveling to and from concerts with her driving and me sitting on the passenger side of the van practicing on Excellent. During these trips Excellent has never been in a case. In fact she's never had her own case since the one she came with disintegrated on our cross country motorcycle trip. She still stands or lays around the house, ready for anything. I'm still working out new tunes on Excellent. In fact, just today I sat with her on our front porch overlooking the garden and mountains and worked out John Standefer's arrangement of *In the Sweet Bye and Bye*. Even though she's not as worn as Willie Nelson's guitar, she's seen fire and rain and everything in between. Excellent doesn't much resemble what she was thirty-seven years ago, but then neither do I. Age has taken quite a toll on us both, and yet I can't help thinking that we've got a few good miles and a few good songs left to go. She probably wouldn't bring over $30.00 in a pawn shop, but

> Excellent doesn't much resemble what she was thirty-seven years ago, but then neither do I. Age has taken quite a toll on us both, and yet I can't help thinking that we've got a few good miles and a few good songs left to go.

money can't buy memories, which is really about all she's worth anymore.

A few years ago I took Excellent to see Orville and Bob Milburn, my favorite guitar makers here in Oregon, in hopes that they would help her play in tune. The top between the sound hole and bridge has sunken in from tension, causing the bridge saddle to lean forward and throw her badly out of tune. My kids were collecting stickers at the time, and had placed an "Excellent" sticker on her head right next to a smiley sticker they'd put there earlier to replace the worn out one a student of mine had stuck on her head twenty-five years ago in Santa Barbara. During our visit Bob Milburn started calling the guitar Excellent and the name stuck.

> The history of Excellent corresponds to my life history as a fingerstyle guitarist—the story of her life is the story of my life.

The history of Excellent corresponds to my life history as a fingerstyle guitarist— the story of her life is the story of my life. The longest we've been apart was a little over a month when I traveled to Europe to look at guitars and other things with a fellow guitar teacher and his wife from New Haven. Like a good wife, Excellent will be with me forever or until death do us part. Although there's no way of knowing, there may not be another guitar that has produced more sacred music than Excellent. In this world Excellent will probably outlive me, but she'll eventually disappear forever. Even so, I believe that the music we've worked on together will live forever in the lives of those who have in some way been touched by the sacred music we've given to them. Who knows, maybe the music has served to draw someone closer to Jesus, who taught us that the path to greatness, peace, and eternal life is a path of service. Excellent has served me well.

Visit Rick Foster at www.rickfosterguitar.com

There are two major impediments to learning the fingerboard:
1) Unlike the piano, the strings are not marked; 2) We learn
chords as isolated forms, without understanding why
they look the way they do.
—*Howard Morgen*

Doyle Dykes

A WHITE ROSE FOR HEIDI

Some time ago, Bob Taylor approached me with some interesting ideas for a new electric-acoustic stage guitar. In time those discussions yielded what has become the Doyle Dykes Signature Model Guitar, Taylor's best selling signature model. One particular design detail, though, would be the final flourish on what, for me, has become a dream come true: a single white rose beautifully inlayed on the guitar's headstock. And wherever my musical travels take me, I always tell the story behind the white rose.

In 1980, I moved my family to our home state of Florida after leaving the Grandpa Jones show in Nashville to follow my desire to play concerts in churches. I came home late one night from a show, and my wife, Rita, met me at the door with our two young daughters, Holli and Heidi. After giving me a hug and a kiss, she put Holli in my arms and said, "Good night… they're yours now. Have fun!" I played with the girls, age two and four at that time, for a couple of hours before putting them to bed at about 2:30 AM. I started to say a quick little prayer with Holli, but she fell fast asleep before the "Amen." I went over to Heidi's twin bed across the room and repeated the prayer, kissed her good night, and turned back only to see that she was wide awake. I returned to her bedside and said, "Heidi, it's very late, but was there something special you wanted to ask God for?" She answered, "There is one thing I've been thinkin' about: I've never had a rose of my own, and I've always wanted one." I thought, "always wanted one"—all those years! Four! "Do you think God would bring me one?" she asked. I said, "Heidi, what do you think?" She said, "I think God can do *anything*, Daddy!" So we asked God for a rose.

I left the room wishing that I had someone to pray with in such a child-like manner. At that moment, I turned around, sensing in my heart, that I did have someone I could pray with—Heidi. Admittedly, I felt a little strange asking a four year old to pray with me—a mature adult, a husband, and her father! But I obeyed that feeling in my spirit, and knelt beside her bed and with a little difficulty, I began to say something like, "Heidi, do you believe God can…" and before I could speak another word, Heidi spoke out, "God can do *anything*, Daddy!" She said it again, just like before, and I thought to myself, *I know that, but I needed to hear it again.* You see, I had been carrying a heavy burden in my heart for awhile then. Among other things, we needed a bigger home, and so I shared that with Heidi. After we prayed, I felt as though a heavy weight had been lifted from my shoulders. Unfortunately, though, with all the things on my mind, I forgot about Heidi's rose.

The next day I took the kids to the "Treaty Oak" in Jacksonville—an 800-year-old oak tree where the Spanish signed treaties with the Indians many years ago. The city of Jacksonville made a beautiful little park of the area that included a rose garden. They were the most beautiful red roses you could have imagined. Oddly enough, it didn't jog my memory about Heidi's wish for a rose.

Later that evening at prayer time, as we were beginning to pray, Heidi became upset. Her lips began to quiver and her eyes began to tear up. "What's wrong Heidi?" I asked. "How come God didn't bring my rose to me today? Do you think he forgot?" Suddenly I remembered the Treaty Oak rose garden! I said, "Remember all the beautiful roses in the park today? God made those for you and he made them for me just so we could enjoy them today!" It sounded pretty good to me, but Heidi didn't buy it. She said, "If they were ours, then why didn't you pick one for me?" I explained, "Because there was a sign that said *Please don't pick the roses—City of Jacksonville.*" Heidi said, "But Daddy, I want one I can hold in my hand!"

The scripture suddenly came alive to me in Hebrews 11:1: *Now Faith is the substance of things hoped for, the evidence of things not seen.* I said, "Heidi, we didn't mention the color of the rose…" She answered, "Is that why he didn't bring it? Did he need to know the color?" I explained that maybe he did! "Well, then," she said, "I've been thinking of a white one. Let's ask him again!" Heidi reached out her little hand and took mine, and the scripture then came to mind from Matthew 18:19 where Jesus said, "If two of you shall agree on earth as touching anything that they shall ask, it shall be done for them by my Father who is in Heaven." As I shared this with Heidi, she said, "Well, I agree Daddy!"

Needless to say, I did not forget about Heidi's rose after that! In fact, it was difficult to go to sleep, and when I did wake up the next morning, my first thought was the white rose. I was scheduled to leave town that day for a concert a few hours away, and I couldn't help but think of calling the florist down the street, or asking a friend to drop one by, but I didn't. I wanted Heidi to know it was "Him," and not me.

After my concert, I started packing up my guitars and equipment. The Pastor was in the foyer talking to an older couple whom I supposed to be the last ones there. Suddenly, I heard a voice asking, "Are you Doyle Dykes?" I thought it was an odd question to ask, considering I had just finished a concert there. I bit my sometimes sarcastic tongue, and just said yes. She walked slowly up to the stage area with a slender aluminum foil package in her hand. "I was in my garden today," she said, "and God told me to bring this to you Mr. Doyle Dykes." By this time, I could see that this little lady was "special." Although she was perhaps in her thirties, she was still a little girl. I asked, "God told you to bring me that?" "Yes," she answered. "I was in my garden today and God told me to bring this to you from my garden." She handed me the carefully wrapped foil package. "Thank you so much," I said. "I'll certainly enjoy eating this from your garden." She said, "Well, I don't think you should eat it. You'd better look at it." She stood there watching me as I opened the little package where inside I found a single white rose.

> I stood there amazed as she left, watching her every step. I was waiting for her to fade away, thinking perhaps she was an angel.

I couldn't believe what I was seeing. It was truly a miracle that I was holding in my hands. It was as though the Lord had allowed me to be a part of this event not only for Heidi's sake, but for my benefit, as well. Suddenly I felt ashamed. "Yes," I told her. "God did tell you to bring me this rose." I told her about Heidi's prayer, and that God had chosen her to bring it. "Well, that's nice," she said, as she turned and walked away. I stood there amazed as she left, watching her every step. I was waiting for her to fade away, thinking perhaps she was an angel. But she didn't. She had been attending that church for many years, and everyone knew her and knew that she was special. Indeed, she was!

I kept the little rose in a vase all night, and then wrapped it again in its original aluminum foil package and headed home. When I pulled up in the driveway, Heidi ran out to meet me. She climbed up into my van and gave me a big hug. "I'm glad you're home Daddy," she said. I reached over and handed her the little package and said, "Here's a present for you, Heidi!" Without any hesitation or doubt, she saw the package and said, "He brung it, didn't he Daddy!" She got so excited and ran through the house saying, "Mommy, Mommy, Mommy! God brung my rose to me today!" I can still hear her little voice crying out those words, and the slam of the screen door, while she so excitedly shared the news with my wife.

Maybe by this time, you've forgotten about my prayer for a bigger house that night when it felt as though the weight of the world was on my shoulders. We got our home. It's funny, though—I couldn't tell you the address of that house today. We've moved a number of times since then. Houses come and go. And the things that seemed so important then have been banished into forgetfulness. But the white rose I'll never forget. In some ways, this little incident changed my life. I wrote a song about it, *White Rose for Heidi*, and had the opportunity to record it with an orchestra. And of course, it adorns the headstock of my Taylor guitar model.

Heidi's all grown up now. She's a nurse anesthetist and she still loves white roses.

Visit Doyle Dykes at www.doyledykes.com

It all seems a pity at first, for I have overcome a fiercely anti-Catholic upbringing in order to attend Mass simply and solely to escape Protestant guitars. Why am I here? Who gave these nice Catholics guitars?
—*Annie Dillard*

Eliot Fisk

GUITAR DIVINE

The birth of my only brother, Matthew, when I was three, was probably the defining event in my life, and probably also the reason I was destined (or damned, depending on your perspective!) to become an artist. Matthew was born with Down's Syndrome, caused by an extra Y chromosome on the 21st pair of chromosomes, the result being mental retardation. In 1957, the year of his birth, not much was available in the way of early detection, let alone proper care and support for middle class families with Down's Syndrome children. In fact, it wasn't until Matthew was more than a month old that my parents received confirmation of his condition.

It was a tremendous family challenge to try to find proper care for Matthew, a problem that grew until as time went on the agonizing decision was made to institutionalize him, although he continued to come home most weekends. It was this psychic wound, ritually reopened several times a month, that caused me to have not just a desire to make music, but a psychological necessity to do so. Looking back I realize that it was the only way I could deal with the situation in which our family found itself, without going insane.

Nonetheless, during the early years before Matthew went away to school, it occurred to my mother that one thing we might do as a family could be to sing songs to the accompaniment of a guitar. God knows what impulse moved her to send my father out with orders to buy a guitar, but he returned from this little outing with a $60 guitar, and, because he had played one in college, also a $40 banjo—neither of these specimens was very good, as you might imagine.

Nonetheless, I started playing the banjo, but, of course, it was a very bad banjo, and perhaps a banjo was anyway not the ideal instrument for a seven year old. After a month of very sore fingers and equally bruised eardrums, I picked up the guitar. In short order I was teaching myself to play with the help of a two-record set and book. I remember playing *Home on the Range* in A Major and learning a few basic chords from the diagrams in the book. When three months later I was still picking away at the guitar, my parents offered me the chance to take lessons. I remember thinking that the chance to have private guitar lessons at extra expense was very near to being a frivolous luxury.

Roger Scott, a member of our Quaker Meeting in Philadelphia, was the principle double bass player in Eugene Ormandy's Philadelphia Orchestra. Asked for advice about what to do with me, Roger told my parents that, if I were going to play the guitar, I should play classical guitar. He asked around and was referred to practically the only person in Philadelphia at that time with any real credentials, a man named Peter Colonna, who had actually taken some summer classes with Andrés Segovia at the famous summer course at the Academia Chigiana in Siena, Italy. (When a couple of summers ago I myself had the honor of teaching a seminar there, I really felt that things had come full circle!)

Although Colonna was not a demanding teacher, he did his part to bring the music of Segovia into my life. And Segovia's guitar just got to me, captured me hook, line, and sinker. Even though I didn't practice that diligently (I would go an entire week without taking the guitar out of the case!) the guitar was beckoning. It seemed to speak of another world—a more elegant, wonderful, magical world than the one we inhabited in our every day life, and I wanted to find out what that world was about.

It wasn't until I was eleven that I got serious about the guitar. Again it was a chance occurrence that impelled this change of heart. My father decided to use his sabbatical year from the Wharton School at the University of Pennsylvania to exchange jobs, houses, and countries with a Swedish colleague. Thus, after a nine-day boat trip to Sweden, during which I had my first experience of sea sickness, we arrived for ten months in the southern Swedish city of Lund where I attended a Swedish elementary school. I spoke not more than a few words of Swedish when I entered, and although the kids were nice to me, I still felt isolated and alone a lot of the time. For lack of anything better to do, I began to practice the guitar. Also for the first time, at the insistence of my Swedish guitar teacher, Gunnar Rosen, I even stopped biting my nails (at least on the right hand) and began to play with fingernails.

> That's the way it was at that time: Segovia was like the Pope and you just waited for the latest encyclical to come down.

When we came back from Sweden, I was fluent in Swedish and also more advanced on the guitar. I then began to study with a man named William Viola—the only serious regular guitar teacher I have ever had in my life. He was an engineer at IBM but taught guitar on the weekends. A very smart, disciplined man, he was also a very demanding teacher. He had taught himself many of Segovia's tricks by listening to the records thousands of times. That's the way it was at that time: Segovia was like the Pope and you just waited for the latest encyclical to come down. When it did, you rushed out and tried to figure out how the old man was achieving all these wonderful results.

So with Viola came a disciplined approach to the guitar. He demanded excellence from me, requiring me to keep and maintain a list of my repertoire. Every week he would go down the list and make check marks, marking five or six difficult pieces to be prepared for the following week's lesson. When I played, he was extremely demanding, not allowing any dirty notes. In the two years I studied with Viola in Philadelphia, he never gave me an outright compliment. If something was good, he'd say, "All right, what's next?" and I would then continue to the next difficult piece he had assigned me. I was determined to prove to him that I was worth something, and I started to practice in earnest. By the time I was fourteen, I was getting up of my own volition every morning at 5:00 in the morning. My parents, if anything, were trying to discourage my driving myself so hard. I remember my father asking me not to practice the loud parts of Albeniz's *Leyenda* at that hour because the sound would travel up through the heating vents directly into his bedroom! But I continued setting the alarm clock for 5:00 in the morning, and by 5:15, I would already be practicing.

> I've done many things in my life, but nothing has challenged me more in purely intellectual terms than playing contrapuntal music on the guitar.

After two hours of practice, I would go upstairs and basically inhale breakfast before running down the street to catch the school bus. I'd be in school till 3:30 or 4:00. I'd get home and practice another hour and a half or so. Then I'd eat dinner, do my homework, and set the alarm for the next morning and start all over again. I did that through all my high school years without any teacher to guide me. In my high school of 1,500 kids I was aware of no one who was this serious about classical music. This was really marching to the sound of your own drummer. But that work laid the foundation for the whole basis of my future technique.

During the summers beginning in 1970, I also took summer classes, most especially with Oscar Ghiglia at the Aspen Music School. For me, these classes were reality and everything else was treading water, waiting for the next summer to come around. Finally in 1974, when I was a sophomore at Yale, I played for the first time for Segovia in his hotel (always the Westbury!) in New York City. That's when the tremendous association that we had from then until his death fifteen years later began.

Looking back now, it all makes sense, but at the time it seemed liked the most impossible thing—really something unusual. Nowadays there is so much more information of every sort available, and it all flows so much more rapidly. Yet I still feel that those involved in art music as a whole need to work much harder to find people like the boy I once was to locate those kids in all social classes and ethnic groups who may not even come from musical families but who are or could fall hopelessly in love with music. We also need to do a much better job of communicating to nonmusicians about the beauty of music, and particularly the beauty of *making* music.

It's a great danger to a democracy when pushing a button on a machine becomes people's idea of what music is. I'd rather hear people playing music however imperfectly than have them think that the way music is made is by putting a CD in a CD player and pushing a button. I think that even *trying* to play music is good for people. Music—and particularly art music—has a lot to give to our country, particularly in this time of multiple challenges from within and without. Music challenges a person in such a way that he or she can't help but be better for it.

To do art music well, you have to be gifted in many ways. You have to have the physical coordination of a great athlete. On the classical guitar the right hand needs the elegance of a Michael Jordan and the left hand the power of a Shaquille O'Neill. Of course, in the case of the guitar, your fingers do the walking, but it is in purely phsycial terms extremely demanding. The two hands are doing totally different things simultaneously, yet they have to work together with perfection of a smoothly running machine at the service of the most subtle and continually evolving human emotions. In terms of tone production, you're dealing with five fingernails—the equivalent of five problematic oboe reeds, again five elements that need to dovetail perfectly.

The classical guitarist plays contrapuntal music. Again, this in and of itself presents an enormous intellectual challenge. Almost any particular passage can be fingered in seemingly endless ways. Think about the number of permutations that we're dealing with on the acoustic guitar! There are thousands and thousands of permutations! To pick the right one—or at least one of the several good possibilities—takes a great deal of work and concentration even for experienced players. And of course, one is continually revising and changing in the hope of improving what one has already done. I've done many things in my life, but nothing has challenged me more in purely intellectual terms than playing contrapuntal music on the guitar.

Another fascinating aspect of art music is that it reaches back into five or six centuries of history. This means that we have to know about all sorts of cultures different from our own. Familiarity with, or better yet, fluency in foreign languages is practically a prerequisite. Of course, where all the work is really leading is to the great, intangible, indefinable realm of spirituality, a final aspect to the great challenge of trying to be a good musician.

Something that is not commonly understood, however, is that these four big areas—the physical, intellectual, historical, and the spiritual—are of tremendous benefit in any society that aspires to be an effective democracy. To top it all off there are tremendous benefits in interpersonal skills that are necessary in any successful musical endeavor. In music (outside of the very strange and questionable institution of musical competitions) you're not dealing with winners and losers. The only way for the event to be a success is for a win-win situation to be created. A symphony orchestra is not going to get up on stage and play well if people are fighting—at the very least not while the members are onstage! They may hate each other offstage, but on the stage, the only chance for success is to subsume petty personal egotism to the great common good represented by the music.

> The fact is, in the world of art music we are selling a Rolls Royce at Chevy prices, and having difficulty selling it.

So I think society as a whole has a lot to learn from art music. Nonetheless, we musicians need to do a much better job of getting the word out. And I understand this isn't an easy thing to do in this culture. The fact is, in the world of art music we are selling a Rolls Royce at Chevy prices, and having difficulty selling it. But I'm convinced that the only reason for that is bad marketing. I know we can do a better job.

I try to take any opportunity to get this message out—particularly to young people. For this reason I have played all over the world in all manner of unconventional venues from churches to prisons, from juvenile detention centers to elite schools, from logging camps in southeast Alaska to palaces in Europe in an effort to (to borrow Milton's words from the invocation of *Paradise Lost*) "Justify the ways of God to man." One very important thing about this sort of "outreach" activity is that it needs to be part of a regularly ongoing program. When you do connect, the rewards can be astounding.

In the same way I try to transform the students who come to work with me. I'm not just interested in teaching them how to play the shit out of the guitar. I want to transform their lives! Students sometimes come to me with their entire demeanor suggesting a lack of self confidence: shoulders slumped, looking down at their feet, shy, and insecure. To see these same people grow and blossom into active, creative, empowered adults is a wonderful thing. As a teacher, I want to take their fear away, and I want to give them real ways of dealing with actual problems that they're going to face in life.

It remains a real worry of mine that people who come from nonmusical backgrounds may be slipping through the cracks—particularly since in the last twenty years, we've all but demolished good music education in the public schools of our country. That's something that no patriot should ever, ever acquiesce to. Anyone who loves this country and what it stands for has got to be for music in public education. You just can't come down on any other side of the issue. The research is so overwhelmingly in favor of the importance of music in education and what it does for young people. It doesn't matter what political party you're affiliated with, this ought to be a nobrainer. And we musicians who love music and care about music have got to do a better job convincing our fellow citizens. Quite apart from the great personal pleasure I derive from playing music, is this larger imperative.

I'm actually very proud that a few of my students haven't become professional musicians, that they have gone into business or have become fine doctors. Most of them, of course, *have* stayed in the field, and a number have become leading figures on many continents. Now some of them send their own students to me so that I have now become a "grandteacher." But even those who did not become professional musicians have been extremely well served by their music education, simply because music demands so much of a person at so many levels. If you can do music, almost anything else is going to be easy.

You can speak of talent, but talent also has something to do with a love for something. At a certain point, it's difficult to separate the two. When asked how he became so great, the great cellist and conductor Mtislav Rostropovich answered, "Maybe I loved music just a little bit more than some of my colleagues." I can certainly understand this sentiment. For me, music *hurts*. It's so beautiful that it hurts. And it pains me to play in a way that is not beautiful, or to make a note that is not beautiful or not true. It hurts me *physically*. And it's much more than a mere love for beautiful sounds. For me, music has an almost religious significance.

The best music of the western classical tradition is, for me, a communing with God. In fact, most of it was written with that in mind, particularly that of my favorite composer, Bach. There are very few of his pieces that are not religiously

> It remains a real worry of mine that people who come from nonmusical backgrounds may be slipping through the cracks—particularly since in the last twenty years, we've all but demolished good music education in the public schools of our country.

inspired—even when he writes purely instrumental music without text, Bach seems to be reflecting on some aspect of the Christ story. He was profoundly religious in the most beautiful sense of the term.

You might say that Bach's music compares to a lot of other music the way the Amazon rain forest still does to most of the forests most of us have experienced. In terms of the variety and richness of species, the beauty of the flora and fauna, the ratio in favor of the Amazon in comparison to the manmade replanted forests most of us know is about ten-thousand to one!

Great art music brings us very near to this manifestation of the Divinity that we can sense in this most wondrous part of our planet. Looking out into space, we look back into time and see light that is thousands of light years away. When we look into the microscope we see the astonishing richness and variety of the miraculous submolecular world that we're only beginning to discover. This same wonder is what attracts me to great music. I hold it in a similar awe and reverence. Great music inspires in me the passion to preserve and carry on the great tradition I have inherited from mentors like Segovia, the late composer Luciano Berio, the harpsi-chordist Ralph Kirkpatrick, with whom I worked at Yale, and many others too numerous to name. The guitar is my own little way of seeking what for want of a better word you might call the divine.

Visit Eliot Fisk at www.eliotfisk.com

Music is moral law. It gives a soul to the universe, wings to the mind, flight to the imagination, a charm to sadness, and a gaiety and life to everything. It is the essence of order and leads to all that is good, true, and beautiful.
—*Plato*

Muriel Anderson

MUSIC FOR LIFE

I t began with a string of crimes on Linmar Street, one-block long in the Green Hills area of Nashville, a reputably safe, family-oriented neighborhood. During a period of two weeks, virtually every night one of my neighbors had their house or car broken into. My next-door neighbor Margie kept an eye out at night and twice saw two thin teenage youths skirting around the bushes. Every time there was a break-in I called the police and asked them to put an extra watch on the street, or at least drive down the block once. However, regardless of whom I spoke to I got the same response: some combination of "Our funds have been cut back," or "We've been getting calls from all over the city," or "We don't have the staff to send a car to your area."

I flagged down a policeman in another part of town, and asked him what the problem was. He told me that 98% of the people they arrest for break-ins are actually on drugs at the time. Most of the police force they have left after the cutbacks were allocated to downtown, where the larger businesses are. Morale was so low in the police force that he was only counting the days to his retirement.

At that point, I began calling the mayor's office, my representatives, the juvenile court, the newspapers, and Channel 2 and Channel 5 News. I received polite letters back from the mayor's office and my representatives, and a call from Channel 5. The television news crew came to my house to do a story for the 6:00 news. They did a long interview and at one point asked, "What would you like to have happen as a result of this interview?" I joked, "Well, I'd like them to move on to another block! Actually, we need to fund the police force and at the same time fight the drug trade and support programs that would give youth alternatives to drugs."

That night I watched the news. It showed my neighbor who had simply had some change stolen from her car, then panned to my mailbox showing my address. The camera held on the street number, and a voice came on, "This woman, who lives at…" They gave my address and directions to my house, and then cut to me

225

in my living room saying simply, "I hope they move on to another block." The camera cut, and that was pretty much the end of the story. I could hardly believe it. Immediately, I called the police department. "It's me again. Before, I was concerned for our possessions, but now after watching the 6:00 news, I'm concerned about my personal safety! Please put an extra watch on my block." Channel 5 also apologized for their careless coverage, saying they didn't know until they aired the segment that I was a prominent performer, and they had just showed the entire city where I lived. That night I heard a car drive slowly down the block once. They had finally put a temporary watch on the block, and that was the last of any crime in the area to my knowledge for as long as I lived there.

Concurrent to this, I got a call from Andy Shookov, the head of the juvenile court, and we set up a meeting. Andy also invited one of the prominent leaders in the black community to join us. Over tea and scones we discussed the roots of the situation. I wanted to know what I, as a musician and a citizen, could do to hit at the foundations of the problem—the crime that was perpetuated by drugs, which was perpetuated by many factors, one of which was fewer alternatives to drugs, to combat the sense of futility and purposelessness. As the music programs had been cut back to nearly nonexistent in the lower-income public schools, I realized that perhaps I was in a unique position through my associations with the *All Star Guitar Night* and with the music community at large to create a program by which kids could learn the guitar and earn the right to keep their instrument. Harold Bradley of the Nashville Musicians Union offered his support and expertise, as did Jonah Rabinowitz, who heads up the W.O. Smith School of Music, a highly successful program in Nashville that teaches a variety of instruments to kids of low income families. I called Washburn guitars, and they agreed to donate as many instruments as necessary for the program. The kingpin in the program was Shookov's associations in local government that could actually implement the program in after-school centers across the city. All was coming beautifully into place, except for one variable. It was just before the elections, and unfortunately, Shookov lost the election that year, despite his profound dedication to his work. Without his energy, the entire program was scrapped. Or so I thought.

> I knew all so well that in the folk process, ideas often get passed around but authorship doesn't.

Several years later I was looking for an appropriate benefit for my annual Saturday-After-Thanksgiving show in Downers Grove, Illinois. I learned that the House of Blues in Chicago had begun a program very similar to the one I had envisioned in Nashville. I toured their facility, was impressed with the program, and coincidentally Washburn Guitars had donated their instruments, as well. They appreciated the help, and my friends at GHS also donated guitar strings that were much in need at the time.

It occurred to me that there must be some umbrella organization to unify and support all the grassroots efforts that have sprung up across the country to address the problem of the way access to playing an instrument has been disappearing from the schools and from the lives of the kids who most need it. In particular, I wanted my *All Star Guitar Night* show to benefit such a program. Finding no such organization, I decided that what was most needed was not another Music for Life program, but a Music for Life *Alliance*.

About a year or so later I was on concert tour passing through Santa Cruz, California, and was invited to stay with Jessica, an old friend I used to work with at the Old Town School of Folk Music in Chicago. She had married luthier Rick Turner, also a longtime friend who currently designs my pickups. Jessica coordinates a national program called *Guitars in the Classroom*. I thought it would be good to find out a bit more about her program, and to make sure it was a good match to receive a small grant from the Music for Life Alliance, which had just gotten up and running.

It was great to see Jessica again after so long. "What have you been doing all these years?" I asked. "I was hired by the International House of Blues Foundation to assist in the development of their *Make an Impression* guitar program." she told me. "They recently started a program at the House of Blues in Chicago." "Really?" I exclaimed. "I didn't know you designed the curriculum. They were the first recipient of what was to become the Music for Life Alliance. I was impressed at how much the program resembled one I had envisioned in Nashville." I looked in my laptop computer, and found I still had the old outline I had submitted to Washburn many years ago. I showed it to Jessica. "That looks very similar to the outline they gave me to work from!" she said. "Doesn't that make you wonder?!" I knew all so well that in the folk process, ideas often get passed around but authorship doesn't. "No, not at all," I said as I felt moisture welling up in my eyes. "You've helped to develop this idea into a flourishing program. I could have never done that. It's like a seed that I thought fell on the pavement, but instead, has grown into an orchard."

Visit Muriel Anderson at www.murielanderson.com

Playing scales is like a boxer skipping rope or punching a bag.
It's not the thing in itself; it's preparatory to the activity.
—*Barney Kessel*

Laurence Juber

A GUITAR WITH A SILVER LINING

I t started with a phone call from Jessica Turner. She is the founder of a program called *Guitars in the Classroom*, the creator of the *Smart Start Guitar* method for kids, and the wife of luthier Rick Turner.

She was calling with bad news, and was clearly upset. My immediate concern was for the welfare of Rick or one or other of the musicians who are our mutual friends. However, it transpired that Jessica was grieving over a guitar—a trashed guitar. A "six-stringed friend that was now only good for kindling."

A classroom at Soquel elementary school near Santa Cruz, California, had been vandalized, and Jessica's teaching guitar had been destroyed. The timing was especially frustrating, as she was putting together a new program to provide guitars for the kids and the teachers to use.

> "I certainly don't need another guitar, but it sounds like your school kids could use some. How many do you need?"

Technically, this was my instrument, being a prototype made for me by Taylor Guitars. I had loaned it to Jessica for a video shoot, and she had fallen in love with it (it sounded great in open-G tuning, her favorite) so I let her hang onto it. The school had insurance for this kind of thing, Jessica reassured me, and we would be able to replace the guitar, but she was concerned that I would take the loss badly.

I said, "I certainly don't need another guitar, but it sounds like your school kids could use some. How many do you need?"

"Twenty-one." I immediately called Ed Alves at Taylor Guitars and reported the untimely demise of the prototype. Ed agreed to write up a valuation for the insurance and, this being a one-of-a-kind piece, it had some additional intrinsic value. Then I told him that I would like to buy twenty-one Baby Taylor guitars. By coincidence, the cost was equal to the value of the "ex-instrument."

A few months later Jessica and I led a group of teachers strumming their new guitars in a rousing rendition of *Yellow Submarine*—in open-G tuning—with three-hundred eager kids singing along!

In the hands of the students, every guitar has its own personality and its own story. Some become famous instruments—Jimi Hendrix' white Strat, Eric Clapton's pyschedelic SG, Willie Nelson's Martin. Others exist as "objects d'art," treasured possessions, or simply workhorses. Ironically, the wanton destruction of our rough and ready prototype created a glorious opportunity for elementary school kids and their teachers. Its spirit lives on in their music-making.

Visit Laurence Juber at www.laurencejuber.com

Among God's creations, two—the dog and the
guitar—have taken all sizes and shapes in order
not to be separated from man.
—*Andrés Segovia*

Peter Huttlinger

THE ROAD TO WINFIELD

They say things happen for a reason, and I suppose they're usually right. I was driving from Nashville, Tennessee to Winfield, Kansas to compete in a guitar contest. I had made it almost all the way without any problems. No oil leaks, the CD player and the air conditioner both worked, and I hadn't made any wrong turns. Of course, making a wrong turn would be hard to do on this trip, since all I had to do was get on I-40, drive west for a lifetime and turn right in Oklahoma.

It was early in the morning, and I had all day to kill, so I got off the highway to enjoy a ride through the country. And I didn't mind when I realized that I had actually taken a wrong turn in El Dorado, Kansas, which took me about fifty miles out of my way. Truth be told, I'm great on an interstate highway, but I usually go the wrong direction out of my own driveway. I was in the town of Eureka by the time it dawned on me that I had to turn around and go back to El Dorado to get back on the road to Winfield.

On the way back to El Dorado I saw the most beautiful rainstorm. In Kansas the plains go on forever, so when you are driving through the farms and wheat fields you can watch a rainstorm that is miles away on one side of you and on the other side it's nothing but blue skies and puff clouds. This was a new sight for me, because in Tennessee, if you see rain, you're wet. Eventually the highway led me inside the storm and the sight there was spectacular, because I could still look out and see the blue skies in the distance all around me. The rain was falling hard on the windshield, but I kept my window down as I drove so I could continue looking beyond the storm.

That's when I saw the car in the ditch. All at once there were several thoughts running through my mind. The first of which was that even though there wasn't much traffic on the road, I couldn't believe someone hadn't stopped to help. In the city, I could understand it; folks are always in a hurry to get somewhere. They don't

230

have time to stop and say hello and, as much as I hate to see it, they often don't have time to stop and help someone in a stranded car. But out here in the country where people always have time to stop and ask about family or talk about the weather or share the latest gossip, it surprised me. It was a long way to the next town—a long way to the next anything for that matter—and whoever was in the car would surely need a ride.

My second thought was the hope that the folks in the car were not hurt. As I turned my Jeep around and headed to offer my assistance, it occurred to me that things happen for a reason, and maybe this is why I made a wrong turn back in El Dorado. It's nice to help folks out when they need it.

I put on a hat and a flannel shirt, since it was still raining, and hurried over to the car. I could see someone in the car but he wasn't moving at all. I thought, "My God, he's dead!" But right away I saw that the windows were fogged up and that who ever was inside the car had to be breathing. Gerald Merwin was alright. He was a farmer and I guessed him to be in his late fifties or early sixties. But hard working folks can surprise you; he could have just as easily been seventy-five. He said he was going too fast to make his turn and wound up in the ditch. I offered him a ride. He had planned to wait until the rain stopped but now that I was there, a ride sounded like a good idea. As we drove the mile and a half down the muddy road to his farmhouse, we talked about how to get his car out of the ditch and about Winfield. He'd heard of the festival but had never been there. He's got a band that plays once a week at local retirement homes. (Then a thought occurred to me—when you live in the middle of nowhere, how far can you go and still consider it local? He could be driving fifty or sixty miles to play for the old folks.) Mr. Merwin said his band isn't very good but that the old folks like it when they come and play. I supposed that they were just about as good as they needed to be—and that was good enough. I told him so. And I'm sure the band probably enjoyed playing as much as the old folks enjoyed hearing them.

> I was a good guitar player but, at that moment, half of my brain wasn't sure what a guitar was, half my brain knew but couldn't remember how to play, and the third half was dreaming of fly-fishing somewhere far away from the stage.

After I dropped Gerald Merwin at his house, I drove to Winfield and entered the contest I had come for. My number was called and I got nervous when I sat down to play. I was a good guitar player but, at that moment, half of my brain wasn't sure what a guitar was, half my brain knew but couldn't remember how to play, and the third half was dreaming of fly-fishing somewhere far away from the stage. I played poorly. I didn't even place, but I had a good time just the same. I met some great folks, and we played all night at my campsite.

The next morning, after driving most of two days and sleeping on the ground all night, my back was killing me. So much so that I decided to leave the festival early and head for home. So I packed up my guitar and my wounded pride, a bottle of Advil for my back, and I hit the road. I had over seven-hundred miles to drive to get home and a lot of time to think. I had come a long way to compete and I thought a lot about how to come back and win. What did I do wrong? Why did I get so nervous? I had played professionally all my life, but I'd never competed before. That was it. Never had every single note meant so much before. The judges were listening closely and heard every nuance. Every finger squeak. Every muted note. Everything. And so did I. The problem was that when I heard them they were magnified a hundred times and I lost confidence. I had to learn to play through that next time.

Then it dawned on me that maybe I didn't just take a wrong turn in El Dorado for a reason, maybe my whole trip was for a reason. It's a long way to go to help a guy out of a ditch, but I drove the rest of the way home with a smile on my face.

Visit Peter Huttlinger (who did return to Winfield to win the contest) at www.petehuttlinger.com

I think there is a certain melodic core to what I do that
can't be changed. Believe me, there have been many,
many times in as many years when I wished that I didn't
write the way I do. But I think it's me.
—*Paul Simon*

John Standefer

A WINDFALL AT WINFIELD

At the urging of my friends Todd Hallawell and Pat Kirtley, I decided to enter Winfield's National Fingerpicking Championship Contest in September of 2002. I began in the early spring to develop arrangements and practice fairly regularly, but as the time drew closer, I started to develop tendonitis in my right forearm. And for the first time in decades, I actually began getting nervous. I can't remember *ever* getting nervous just practicing— and a month before a contest! The combination of nerves and the pain in my arm was getting to me by the time September rolled around, but I persevered. I knew that if I could just win this contest, the title would do a lot to inspire more people to turn out for my concerts and workshops. So after completing a show in Garden City, Kansas, I found the hood of my rental car pointing across the state to Winfield, the best part of a day's drive away.

The conflicts I had been feeling concerning the upcoming event began to weigh on me during the first hour of the silent drive. I began a sort of prayer-conversation with God. I needed a good listener—not to mention some answers. I was questioning things like why I was doing this, if it was just a pride trip, and where this all was leading. And of course, what about the pain in my arm? I couldn't play more than fifteen minutes without hurting. And on top of it all, I was nervous as a cat.

Then came some answers. It was as though God had said to me it's time to shut up and listen: "Are you kidding? Why wouldn't you win? Just keep driving." I finally began to relax, and made the decision to not sweat it. I'd just try to enjoy the experience while it lasted. When I got to Winfield, I actually practiced very little. More than anything, I jammed and hung out with friends.

When the time came to draw numbers and get down to business, I drew No. 7. A good sign, I thought! Then I heard my number called. I was just nervous enough to keep focused, but not enough to instill panic. I began playing my first tune, *I Am a Pilgrim*. I was really smoking along through the first half or so, feeling confi-

233

dent and playing well. Then I came to an accented note, dug in, and broke my third fingernail completely off. I continued to play as I watched it fly across the stage.

I didn't fall completely apart, but without that nail, my three-finger picking patterns sounded like an engine cylinder missing; every third note simply wasn't there. I had to rearrange the fingering and the order of the tune, and fake my way to the end. It was a nightmare. I've never had a fingernail break like that in my life—and I had just begun having an acrylic coat put over my nails to strengthen them to avoid any possibility of breakage. I couldn't believe it. But then an even worse thought passed through my mind: "I still have to play a second tune," which was *Paper Moon*—the toughest of the four tunes I had prepared to play. But I just plowed through it with a "show must go on" attitude. When I finished playing I thought,

> Then I came to an accented note, dug in, and broke my third fingernail completely off. I continued to play as I watched it fly across the stage.

"Well, that was it." I had lost for sure. All that time and work and expense getting to Winfield was shot. I left the stage practically dragging my guitar behind me. I then did what you're never supposed to do in a competition: I went out and watched the rest of the lineup play—hours' worth of them.

At an intermission Todd Hallawell found me and said, "Okay, we have a break. Let's go fix that fingernail." I thought, "What for?" but Todd was insistent. We went to his trailer and built a globby-looking acrylic nail. It was mighty thick, but at least it worked. Then I went back and watched the rest of the contest. While the fortieth and final contestant was playing, Todd found me again and asked where my guitar was. By then I knew that I wasn't going to make the cut, but Todd, who had been keeping an unofficial score sheet assured me that I was still in his top five. So I ambled over and got my guitar. I returned just in time to hear my number called. I couldn't believe I had made it! If I had thought there was a chance, I'd have been practicing, resting, eating correctly—anything but sitting out in the audience for hours. I suddenly realized that my hands weren't clean, I wasn't in tune, and I was the second of the finalists to play. I got back from the washroom and got tuned up just in time to be called back to the stage. No time to think. This was it.

I started with my original tune, *As a Little Child*, then went into the "clincher" finale—a slammin' hillbilly arrangement of *Man of Constant Sorrow*. I listened intently to the other players, and realized that it was anyone's guess as to who would win. The judges, in an unprecedented move, sent the top five players a note saying how close it was and that we were all great. But as it turned out, I ended up with the first place prize! I was so shocked that it took me days just to get happy about it. I had gone from the depths of despair to the heights of glory in just a few minutes. And I had also won a great Larrivee LV-10 for my trouble. God is good.

Visit John Standefer at www.praiseguitar.com

RIP-OFF ARTISTS

If you learn from other stringed instruments, you can learn more about your own stringed instrument. Fot me, the banjo is a terrific influence. You can steal this lick off a banjo, you can steal that lick off a banjo. You can steal all this stuff from banjo players—and they won't mind!
—*Adrian Legg*

I've shamelessly helped myself to everything around me.
—*Harvey Reid*

Bob Bennett

THANKIN' THE LORD FOR MY FINGERS

It seems almost all of my life
I've held onto this piece of wood
And sometimes I am tempted to think
It's the only time that I can do any good
Sometimes when I stand up to play
I am a lonely and desperate man
These songs are the only prayers I can pray
And I sing them just as hard as I can *

For as long as I can remember, I have never been very far away from a guitar. At first it was simply listening to my older brother's record collection: The Kingston Trio, Peter, Paul & Mary, The New Christy Minstrels, Gordon Lightfoot. To be sure there was also some bluegrass, flamenco, jazz, and bossa nova—even some early Shel Silverstein music—in the mix. This was mostly during what Martin Mull referred to as "…that great folk music scare of the sixties—when that stuff almost caught on!" I suppose I missed a lot, too. I'm more than a little embarrassed to just now be carefully excavating, dusting off, and analyzing all the songs on *Blood on the Tracks*. A little bit like presuming to be interested in painting and then suddenly checking out that "new" Rembrandt guy!

At about age ten, my parents brought me back a scaled-down guitar from a trip south to Tijuana, and my older brother Michael immediately began teaching me how to play. Already Mike had been taking me to concerts (remember the actual folk/bluegrass hootenannies, anyone?), and that live music made an incredible impression on me. The first two songs I learned were *This Land is Your Land* and *Tom Dooley*. The best piece of advice he gave me, though, was to keep strumming with my right hand, even if it took way too long to get my fingers to change chords with the left hand. When my left my hand improved, it actually started to sound

236

like music. And that was the ball game.

Music, on records and live, was my window into a larger world. I was ten years old, I lived in a totally white bread town where everybody clapped on one and three instead of two and four, and I was what they called a "husky" kid (still am, I'm afraid). Eventually it worked out that my most effective rejoinder for being a social outcast, not being picked for the team, and all the usual conflagrations and peer terrorism of childhood, was to grab my guitar, start playing, and say, "Well, yeah, but can you do *this*?" I think psychologists call this consolidation, the idea being that you try to compensate for your deficiencies, real or perceived, by simply getting as good as you can at "that one thing."

I went through a brief flirtation with a swap meet electric guitar, and like many unfortunate acoustic players, I found out that I play electric guitar just like an acoustic player: I suck! But as the '60s threatened to turn into the '70s, I was most swayed by singer-songwriters. Not only for the songs, but because nearly all of them were guitar players. People who played self-contained, imaginative, and "I can hardly believe it's one guitar" accompaniment to their songs. Stephen Stills, Paul Simon, James Taylor, Bruce Cockburn, Joni Mitchell, Dan Fogelberg, John David Souther, Stephen Bishop, to name a few. Later, I discovered Pierre Bensusan, a guy who apparently simply couldn't be bothered with the fact that it was just one guitar. In his hands, it a flippin' orchestra! Years later when I met Pierre at a Southern California house concert, I thanked him for not being omnipresent so that the rest of us lesser players could still have jobs.

Although I enjoy all kinds of guitar playing, I have a special soft spot for a guitar in service to, and support of, a great song. A solo guitar in the hands of an artist is, perhaps, the most reliable test of a song. If it can stand on its own two feet with a guitar and vocal, that means something.

David Wilcox is one of the most distinguished practitioners of "all by myself with a guitar" music. I've heard him speak along the lines of the guitar being something that literally beckons us to discover and give shape to music and ideas that are, perhaps in some mystical fashion, waiting in store—a little like the traditional Christian sacrament of the Eucharist, where grace is believed to be conferred through bread and wine regardless of your full understanding of the mechanics involved. Whether the guitar itself actually has something to bestow, or whether there is simply a wonderful and reliable alchemy that occurs when a guitar is placed in creative human hands, I suppose I don't really need to know.

> Later, I discovered Pierre Bensusan, a guy who apparently simply couldn't be bothered with the fact that it was just one guitar.

A little late in my guitar-playing life, I've also come to appreciate the work of guitar builders. Some years ago, I met my friend and world-class artisan Kevin Ryan. Each year, in conjunction with the National Association of Music Merchants convention, he hosts a luthiers' dinner. Over the years, many of the well-known and less-well-known guitar builders have dropped by the annual event. Kevin has let me attend and eavesdrop on these occasions, even though I can't nail two boards together without injuring myself. And it's fascinating to listen to the guys the guitars are named after: Bob Taylor, Jim Olson, James Goodall, Jean Larrivée, for example. And what do they talk about? Jigs, processes, and the occasional, "Have you tried *this*?" It's hilarious, because you know on one level they have a keen appreciation for what their instruments enable artists to do. But they're too busy to let that overtake the one-after-the-other tasks at hand.

One of the sweetest Cinderella stories I ever heard was Jim Olson talking about his early days as the clean-up/maintenance guy at a local church. As he tells it, he's already been building for years, but he doesn't quite yet have the nine-year waiting list. He's in the middle of cleaning toilets when a cordless phone rings. And it's Sting. Or James Taylor. Or Phil Keaggy. Amazing. But at the get-together, in between bites of tacos and cilantro pesto, everyone shares and shares alike, and all feed off the energy that comes from birds of a feather flocking together to talk shop.

When I visit Kevin's shop, it's easy to sense that it's *never* just about wood and measurements and skill; there is clearly something inherently good and right being done there. There is a sacred awareness of all of the songs that will be written and played and sung using those instruments.

And I have been a grateful beneficiary of these many labors. As a listener, I have been given an indelible soundtrack to accompany my years. As a player, each album was another volume added to the library of guitar school. So I extend my sincere thanks to all the players and songwriters (many of whom are represented in these pages) who have unknowingly mentored me through speakers and headphones. Paul Simon put the right words in Lincoln Duncan's mouth over thirty years ago:

> *I was playing my guitar*
> *Lyin' underneath the stars*
> *Just thankin' the Lord*
> *For my fingers* **

Visit Bob Bennett at www.bob-bennett.com

* "Singing for My Life" written by Bob Bennett, © 1991 Bright Avenue Songs (ASCAP)

** "Duncan" written by Paul Simon, © 1971 Paul Simon Music (BMI)

Earl Klugh

WITH A LITTLE HELP FROM MY FRIENDS

As I look back on it now, I can see the many connecting threads that have run through my musical life—friends, teachers, the many musicians that mentored me—so many people who at one time or another came alongside and helped me on my way. But the most significant of all was my mother; so much of what I enjoy in music and what I was able to do at a young age came through her.

I was thirteen when my dad passed away, leaving my mom to raise two young boys. I didn't really appreciate it then, but those weren't easy times for her; she really struggled to do all the things she did for me. But music was one area where we really connected, and she always made time for that; she knew I wanted to be a musician and was incredibly supportive. And we enjoyed the same musical tastes. She was from Mississippi and grew up listening to country music—she especially loved Patsy Cline. And through my dad, there was always jazz in the house: Count Basie, Harry Belafonte, and Errol Garner. So I was exposed to all of this music, and I had a love for it very early on.

> Chet's style of playing opened up a whole other world; I had never heard the guitar being playing like that.

Probably the one person who combined the best of both country and jazz like no other was Chet Atkins. And I would never have known about him had it not been for my mom. We'd watch a lot of the variety shows on TV together, and one night in January, 1967, we were watching the Perry Como Show. Chet Atkins was one of his guests that night. And though a lot of kids got turned on to the guitar watching TV one night in 1964, for me, the watershed was that 1967 Perry Como

239

show—it pretty much marked my destiny. That experience changed my life. I really enjoyed playing guitar, and even at that young age, I was pretty dedicated, but Chet's style of playing opened up a whole other world; I had never heard the guitar being playing like that.

The next day I bought a couple of his records. And like all of us back then, I learned to play guitar by listening to records, lifting the needle, and figuring out the licks. Shortly after watching that show, my mom bought my first electric guitar— a Gretsch Tennessean—just like the one Chet played.

When I was fourteen, my mom started taking me to Baker's Keyboard Lounge so I could hear the great players in person. On our first outing, we saw George Benson, and it was just amazing. It was also the start of my getting musically plugged in. At sixteen, I was offered a job at a local music store, teaching guitar after school to the younger kids in the neighborhood, and it was there that I met Yusef Lateef, who offered me an opportunity to record.

I was taking lessons at that time, as well. Jose Martinez was an excellent teacher. He played great fingerstyle, mostly Mexican folk styles, but he had really strong technique. He really pushed me hard to develop my right hand, and that really helped solidify my fingerstyle approach.

My mom would continue to take me to the clubs, sometimes a couple of nights a week, so I could watch the musicians— Kenny Burrell, Grant Green, Barney Kessel—all the great players. Once I got my driver's license, I could get there on my own and the club owner acted as my guardian. And during the off-season in winter, he would have me come in and play with my own little group. All these things were happening while I was still in high school!

I met countless people at Baker's Keyboard Lounge—Bill Evans, George Shearing, George Benson, Chic Corea. I was only seventeen, but I was on a first name basis with so many of them. And I ended up working with all of them on some level. I joined George Benson's band right out of high school, and toured with him for a year and a half, which really speeded up my education—the good and the bad about the road. It was the first time I had been away from home. And seeing the various cities and hanging out with the guys in the band made a pretty strong impression on me. And it's true that a lot of the jazz musicians were into drugs and alcohol. Most of them were straight, but even the ones that weren't would watch me like a hawk. I never did anything wrong—that was just totally taboo—but they did look out for me.

George Benson was just the greatest guy, and a bit of an older brother. Besides all the playing we did, he was very supportive—especially of my playing classical guitar. He first heard me play when I was seventeen, and he'd never seen a black kid play with that much classical influence. He liked that; he thought it was something different. At that time there really wasn't much going on in the way of acoustic jazz—the whole fusion thing was electric—but George really encouraged me to stay with the nylon string guitar. He said to me, "Earl, this is what you do. Just do it, it's going to work for you. You've got your own spin on things, so don't worry about what other people are doing—don't let that even cross your mind! Just keep going forward." So I did.

Even after I left his band, George would continue to look out for me. There was an all-guitar night at Carnegie Hall with Les Paul, Laurindo Almeida, Jim Hall—just a herd of guitar players. George called me up on a Wednesday and said, "Earl, what are you doing Friday night? You need to come out to New York. We're doing a big guitar show at Carnegie Hall, and I want you to be there; I want everybody to hear you." So these one-in-a-million things just seemed to keep happening. It was pretty remarkable.

> His level of playing was so extraordinary, and it showed me that to play at that level, you had to put in a lot of hours.

Working with George was a learning experience in so many ways. I was nineteen at the time, and we would play in clubs from 9:30 to 2:00—three long sets—and he then would go back to his room and practice some more. He would practice all the time! His level of playing was so extraordinary, and it showed me that to play at that level, you had to put in a lot of hours. I adopted that ethic because of his example. I would always practice too, but to practice like that when you were on the road was something that never would have occurred to me.

I also met Chic Corea at Baker's Keyboard Lounge. But it was through my friendship with his drummer, Lenny White, that I came to join his band. It was the first incarnation of Return to Forever in 1974 that featured Stanley Clarke on bass, Joe Farrell on reeds, and the Brazilian husband-and-wife team of percussionist Airto Moreira and singer Flora Purim. The band had a more acoustic, Latin-tinged sound, and the music was great. Billy Conners had left the band, and they knew they'd have a hard time replacing him. He was such a great player—every bit as good as Pat Martino. Then Lenny said to Chic, "What about Earl?" So thanks to Lenny, I had an opportunity to work with Chic.

I had to have a crash course on all of their music—we only had four days to get it together before we left for a four-week European tour. I was working on the music day and night trying to learn it. At that time it was a pretty big a feather in my cap, because Chic had one of the top groups at that time; all his sidemen went on to front their own bands. And though I was in Return to Forever for only a brief time, that association, along with my work with George Benson and George Shearing created enough interest in my work that when I started shopping my demo around I was able to get a record deal pretty quickly. But it was a different time then; the labels were really looking for people to sign to record deals. There was a lot more optimism about instrumental music. The seventies were a boom time.

But also at that point, I was really debating some things. I had been in George's band for a year and a half, and so I asked Chic for some advice. I had been accepted into a couple of colleges, and I wondered if I should go back to school for a couple of years or just try to continue with my music. Chic just looked at me and said, "Well, do you want to be a musician?" I told him yes, that's what I want to be. And he said, "Well, that's what you need to do." But when I asked him about college, he said, "Well, let's analyze it. What are you going to gain in college that's going to help you do what you're doing now? Think about that—you're in a really good position, things are starting to happen. But if there is something you need to gain from school to do this, then that's where you need to go. But whatever you choose to do, just do it to the full extent of what you can do. You can't be half way in or half way out. You've got to go for it."

> As far as the guitar was concerned, I wasn't going to let anything stop me—not even Stevie Wonder.

It's not that he talked me out of going to college; he really just helped me to focus in on what it was I really wanted to do. But coming from someone like that who also gave me the feeling that I had a real shot, it was pretty a powerful thing for me at that time.

I was disappointed when Return to Forever became the Electric Band, because that direction was not my calling; I couldn't play that new style with any real conviction; I'm not an electric player. So I was frustrated by the change—I didn't want that to end. But it did. Chic did alright, though—he brought Al DiMeola on, who was just nineteen at that time. So taking Chic's advice to heart, I decided it was time I really focused on my solo ideas.

As far as the guitar was concerned, I wasn't going to let anything stop me—not even Stevie Wonder, who almost immediately after I made this decision invited me to join his band! At that time he was on the threshold of becoming the biggest star in the world; he had that long string of incredible hits in the '70s. So naturally, I was tempted. But then I really started to think about it. The fact is I'm not a great electric player, or rhythm player for that matter. So I did something that probably a lot of people wouldn't have done: I told him that I was going to pursue a solo career, it's what I had to do, and I recommended David Miles, a great player who would be much better at this than me. That was a gamble for a twenty-one year old guy who didn't have a real job at that point! I just knew that I needed to. But I never burned a bridge; I ended up doing some recording work with Stevie, anyway. There's no question that it would have been a wonderful experience, but I knew it was going to take me in a direction that was different from the one that I ultimately wanted to go. And for me, it was the right decision.

The guitar has taken me all around the world so many times. My greatest vision was being able to play the guitar, to play the music that I loved, and make a living doing it. And because of so many people who supported me and opened doors, I've been able to do that—and I still do. I'm very thankful for that; I've been very fortunate. I'm especially fortunate to have had such a wonderful mother. She's the one who planted the seed, watered it, and nurtured it. She always believed in my music. And like the line from the Barbara Mahone poem about her mother, "Her music does not leave me."

Visit Earl Klugh at www.getaklugh.com

For him to be playing so much at nineteen, it scares me to
think about what he'll be doing in ten years.
—*George Benson (January, 1974)*

Frank Gambale

CLOSING THE CIRCLE

Although I had started playing guitar when I was seven, by the time I was seventeen, I decided that the guitar wasn't for me at all. While all my friends were listening to Led Zepplin, I had discovered Chic Corea. Already a jazz nerd, Chic's playing just blew me away. I gave up guitar and took up piano.

I went deep into Chic's music, transcribing his solo piano works, playing them, and really getting my stuff together on keyboard. My brother Nuncio, though, had other ideas. He was putting a new group together, and he wanted me to play guitar. "Frank," he said. "We don't want a piano player. Besides, you suck at the piano. Come and play guitar with us." Well, at that point, I thought that maybe I shouldn't throw away ten years of guitar playing, so I got back to it and decided to do both things.

The spell of Chic's music, though, continued its hold on me. I wanted to be closer to it. I wanted to somehow be a part of it. And I knew that I could have been the greatest guitar player in the world sitting in my bedroom in Canberra, Australia, and who would ever know? I had to move myself to where the action was. I had to be in the game. To me, that meant moving to Los Angeles.

I was twenty-three when I got to the States, studying music in school and really getting my stuff together as a guitar player. A few years later, I was recording an album with bassist Jeff Berlin. And the sessions took place at Chic Corea's studio. I was in awe. I was in the very place where some of my favorite records had been made. And on one of the walls hung the original *Romanic Warrior* album artwork. I was just overwhelmed.

After the session I was loading my car, and happened to see a woman leaving Chic's office. I thought, "What have I got to lose?" I approached her, gave her my card, and said, "You don't know me, but if Chic Corea ever needs a guitar player, you *have* to call me for an audition." She looked at the card and said, "Oh, Frank

Gambale. I've heard of you. I think my husband played with you." It turned out that her husband, Tom Breckline, played drums for Chic. In fact, I had seen him play with Chic's band when they came to Australia many years before. So the connection had been made. "If anything comes up," she said, "I'll let you know."

Six months later, I got a call for an audition. I was beside myself. The instructions were pretty basic: "Learn some of his standards, and perhaps one tune off the new Electric Band record." Well, of course I had the album, and I had actually already transcribed much of it by ear. I was prepared to give him more than he expected. That's a good philosophy for life in general! I understood that nearly one-hundred players had been considered for the gig, and that the list had been whittled down to four live auditions. I think they were surprised by me, because the day after I got the call, I FedEx'd albums, CDs, videos, and cassettes of all my stuff. I wanted to send my material in every format just to make sure there wouldn't be any problems. And as it turned out, I was the only guy out of the hundred people who were called that actually did that.

I was the second player to audition. Tommy Breckline was sitting in for Dave Weckel, who was on the east coast at the time. That was good. And I had played with bassist John Patatucci, so the only unknown was Chic. He walked in the room, we shook hands, and we settled down to play.

Now, most musicians will get nervous in most any audition setting, let alone a heavyweight one like this was. But before the audition, I had been reading a book called *The Magic of Thinking Big*. One chapter in that book really helped me get through the audition with confidence. It referred to the idea of not selling yourself short. And as I thought about how this concept might apply to me, I became aware that was looking at Chic Corea as a giant monolith of output and music and ability. And here's Frank Gambale—an amoeba, ready to divide at any moment! The disparity in my mind was just

> He needs a good guitar player. And you know what? I consider myself to be a good guitar player. In fact, I'm a darn good guitar player!" With that, I felt myself move up the food chain from amoeba to Cro-Magnum man.

so vast. I knew that if I went into the audition with that kind of mindset, I'd blow it. So I had to balance this. And as I thought about it, I said to myself, "You know, Chic Corea needs a good guitar player. Why else would he be auditioning? He needs a good guitar player. And you know what? I consider myself to be a good guitar player. In fact, I'm a *darn* good guitar player!" With that, I felt myself move up the food chain from amoeba to Cro-Magnum man.

I decided that I could take it even further. I said to myself, "Chic Corea, as wonderful a musician as he is—and a most mind-boggling keyboard player—really sucks on the guitar. As I guitar player, I'm better than him!"

That thought process really, really helped me. It gave me an area of expertise that was beyond his. So I went into the audition like it was my last performance. He counted off the tune from the top, and I played it mostly right. And they were knocked out. Chic was knocked out. He'd never before heard the sweep picking technique I had developed. The whole thing was just fresh and exciting to his ears. Chic jumped off the keyboard, shook my hand and said, "You know Frank, your amp will be pointing across the stage sort of at an angle toward me..." I was astounded. I was thinking, "You mean it only took one song?" This was amazing. And then the other guys had to remind Chic that there were still two other players they needed to audition. And with that, he snapped out of it and said, "Oh yeah, you're right. Okay. We'd better listen to these other two guys. Frank, that was fantastic. We'll call you."

> **Chic, I can't take this anymore! Do I have the gig or don't I?**

Monday rolled around, and I didn't hear anything. And then it was Tuesday. And then Wednesday, Thursday. I began to think that maybe one of the other guys got the gig. I was feeling pretty bummed. And then Friday I was coming home from a day of teaching, and as I was unlocking my apartment door, I heard Chic's voice on my answering machine. I was hurrying up to get in and pick up the phone, but I just missed it. Playing back the message, Chic, just matter of factly, said, "Hi Frank. Well, you're not there. Look, I'm just about to get on a flight to New York and I'll call you when I get there." Nothing else. And I thought, "Oh God, now I've got to wait another five hours till he gets to New York!"

Later that evening he called. And after ten minutes of small talk, I said, "Chic, I can't take this anymore! Do I have the gig or don't I?" He answered, "What?! The office didn't call you?" I told him no, nobody called me. "Oh, I'm sorry," he said. "Yeah, we absolutely want you to do the tour!"

That was in 1986, and I'm still pinching myself. We just finished a three month tour of Europe, and I still can't believe it was real. Playing what I consider to be some of the most important artistic music on the planet—uncompromisingly artistic music with some of the best players in the world. It's just incredible.

And so I firmly believe now that anything is possible if you are driven, and have the desire and passion, and you are willing to work hard at your skills. But you also have to get close to the music source—you have to motivate yourself, and you have to move toward the target.

When I think back on that audition, Chic had been such an influence on me that when I played for him, he must have heard the kinds of things that he loves to hear—but coming out of a guitar. I had internalized so much of his music that I was talking his language. But what's so remarkable to me now, the relationship seems to have gone one more level. I'm beginning to hear his keyboard emulating the sounds of sweep picking on the guitar. Giant, sweeping arpeggios that he does with two hands right up and down in harp-like fashion on the piano—something that hasn't appeared in his music before. And I hear him following my phrasing from time to time when we're trading. And I go, "Well, there it is. I've been an influence on him, too!" That blows me away.

Visit Frank Gambale at www.frankgambale.com

The guitar is like a friend. Better, it is like trying to relate
to a gorgeous, but intelligent, woman. It is an enemy until
technique is conquered; you feel impotent or stupid.
—*Paco de Lucia*

Paul Yandell

MISS WANDA, HER GUITAR, AND ME

I grew up in Graves County, in western Kentucky. And like most of the people in that area, we were tobacco farmers. Ours was a thirty-acre farm, and as the oldest son, I worked it as a kid with my father. I don't mind telling you, it was hard, backbreaking work—probably the hardest work you can do, next to picking cotton.

In 1948, when I was about twelve years old, my family had gone up the road to Clear Springs School to see a country music show. Hearing the music that night gave me the bug to play guitar. But being fairly poor—at least by today's standards—I wouldn't have a guitar for quite a while. In time, though, my mother and father gave me a calf to raise. When it got big enough, we took it to town and sold it. With some of the money that it brought, I bought myself a baseball glove and a Stella guitar. I paid $12 for that guitar, but I couldn't play it.

Every Wednesday afternoon, the peddler would come rumbling down the road with his truck full of groceries and wares. And on one of those Wednesday afternoons at the peddler's truck, I met Miss Wanda, our neighbor across the field, and told her that I had gotten a guitar. Wanda, a sweet, fifty-something woman who stood all of five feet tall, told me that when she was a girl, she played the guitar. And she offered to teach me.

Every week, I'd walk across that field, and she would give me a lesson. And Wanda, who always wore a bonnet and apron, would go to her bedroom where the guitar hung on a wall, and she'd bring it over by the fireplace and we would play.

She taught me right out of the *Broadman Hymnal*—the one all the Baptist churches in the area used. I knew many of those hymns—*In the Garden, Are You Washed in the Blood*—and she would mark the chord changes above the words. And once I got those chords under my fingers, she taught me other tunes, like *Little Brown Jug, Little Willie,* and *Spanish Fandango*.

After my lessons, I'd walk back home across that twenty-acre field, but I'd always

248

stop under a big tree that stood right in the middle of it. I'd sit down in its shade and practice what she had shown me that day so that I wouldn't forget it. I remember one day after a lesson I had forgotten it already, and I sat there under that tree and cried.

As I got older, I got better and started playing with other musicians in the county. And eventually, I got good enough to land a job at WNGO, the radio station out at Mayfield. It began to occur to me then that I could be a professional musician, and so I practiced. Working on that tobacco farm is another reason I practiced so hard. I practiced day and night just to stay out of that tobacco patch. And believe me, working in a tobacco patch will make you practice your butt off. People knock tobacco, but I love it—it got me to Nashville!

> I practiced day and night just to stay out of that tobacco patch. And believe me, working in a tobacco patch will make you practice your butt off.

As the years passed, I would get back home from time to time for visits, and I would always be sure to see Miss Wanda. The last time I saw her was in 1995. I had gone home with my family for Christmas, and by then, Miss Wanda was living at a rest home, her husband having passed away many years before. They had been married for seventy years. She seemed so happy to see us, and she told us a wonderful story. She was a hundred years old. She was frail, and her sight was failing, but she was as sharp as a tack.

As we got up to say goodbye, she stopped me to tell me she wanted me to have her old guitar. It was over at her sister's house; we should stop by to get it.

We went to her sister's home, and she brought the guitar out to me in a pillowcase. Amazingly, it still had the same strings that were on it when I was a young boy taking lessons from her all those years ago. Miss Wanda had owned that guitar since she was ten years old.

Today, that old guitar hangs on a wall in my music room. And every time I look at it, I think of the days when I was so excited to learn something that Miss Wanda had played on it. It is a treasure.

Miss Wanda passed away at the age of 103. She was a fine Christian lady—the sweetest woman who ever lived.

We're more than roots; we've got leaves and bark.
—*Billy Gibbons*

Stefan Grossman

WHO WOULD HAVE KNOWN?

I love the country blues—the music of Charlie Patton, John Hurt, Son House, Lonnie Johnson, Blind Blake, Big Bill Broonzy, and of course, Reverend Gary Davis. The music always has such great melody, great lyrics, and great guitar playing. And the music is so direct. It's so "man with guitar." It's so "one plus one."

It was a world I discovered when I was fifteen, growing up in New York, in the early 1960s. The blues, though, was the last thing on my mind when I picked up the guitar. Going to an all-boys school, I wanted to meet girls, and playing guitar was a great way to do that. But as it turned out, I met a whole lot more than girls. New York at that time was a particularly vibrant and fertile place for blues and folk music. And as I became exposed to more and more of it, I discovered the joy of meeting a whole class of people that I knew nothing about—a poor black community playing country blues. And the sounds changed my life.

The passion was ignited, and from that point on, I would dedicate my life to its pursuit. The Rev. Gary Davis was the dominant influence for me at that time. I was referred to him by a friend, who gave me his phone number. When I called him up he said to me, "You want lessons? Bring your money, honey." The lessons were five dollars, and he gave me his address. My father, knowing it was a pretty rough north Bronx neighborhood, drove me. And it was rough; the houses looked like they had been destroyed in a war. But Davis didn't live in one of those homes—he lived in a shack *behind* the tenements! You had to go down an alleyway and up some stairs to get to his place. I knocked on the door, and he poked his head out and said, "Is that you, Stefan? Did you bring your money, honey?" He really scared me, because one eye socket was empty and the other had a huge, bulbous cataract. I went in anyway and stayed for two hours.

That afternoon with Davis was a watershed for me, as I would continue to study with him for years, trying to learn all I could. I taped a number of my lessons

250

with him, which was no small task. In those days you didn't have a portable DAT recorder that you could stuff in your coat pocket; I'd have to lug my heavy reel-to-reel Tanberg tape machine up those stairs. In fact, I lugged that machine around quite a bit, and recorded a number of the players I'd get to see. But who would have known that I was recording history? In retrospect, I should have made sure to keep the tape machine rolling. I should have taken a million photographs. I should have gotten some kind of film equipment. But the fact is, we were just living life in the moment then, and really didn't have that kind of appreciation or foresight.

> He really scared me, because one eye socket was empty and the other had a huge, bulbous cataract. I went in anyway and stayed for two hours.

Rev. Gary Davis had other students, as well, and he developed close relationships with all of them. I'd spend eight to ten hours at a stretch up there with him, talking and playing and recording. He really was a great teacher. Two things I remember him telling me were always play first thing in the morning when your mind is fresh, and the second was to never put your guitar in the case—always keep it out and available.

Gary Davis was also a very proud man. He wouldn't allow me to go out and perform until he determined I was ready. He said, "You'll be taking *my* name into the public when you perform, so I have to be the one to tell you when you can."

I didn't have paternal grandfathers; they had passed away before I was born. Rev. Gary Davis very much took that place in my life. He filled that gap with warmth, knowledge, and humanity. And though he didn't have any children, he had many sons.

Visit Stefan Grossman at www.guitarvideos.com

The hands find a way to do what the heart wants to say.
—*Paco de Lucia*

Tuck Andress

LIFE IN THREE LESSONS

Some people learn quickly, some the hard way. It took me three shots before I learned my lesson. My first club gig was arranged by my guitar teacher, Tommy Crook. He generously allowed me to substitute for him in his band, consisting of guitar, pedal steel, and drums. These were the top guys in Tulsa. Of course, they were playing at a topless bar, but even at the age of sixteen I barely noticed this, being so wrapped up in trying to fit in musically with these awesome musicians. It could have been Carnegie Hall to me.

There were no rehearsals or charts, I just caught what I could by ear as it went by. I did a pretty decent job of not drawing attention to myself, playing defensively and quietly. Of course, I knew I had a long way to go as a guitarist (I had been playing less than two years), but I also thought part of the weakness of the sound was my guitar—a Mosrite Ventures model. Its strings were too close together, its action was too low, its frets were too small and flat, and its pickups were weak.

Along about the third set Tommy Crook came in to see how I was doing, then sat in with his own band on my guitar. It was as if Godzilla had wandered through the club swishing his tail. I realized for the first time that it had nothing at all to do with the guitar. It had everything to do with the guy *playing* the guitar. He sounded just as overwhelming as when he played his own vintage Gibson archtop. Yet his hands looked just like mine. Lesson number one.

> I realized for the first time that it had nothing at all to do with the guitar. It had everything to do with the guy *playing* the guitar.

A few years later I was out of high school and alternating between going to Stanford in California and playing with the Gap Band back in Tulsa. The other members were seasoned professionals. I could never figure out why they invited me to play with them. When they first called I was playing

252

rock at high school dances and dabbling with jazz. The Gap Band was terrifying and I was completely out of my league, but I knew a good musical opportunity when I saw one. Again, there were no rehearsals or charts, and I played the only chording instrument (this was before Charlie Wilson finished college and joined the band on keyboards). None of the music was familiar. Definitely a cold plunge under pressure. Fortunately I had a good ear, was smart, asked questions, exhibited humility, and worked like a dog.

We most frequently played at the Gallery Club, where on Sundays we'd play for eight hours straight, or at J.D.'s International Cafe across the street, where we'd play from midnight until 5:00 AM.

After I had played with the band for a while, Odell Stokes rejoined the band. I had been looking forward to this. He would play with the Gap Band whenever he was off the

> **Figuring out the notes came much more quickly than figuring out his technique, which was inscrutable. It was like asking a lion in mid-pounce, "How do you do that?"**

road from playing with Ike and Tina Turner, Bobby "Blue" Bland, Johnny Taylor, and other famous soul bands. All of a sudden I had a titan standing next to me on the bandstand—he even knew the songs! To me he was Wes Montgomery and Jimi Hendrix rolled into one, and he was the sweetest, most supportive guy in the world. His nonchalant rhythm parts were the stuff musicologists could analyze forever and yet still not explain the beauty of. But he would never talk about his playing, which he considered insignificant. He would always dismiss my questions with statements like, "You're the man." If there was anything that his presence in my life illustrated, it was that I definitely was *not* the man. He was the most humble person I ever met.

At this time I was playing a very nice old Telecaster through a Fender Twin with JBL speakers. But I soon bought the same guitar (Gibson ES-175) and amp (Acoustic) that Odell used, and copied his knob settings, strings, and pick choices. I just loved his sound, as well as his playing. Guess what! I still sounded just like me. He still sounded just like him. Lesson number two.

So I very seriously began to observe and dissect his playing and technique. Figuring out the notes came much more quickly than figuring out his technique, which was inscrutable. It was like asking a lion in mid-pounce, "How do you do that?" So it was years later that I began to understand what was at work, and longer still before I was able to imitate it. Much of my analysis of how to use the body to support a pick came from watching this giant play instinctively.

Another three years later, I was back in town playing with the Gap Band when

Leon Russell sat in. On guitar. On my guitar (a beautiful Les Paul Custom). Leon was producing the band's first album. He was a brilliant pianist in all styles; I knew his playing well. He was a Tulsa success story. I had also worked with a number of the musicians from the Joe Cocker Mad Dogs and Englishmen band in Los Angeles. I had studied this band and knew that Leon was a man of few notes on the guitar. On this night I found out why. He only played on one song, and during that song he only used two or three notes. But he played with such authority and with such a stinging tone that the audience of hundreds of drinkers and dancers literally gasped and fell silent when he played them. I noticed that they did not do this later when I played my usual thousands of notes (including the ones he played) and chord variations. Lesson number three. At least this time I did not have to buy another guitar and amp to learn the lesson.

> He only played on one song, and during that song he only used two or three notes. But he played with such authority and with such a stinging tone that the audience of hundreds of drinkers and dancers literally gasped and fell silent when he played them.

At that point I decided to move on to new lessons. Finally understanding clearly that assertiveness was not a key element in my personality and therefore my playing, I realized that I would have to train myself musically to compensate for this. Otherwise I would be lost blending into the background for the rest of my life, not playing the music it was given to me to play. It had been gently proven to me that incredibly powerful music was coming out of regular hands on ordinary instruments. During the next couple of years of woodshedding I simply taught myself to play as if I had the authority to play. Through the process I even began to feel that I had the authority to play. It's somewhat like a shy person acting like an extrovert long enough that he even fools himself (I know because I practiced this, too). And I vowed never to forget Tommy's generosity, Odell's humility, or Leon's simplicity and clarity of purpose.

Visit Tuck Andress at www.tuckandpatti.com

There's a basic rule which runs through all kinds of music—kind of an unwritten rule. I don't know what it is, but I've got it.
—*Ron Wood*

254

George Benson

I REMEMBER WES

My earliest recollections of music involve recordings I heard when I was seven years old—records by Charlie Christian with the Benny Goodman sextet and George Shearing on the piano. Those amazing performances set the tone for the quality of music that I would enjoy for a lifetime. Very few things came up to that quality for many years, and they certainly planted in me a desire to learn to play.

My stepfather allowed me to play his guitar, but he soon realized that my hands were too small. He dug an old, broken-down ukulele out of a garbage can, glued it back together, and presented it to me. My first instrument!

When I was nine, my mother bought a guitar for me—a $14 Stella. And boy, was I happy! I learned to play in no time, and almost immediately found myself on the street corners in Pittsburgh playing that guitar and singing. I made a lot of money on weekends as a kid. It was quite exciting. I'd sing my favorite songs by people like Nat King Cole, Frankie Lane, and so many others. Later I would hear from fellow Pittsburgers like Art Blakey that they remembered seeing me as a little boy playing on the street. And my father used to hang out with Charlie Parker, and he told me that Charlie saw me playing on the street corner. Those were some good audiences! And though I always had a guitar in my hands, I was considered "Little Georgie Benson the Singer" for many years.

As time went by, though, the guitar rose in prominence, especially with the advent of rock and roll. The guitar really came to the forefront then. And in those days, being one of the few guitar players in town, I'd be called by various bands to play guitar. I'd tell them that I wasn't really a guitar player, that I was a singer who plays the guitar. "That's close enough," they'd say, "If you want to, you can sing with us too, but what we really need is a guitar player."

By the time I was seventeen, I was working in an organ trio, singing and playing. And at that time, my guitar playing began to step up a bit. I would also be

255

invited to Saturday afternoon sessions at a friend's house. He was a "mature" guitarist, and he played nothing but jazz. We would hook up at his house where he would teach us the new chords—all the slick stuff that we couldn't figure out on our own. We played records by Jimmy Smith, Kenny Burrell, Grant Green, and then Wes Montgomery came along and showed us all how to play guitar! But it was a 1961 Hank Garland record called *Jazz Winds from a New Direction* that really changed our opinion of what the guitar should sound like. A "new direction," as the label said. And it was.

> You might get stuck, but when you break through that wall, you'll find another one waiting up the road for you. Enjoy your little breakthrough while you've got it!

As I grew as a guitarist, it helped my singing, as well. Adding the guitar to my scat singing created something that gave the guitar another dimension. And it's a challenge. The guitar is always a challenge. You might be able to play one day, and wake up the next morning not being able to put your finger on anything. That seems especially true for jazz guitar players, because we're trying to create something new every day. It never gets boring when you're looking for something new to play. You might get stuck, but when you break through that wall, you'll find another one waiting up the road for you. Enjoy your little breakthrough while you've got it!

Perhaps the greatest breakthrough for me—an epiphany, really—occurred in a hotel room in Buffalo, New York. A number of jazz artists were performing in Buffalo that week and in the hotel were some really big stars, including Kenny Burrell, John Coltrane, and Wes Montgomery. I was there with organist Jack McDuff. There was a party going on in Elvin Jones' room—he was Coltrane's drummer—so we all went down. I had to be about twenty years old at the time. I had just gotten a test pressing of a record I had made—my first one as a featured guitar player. I told Wes about it and he asked me to bring it down. "Go get it," he said. "Let's check it out." So I bought it down and I played it for him. It was called *The New Boss Guitar*. Now, by that I meant the *instrument*, not the player! There was only one boss of the guitar, and that was Wes Montgomery! He listened and was very kind to me, and gave me a nice review on it. And then he said, "George, you know I just got my new test pressing, too." So he went upstairs and got it and came down and he played 'Round Midnight. And brother, it was incredible. After that he said, "I gotta leave now." I said, "Where are you going?" And he answered, "I gotta go upstairs and practice." I thought, "Practice?! You've got to be kidding!" And then my eyes opened. John Coltrane already had his horn with him there in the room. He had never stopped playing. When he came in the room, he was playing. He was playing while we were listening to the records. *He never stopped practicing!* So I learned my lesson back then: if you're going to play this instrument, you've got to play it!

Visit George Benson at www.georgebenson.com

I can't play fast. George Benson and those guys run off
and leave me in four bars!
—*Chet Atkins*

Howard Morgen

IN MY OWN WORDS

In my mid to late twenties I began experimenting with applying fingerstyle techniques I had learned from my study of classical guitar to jazz and pop-oriented material. I had heard recordings of Merle Travis, Chet Atkins, George Van Eps, Charlie Byrd, and Laurindo Almeida, and was fascinated with the idea of sounding like two guitar players.

One day, I decided to call guitarist Billy Bauer, with whom I had studied when I was seventeen, and ask him if he would critique some of the things I had come up with. Billy is a great, innovative player and teacher best known for his work with the Woody Herman band and jazz pianist Lennie Tristano. Billy was also an early disciple of Tristano who, though gone now, remains a highly influential figure in the evolution of jazz, so I was anxious to hear what Billy would have to say.

Well, Billy came to my house and listened attentively to what I played for him. When I finished playing he nodded, smiled and said, "Yeah man, you sound like two guitar players… but you didn't say *nothin'* to me." As you can imagine, I was disappointed to hear that, but I listened as he continued. "All the guys you dig, whether they play jazz, country, Latin, or whatever, have developed a musical *identity*, a voice that their fans can recognize. To get recognition in this business you need to find your own voice. *How* you play, whether it's with a pick or fingers, is part of it but it's probably the least important part. A technique alone without musical content becomes a gimmick and it's not enough to be a voice. So it's more about *what* you play than how you play it."

He went on to suggest that I try to pinpoint what appeals to me most in a musical performance, and also what comes most easily and naturally for me to recreate for myself. "Because," he said, "those probably are the areas where your strongest talents lie. Concentrate on developing and capitalizing on your strengths and avoid your weaknesses." Billy also suggested that I work hard to find original ways to approach my music. To illustrate he told me how Lennie Tristano, seeking to find his own voice early on, would listen critically to himself to discover those aspects of his playing that were unique from other pianists, and how he deliberately and systematically set about to develop, amplify, expand, and finally emphasize those differences.

The advice Billy so generously gave me that day helped me to clarify my career choices and set the direction of my entire professional life. Very soon after our meeting I remembered that whenever I listened to a musical performance my ears always tended to gravitate to the chord changes, the rhythm section, and the bass line. All my LPs attest to this because those were the sections on the records that were the most worn! Soon I began using my ear and intuition to discover more personal ways to voice my chord structures, and in time, they began to sound less "garden variety" than the ones I had been using. I also began thinking horizontally in lines rather than chord forms, and started exploring in greater depth the harmonic possibilities for each of the songs I had chosen to arrange. Technique became a means rather than an end. My arrangements were starting to sound more like *my* arrangements. I was starting to find my own voice!

> My musical background, like most guitarists of my day, was full of black holes, and I very much wanted to become a teacher who would fill these holes with light.

In time it became increasingly clear that to establish an identity in terms of a life-long career, my "voice" would also need to include all my interests and strengths. Teaching always came easily and naturally to me, as did a knack for organizing the material I wanted to teach. My musical background, like most guitarists of my day, was full of black holes, and I very much wanted to become a teacher who would fill these holes with light. Writing and publishing became the obvious next step toward reaching a wider audience.

I've never regretted taking Billy Bauer's advice. I've never lost my passion for the guitar, for teaching, arranging, or writing, and I did achieve a degree of recognition in my field. I found my voice by capitalizing on all my strengths and avoiding most of my weaknesses—and let's not forget that my chosen instrument became so popular as I was coming up. Luck is also a factor, I guess. I often wonder what would have become of me had I chosen the accordion… or possibly the trombone!

Visit Howard Morgen at www.howardmorgen.com

There's nothing like the smell of a new guitar.
—*Jonatha Brooke*

Keola Beamer

HAWANAWANA (THE WHISPERING)

For many years *Ki Ho'alu* (Hawaiian Slack Key Guitar) has been passed down from father to son in a way that is typical for Island folks. When the house is quiet and the day's work is done, the father takes his old guitar out of its battered case. Moving to the back porch, he finds a favorite chair, stretches out his tired legs, and cradles the instrument gently in his arms. At his feet, a young boy's face lights up in wonder as a sweet sounding melody fills the warm evening.

It is difficult to explain, but I believe this to be the defining moment of our music. This silk in the air. It's what we Hawaiians call *nahenahe*. Soft, soothing, satisfying music. The kind of music that swells up in your heart like a big blue wave. The kind of music that whispers in your soul. The kind of music that accepts your cares and troubles and dims them down, like the fading light on the old man's porch.

I began to hear that beautiful whispering when I was about nine years old. We were at a family gathering in *Nu'uanu* and as the sky turned orange-red, there was a kind of magic in the air. Something wonderful was going to happen. I followed a small path that wandered beneath the mango trees and as I walked, the air overflowed with the sweet scent of jasmine. I paused for a moment to look at the fading light through the trees, when I first heard the music that whispered. It was flowing in the cool air, drifting down through the mango leaves.

At first, I couldn't believe it. What was this sweet sound? I searched for the source of the music and in a clearing beneath the faintest of stars, I saw an old man playing a guitar. He was making the most beautiful music I had ever heard. Taken by the flow of the rhythm, the old man had closed his eyes. I approached slowly, entranced by the music and as I sat down, I made a small rustling sound in the dirt. The old man opened his eyes and a puzzled expression came over him. In the dim light, I felt his eyes searching my face as I sat there quietly at his feet.

260

He hesitated for a second. Then abruptly, the old man stopped playing and coldly turned his back to me.

On that warm evening, the stars continued to glow, the ripe mangoes still hung from the trees, but the beautiful whispering music was gone. In the first rush of that silence, I looked at the old man's back and felt something leave my heart. I was too young to know it then, but I understand it now. The bitter disappointment, the thickness in the throat, the aching in the chest. The old man had broken my heart. I found out later that because I was not a member of his *ohana* (family), there was no way on earth that he would share his music with me. I was to be left outside. Outside in a world without the whispering.

> The old man had broken my heart. I found out later that because I was not a member of his 'ohana (family), there was no way on earth that he would share his music with me.

I was just a boy, and it was a difficult moment for me that evening, yet I did not give up. The sweetness of the music seemed to have found its way into my heart. It began to change me somehow. As the years went by I worked hard to understand the nature of *Ki Ho'alu* and my path expanded beyond my youthful dreams. My world began to change. It wasn't always for the better. I would be rich. I would be poor. Over time, those beautiful old mango trees were cut down and the soft rustle of an evening breeze transposed into the roar of jet engines.

Recently I sat with my wife in an airplane on my way to a concert, and I wondered what I was looking for. I wondered if my whole life has been about trying to find that same, stubborn old man. To sit at his feet, to pry open his heart. To study carefully the movements of those gnarled hands on the shining, singing strings.

I marveled at how that evening of so many years ago had changed the outcome of my life. Are we all this vulnerable? Do such small moments in time irretrievably change the future? I closed my eyes, determined to re-trace my steps beneath those ancient trees. At first, I had trouble quieting my thoughts, but after awhile, I begin to feel a mysterious resolving power, some precision beyond memory. I recalled hearing the first, faint notes of the old man's guitar and I moved backwards in time. I saw the blades of grass in that bountiful twilight and a river of red earth beneath my bare feet. What a beautiful gift this journey has been, I thought as I settled back in my seat and drifted down through the music, down through the years.

Recently, I was given a grant by the Hawaii State Foundation for Culture and the Arts to teach an apprentice. I wasn't quite sure where to start, but I had heard of a young man who played guitar and made his living from a pink lunch wagon.

He lived a simple life, waking up early to make chicken and noodles. The young man was a good cook, but when I heard him play, I knew that his real love in this world was for a special music.

He became my apprentice, but something in my heart told me that he was here to teach *me* something. He has come into my life for a purpose that I can't quite figure out.

We walk down by the park listening to the sound of the wind and we talk about music and how it changes peoples' lives. I sit on a bench with my guitar, the young man sits in the grass at my feet. I look in his eyes and I see how earnest he is, how important it is to him, this time that we spend together.

I really don't mind being here too much. The gift he has brought me is more valuable than I expected. It is the hope in his heart.

It is getting late. I am feeling old and tired. He is not of my family. He is not of my own race. I study his face for a long time.

My guitar sings, as the evening light floods the valley.

Visit Keola Beamer at www.keolabeamer.com

You have a lifetime to get your first CD together. After that, you have
six months. You have to learn to cut right to what's important.
—*Keb' Mo'*

Johnny Smith

with John Schroeter

THE RELUCTANT GUITAR HERO

In a list of shorts lists, perhaps the shortest would be the one of musical legends that Johnny Smith did *not* play with at the height of the big band era. And that was by design. "My greatest ambition," he says, "was to work with the best musicians in the world. And that dream came true when I got to New York."

Smith's humble spirit, though, would render him oblivious to the mutual esteem of his legendary peers, who included the likes of Count Basie, Benny Goodman, Charlie Parker, Stan Getz, Bing Crosby, Sarah Vaughn, Stan Kenton, Meredith Willson, the great Dimitri Metropolis—a catalog that would comprise a veritable *Who's Who* of the world's most celebrated musicians and bandleaders. And as far as guitarists were concerned, Smith reigned at the top of their "A" lists.

The post-war years in New York City were witness to the very apex of live music, and its epicenter was 52nd Street. "Everything was live," remembers Smith, "the clubs, the radio programs, the commercials—everything. And 52nd Street was live music door to door."

Smith kept a full calendar recording, performing, arranging, and touring, somehow keeping all the balls in the air. "I'd finish up playing at Birdland at 4:00 in the morning," he says, "and at 9:00 that same morning, I would be sitting in the middle of the New York Philharmonic. Talk about a transition! And then I'd be back at the studio writing and scoring music for the Benny Goodman Sextet, and a very early TV show called *Star Time* with Francis Langford and Benny Goodman."

Smith could attribute the demand for his services to his highly unusual and

innovative approach to the guitar—to say nothing of his well-honed musical sensibilities. But that, too, was by design. The musicians who tended to capture Smith's
attention were pianists. "I've always leaned toward copying techniques of other
instruments," he says. "Especially the piano. And I had developed some disciplines
and techniques to emulate them. I figured if these guys could go from one end of
the keyboard to the other, I ought to be able to do it on the guitar." And he did.

Foremost among those that he admired was Art Tatum. "This man was so
incredible," Smith says. "Just unbelievable. When I first got to New York, I would
sneak into the clubs where he was playing. You couldn't get near the bar in these
places, they were so crowded. It didn't matter; I didn't have any money to buy
drinks with, anyway. But I'd make my way to the piano and sit as close as I could.
People would send drinks up to him—shots of Scotch and bottles of beer. On one
occasion, he was playing an upright piano, and the top of the piano was lined up
with bottles and shots. He be playing with one hand, and with the other hand, he'd
throw back a shot glass. He'd follow that with the beer chaser and never miss a
beat."

One night in Birdland, Smith spotted a mysterious figure entering the club and
taking a seat in the back. "We called him Lamont Cranston—*The Shadow*," laughs
Smith. "He wore a black hat and a long overcoat, and he just slipped in and out of
the place. It was Vladimir Horowitz. He would come in and listen to Art Tatum
and just leave. I couldn't believe it."

Smith would go on to do a series of seventy one-nighters with Tatum when the
pair toured with Stan Kenton's band. "There were two busloads of us," Smith
remembers, "and I sat right across the isle from Art. He kept after me to teach him
to play the guitar. I said, "I will not." He asked why, and I explained to him that
there was enough competition out there without him joining in! As it was, when
he played, there was never anything left for anyone else to play! But he kept after
me."

Traveling from city to city through the segregated southern states, Smith and
Kenton would have to order food from the restaurants for Tatum and bring it out
for him to eat on the bus—a situation that would increasingly anger Smith.
Though Jim Crow laws were commonplace, as far as Smith was concerned, they
had no place. "On another occasion," he says, "I was traveling with Benny
Goodman. When we got to the hotel to check in, the concierge said to Teddy
Wilson, the pianist, 'Mr. Wilson, I'm sorry but we'll have to put you in different
quarters.' Teddy was used to that. But I went up to register and I told the guy, 'I'm
staying with Mr. Wilson.'"

Although he'd become a fixture on the thriving New York scene, Smith arrived
in the city without a guitar. "Just before I left for New York," he explains, "I was

working at a nightclub in Portland, Maine. One night I made the mistake of leaving my guitar—a Gibson L5—in the checkroom. Somebody came in later and said that I had told him to pick it up. I didn't see that guitar for ten years. Then out of the blue, I got a call from the police saying that they had recovered a guitar that belonged to me. And it still had the same strings on it, with my guitar pick still slipped under the strings. It hadn't been touched!"

As it turned out, being without a guitar— at least professionally speaking—was a moot point. Smith couldn't work in the studios or the clubs until he got a union card—a rite of passage that took six months to acquire. In the meantime, though, a friend, swing guitar great Harry Volpe, took Smith to the Gretsch factory to find a replacement. Gig or no gig, Smith couldn't do without an axe. "Gretsch made a guitar for me," he says. "I had it for about two weeks and the neck turned out to be a roller coaster. So I ended up with a big Epiphone Emperor. And that guitar was stolen out of the studio just before a broadcast. I was doing a fifteen-minute show with the singer Mindy Carson. We did a short rehearsal and went down to Hurley's for a little fixer-upper. When I got back to the musicians' lounge at NBC, the guitar was gone. I never kept the guitar in the case; I just kept it in the locker and would take it out and go up to the studio when I needed it. I just figured somebody was playing a joke. But it was no joke. I've not seen that guitar since."

Many other guitars would follow, though—some of which would meet more tragic ends. "John D'Angelico made a guitar for me," he says. "A beautiful guitar, but I lost it. I'd gone over to Mary Osborne's house for dinner. And Mary was an amazing guitarist in her own right. When I came home that night, I turned into my driveway to discover that my rented house on Long Island was completely gone, destroyed by a fire. Everything was gone, including the D'Angelico. I also had a little Bedlington terrier that was killed in the fire. When that happened, a dear friend of mine, the late John Collins—the guitarist with Nat King Cole—had an old D'Angelico that he let me use while John was building another one for me. And when he finished it, I wouldn't give the other one back to John Collins. It had a neck like a plow handle, but I had fallen in love with it. So I had John D'Angelico give him the new guitar and I kept that old one."

Smith would go on to design a number of signature models for Epiphone, Gibson, Heritage, and most notably, Guild. But due to differences over design and quality, Smith would eventually terminate the relationships. And while the Guild Artist Award model bore his name, Smith never played it. "But a couple of years ago," he adds, "I got a call from Fender, who now owns Guild. It was a very nice fellow who asked if I'd consider endorsing a Guild guitar, specifically the model called the Artist Award. I said to him, 'I hate to tell you this, but I designed that guitar.' There was a long silence. It was pretty funny. Well, Fender had worked out an arrangement with Bob Benedetto to design their high-end archtops and oversee the making of these models. And I was very happy about that. Bob Benedetto is among the very best that ever were. So we talked it over, made a few changes, and it's a beautiful instrument. They finally got it right."

In his early years and through his time in the service, it seemed that Smith was the only one who recognized his calling as a guitarist. "My dad wanted me to play the violin," he groans. "But I always loved the guitar. I'd go into pawnshops and offer to tune up their guitars just to play a little bit. My father bought me a violin, but he wouldn't buy me a guitar. I didn't own one until I was thirteen—and that was given to me by a man I was giving guitar lessons to!"

Smith, though, had never taken a lesson. "The radio was my teacher," he says. "I would listen to all the big bands and play along. I played as much as I could. In fact, I slept with my guitar. I'd be dreaming about a new chord, and then I'd fly out of bed, grab the guitar, and sure enough, there it was. I used to really drive my folks crazy."

The Smith family moved to Maine as Johnny entered high school. It was there that he joined the hillbilly band, Uncle Lem & His Mountain Boys. "This was back during the depression," he says, "and I was making four dollars a night. And working five or six nights a week and traveling all over the state, well, *that* was big money."

> I'd go into pawnshops and offer to tune up their guitars just to play a little bit.

His days would begin with a 6:00 AM radio broadcast, advertising the upcoming performance. Then it was off to school until 1:00. "My band mates would pick me up at school, and we'd go fifty, seventy-five, or a hundred miles and play. I'd get back in time for bed, and I would have a hell of a time trying to wake up the next morning. My brothers used to slap me in the face with a wet washcloth to get me up. And that's the way it went, five or six days a week. Needless to say, I didn't graduate from high school."

Smith, though, did see a steady improvement in the quality of his guitars. "A music store in town issued me credit," he says, "and I bought a Martin guitar—an orchestra model. On one of our dates, we played on the Fourth of July. There was an overhead fan above the stage, and when we finished up our set, I stood up and stuck the headstock of the guitar right into the fan blades, which just chewed the heck out of it. It went through it like a buzz saw. So I went back to the music store and traded it in—such as it was. They gave me some credit on the L5, which was what I really wanted."

Then the war came along. But Smith credits his stretch in the military with opening doors in New York. "I had started flying before the war," he says "and I was supposed to be a pilot. But because of a little deficiency in my left eye, they wouldn't let me. So they stuck me in a band and issued me a cornet and an Arban method book, and told me to get in the latrine and work up a lip. I had a couple of weeks to get it together if I wanted to stay. During that time I learned to read music, and I started writing, and did arrangements for our small group. That's where it all began. So I can be thankful for my years in the service—it really prepared me for New York.

Smith would hit the road with the military bands to perform for bond drives and recruiting rallies. Upon one return to his home base in Macon, Georgia, a requisition awaited him—an invitation from Glenn Miller to join his orchestra. "That was really the big time," Smith says. "But my Commanding Officer wouldn't release me. I was

> Poor Chet. The look of shock on his face! I think he became a man that night!

furious, to say the least. But as it turned out, when Miller got killed, they sent the band members to Belgium, where they lived in the mud and tents. These guys were hated. They called them 'gold bricks' because they had such a great life in the service. All but one of the Glenn Miller band came back chronically ill from that, so I guess somebody upstairs was looking after me. But it sure was upsetting at the time."

During the post-war glory days in New York, working for the studios, Smith would distinguish himself among his colleagues, but as far as the public was concerned, the man behind the brilliant guitar work was virtually anonymous. Content to work behind the scenes, he had no aspirations for fame and fortune—he was in it for the music. In a comically sardonic twist, when Smith did make his radio debut as a solo artist, he was the last to find out. In 1951, His *Moonlight in Vermont* was released on a 78 just as he left town for a vacation in Florida. He returned three weeks later to discover that the record was on its way to becoming the best-selling jazz record of the year. "You've got to be kidding!" he said upon hearing the news. With the surprise success of the record, he began doing more work for the small label, Royal Roost.

"The owner of the record company asked me to come up with some originals so they wouldn't have to pay royalties to the copyright holders. So for one particular session I took the chord changes to *Softly as in the Morning Sunrise*, put a counter melody to it, and called it *Opus*. The owner of the label changed the title to *Walk, Don't Run*."

Chet Atkins heard the record as it started to enjoy some airplay in early 1954. "One night Chet came into Birdland to see me," remembers Smith. "He told me that he'd like to record the song, but he wanted me to hear his version before he did. So I invited him backstage where there was a small dressing room, and as we walked in, some of the musicians back there were snorting, some were shooting up, and others were lighting up. Poor Chet. The look of shock on his face! I think he became a man that night! Anyway, we sat down on a couch, and he played his version of *Walk, Don't Run*, and I said, "Sure, man. Sounds great. Go ahead.'"

Later, the Ventures would hear Atkins' version, and record one of their own—the one that became the huge Top Ten hit in 1960. "And to this day," marvels Smith, "*Walk, Don't Run* is still played all over the world. It's just incredible. And I had nothing to do with the success of the song—I didn't even name it!"

> "The most beautiful thing I ever saw," he says of his sudden departure, "was the skyline of Manhattan in my rearview mirror."

Smith had recorded a great number of tunes with his small groups, many of which were featured in live weekly broadcasts. "The records, though," Smith explains, "had to be limited to three minutes or the disk jockeys wouldn't play them. So there were a lot of things I did under these constraints that I wish I could have done better. And there are things that I wish would have remained buried! The record label changed hands several times—I don't know where it ended up—but the old masters were found in England, apparently only recently discovered in EMI's tape vault at Abbey Road. Then someone decided they needed to fill up a catalog, so they re-mastered these things. They did a really good job. They didn't erase the things that I would have liked to have seen buried, but I was really pleased with the way they released it as a boxed set."

Smith's musical successes notwithstanding, the New York lifestyle didn't suit him particularly well. "I very much disliked living in New York," he says. "The hustle, the rat race, the rudeness of it. I always hated New York for that reason—but I loved being there for the music. And I'm so grateful to have been in circulation at that time. But I'm also grateful that I was able to get out of New York at the very changeover in live music. So many fine players moved right along with that change, but I was spared that."

In 1957, the entire landscape of the music business was forever altered with the tidal wave of rock and roll. "The studios had fired all their staff musicians," says Smith. "All of that just disintegrated. The big studio orchestras were out. I remember a guitar player who would come in with a big trunk on wheels, and he had an acoustic guitar, a classical guitar, a Telecaster, a banjo and a ukulele and a mandolin— all in this one big box. We called him 'The Exterminator.'"

The landscape of Smith's own life changed, as well with the untimely passing of his wife. Raising a daughter in New York as a single parent was out of the question for Smith. So he picked up stakes and headed west, to Colorado Springs, where family awaited. "The most beautiful thing I ever saw," he says of his sudden departure, "was the skyline of Manhattan in my rearview mirror."

Smith would return to New York from time to time to tie up loose ends, record, and play the odd gig at Birdland, but as he settled in the small Colorado town, New York became an increasingly distant memory. In 1961, he and his new wife, Sandy, opened a music store. Smith began to teach, as well, imparting to students the secrets of his guitar work, arranging, and improvisation.

Today, seventy-five years after entering the music business (he made his first broadcast at age six) Johnny Smith is content to sport fish marlin in Mexican waters, preferring the rod and reel to the six-string. "I don't play anymore," he says with some ambivalence. "I just can't stand to sit around and plunk on the thing; it's nothing but frustration. As far as I'm concerned, you're either playing it or you need to give it up. I still have a few guitars around the house, though. My wife would love for me to have a yard sale!"

Learn more about the legendary Johnny Smith and his recently reissued recordings at www.mosaicrecords.com

---

You can't tell lies on the acoustic guitar; there's no forgiveness.
If you can't play, it's obvious.
—*Lee Ritenour*

Christopher Parkening

SUFFICIENT GRACE

I had a very frightening experience several years ago when I smashed my finger only days before an appearance at the Hollywood Bowl. My sister and her family were visiting me at a fishing ranch in the Sierras. Her boys were sleeping on a roll-up couch bed with a metal frame. As I was starting to close up the bed, unknown to me, my ring finger had slipped between the metal "scissors." My sister ran over and said, "Oh, I'll help you!" She threw the bed up from the other side and—CRUNCH! It cut right into my finger. I thought the bone was broken.

A doctor, who was a member at the ranch, happened to be at his cabin. He came over, looked at my finger, and determined that it was not broken. "However," he said, "it is severely lacerated. You need to put ice on it, head back home, and see your doctor immediately. You must worry about the possibility of infection."

> So here it is, three days before the concert, and I could barely play because my fingers were so bruised and stiff.

This accident occurred six days before I was scheduled to play Joaquin Rodrigo's *Concierto de Aranjuez* with the Los Angeles Philharmonic at the Hollywood Bowl, an outdoor concert venue that seats over 15,000 people. After the accident, I couldn't practice for three days; my finger and hand were so stiff and sore. I prayed about what to do, but did not feel I should cancel the concert.

So here it is, three days before the concert, and I could barely play because my fingers were so bruised and stiff. The next day I started playing, but my fingers and whole left hand felt so stiff. One day before the concert, I started to go through the concerto slowly. I had lost so much practice time, and was worried how the concert would turn out. Later that evening, I found a cassette of a sermon that my pastor,

John MacArthur, had preached that meant so much to me. He spoke about "The Sufficiency of God's Grace" from one of my favorite passages in the Bible, 2 Corinthians, chapter 12, verse 9-10: "My grace is sufficient for you, for My strength is made perfect in weakness. Therefore most gladly I will rather boast in my infirmities, that the power of Christ may rest upon me… For when I am weak, then I am strong." Pastor John explained, "So the suffering that humbles us, the suffering that forces us to God in prayer, the suffering that makes us cry out for a grace to endure is the very source of power in our lives. It is when the Christian has lost all human ability to deal with his difficulty, when he is weak, without resources and destitute and left totally to trust in God's power in grace to sustain him, that he becomes a channel through which God's power can flow."

After I listened to the tape, I went to bed the night before the concert, feeling at peace. I thought, "I have to totally trust in God's power in grace to sustain me." So, besides my family, I didn't tell anyone what had happened to my finger. I went out on stage that night with all those bright lights and all the people and thought, "Lord, I am playing this concert for you and I will totally trust in your grace tonight as I play." I had such peace that night, and it turned out to be one of the best concerts I have ever played. I came off stage and the manager of the Los Angeles Philharmonic congratulated me on my performance. I said, "This was all God's grace." Then I showed him my finger. He gasped and asked, "When did that happen?!" I said, "Six days ago, but I didn't want to show it to you." I told him that it was only by God's grace that He allowed me to play this concert tonight. *Soli Deo Gloria*!

Visit Christopher Parkening at www.parkening.com

Young people don't listen. And if they listen, they listen to that guy in England—Eric Clapton. He's a good player, but so is Christopher Parkening.
—*Chet Atkins*

El McMeen

THE SILVER LINING

It was July 3rd, and more sensible people were preparing for the July 4th holiday—perhaps traveling to visit relatives, playing hookey from work, anticipating the holiday festivities, or even playing guitar. I, on the other hand, joined my young sons who were taking turns riding the newest McMeen acquisition—a "Runt" miniature bicycle, in fire-engine red. At this point in the telling of the story, the facts become a bit clouded. I contend that one of the children goaded me into riding the bike; their story is that they counseled me *not* to ride the bike. In any event, I got on the bike, and after approximately three seconds, pitched over the handlebars. I put out my hand to break the fall, but what I broke was the pinky on my left hand. To visualize the end result of this maneuver, hold your left hand out, spread the fingers, and pretend that the first joint of the left pinky is sticking out to the left at a 45 degree angle from the rest of the finger. Gruesome, to say the least. With my guitar playing days apparently behind me now, I grabbed the displaced joint and yanked it back into place—at least roughly—where it generally resembled a finger again. However, I couldn't bend it. Time to go to the emergency room.

After the obligatory wait, occasionally punctuated by my mumblings of words like "broken finger," "professional guitarist," and "bad," we got some attention. The attending doctor did an X-ray, pronounced the finger broken and dislocated, and said, in medical terms that it had to be yanked back into place. I scored points with the kids by forgoing any anesthesia. He indeed fixed it, but it was sore, and needed to be splinted for six weeks. It was during this time that I would have dealings with a very nice, very attractive, 88-pound woman who would terrorize me in her capacity as "physical therapist."

I had recently finished my Spring tour of the Eastern US with my sometime touring partner Larry Pattis, and the next tour would begin in the fall, so the first matter of good fortune was the timing. Perhaps I might live to play again, and even, perhaps, to the extent that people might want to continue to pay to hear me play. Somehow I would try to cope with this.

I was fitted with a straight splint, which would give way to a curly one. I decided, for no particularly good reason, to go through my repertoire to see whether I could play pieces without resorting to the pinky. The experiment was only a qualified success. The pinky was quite important in a lot of the tunes. I did harbor the nagging idea of re-learning the pieces without the use of the pinky, but I knew that once the pinky was back in operation, I'd be totally confused. I began to brood.

I decided to try to play guitar without the splint. Many chord positions put a strain on the finger, but one chord position—an E minor in my favorite tuning, CGDGAD—was actually comfortable and provided some therapy for the finger. I started experimenting with fingering notes around this chord, and what began to evolve was an original tune. At first I called it *On the Trail*, owing to its somewhat loping quality, but as I became more confident and the tune picked up speed, it became *Le Mans*. I had only ever composed one other original tune, so my injury had already led to at least one positive result.

> I grabbed the displaced joint and yanked it back into place—at least roughly—where it generally resembled a finger again.

As I was going through my repertoire, I began to emphasize some melody lines, since I was still in my re-fingering mode to some degree. One was the famous Irish tune *Sheebeg and Sheemor*. I began the first few notes of the tune, and then almost absent-mindedly took the melody line in a different direction. It was becoming another original piece. It evolved over a period of nine months into *Song for Sheila*—a song in honor of my wife of over thirty years, and one of my most popular tunes at my concerts. Finally, in this period, one other original tune came about. I called it *Breakout*, in reference to my "breaking out" from my primary approach of only arranging tunes for guitar, rather than creating original pieces.

It's fair to say, I think, that this bicycle accident and the therapy that followed led to my composing three times as many original tunes as I had ever done before! But there was more. A few months earlier I had recorded my seventh CD—*The Lea Rig*. It became quite popular, and had even found its way onto at least one DJ's list of top ten discs of 2001. It had taken a lot out of me to do that CD, which involved the services of some terrific musicians. But when it was finished, I told myself that it would be my last CD—with the qualification that I might do another if I were able to write a significant amount of original music for the guitar. A prospect at that time I considered highly unlikely. The bicycle accident changed all that.

That broken finger ultimately liberated me in myriad ways, opening doors I didn't know existed. And I did, in fact, begin to look toward recording a new CD—one that would include a number of original pieces, as well as others arranged in original ways. And some of the pieces would be difficult, and stretch me in new directions.

In the summer of the next year, my CD *Breakout* was born—something that proved to be the best therapy of all.

Visit El McMeen at www.elmcmeen.com

Too often, newly-learned skills, improved technique, and the stoking of creative fires yield the fanciest guitar arrangements this side of guitar heaven. But there's a downside. That's when what is interesting to play turns out to be uninteresting to hear.
—*Rick Ruskin*

Johnny A.

BAD CAST, GOOD PERFORMANCE

It has been said that there is nothing the body suffers which the soul may not profit by. Certainly my music has profited from a fair amount of physical adversity. As a young boy I had scoliosis—a curvature of the spine that results from an unequal development of the muscles on either side of the spine. And the treatment for my particular condition was a full-body cast for fourteen months, followed by a back brace for another two and a half years. To add insult to injury, this state of affairs coincided with the bulk of my high school years.

Now, the burden of a forty-pound cast on your back eliminates a lot of options for a teenager who only wants to play sports and hang with the guys. And just imagine trying to find a date, let alone have a girlfriend! It was a tough time, to say the least. But fortunately, I did have a friend that saw me through that rough period.

In the years prior to my going into the hospital, I had taken up the guitar. Musically speaking, growing up in the mid to late '60s, I was most definitely a product of the British Invasion. It was such a musically fertile time, and like many who loved the Beatles and idolized George Harrison, I wanted to be a guitar player. That was it.

When I was eleven, I spotted a Vox Clubman in the window of a Medford, Massachusetts music store. Of course I wanted it! I swept hair off the floor of my aunt's beauty salon every Saturday until I earned the $88 to buy it. At thirteen, though, I went into the body cast, and that's when things really got interesting. At that time, my dad bought for me what would be my first really good guitar—a Gretsch Viking—which happily, I still own.

Once I was in the cast, the angle at which it held my head was pretty severely restricted. I couldn't really see the fingerboard when I played; I couldn't move my head in that direction. Imagine holding a guitar as you normally would, but keeping your head totally straight ahead and up. You can only glimpse the left hand

275

through your peripheral vision. For the next few years, that's how it went.

The upside to this for me, though, was that it forced me to develop a feel for the fingerboard that I never would have otherwise achieved. And I actually used to gig like that while I was in the cast. I had no idea it was… odd!

I think, though, that when you're that young, you're so resilient that you don't appreciate the gravity of the obstacle you're trying to overcome—you just do it. It's when we get older that fear enters the picture and you begin to convince yourself that you can't do this, or you can't do that. But when you're a kid, you just go for it.

> When you're that young, you're so resilient that you don't appreciate the gravity of the obstacle you're trying to overcome—you just do it. It's when we get older that fear enters the picture.

Even today, when I have total freedom of movement, I often play with my eyes closed and my head lifted up. And people ask me how I do it. Well, how does Stevie Wonder know where he is on the piano? When you learn something a certain way, it just becomes second nature. And amazingly, something that might be an obstacle at the time actually serves to mold the player, and ultimately, the person.

The guitar has been the one constant throughout my life, and through all of the periods that really mattered to me. That's made an indelible impression. It's always been there. It's easy to say that the guitar has served me well, but I'm trying to serve *it*. The fact is the guitar has served me far better than I've ever served it.

I had never in my wildest dreams imagined that I'd have a signature model with Gibson. It's very humbling. To realize that I have a model with a company whose artists have included people like Wes Montgomery, Les Paul, Tal Farlow, Johnny Smith, and Chet Atkins is just overwhelming. But it's just one more thing the guitar has given me.

I think I know just how Jack Benny must have felt when he said, "I don't deserve this award, but I have arthritis and I don't deserve that either!"

Visit Johnny A. at www.johnnya.com

The minute people say, 'This is the definition, and this is
how it's got to be played," you've lost me.
—*Roy Rogers*

Pat Martino

with John Schroeter

ONE DAY AT A TIME

Upon waking from the hours-long surgery, with the lingering effects of the anesthetic still hanging on like a dense fog, Pat Martino struggled to bring into focus the unfamiliar faces encircled about his recovery room bed. Nearly fifteen years of misdiagnoses had left a growing brain aneurysm virtually unchecked. In time, though, a CAT scan would reveal the source of the seizures that had grown from their pianissimo beginnings to their forté climax—seizures that brought the brilliant jazz guitarist horrendous headaches, blurred vision, and onstage blackouts.

Immediately upon receiving the diagnosis for a condition that concealed itself behind many masks over many years, he boarded a plane in Los Angeles to fly back to his hometown of Philadelphia, where the delicate yet critical operation would take place. And while the procedure successfully removed the aneurysm, it also erased large segments of his memory. Two of those unfamiliar faces gazing down upon him belonged to his parents. Yet the surgery saved his life, with what was determined to be only hours to spare.

"The amnesia," Martino explains, "took place in every context with regard to personal relationships, my career, my craft, my penmanship, my writing, my very *identification*. All of these things were a total blank." And that included the memory that he had ever played the guitar. Yet in spite of this horror, he has come to view the experience as one of the most positive things that ever happened to him. "What really got erased," he explains, "were all of the identifications that resulted from having to please others, the expectations to live up to the rituals that a family naturally produces. Things like wanting to be a great guitarist to please my father, to uphold the family name, to stop playing so much and do my homework, to do

277

the many things that all of us are expected to do. Certainly, there are responsibilities in terms of the growth process, and they are important, but when all of this was erased, I had to start from the beginning. The difference this time is that there were no expectations from anyone else. It was left to me to make these decisions. I had a clean context, a clean slate."

In time, though, things that were remembered only subliminally eventually began to reemerge as whole memories. Recovering at home with the help of his parents, Martino was surrounded by material fragments, reminders of the past that had slipped his grasp. "There were details of my experience throughout the house," he says. "There were pictures, stories, interviews and write-ups, there were magazines, descriptions of my career, albums upon albums, as well as contact with old friends. One thing that this did provide was a solid position in the midst of a vortex. It was the solidity of the here and now. That was the only thing I could really identify as realistic."

> The guitar is of no great importance to me. The people it brings to me are what matter.

Martino began to pick not where he left off, but from what he left behind. "More importantly," he explains, "I began to pick up on the authenticity of my own intentions as a child. As I went through the serious confrontations brought on by the operation's results, playing became more of a healing power than a continuance of responsibilities. I began to play like a child would play with toys. And when one of my therapists suggested that I get a little more serious about play, I began to play with computers. And the more I did that, the more lost I became in that playfulness."

The computer—one of the original little 128K Macintoshes—included some music software. "That program became more playful than any of the other toys that had been presented to me in the course of my therapy," he says. "And as I began to play with more and more seriousness, it began to expand. And that opened up a new future and a new decision: to enjoy my life, and to enjoy playing."

It was in this context that the guitar reentered the picture. "It came back as a favorite friend," he says. "…a reemergence of my most intimate partner. It enabled me to express myself with intricate precision—more intricately than any of the other tools. And when I picked it up again, it began to provide a taste and an experience that I otherwise would have no access to."

The loss of conscious memory notwithstanding, Martino's muscle memory was still very much intact. With that much in his favor—and at what should have been the apex of his career—he set out to learn again. Absent this time around, though, was the competitive, business model-oriented agenda that had, in part, fueled his spectacular rise in the jazz world. This time, it was just for the music. And remarkably—miraculously, really—he's once again at the top of his game.

"Now that I am flowing and emoting with a deep love for this universal language," he says, "it allows me a larger creative perspective, without the distractions and free of the trappings. And what brings this into every day living is that everything seen, heard, smelled, and touched ignites an ongoing participation in this universal language. In my previous musical life, I was very successful. It's true. And that's because I was totally dedicated to it, just as I am now. There is no difference now in terms of the dedication and commitment. But the motive has changed. I'm going to the next moment and what it contains, and I want it to be as artistically enjoyable as possible. And somehow, the moment those things are activated, they are out of my hands, and they're invisibly evolving into the next moment. I enjoy participating in that process. And there is something inherently and wonderfully unscripted about following the muse without deliberate manipulation of direction. It's called *play*."

And to that end, Martino regards the guitar as just another vehicle. "The guitar is of no great importance to me," he says. "The people it brings to me are what matter. They are what I'm extremely grateful for. They're *alive*. The guitar is just an apparatus, a vehicle. It has nothing to do with the nature of its destination. Each *day* is a vehicle. And music is a doorway into other portions of the house. And because of that, it transcends the craft. But ultimately, the only advice I can offer is the most simplistic of all, and that is to be focused and concerned with the best that can be done—the best that you can do—and to take that not one day at a time, but one *moment* at a time."

Visit Pat Martino at www.patmartino.com

I look for someone who's 100% man. If he's only 50% musician,
that's okay; we'll turn him into 75% musician after a while.
But if he's not 100% man, there's nothing I can do.
—*B.B. King*

279

Tony Melendez

A GIFT OF HOPE

The white papal helicopter bearing the coat of arms of John Paul II landed near the stage entrance of the Universal Amphitheatre in Hollywood, California. I couldn't see the fleet of helicopters carrying television camera crews, secret service agents, and reporters from the world's press. But all 6,000 young people sitting in the Amphitheatre with me could hear the noisy armada as it hovered over us in the cloudless sky.

The Pope had come to visit America on his 1987 tour. And on this stop in Los Angeles he was about to meet with 15,000 teenagers and young adults. Besides the 6,000 of us filling every seat in the posh red-and-gold Universal Amphitheatre, another 4,000 were packed into a cathedral in St. Louis, Missouri. In Portland, Oregon, 3,000 more were crowded into the Portland Civic Auditorium. And in the Regency Hotel in Denver, Colorado 2,000 young people were jammed together in the spacious ballroom, awaiting the Pope's appearance.

History was being made, and we could feel the excitement mounting. Through the miracle of a television satellite, youth in four different locations across the western United States would be meeting simultaneously with John Paul II to discuss the issues that concerned us. Television crews in each location projected all four congregations on giant screens. We had been talking, singing, and worshiping together for almost an hour. Now, in just moments, the Pope himself would enter this "Papal Spacebridge: Satellite Youth Forum" to greet us.

I was sitting on a small raised platform about twenty steps from the primary stage, where the Pope would enter. I was barefoot, and my guitar rested on the floor in front of me. Somehow the Spacebridge planning committee had heard of my name and my music. Early in the summer they had interviewed and auditioned me. Days later I received their invitation.

"Tony, we want you to sing and play for Pope John Paul II," they said, "and for a potential television viewing audience of more than one billion people."

A "thalidomide baby," I was born without arms, because my mother was prescribed thalidomide—a drug used to help calm morning sickness during her pregnancy. I was fitted with artificial arms at one point, and I wore them until I was ten, but I disposed of them. I just never felt comfortable; I could use my feet so much more.

After Dad retired his old Spanish guitar several years before he died, it stood in the corner of our living room like furniture or a piece of art. One evening when I was just fifteen, I leaned down, grasped the old guitar between my neck and shoulder, and carried it into the bedroom that my brother and I shared.

Looking back now, I realize that when I placed the guitar on the floor at my feet for the first time that night in 1977 and began to brush my callused toes against its strings, one life ended for me and another life began.

I was a sophomore at Chino High School when I first picked up that guitar, and I was singing in Beth Ann's choir at Saint Margaret Mary's. Ray Jansen who accompanied the church choir one Sunday morning noticed my interest. I explained to him that on the several times I had tried to strum my father's guitar with my toes, the only noises I made were harsh, unmelodious, and unpleasant.

"Have you tried an open chord?" he asked me, strumming the strings and turning the little tuning screws. "Now strum this," he said, placing his guitar on the floor in front of me.

When I brushed my big toe lightly across his strings, a beautiful major chord sent shivers up and down my spine. With one quick movement of my foot over six little strings, I had made music that echoed on throughout the church.

"And you can change the chord simply," he added. "As you place your toes up or down the fret, a new chord will form."

I placed my left foot on the neck of his guitar, held down the strings, and strummed again. This time the chord sounded higher on the scale than the first. Quickly I moved my foot and strummed again, and a third chord sang from the instrument. I was making music!

Later than night, alone in our bedroom, I struggled to tune my father's guitar to that amazing G-chord without my friend's help. It wasn't easy holding the guitar in place and turning the little tuning screws with the toes on my left foot while simultaneously picking the strings with my right. At first all that my grunting and groaning produced was discord. Then suddenly the strings stretched perfectly into place, and a beautiful G-chord sounded once again.

Today, Dad's old Spanish guitar is my most prized possession. I can't imagine what my life would be like without it. During my last three high school years I practiced on that tough little instrument for four or five hours a day. You can still see the imprint of my heel where it rested on the rounded wooden frame.

Between the two largest toes on my right foot I learned to hold a pick shaped like a triangle with rounded edges. I then formed the chord by pressing the strings down with the toes on my left foot and by strumming with my right. It wasn't easy to learn to play with no hands or fingers, but in a very short time the noises echoing from that old guitar sounded a lot like music.

I admit that my family suffered in the process. I played and replayed each chord a million times—or so it must have seemed to them. From the moment I returned from school until nine or ten at night I practiced, while my sisters watched television or did their homework and my mother worked in the kitchen. Our house is small, and the walls are thin. But my family seldom complained, even though the first few years I sounded pretty terrible.

Just three weeks before the Pope's visit, I had been singing on a street corner in Laguna Beach for townsfolk and tourists who chanced by. Occasionally they would stop to listen or place a coin in my open guitar case. Now I was sitting on a little red platform that had been built for me, waiting to perform for the spiritual leader of hundreds of millions of Catholic Christians and for a live television audience so large I couldn't even imagine it.

Suddenly he was there on the stage before me. The young people in all four cities leaped to their feet and broke into an ovation that lifted the roof and sent chills up and down my spine. I had never seen a Pope in person. John Paul II was wearing his traditional white robes, a white cap, and a simple gold cross. As he walked through the crowd, greeting the enthusiastic kids in English, Spanish, and other languages I couldn't understand, the people began to chant, "We love you" and "*Te amo*, Papa." He waved, nodded his head slowly, and grinned at our wild and noisy welcome.

When the last trumpet fanfare had sounded and the crowd grew quiet at last, the Pope greeted us in the name of Jesus and then invited us to pray the Lord's Prayer with him. He preached briefly about hope. "The people of hope," he said, "are those who believe that God created them for a purpose and that He will provide all their needs as they seek to fulfill His purpose in their lives."

It was the same truth that my mother had passed on to me since my earliest childhood. She had believed from the moment of my birth that God had created me with something wonderful in mind, and she never let me forget it. When I grew discouraged or wondered just how I would make it, she said simply, "Trust God, Tony. He made you, and He will take care of you."

After the Pope's sermon, young leaders in all four cities asked him a series of frank, probing questions. The Pope answered each one honestly and openly. He didn't beat around the bush, nor did he say what was easy or popular. And whether they agreed or not, the crowds applauded each answer with growing respect for this courageous man.

"Now, Holy Father," a young man said into the microphone, "we have a special gift that we would like to present to you."

John Paul II, sitting on a chair in the middle of the stage, turned to face the speaker. And then, as he realized that I was going to be his "special gift" that day, the Pope looked directly at me.

"Our gift represents courage," the young man said, introducing me, "the courage of self-motivation and family support."

The Pope nodded at those words and smiled at me.

"The gift is music," the man continued, "in a performer who says when he sings, "I hear the Lord.'"

I moved my feet up to the strings of my twelve-string guitar. The lights dimmed, and a spotlight lit up my small red platform.

"Holy Father," the young man concluded, "we are proud to present to you Tony Melendez."

The audience applauded politely as they turned in my direction. Only then did they notice that I had no arms and that I was strumming the guitar with my feet. I'm used to surprised gasps and quiet whispers, and I heard them then. But I wasn't there to impress anybody. I've never felt handicapped, let alone gifted. *You* could play the guitar with your feet if you were willing to practice hard enough. I didn't play that day because I had no arms and the program needed a novelty; I played to celebrate the presence and the power of God in each of us. And I think that the people could tell, as I sang, that I wasn't a performer at a circus. This was a singer of the Song of Songs.

I didn't look at John Paul II. I didn't think about that huge arena filled with people or about the millions watching me on television. I just closed my eyes and sang the song as a prayer to God, as always.

> *You* could play the guitar with your feet if you were willing to practice hard enough. I didn't play that day because I had no arms and the program needed a novelty; I played to celebrate the presence and the power of God in each of us.

It was a simple song, and I sang it from my heart. It was a gift to our visitor, to the millions watching, to my family, and especially to my Heavenly Father, whose presence makes every day like no other day before.

When I finished the song, the audience gave me a standing ovation; even the Pope was standing and clapping his hands above his head enthusiastically with the crowd. It was truly a day like no other! I could have died at that instant and felt my life fulfilled.

Then something totally unpredictable happened: the Pope walked down from the stage. He had to descend several steps and then jump down off the edge of the platform to reach me. Security people scrambled to keep up with John Paul II's unscheduled journey, and television crews tried to follow. Hands reached out to help him.

Suddenly the Pope was standing at my feet. At that moment I wished I had arms. I wanted to reach out and take his hands in mine. I wanted to lean forward and embrace him. Instead, he held his arms out to me. My heart was pounding with emotion, and my eyes were blinking back tears. As I leaned forward, the Pope took my head in his hands, stood up on tiptoes, and kissed me gently on the right cheek.

The crowd of young people went wild, cheering, singing, and clapping their hands high in the air. The Pope looked me in the eyes, then turned and walked back to his central place on that impressive platform.

I thought that my heart would burst. As I tried to take in what had just happened to me, we were once again surprised by this insightful man. I couldn't believe it, but John Paul II was calling my name above the cheering crowd.

"Tony," he said. But the young people wouldn't be silent.

"Tony," he repeated a second and then a third time.

Finally he people in the gigantic room grew still.

"Tony," he began a fourth time, "you are truly a courageous young man. You are giving hope to all of us. My wish to you is to continue giving this hope to all the people."

I tried not to cry, but tears brimmed up in my eyes and a few uncontrollable strays trickled down my cheek and into my beard. For the last months I had been praying for God's direction. Now Pope John Paul II himself was delivering God's word to me.

"Give hope to all the people," he had said, and a voice inside me answered, *Yes, it was for this that I was born. It was for this that I came into the world.*

Learn more about Tony Melendez at www.tonymelendez.com, the home of Toe Jam Music.

This story was adapted from the book, *A Gift of Hope: The Tony Melendez Story*, Copyright © 1989 by Tony Melendez. Used by permission.

Musicianship really boils down to what sort of soul you have.
—*Christopher Parkening*

The Beatles

IT WAS FORTY YEARS AGO TODAY

It was all rather inexact. I never had a really good instrument, but it didn't matter. The whole thing with the Beatles was we never really had great instruments, we never really had great headphones, we never really had great microphones or PAs; we somehow learned to muddle through. In fact, I think it was quite good for us, because now all this sophisticated stuff seems such a luxury; it's wonderful. We always made do with whatever we had.

—Paul McCartney, from "Many Years from Now"

You can't appreciate anything if you have no respect. I never was into those people smashing up their guitars anyway. That was just rubbish.

—George Harrison, from "I Me Mine"

For a long time I wasn't listening to music—to the rock and roll stuff on the radio—because it would cause me to get sweaty. It would bring back memories I didn't want to know about, or I would get that feeling that I'm not alive 'cause I'm not making it. And if it was good, I hated it 'cause I wasn't doing it. And if it was bad, I was furious 'cause I could've done it better.

—John Lennon

I had a £15 acoustic Zenith guitar, which I still have in my studio. I swapped a trumpet for it at Rushworth and Dreapers. My father had given me a trumpet for my fourteenth birthday, and I used to play it a little bit because that was the hero instrument then, *The Man with the Golden Arm* and everything. But it became clear to me fairly quickly that you couldn't sing with a trumpet stuck in your mouth. If you had aspirations in the singing line it had to be something like guitar, so I asked me dad if he would mind and he said no. I went into town, swapped it in, got a guitar, came back home, couldn't figure out at all how to play it. I didn't realize that it was because I was left-handed, and it wasn't until I found a picture of Slim Whitman, who was also left-handed, that I saw that I had the guitar the wrong way round.

—Paul McCartney, from "Many Years from Now"

He had rested it up against a wall and was talking to a mate when someone suddenly pushed back a chair right into it! Although George had it repaired, it was never the same again. What he really wanted, though, was an electric guitar, but Dad wasn't keen on him having it on hire purchase. He always said you shouldn't buy anything unless you had the money to pay for it.

Anyhow, one night George, who was then working for Blackler's, came round to my flat. He went into a long speech about how much better an electric model would be. I realized he was working up to something, but said nothing. Then he finally came out with it. He knew Dad wouldn't let him have anything on hire purchase, so he wanted me to sign the guarantee forms. I wasn't very keen, but he persuaded me to go to Hessy's, the Liverpool shop where all the groups bought their instruments. There he showed me the guitar he wanted. It was priced at £120. George fiddled with it, trying to look like an expert, but no sound came out. So the salesman pushed a button on the amplifier, and suddenly there was a tremendous blast and all the instruments on the opposite wall crashed to the floor. After that, I just had to let poor George have his guitar!

—*Harry Harrison, on brother George, from "Dark Horse"*

I'm not interested in a marketable product; I'm interested in what
I know from my life experience to be standards of excellence.
—*Barney Kessel*

Noel Paul Stookey

SEBASTIAN

Sebastian arrived in a cardboard suitcase;
Sealed with a kiss from his mom
With a newspaper under his arm and behind his head
Alone in the hall with his back to the wall
You could see he was one of a few
He spoke only when spoken to
And sometimes alone in his bed

Small and jocular was the group that sat cross-legged in the middle of the cabin's living room. Some on the couch, some leaning against the walls, and enough of us to spill out into the kitchen where the bourbon and beer sat bag by cooler on counters.

Betty and I were attending our first "rinctum"— a term which contrary to its sound, has nothing whatsoever to do with anatomy. Gordon Bok, a former schoolmate of Betty's brother, had visited us several times at the house in Rye. And now he had invited us to Camden, Maine to join in an informal "down-east" folk gathering where perhaps thirty musical friends came together to renew themselves with traditional folk music. Guitars and mandolins, fiddles and pennywhistles (some carved out of PVC plumbing materials). This was my first opportunity in a long time to relax musically and be known as Noel, brother-in-law of one of Denny's schoolmates at Hebron Academy—somebody other than the "Paul" of Peter, Paul, and Mary.

Denny picks up a boxy looking twelve string and begins to play music from the Hebrides Islands. I'm hypnotized. The growl of the low strings on the guitar pluck my imagination... like a Hauser flung ashore from some ketch; fastened around a piling and stretching taut against the swell of the ocean and the rhythmic flug-flug-flug-flug of the ship's engine at low idle. Though it is, after all, only a guitar he's playing, it seems as though Denny's right hand is hauling lines and his left hand is setting sail. And then, in a knowing, loving voice, from under his walrus moustache comes the tragic tale of a mystical union between a seal and a beautiful woman; a son who grows handsome and strong and wise in the ways of the sea and fishing. And, borrowing a page from Shakespeare (or not knowing the age of this old folk song, perhaps it's the other way around), kills his own father... or was it that he leaves his mother to join his father in the ocean never to return? Sigh. Sometimes I suspect that these tales are composed with a variety of verses and endings and sung simply for the pleasure of expressing exquisite sadness and lament that can't be understood in any other form. And then somehow they all get collected together and made available for whatever circumstance might call for them.

> With your eyes closed, hearing the chug of the tempo and the crystalline harpsichord sounds of the top strings, you'd swear that Bach was Irish and that some sea captain was playing his variations as a well-tempered jig.

Following the *Skule Skerrie* song there are several others sung and accompanied by this magic strung box. Then an instrumental is played upon it. With your eyes closed, hearing the chug of the tempo and the crystalline harpsichord sounds of the top strings, you'd swear that Bach was Irish and that some sea captain was playing his variations as a well-tempered jig. There was a salt breeze blowing, the middle strings flapping like petulant sails in a sloppy tack. It could be covered in barnacles or dripping in seaweed or plucked from a leather satchel by Alan Adair in Sherwood forest... and say, "where *did* this guitar come from?" I ask the fellow next to me. "I made it for him," he replies. "You *made* it?!" I respond in surprise to this modest, soft-spoken unassuming fellow in a checkered shirt with whom I've been sharing the wall for the last twenty minutes or so.

"Is it a one-of-a-kind instrument?" I asked. "What do you mean by that?" He cocked his head and smiled slightly. "Well, uh..." I stammered, "Did you make it as a gift for Denny?" His smile widening, he said, "No, I make them for a living."

I asked him if he'd consider making one for someone else while my mind tumbled over itself with questions. I mean, you can't just go to a magic concert and order a mystical guitar, can you?! "Sure," he replied. "Just like that one?" I asked, still disbelieving. "If you want," he allowed. "Well, uh," I began tongue-tied, "uh... that's great. Do you want a deposit or should I write my address down or, I mean, how long would it take… wow this is terrific. Uh… oh, I'm Noel Stookey," I say finally realizing that I've been babbling away and haven't introduced myself. "Oh, I know who you are," he says. "I'm Nick Apollonio." He nods in Denny's direction. "Denny's got your address, and…" He pauses for just a moment to consider something, "It'll take me a couple of months." Assuring him that was fine, I added, "I do a lot of traveling, anyway." With an almost conspiratory reply, he said, "Yes, I know."

> *Sebastian is led to a black-walled room*
> *Red carpeting covers the floor*
> *Someone is closing the door and raising the blind*
> *Hiding his eyes so they won't be surprised*
> *When the hand reaches down for the note;*
> *The one that his mother wrote*
> *And tied by a string to his neck*

Another concert week had finished. And though Peter, Mary, and I were doing far fewer concerts than the almost two-hundred per year of the mid sixties, it was still unusual to find myself around the house with ten uninterrupted days.

"How weird," I thought as I walked from the kitchen through the pantry to the dining room, "to be a stranger in my own house." Oh, not the physical layout; Betty and I had made all the decisions regarding this thirty-room, four-floor Westchester Tudor. But rather a stranger to the flow *within* the house; the day to day activity.

It's 10:00 AM, and I've just awakened. Betty says I'm a night person, but I really *do* like the morning (she laughs when I say 10:00 AM is the morning, and I know what she means, but just give me some time—I'll be up at 6:00 AM… she'll see!).

I'm so out of touch with the day to day around here. I mean, after a week or so away I usually catch up on the big stuff, like Brett's over her cold or the raccoon got into the garbage again. But the little delicate day to day wonders (like discovering the spider's web behind the refrigerator or the A+ on the test that's now week-old news) don't get mentioned, and it hurts being "out of the loop." No wonder some folks just pour themselves back into their work—at least their work understands them! Sigh.

Well, hopefully those self-pitying thoughts will be more and more behind me, what with the decision I've made to get off the road. I glance through the paneled den off to the left into the tiled gazebo. Nobody there. Hmm, let's see. It's Monday and what happens on Monday? Oh yeah, Brett (used to be Button, but she's four years old now, and aside from an intense six months where she wanted to be known only as Dorothy—as in Wizard of Oz Dorothy—Button has become Brett. We've endorsed the "changeover" trying to avoid the use of Liz as a nickname, which ironically, of course, finally becomes her operative name starting in her early twenties) is at ethical culture school and Betty, hmm… probably working on *Westchester Magazine*. So I wonder if the mail has come yet.

I walk to the front door where, scattered on the slate floor is the mail of the day, and of course, that package that came for Betty over the weekend. Hmm, that's odd. Betty usually opens her department store items right away. I bend over and check the mailing label again. Hey! This package isn't for Betty; it's for me! From Maine… hey, this must be my guitar! Hey, wow! The mail forgotten, I pick up the large cardboard box and head for the basement studio.

"This is Sebastian," reads the note. "Treat him with love and care, for that is how he came to be built."

In the unreal, almost vacuum quietness of the black-walled, red-rugged room, I cut the twine that holds the package together, and gently lift off the top. There are crumpled newspapers and, "Oh my gosh—there's no case here!? Just the guitar?" Fortunately it appears as though the box was handled by the carrier with kid gloves.

I lift the casket-shaped instrument out of the box. It's fully strung, and there's a note threaded between the strings that says, "Read before playing."

"This is Sebastian," reads the note. "Treat him with love and care, for that is how he came to be built." I look once again at this strange, flat-sided twelve string, and think how inauspiciously he arrived. I return to reading the next several pages of the note, which suggest the brand and tension of strings to use, a bit about the wood, and a brief history of the casket style. It seems that long voyages on the sea made for a certain kind of musical vacuum, and when the desires of the crew ran beyond shanties and the little squeeze concertina, several planks from an empty packing case could be fashioned together into a box and joined with a long sturdy neck (made perhaps from a split oar) to produce a fair facsimile of a guitar, without of course, the tonality that results from shapely curves of steamed, pressed, and clamped hardwood.

I pick up the instrument, and laying my fingers at random somewhere in the middle of the neck I strum Sebastian for the first time.

Any musician, from serious composer to jazz virtuoso, knows the extent to which coincidence often creates a new set of melodic options. I could be wrong, but it seems to me that most musical "accidents" just challenge the status quo; the "established" way of presenting the inversion of a chord, for example. The twelve-string has so many overtones, and particularly because of the third string's octave tuning, the combination of high notes with the non-fretted open strings produce a tonal range that more resembles a harpsichord than a guitar. And so it was with astonishment that I discovered the opening chord for the chorus of a song that later became *Sebastian*. Equally astonishing was the fact that the entire guitar arrived in tune! It's hard enough to keep a twelve-string in tune from song to song, but this box had managed to travel from Maine to Westchester County intact and in tune!

But about the song: originally begun as a description of Sebastian's arrival, the song lay around in its one chorus-two verse state for a year or so. Though my songs are usually grammatically correct, I must admit I looked the other way when producing the sentence-with-no-subject in the second verse: "…hiding his eyes so they won't look surprised when the hand reaches down for the note; the one that his mother wrote and tied with a string to his neck." It was just too delicious a chain of events to make "proper." However, current pop music examples to the contrary, a chorus and two verses doth not a song make, and it wasn't until well after Abilene, Texas that a last verse could be written. But that's for later…

Waiting for the sunrise
And the rest of his life to begin
Sebastian is wearing a grin under his nose
And out on the grass
He can hear it at last;
The rush of a bird to its home
And then while unpacking a comb
He thinks of a song that he knows…

Sing sweet Sebastian; sing the sweetest song
Sing so sweet that while you sleep, your melody lingers on

Visit Noel Paul Stookey at www.noelpaulstookey.com

My only rule is to play what you want to hear. That may
be the only way you're gonna get to hear it! I'm going to
run out of Lightnin' Hopkins records to discover, and
then what am I gonna do?!
—*Jimmie Vaughan*

Michael Gulezian

A LESSON IN HUMILITY

The more a man knows, the more he forgives.
—*Catherine the Great*

Early in my career as a professional solo guitarist, I knew I was very, very good. I was signed to a big record label, and big record labels have a way of making their artists feel like they are more important than they really are. I don't think I ever bought into that mentality completely, but I'm sure it did have at least some effect on me. The big record companies certainly do not have anything to teach their artists about humility!

So there I was, this young kid, out on tour, totally independent, playing concerts all over the country, and getting great reviews. In the early 1980s, Michael Hedges' first album *Breakfast in the Field* was released. I thought it was good, but it didn't knock me out. I was scheduled to perform at Phillips University in Enid, Oklahoma. I got a call from Ray Parker, the Dean of Students, asking me to approve an opening artist, who happened to be a Phillips alumnus. He also was an acoustic guitarist, and apparently a big fan of mine. His name was Michael Hedges. I'll never forget what I said—and I'm sure Ray won't, either. I replied that I would probably blow him off the stage, that I might make him look bad. I turned him down.

That is the truth. I refused to allow Michael Hedges to be my opening act, on the grounds that my own playing was so good, Michael would be embarrassed. Can you believe that?

Soon afterward, I met Michael for the first time at a concert in Santa Cruz. He was playing with Preston Reed and John Fahey. We were backstage, and John introduced me as—and I am not kidding—the best guitar player in the world (remember, John was working for Chrysalis Records at the time). Michael was very gracious, and played some new compositions for me. I was startled to see and hear him doing things on the guitar that seemed impossible. I asked him, "How do you *do* that?" He just laughed. We never talked about my refusal to let him appear with me at Phillips University.

292

A couple years later, Windham Hill released Michael's *Aerial Boundaries* album. I would not be exaggerating to say that upon hearing it, I went into a state of mild shock. This was the most powerful, majestic, original, and beautiful solo guitar music I had ever heard. It was nothing short of revolutionary. I still remember that day very clearly. I was on tour, in Oneonta, New York. I was staying at a cabin on a lake. I replayed the first side of the album all afternoon, and all night.

As awed as I was by that recording, nothing could have prepared me for hearing Michael live in concert. It was a completely transcendent experience. There are no words to describe the *hugeness* of that sound, the technical command he held over his instrument, the grace of his music, and his utter authority on stage. It was 1986, in Tucson, Arizona. The concert promoter happened to be my old friend Larry Berle, from SRO Productions. He had flown in from Minneapolis that night for the show. We sat together, and he saw how deeply I was moved. So I told Larry the whole story of how I had once said the most absurd, arrogant, and awful thing possible about Michael, and how heavily it had been weighing upon me.

> That is the truth. I refused to allow Michael Hedges to be my opening act, on the grounds that my own playing was so good, Michael would be embarrassed.

Thank God for friends like Larry. He didn't tell me what he was planning to do. After the concert, Michael, Larry, and I were all gathered in Michael's hotel room. Larry turned to Michael and said, "Michael has something he wants to tell you." So I told him the exact words I had spoken to Ray Parker years before. I confessed it all. By the time I finished I was practically in tears. And once again, I was not prepared for what happened next. Michael smiled and shook his head, then walked over to me, gave me the biggest hug, and started laughing, and kept on laughing until all I could do was laugh with him. I laughed at my own stupidity. I laughed because the burden was gone. I laughed because it was all so funny.

Michael and I went on to become good friends. We would bump into each other whenever our paths crossed when we were on the road, and we saw each other every time he came to Arizona. Michael died very tragically in a car accident in December, 1997. As far as his place in the world of guitar music is concerned, I believe he was by far and away the greatest musician ever to touch an acoustic guitar. As a human being, he was a gentle, kind soul. He taught me the true meaning of humility. And he taught me a lesson in the power of forgiveness.

Visit Michael Gulezian at www.timberlinemusic.com

Michael Chapdelaine

BETTER THAN AN ENDORSEMENT LETTER FROM SEGOVIA

In the '70s, when I began my quest to become the world's greatest classical guitarist, one of the credentials possessed by most of the existing "world's greatest classical guitarists" was "Studied with Andrés Segovia." And the real kicker was for those who had a quote from the maestro, saying that he thought that the player was well on the way to *becoming* the greatest.

Being a barefoot surfing cracker from Tallahassee, Florida, who listened to Duane Allman a thousand times more than J.S. Bach, the odds were pretty long on my getting to hang with Segovia (who was about fourteen-million years old by then), so I assumed that I would just do without that ticket punch in my sure-thing career. I finished my Master of Music degree in 1980 and forgot all about chasing the Segovia dividend.

Then in 1986 I was invited to study with Segovia at USC in Los Angeles in what was to be the last great prestigious master class of an era. Whoa… finally, I thought, I would get my Segovia credential. If that sounded glib, don't be confused; I really had no interest in what the old maestro had to offer as a teacher. I planned on knocking him out with my incredible, brilliant, mature, "Oh! My! Gott!" playing, and then have him write something like:

I have been playing the guitar and studying and living classical music for seventeen decades, speak six languages, have known most of the great artists of the last two centuries, and have some very solid ideas about how one should play the guitar—particularly the music of composers who wrote the major works of our repertoire for me and who were all drinking buddies of mine. That being said, and furthermore, it being obvious that Chapdelaine never listens to my records and does nothing like me

294

(and, in fact, seems to do most things in the opposite), I believe that he is the greatest guitarist in the world.

Love, Andrés

Yeah, right. In my defense, though, I came up in the generation that didn't really listen to him very much. And during my college years, his highly romantic, personal style of interpreting music was way out of fashion to the point of being frowned upon by all us future "world's greatest classical guitarists" (a.k.a. fools.) Our teacher, Bruce Holzman, told us to listen to him, but we knew better. Williams played perfect, fast, and loud, and kept the music clean and simple to understand, without all that schmaltzy stuff; he was our man. By the time I played for Segovia, I believed that a performer's job was to render the music cleanly and intelligently without a lot of soppy selfish emotion spread over it. It is an endless source of amazement what a young man will come up with while trying to deal with the relentless ache to be unique in a world where everything has already been done and felt. But back to the story!

So off I went to LA to show the maestro how to kick ass and take names on six strings.

So off I went to LA to show the maestro how to kick ass and take names on six strings. The ground rules of the class were that the cast of twelve international players had to play repertoire that Segovia had played, recorded, and, in most cases, edited. In past classes, he had been annoyed when someone played a modern (dissonant) work that had not been accepted into his repertoire, and so the 1986 class director, James Smith, wisely arranged to avoid that discord in the class. (But don't you worry—there were other ways to let the atmosphere of joy and harmony out of a Segovia class.)

Okay, it is pretty well known that there were two ways to make it likely that the maestro would like you:

1. Play like him, or in a way that showed that you had listened to him a great deal and walked down a common artistic path.
2. Be a girl.

If you wanted to assure that he would get pissed off and throw you out of class, there was a method for that,too: Change his fingerings.

So the good news was that I wouldn't be playing any works that he didn't like.

The bad news… fingering. I considered—still do—any editor's fingerings to be a good place to start. Then I finger it lots of different ways and just see what sticks. *Baaaaaad* way to pursue the Segovia endorsement.

Sooooooo… the first night I played Ponce's *Sonata III, First Movement*. We had a great time. He gave a really long lesson and seemed to enjoy it. The first movement is somewhat more abstract than romantic; one can make it work without being overly expressive. And the textural and harmonic properties make it less subjective for fingering choices than most guitar pieces. Safe stuff for the mission at hand. We ended the lesson smiling and well on our way to a juicy Chapdelaine-is-a-genius letter.

> Segovia appropriately fingered on the 2nd and 3rd strings, up the neck where the tone is really rich and luscious. I played them in other places.

The second lesson was a little less chummy. I played the second movement from the same sonata. It is an extremely expressive piece with lots of dark lovely melodies that Segovia appropriately fingered on the 2nd and 3rd strings, up the neck where the tone is really rich and luscious. I played them in other places.

I played the piece a bit on the academic side, meaning, not terribly expressively. In other words, boring. He got pretty crabby, and progressively more so, during this lesson. By the end, I'm sure that he would have smiled upon learning that I got a tax audit that year.

Well, batting .500 so far, but we must have two more grand slams. I decided to play *Mallorca* by Albeniz. He'll love me when I play that! *Mallorca* is a very, very romantic Spanish piece that begs for lots of expression from the player, and lots of melodies played up the neck for that sexy Spanishy, this is *sooooo* beautiful sound. At this point you're probably thinking, "C'mon, Mike… you didn't. Fingerings? Please, no!"

I did.

Changed 'em all. Just went through it like the Terminator with PMS. Segovia got restless, then ornery, then downright hostile. He stopped me a lot. "Tune the guitar"… "Don't leave out that portemento (slide)"… "That is very ugly." More and more anger. And finally, the SHOWDOWN!!!

SEGOVIA: "You bring me my edition, but you change all the fingerings. Why do you do that?" (The traditional and correct response to this is to pee your pants, sob, and say something like, "I'm sorry, Maestro. I am slime. I won't ever question your genius again.")

CHAPDEAINE: "It's just decisions that I make." (Segovia's "HMMMMMMM-

MMM" echoes through the hall like the voice Noah might have heard when he suggested that a real nasty drought might be sufficient.)

SEGOVIA: "Very well. This is for you… continue."

I play one more phrase. Segovia wacks the music, looks up disgusted, and stops me. He launches WMD though his coke-bottle glasses and says, "Do you think what you have done is better than what I have done?" I reply, "No." (At this point, I'm also thinking, maybe no endorsement this time out.)

SEGOVIA: "Then why do you do it?"

(*Nooooooo*, don't do it, Mike! Don't! *Pleeeaase!* Don't give him that…)

CHAPDELAINE: "*Because it's good!*"

The room fell silent. For a moment it was like the vacuum of space. And then he growled, began sputtering, and came to a screaming crescendo with, "*Afuera!*" That's Spanish for "Get out, you disrespectful-not-going-to-get-an-endorsement-from-me-scumbag!"

Well at this point I am seeing red, too. I don't need this. I am a University Professor with a pregnant wife and enough guitar prizes to… well, you get the point. I grew up taking that kind of crap from my dad, and I had no stomach for it at twenty-nine. He hands me my music, and I am an eighth-note rest away from firing off a few profanities of my own at the maestro, and in front of thousands of people and PBS TV cameras. Then suddenly, in a moment, like the shadow cast from a fast moving cloud, something made me stop. "Just take the music and walk calmly back to my seat," I say to myself. The other players were eyeing the exits like a tomcat at the vet. In that rush of rage, probably all that would have come out anyway would have been something like, "*Hop buntachly moochag nall pupnyborf wapunzarple!*" Stoicism really works sometimes.

> Just went through it like the Terminator with PMS. Segovia got restless, then ornery, then downright hostile.

I got a lot of support from my colleagues after the class. And several of the "world's greatest classical guitarists"—stars, former Segovia students who were there as part of the event—said, "Feel good. He does that with all his favorite students." Oh goody! Can I have another?!

Didn't help. I went directly to Jim Smith and told him that I was resigning from the class. Let one of the alternates take a little love from the old curmudgeon. But, Jim said, "Look, right now, everyone thinks that he mistreated you." No, duh. Really? Yer pullin' m' leg, like honest, Wally? He continued, " If you don't show up for your next lesson, they are going to think that *you* are the jerk." Oh, yeah, I'm a regular Richard Nixon... thanks!

> The traditional and correct response to this is to pee your pants, sob, and say something like, "I'm sorry, Maestro. I am slime. I won't ever question your genius again."

So I decided to face my beast again. But here is where it turns good. My old teacher Bruce Holzman was in town for the class. I asked him if he would give me a lesson on how to not get thrown out of a lesson. He came by right away. He said that all I had to do was play very expressively (like he taught me before I got smarter than him). Practice slowly, and find all the beauty in the music and magnify it. Exaggerate the expressiveness like a stage actor does with gestures. Basically, just do what Segovia was telling us all to do. And above all, DON'T CHANGE THE FINGERINGS!

I spent the next day playing slowly and expressively. I mean, *really* slow and expressive! I tried to do what Segovia had been trying to get us to do for ten days, which is to make every note be a personal statement, and a conduit between me and the rest of humanity. Oh, and I chose a multi-movement piece to play for him—one that had no fingerings written in it. By the end of this seclusion (my wife had bailed and taken her frail, pregnant self to hang with friends in the Valley), and refocusing, I really was transformed into a new player.

When I next played for him, he seemed to really enjoy it. Instead of stopping me every two measures for tuning or instruction, he just let me play! Like he didn't want to change anything. I played great. And he dug it, and then asked for another, and another, and another. It was amazing. He never did that in a class! It was like a private concert for Segovia. He was like, "Show me what you got"... "Yeah, go boy!"

I knew that I would not get the endorsement, but I had gotten something much better. I learned. And I had made Segovia happy when I showed him what I had learned.

I worked like an animal after the class to become a more expressive player, and that lead to many great things. But I never changed my mind again. If one doesn't take the music and mold it to his or her own soul, and play with total emotion, then why bother.

I have thought about my special relationship with Segovia many times. I believe that he knew what I was as soon as I touched his hand the first time: an over-confidant know-it-all. I think that he knew that the only way that I would learn from him was if he treated me exactly the way he did. To break me down night after night and kick me out of class. And then finally just let me play for him in front of thousands of people, like we were homies just trading licks. And then sit back and smile while the audience went nuts when I finished playing.

He was a clever teacher, as well as the World's Greatest Classical Guitarist.

Visit Michael Chapdelaine at www.michaelchapdelaine.com

HOUSE OF BLUES

Sounds like the blues are composed of feeling, finesse, and fear.
—Billy Gibbons

When people play blues guitar, it is a matter of pushing the string the way you can and trying with your own ears to get the pitch right. You know, a lot of current guitar players have no sense of pitch at all, and it doesn't seem to matter.
—George Harrison

The last thing that the blues needs is another smart-ass white boy with an attitude.
—Brownie McGhee

Blues is for gut-bucket people who run around with only half their clothes on.
—Reverend Gary Davis

When you sing cry every word
Flat the seventh and the third
—Henry Hipkens (from "That's how I Learned to Sing the Blues")

What makes a Lightnin' Hopkins or a Robert Pete Williams is what they chose to do with those notes. There's a process that occurs between the fingers and the mind and the heart, and that's what makes the clock on the wall stop and turn backwards. The stuff that's drug behind you gives a note its meaning—those crusty layers of history that led you to the point of making that decision. Let me put it this way: It ain't my first night out.
—John Campbell

I Remember Andrés

I heard Segovia telling a student, "Your thumb sounds terrible. Cut it off." The student was so despondent that he resolved he would throw himself off one of the towers and end it all. Hearing how he had upset the student, Segovia found him, recanted the proposed remedy, and consoled him by saying, "Probably a worse one would grow back!"

—*Ray Reussner*

I first "met" Andrés Segovia via his 33 LP recording entitled *Three Centuries of the Guitar* which contained music by Santiago de Murcia, Sor, Castelnuovo-Tedesco, Rodrigo, and others. I spent hundreds of hours listening to this and other Segovia recordings, and they and my memories of the many Segovia recitals I attended remain the most profound musical influence of my life. Had I not been exposed to Segovia's artistry, I probably would never have become a professional musician. Segovia's art was an incomparable combination of poetry, musicianship, sentiment (never sentimentality!), beauty of sound, and effortless technique. He had a truly unique voice, a voice that touched millions of people from all walks of life the world over. When I finally met Segovia in person in 1974, he was 81 and I, 19. The sum of our ages equaled 100. Although he had no need of any further accolades and certainly not of any new students, he let me into his life. He not only coached me privately for several years thereafter without ever taking one cent, he also responded to many of my letters personally. Segovia was one of those rare human beings who are possessed of genuine magic. What he had cannot ever be learned, although without long and arduous study no one becomes what Segovia was. His love of music and the guitar was absolutely pure. Innately aristocratic, through his music he bared his soul to the world and changed and transformed the lives of those fortunate enough to encounter him in person or merely admire him from afar. In this faster, more commercial and tawdry age I miss his integrity, his purity, his stubborn adherence to his own sincere convictions. There is no day that I do not think of him, no day that I do not try to steer by the great North Star that he represented for all of us. All classical guitar playing of today is a footnote to Segovia.

—*Eliot Fisk*

300

I remember leaving Segovia after studying with him in Spain. He gave me a hug goodbye and then pointed his finger at me and said, "Christopher, work very hard." And I remember thinking to myself, "Does he mean I *haven't?*" I now know what he meant was that in order to be the best that you can be, you need to work very hard; you can't rely on talent and natural ability.

—*Christopher Parkening*

This continuing Segovia worshipping does more damage than good. It puts off and holds back the development of the guitar in this wider world sense.

—*John Williams*

ANDRÉS SEGOVIA

I was struggling for the attention of the public and the critics and the musicians, to establish the real value of the guitar. Such things were necessary, because at that time—in spite of Tárrega and Sor—the guitar was captivated by folklore, and I had to take the guitar to a place that people didn't believe it could be: *a very noble instrument.*

Unlike the piano, which is a more indifferent instrument in responding to the artist, the guitar and other string instruments have a sound that is much more dependent on the technique, facility, and instinct of the artist. Every guitarist has a special quality of sound.

The composition lies in the score, and the artist comes and says, "Get up and live!" The artist goes to the score and draws out the beauty that lies there. From that moment, the composition belongs to the interpreter.

Jason Truby

ACOUSTIC: RELOADED

It's hard to imagine that only two weeks prior I was laying sod in a yard in Little Rock, Arkansas. I had resigned myself to happily working with my hands, raising a family, and leading this quiet, Middle-American life. I had a beautiful family, a prosperous landscaping business, and peace about the decision I had made. But then the phone rang. It was, at first, a seemingly innocuous call, but it soon transformed itself into a bolt of lightning, finding its target and shattering all notions of this scripted life of mine.

I hung up the phone, and let go with a long, deep breath. If I wasn't in a mild shock, I was certainly dazed—but I was also very, very excited. I needed to step away from this for a moment to regain my balance. After all, I had just been invited to write the title track to *The Matrix: Reloaded* and record it with P.O.D.

I began to reflect on the path that had brought me to this point, to this happy upheaval that would so alter the course of my life—and teach me even more. It was an unlikely journey that had its beginnings in 1980. I was all of twelve years old then, but the memory lives vividly:

A cassette tape had come my way—a compilation of music that included a song called *Spend My Life with You*, by Phil Keaggy. Something in that song really worked its way inside of me. More than the guitar playing, it calmed me, and reassured me in a strange, intangible way at a time when I really needed the comforting.

When I was able to at last get my first guitar, I was immediately drawn back to that song, and I began to pick things out. I'd spend hours and hours with it, alone in my bedroom, capturing more and more of that wonderful tune. Lessons were not available to me, and so I was really on my own with it.

That was a particularly difficult time in my young life. There were troubles and

302

hardships, times of rebellion and running away, but when I picked up that guitar, I found solace. I hid in it. The guitar somehow made sense to me in the midst of all the chaos. I found that I could speak it better than I could speak English. And it spoke to me in ways I hadn't yet begun to understand. I didn't realize then that what I was hearing in Phil Keaggy's music went far beyond the chords.

I came to realize in that crazy time that music—my constant companion—was God's way of holding onto me, of keeping me from going off the deep end and into complete addiction. Even as a preteen, I struggled with drugs, alcohol, and a life lived at the edge. But I also began to realize that God was somehow calling to me through it all. And He spoke through the music.

When I was fourteen, I began to sense something new—that God was somehow seeking more from me—and *for* me. He began to stir in my heart the desire for a personal relationship with *Him*. And soon, all the things of religion that never made any sense to me fell into the shadows as God presented Himself to my spirit. And I accepted that.

I knew that I needed to make a conscious, deliberate decision to step toward God and away from the world. And for me, that meant not drinking, taking drugs, or smoking pot. It wouldn't be the truth if I said I never went back to those things through the rest of my teenage years. But now every time I did, I was strongly convicted. So as a young Christian who struggled with addiction through his teenage years, I had also come to grips with the knowledge that this world and all it offered could not be my source of happiness. That had to be based on what I am in God, not what I am on this earth.

When those things came into balance, I became truly free for the first time to enjoy what God had given me here. And once I realized that God's grace covered me—that He loved me no matter what—something new opened up. God took my passion for music, and He moved it even deeper. I was finally able to understand what it was all about.

Two years later, a band I was involved in, Living Sacrifice, was signed to a label in Nashville. We were a hardcore rock band playing Christian music. And we were on fire. To be signed was just amazing; we were all so young. The producer actually had to call my high school principal so we could get permission to go to Nashville! We recorded, did some touring, and had a lot of fun, but the band just never really broke through. Eventually, it came to an end. When it did, I determined that I'd get a job and just teach music in the afternoons. But I also continued playing for small functions, and writing pieces on my own that I would give to family and friends at Christmas.

At some point in 1998, though, I found myself at another crossroads. I was married now, and Audra and I were looking forward to starting a family. The need to provide for that family led me to abandon my pursuit of what I knew was a less than reliable career in music. It had so many ups and downs, and I just couldn't see holding it all together. But giving up on a dream wasn't easy. Through the many personal battles, prayers, and time spent with Audra, though, I laid it down. And I grieved as I let that part of my life die.

I started a landscaping business. It was a difficult transition to make—emotionally speaking—but I adjusted, and it was good. You'd think that after playing shows and performing for people and being involved in music at a fairly high level that it would be a drag to come back home and plant shrubs. But I was happy. We had our beautiful daughter, and I was still writing and composing and working on my playing. But I'd get up in the morning and do my landscaping work. I'd still play classical guitar for small gatherings and teach a handful of dedicated students, but other than that, I really completely laid it down. I had finally come to grips with how my life was going to be. And I was okay with that.

> I told Audra that I had to make sure I could say no to this. And I knew that I could. She looked up at me and said, "Then you need to say 'yes.'"

A few years later, I heard from an old friend, Tim Cook. I hadn't spoken with Tim in quite some time, and it was good to hear from him, and to catch up. It was Tim, who all those years ago, had given our little rock band the much needed support and encouragement that ultimately led to our label deal. And now Tim was managing P.O.D., a band that in the previous year had gone five times platinum. And a band that we had originally introduced to Tim! But all was not well in that camp, and the band knew they needed to make some changes. That's where I came in.

Tim laid it all out for me over the phone, explaining the band's difficult situation. He had privately consulted with each of the three remaining members, and in those conversations, each of them had brought up my name. And remarkably, none of them had known that they all three had done that. When they found that out, it bonded them in the decision to call me, and certainly gave me cause to listen. I was blown away. I needed to pay attention.

Astonishing as the offer was, though, there were a few things I needed to do before I could make the commitment. I spent that whole night praying about it, remembering my earlier decision to lay this ambition down, and thinking about what the band—my old friends—must have been going through. I watched the sun come up the next morning. I told Audra that I had to make sure I could say no to this. And I knew that I could. She looked up at me and said, "Then you need to say 'yes.'"

I called Tim the next day and told him that if I'm in, I'm in 100%. If things couldn't be restored—and I had hoped that they could be—I was willing to do whatever they needed me to do. With that, I went to work on the *Matrix* song, and a week later I flew out to Los Angeles to meet with the band. We put the piece together relatively quickly, and knocked it out in the studio. Everything went beautifully. Then at the band's suggestion, I went home for a week, and came back out to San Diego to begin writing for the new album.

In the process of working on the new songs, Sonny asked me who had influenced my playing, because clearly, I wasn't a traditional rock guitarist. And I was able to bring some different things into the music—some interesting chord voicings and progressions that they liked. Immediately I was taken back to that old Keaggy tune, *Spend My Life with You*, and all of his riffs that I had learned over the years. And yes, he had an incredible influence on my playing—and probably my very survival! Phil's music was like comfort food to me. When I'd find myself in a trouble spot, I'd put on one of his albums, and it would always help to get me back on center. So I told the guys, "Yeah, I'm a big Phil Keaggy fan." Well they loved that, and wondered if Phil might be up for joining the band in the studio on a few of the tunes when it came time to record. And much to my delight, he was.

I wrote an acoustic piece to feature Phil, to honor him, and present him to a large mass of people that may not have ever heard his music. He came out with his son Ian, and we met at my apartment, where we went over all the songs that we'd be recording the next day. Over dinner, I was grateful for the opportunity to tell him that he had been a very special mentor to me, that he had had a major impact on my life and my music. And now I could thank him. This was, for me, a sacred moment.

In the morning, we took our acoustic guitars into the studio, and just jammed. Phil played his parts and then soloed over *Eternal*, the six-minute piece I had written expressly for him. The band was blown away, as I knew they would be. Phil blessed us all that day. And remarkably, the guitar and Phil had brought me full circle.

When I think back on it all, I stand amazed at how God worked—how he continues to work. How he knocked at my door. How he wove a tapestry for my life using the threads of so many other faithful people, family, and friends. How at different times he put my name on the hearts of my band mates, and theirs on mine.

And I'm reminded of how when you honor God wherever you happen to be, and no mater what you're doing—in my case, cleaning fishponds, laying sod, and digging ditches—God will always lift you up. He'll give you the desires of your heart in his timing, and according to his plan, which is never what we think it is.

And he revealed to me the cords that he holds. He revealed the mysteries that are precious to him, even though they may not make much sense on this planet.

So to those aspiring musicians who are doing the right thing, who are providing for their families, and are out there working and sweating, and frustrated by not being able to use their musical gifts, surrender that to God, and he will lift up and bless the humble heart. If you're digging a ditch, dig it as though you're digging it for God, himself. And when God opens the door, it is miraculous.

Walking up the ladder in the music business is incredibly difficult. I told Audra that I didn't think I had it in me to work up that ladder again—that the only way I could see myself getting back into it was if a positioned opened up with a band that was already established. And that that band is such a bright light in a very dark arena inhabited by so many young people who are absolutely lost—as I once was lost—leaves me breathless. I'm nothing but in awe, humbled, and full of expectations for new miracles—but none that I could ever script.

Visit Jason Truby and P.O.D. at www.payableondeath.com

LIVINGSTON TAYLOR

Regardless of my first guitar teacher's reluctance, he was an unbelievably good teacher. He was my older brother, James. My first guitar was a hand-me-down from him, but not before our other brother, Alex, spray-painted it blue. He proclaimed that that's what Elvis had done to his guitar; he pretty much ruined the thing. So when James got another guitar, the little blue Harmony naturally fell to me.

So as a twelve-year old I'd wait until James was doing something else—reading, eating dinner, anything else he might be doing. That's when I would get around him, as the pesky younger brother, and I would start to play. And I knew what was going to happen next. James would hear me play, and if I didn't do it right, it would drive him crazy. But he wouldn't show me how to do it right without punching me first. So the usual order of my lessons went like this: I would do the guitar lick that I was working on, at which point he would go, "No, that's not how it's done," punch in the arm, then take the instrument and show me how to do it right. And I very quickly learned that the pain-to-benefit ratio was wildly in my favor. He was a great teacher.

Visit Livingston Taylor at www.livingstontaylor.com

Jon Burchfield

ON THE ROAD AGAIN

I was fourteen when my family took a summer trip that would take us from Chicago to California and back. Seven of us, including our dog Bugle piled in a Dodge Station Wagon that pulled a camper loaded down with coolers and blankets. On that summer in '69 we headed for the most beautiful national parks we could find.

For the trip, I bought a little Harmony guitar for around twelve dollars. It would be the perfect companion on those nights while sitting around campfires. My dad showed me a few chords, and I took it from there. I remember the first song I learned was *Wayfaring Stranger*.

By the time we got back to our home in Illinois, I had learned enough chords to play along with our church choir. That was actually a great learning experience, because the teen choir used a lot of Otis Skillings music. He wrote out all these cool jazz chords, and in the back of each book were the fingerings. I was mesmerized at the endless harmonies and chord changes. I spent hours each day discovering new possibilities for progressions and substitutions.

After four years of teen choir and high school jazz band, I entered college with guitar in hand. It was the most exciting day of my life! There were PR groups that would go out on weekends, along with other musical acts needing guitarists. I was considered one of the best players on campus, but then there were only four of us who played in the entire school. Needless to say, it was a thrilling time in my life. And it was all about to end.

While sitting in the student center with other musicians, discussing who would join each group, two men, one of whom was the dean of the college, approached and asked me to step outside. They began frisking me from head to toe, and when they found nothing, they said,

"You're lucky."

I was trying to figure out why I was "lucky" and asked what they were looking for. They said they learned from an outside source that I was the new drug lord on campus. I explained to them the most powerful drug I'd ever taken was a Flintstone vitamin. Nevertheless, I was banned from all music groups and told not to bring my guitar back. When people asked what was going on, I tried to keep it light-hearted and told them I was invited to leave college.

But inside I was devastated. Only days after enrolling, I packed my books and guitar and came back home. And then I wrestled through my "dark night of the soul." To start a new chapter in my life only to have it slammed shut was beyond my understanding. Somehow, though, through all of that I felt that God was saying to me, "Let me do my work. Everything is going to be alright."

Two nights later the phone rang at 1:00 AM. A guitarist I'd met months earlier was leaving a traveling group called The Spurrlows, and wanted to know if I'd like to take his place. I yawned, rubbed my eyes, and asked him when, and he said immediately. I talked it over with my family the next morning, and then I packed my bags. The day before I left, the dean called me into his office one last time and said, "I understand you're joining a tour group. I needed to see you before you left, to tell you that I have an apology to make. We made a terrible mistake thinking you were the person involved in these crimes, but someone has come forward, confessed, and has been sent to a mental institute. As far as we are concerned, you are as clean as a hound dog's tooth. If you ever want to come back to this college, we'll greet you with open arms. And bring your guitar." We shook hands and said farewell. And with a great sigh of relief I left for the road.

> Paydays were on Wednesdays, but I found the money would stretch if I ate at McDonald's Wednesday through Sunday, and didn't eat at all Monday or Tuesday.

I met the group in St. Louis, and the next few months proved to be a whirlwind of concerts and traveling. A whole new life lay ahead of me that was everything I'd dreamed of as a musician.

When I joined that group in the fall of '72, I was told the pay would be $17.00 a week, but most everything was provided, so as an eighteen year old, I didn't really care. I just wanted the experience. But then I learned it was a union gig, and I that needed to pay $5.00 a week for dues. That brought my salary down to $12.00 a week. Let me spell that, twelve dollars a week! That's what I paid for my first guitar!

Well, even that was okay, except we had to buy our own food. Paydays were on Wednesdays, but I found the money would stretch if I ate at McDonald's

Wednesday through Sunday, and didn't eat at all Monday or Tuesday. Then the cycle would begin again. I tried buying bouillon cubes, figuring they would melt in a cup of hot tap water, giving me the illusion of drinking watered-down soup. But they were hard as a rock, and only tinted the water with a faded rust color.

I lost more than twenty pounds in the first couple months, and my face broke out because I'd never eaten that much junk food before. In spite of all that, I was having the time of my life.

Soon Roy Clark heard of us and we became his backup band. He was a huge star in those days and his warm up acts included Kenny Rogers and the First Edition, Barbara Mandrel, Rich Little, and others. I'll never forget the first night we backed him. He wasn't one who liked practicing that much, so he showed up not long before the concert. We were introduced and I was told we would be playing *Dueling Banjos*. I was to simply follow him and play on the guitar whatever he played on the banjo. I walked out on the stage that night at the Cherry Hill Arena in North Carolina and stared at five thousand Roy Clark fans. I'd never seen so many people under one roof, and when it was time for our duet, I nearly fainted. I was so nervous that I just couldn't get my fingers to work on one of the licks, so I quickly bowed and pretended it was part of the show. The audience loved it and Roy seemed to be pleased. Over time I got used to his style, and the fear subsided.

In May of '73 we were booked at the Frontier Hotel in Las Vegas. We'd play two shows a night and mingle with the stars during the days. On Saturdays we'd play softball with the Fifth Dimension, B.B. King's band, and others making the weeks there an intoxicating blend of celebrities and dazzling night life. On one occasion, we were escorted by dozens of police to the Hollywood Bowl for a concert, then back to Vegas for our regular evening show.

> One rule said you would not work for less than $416.00 a week, and we had grossly violated that rule.

Everything was spectacular. Until one night. Two men slipped in the back stage during the performance asking questions about our group. When the show was over, the police came back, only this time we were escorted to jail. We lined up to get fingerprinted and have our mug shots taken so we could get booked. In those days the union was powerful, especially in Vegas. If you didn't comply with the standard rules you went to jail. One rule said you would not work for less than $416.00 a week, and we had grossly violated that rule. I knew nothing about it, and of course Roy knew nothing about it, either; he was an innocent bystander. But he soon learned there was no longer a backup group, and we were all going to pay the price for being law breakers.

The manager of the group was flown in from Orlando, and somewhere along the line he struck a deal with the union. He brought with him a load of money that looked like someone had taken a wheel barrel and dumped it on the table. To keep from going to jail himself, he agreed to pay each one of us everything he owed, including back pay. One by one, we entered a room where we were given a sack of money, and charges were dropped. In private we were told that a new group would be forming, and if we'd give the money back we could continue touring with a substantial pay raise. Most of the members took their share, booked a flight out and that was the last we saw of them. But being the youngest of the group, I wasn't ready to stop touring, so I struck a deal with them. The guitar I was playing was worn out and hard to tune. I told them I'd give the money back if they'd give me a new guitar and a pay raise. They agreed and we were off to New York. I went into to Sam Ash and picked out a Gibson ES 345 double cut away with walnut finish. It was the most beautiful guitar I'd ever seen!

The new group kicked in, touring was better than ever, and we were back with Roy Clark. On many nights we would trade guitars, and I'd play his Gibson Birdland during the show. He would see me polishing my guitar every night, so he went out and bought a case cover for me, which I still have today thirty years later.

I could write a book about all the things that happened during those two years, and all the things I learned as a guitarist. But I'll never forget the biggest lesson of all. When God gives us something and asks for it back, don't sweat it. He's simply going to make it better.

Visit Jonathan Burchfield at www.burchfieldbrothers.com

JONATHA BROOKE

I worked all summer when I was fifteen, saving up the money to buy my first guitar—a 12-string Martin. But that guitar was so wicked hard to play. I have pretty small hands, and it just kicked my butt. Five years later I traded it for Duke Levine's leather bomber jacket. I fell in love that jacket. I didn't have any money at the time, so I offered him my 12-string. I thought it was a good trade.

Visit Jonatha Brooke at www.jonathabrooke.com

Jorma Kaukonen

ON THE BRIGHTER SIDE

The difference between musicians and savings bonds? Savings bonds eventually mature! Or so I've been told. But then, it's also been said that the first sign of maturity is the discovery that the volume knob also turns to the left. Well, I might not want to go that far just yet, but it is true that some things in my life have been turned down, if only just a bit.

As I work on a new album, it occurs to me that my music always reflects my place in the world at the time it was written—for better or for worse. I think it's for the better that that place changes from time to time. And those times and places reflect different thought processes, different frames of mind. The common thread, of course, is I'm always *me*; I still recognize myself when I listen to the old stuff.

It's interesting now to see how my music has tracked my path through life. And I find that my most successful writing has always happened when I was honest with myself about "where I am today." It might be a good place; it might be a bad place. Things are always subject to change.

Over the years, though, I've found it easier to write songs of disaffection and frustration. I have a significant vocabulary of dark language that has served me well in that regard! I wrote quite a lot of that kind of material with Jefferson Airplane. And I've certainly not been alone in that. I recently heard a program on NPR where the guests were discussing the creative process. And one of the conclusions they drew was that angst-driven material tends to have a greater appeal to a wider audience than "feel good" music. Maybe it makes people feel better to know that someone else feels worse. As they say, misery loves company. I really don't know. But that notion presents a challenge to me today. The fact is I just don't feel like that anymore. Much of the darkness in my life has fled, and my life is so much more serene than it used to be. And so, I want to write about more positive things. Yet artistically speaking, I find it a new and interesting challenge to express being in a place of satisfaction without coming off as warm and fuzzy, or worse—trite.

I'm not a pop song writer, and so my first objective is not mass appeal. On the other hand, none of us in the creative community wants to do something that will be unpopular. We like people to like our stuff! I'd be out of work if people didn't! But I've grown, and that growth has to be reflected in the music I write today.

One aspect of that growth is that I've come to realize that there is more to life than what we see. I didn't always believe it. And everybody believes something. For a musician, that belief system gets reflected in the music. I've always been attracted to spiritual music—Reverend Gary Davis, most obviously. And so I would like to think that at some level there is a constant thread of spirituality that comes across in my music. But when that quality comes through in instrumental music, then that's a truly amazing thing. Ed Gerhard is a beautiful example. I was listening to him recently, and his music just touched my heart. It painted pictures. It was beautiful. And for me, that's powerful stuff. That says it all. And today, that's where I want to be.

Visit Jorma at www.furpeaceranch.com, the on-line home of Kaukonen's guitar camp nestled in the rolling foothills of southeast Ohio. The Fur Peace Ranch is a positive place to better explore the potential of your favorite instrument, and to learn from and listen to some great musicians.

VINCE GILL

When I was eighteen, I took off to Louisville, Kentucky to play bluegrass. And if you're going to play bluegrass you've got to have a great old instrument; it's kind of a law. So I felt like I needed a great guitar. I found this old D-28 Martin made in 1942. It was in perfect condition, as if it had sat underneath somebody's bed years and years. So I completely emptied out all my savings account to buy this guitar. That was going to be my college money—my "getting started" money that I had saved my whole life since I was a little kid. And I didn't tell my folks.

Visit Vince Gill at www.vincegill.com

Lee Ritenour

IT'S NOT ONLY WHAT YOU KNOW...

Aside from my family, the guitar has been the most consistent thing in my life—the very key to my being on the planet. It keeps me stabilized on the ground *and* connected to upstairs. Even as a youngster, I was putting strings on broomsticks. And once I got a guitar, it became incredibly clear that that's was I was supposed to be doing.

When I was only twelve years old, my dad would take me to see Wes Montgomery and Kenny Burrell and Joe Pass and Barney Kessel. And it was always an experience. I was so very inspired by all the great players that I totally dedicated myself to the guitar and its journey.

Along with a few other kids I knew in Los Angeles—Larry Carlton, Steve Lukather, and Paul Jackson, Jr.—I was a bit of a prodigy. Larry lived nearby, and I'd meet the others from time to time. We were all in our teens and playing in different situations, various jazz bands, and other groups, and we certainly knew about each other.

Yet, as a student with ambitions and aspirations, sometimes the hardest thing is getting your first significant job, getting a start and that much needed confirmation that you're good enough to make it. One of my first attempts was an audition for Stan Kenton's Neophonic Band, which at that time was made up mostly of college kids and "all stars" from around the country. The guitar spot came down to two guitar players: me and another player whose name will go unmentioned. But his father was a professional guitarist, and he happened to know the gentleman who was conducting the audition.

I could see, even at the tender age of fourteen, that it really was neck and neck between that other guitar player and me. And the bandleader who was doing the auditions really didn't have a clue as to who to choose. At one point, recognizing the name, he said to the other guitarist, "Aren't you so and so's son?" The kid said, "Yes, that's my dad." And that was the end of the audition. He got the job.

313

That always stuck with me as an important lesson, painful as it was. Even back then, you realize that it's not just your musicianship that gets you to the next step; you do have to be in the music business. So that experience encouraged me to look out for my career, and that had to involve more than just the music. And while losing that audition was a very disheartening event, it made me work all the harder. Sometimes, in the bigger picture, the failures can be more positive, if not more so, than successes.

Visit Lee Ritenour at www.leeritenour.com

Steve Lukather on Lee Ritenour

I was nineteen and late to a session, which was a big live orchestra session. Anyway I showed up and had barely plugged in and tuned up my guitar when I saw the score. It was black with notes. I was rattled. On top of that, it was in D-flat. My entire face looked like the blood left it. Lee Ritenour was to play first guitar, and I was to play second, which was the hard part. I looked over at Rit with this helpless expression on my face. He smiled at me, took my guitar part, and gave me his. He bailed me, big time! Lee is one of the best all-around guitarists I've ever heard. And he's a really great guy.

The Edge

SOMETHING TO SAY

I suppose it really starts with picking up the electric guitar, age fifteen, and playing a lot of cover versions, knowing a few Rory Gallagher licks or whatever. Then suddenly you're in this band and there's all this fantastic music coming at you that challenges everything that you believed about what the electric guitar was for. Suddenly the question is, "What are you *saying* with it?" Suddenly guitars were not things to be waved in front of the audience but now were something you used to *reach out* to the crowd. If you were in the fourth row of the Jam concert at the Top Hat Ballroom in Dunleary in 1980, when Paul Weller hit that Rickenbacker twelve-string, it *meant* something and it said something that everyone in that building knew. There were other bands, other guitar players. They all sounded different, but they all had that thing in common which was that there was something behind what they did, which was communicating.

I had to totally reexamine the way I played. It was such a challenging thing to hold up your style against this and say, "Well, what are *you* saying? What is this song about? What does that note mean? Why *that* note?" So much of this bad white-blues barroom stuff that was around at the time was just guitar players running up and down the fretboard. It was just a kind of big wank. There was nothing to it; it was gymnastics. I started trying to find out what this thing around my neck could do in the context of this band. Songs were coming through and, "Well, that sort of works" and integrating the echo box, which was a means of further coloring the sound, controlling the tone of the guitar. I was not going for purity; I was going for the opposite. I was trying to screw up the sound as much as possible, go for something that was definitely messed with, definitely tampered with, had a character that was not just the regular guitar sound.

> "Well, what are *you* saying? What is this song about? What does that note mean? Why *that* note?"

Then I suppose I started to see a style coming through. I started to see how notes actually *do* mean something. They have power. I think of notes as being expensive. You don't just throw them around. I find the ones that do the best job, and that's what I use. I suppose I'm a minimalist instinctively. I don't like to be ineffective if I can get away with it. Like on the end of *With or Without You.* My instinct was to go with something very simple. Everyone else said, "Nah, you can't do that." I won the argument and I still think it's sort of brave, because the end of *With or Without You* could have been so much bigger, so much more of a climax, but there's this power to it which I think is even more potent because it's held back.

I suppose ultimately I'm interested in music. I'm a musician. I'm not a gunslinger. That's the difference between what I do and what a lot of "guitar heroes" do.

Unfortunately when something is distilled down to a simple style, those who copy the style basically are copying something very flat. You take what I do, bring it down to a little, short formula and try and apply it in another context, another guitar player, another song—it's going to sound terrible. I think that's probably what's happened to Jeff Beck and Eric Clapton and Jimmy Page. So many of their strong ideas have been taken up by other guitar players in other bands and the result is some pretty awful music. Heavy metal for one.

INFLUENCE PEDDLING

Everybody who has their own style also has obvious elements
of other players that they learned from.
—*Wanda Vic*

I've internalized all these influences, and when you stick me up in front
of an audience with my guitar, it's like squeezing a sponge; this homogenized
thing comes out that's a mixture of all that plus my own experience.
—*Laurence Juber*

Be a student of whoever inspires you. Don't copy them, but learn
from them. And most importantly, have fun doing it.
—*Wes King*

When you really admire a guitarist, the best dedication, the best compliment
you can pay to him, is to play your own way and to play your own music.
—*Pat Metheny (by way of Pierre Bensusan)*

John Williams

FOR THE LOVE OF BARRIOS

Having been unrecognized outside Latin America during his lifetime and neglected for decades after his death in 1944, Agustin Barrios Mangoré—best known simply as Barrios—is now rightfully appreciated as the outstanding guitarist-composer of his time. And for his qualities of inventiveness and obvious love of the instrument, I would say of *any* time.

In addition to being a virtuoso player, he composed hundreds of pieces, ranging in scope from baroque-inspired and 19th Century pieces to popular songs and dances in the Latin American traditions. But above all, he was a lover of the guitar. And Barrios' poetic nature and devotion to the instrument is shown in his *Dedication to the Guitar*, recited by him at one of his concerts in Brazil:

"Tupa, the Supreme Spirit and protector of my race, found me one day in the middle of a verdant copse, wrapt in admiration whilst contemplating nature. And he said to me, *Take this mystery box and unmask its secrets*. And locking up in it all the singing birds, he left it in my hands. Obeying the orders of Tupa, I took the box. And placing it close to my chest, I embraced it, and spent many moons at the side of a spring. And one night, Jacy, the moon goddess, painted in liquid crystal and feeling the sadness of my Indian soul, gave me six silver rays of light, so that with them I could unlock the secrets of the box. And the miracle occurred: from the depths of the mysterious box there emerged a marvelous symphony of all the virgin voices of our America."

The guitar tradition that he represents in Latin America is unique in the way a classical instrument—the Spanish guitar—could find its way into the indigenous folk styles of so many cultures on that continent. The synthesis of the classical instrument with popular music forms has yielded tremendous music, wonderfully exemplified by Barrios' example.

In 1994, on the 50th anniversary of his death, I enjoyed the privilege and honor of performing several concerts in Paraguay. The President's Medal for that year was issued in Barrios' honor, and presented to me for the work I had done for his music.

I was asked to do a concert in the capital city of Asuncion for the President, and more specifically, for the President's wife's favorite charity. Of course, I agreed to do the benefit, but I thought I would push my luck. I am a supporter of Amnesty International, who were very active in supporting prisoners of conscience under the previous Paraguayan dictatorship. And I wanted to do a concert to benefit the work of Amnesty International in Asuncion. So I said I'd play for the President's charity, as long as I could also do a concert for one of my own. I did think it was a bit cheeky of me to try and be as up front as that, but they agreed to it, as it was the first year of the new democratically elected President.

> On either side of me were the proverbial stacked Marshalls—a bit incongruous to the setting—blasting out into the village square.

It was a most wonderful occasion to be met at the airport by the official car and an enormous group of Amnesty supporters with all their flags and banners. And it turned out to be a lovely concert in the open air venue in the Japan-Paraguay Culture Center square.

I then traveled to San Juan Bautista le Misiones—Barrios' birthplace in the south of Paraguay. I played in the small village church just around the corner from where he was born, the family house now being a museum. The doors of the church opened out onto the square, which was absolutely packed with people. And on either side of me were the proverbial stacked Marshalls—a bit incongruous to the setting—blasting out into the village square. It was an amazing and moving experience.

At one point, in 1932, Barrios traveled to Venezuela, where in a period of two months he performed twenty-five concerts. He struck up a friendship there with a local guitarist, Raul Borges. Borges joined Barrios in a number of his performances, and studied intensively with him. With Barrios passing a torch, so to speak, Borges became known as the "Father of the Guitar" in Venezuela, teaching a whole generation of players, including Antonio Lauro and Alirio Díaz.

Díaz, of course, became a legend in his own time. Over the years he has collected, arranged, and edited a vast amount of Venezuelan music for solo guitar. I first met him as a boy of twelve, and enjoy a close friendship with him to this day. He's been a tremendous inspiration in my love of Venezuelan music.

In 1976, I traveled to Caracas, Venezuela, for the Alirio Díaz Guitar Festival. I accompanied Alirio one Saturday morning to a small town outside Caracas, where a number of his friends were having a party. We arrived, presumably for lunch, at about noon, and we all sat in a wonderful garden patio surrounded by overhung mango trees. They were playing marvelous Venezuelan music on their homemade instruments—cuatros, double bass, guitars, all sorts of things. They just sang, danced, played, and drank quite a lot of wine and whisky—actually, rather a lot of whisky! The celebration went on well into the late afternoon. "Lunch" didn't happen till six o'clock!

Nowadays I am getting more and more interested in traditional techniques of guitar playing—it would be nice to join in on spontaneous occasions more often. "The guitar" and "Latin America"—together they are sure to create great memories and emotions!

Visit John Williams at www.johnwilliamsguitar.com

If your motivation is the music, rather than other
factors, that is never going to leave you.
And that's how it should be.
—*John Renbourn*

George Gruhn

HOLY GRAILS AND BACKSTAGE PASSES

While I have owned many thousands of guitars over the years, my most fond and vivid memories are of my first few. I still distinctly remember seeing the bulletin board ad at the University of Chicago in 1963 for a Conde Hermanos classical made in Madrid which was to become my very first guitar. It didn't take long to discover that while it was a fine classical guitar, it wasn't going to suit Carter Family style playing. About ninety days later I bought my second guitar which was a style O Gibson Artist model with the scroll body made circa 1915. It was a great looking guitar, but it had a huge clubby neck and simply didn't put out very much volume. I kept looking for the perfect guitar. Another ninety days later I bought my third instrument which was a 1937 Martin style F-7 archtop F hole guitar.

Fortunately for me, back in 1963 vintage instruments were remarkably cheap compared to today's prices. As a student I was not rolling in money. Unfortunately for me, none of my first three guitars really suited me personally such that I continued my search. A few months later I found my fourth guitar, a 1924 Gibson Lloyd Loar-signed L-5 sitting at Sid Sherman's Music store on Wabash Avenue downtown. It was $400, an absolutely astronomical sum for a used guitar at that time. I put a deposit down and took several months to pay it off. At the beginning of each month, Mom and Dad sent me money for rent, books, and food to get me through college. I poured all the money into guitars that I would find in pawn shops, music stores, and bulletin board ads. Within a week I'd sell enough to get back all the money Mom and Dad had given so I could pay my bills and still have money left to buy the guitars I wanted to keep.

Guitar collecting was an addiction for me, but I had the good fortune to be able to find fifty or more great deals on items I didn't want to keep for every one that I personally wanted for my collection. As long as I was going into music stores, pawn shops, and scouring classified ads and bulletin boards, I couldn't help but run

320

across screaming deals on instruments which did not appeal to me while looking for those few pre World War II Martin guitars, Gibson F model mandolins, Gibson Mastertone banjos, and Vega Whyte Laydie and tu-ba-phone banjos.

Aside from the Loar L-5 perhaps my greatest score in collecting during the 1960s came about in the fall of 1966 when I got a call from Frank Rizutto in Chicago. Frank collected archtop F hole jazz guitars and was a wheeler-dealer. I had bought and traded a few guitars with him, so he was well aware that I was keenly interested in old Martins. He himself had little interest in Martins since they certainly were not jazz guitars, but he knew enough to call me if he found one. This time when I answered the phone he said, "George, it's Frank. I found an old Martin that is stamped inside D, Four, Five. Is that any good?" I said, "Frank, that's one that I would like. How much do you want for it?" He said, "How about $600?" I said, "That sounds pretty good to me. I could make it over in about twenty minutes. Will you wait for me?" He said, "Sure." Twenty minutes later I was holding a fine looking 1939 D-45 and counting out the money for Frank. Needless to say I was proud of my acquisition. The only other D-45 I had ever seen outside of a photo was one owned by a performer named Fleming Brown in Chicago. Unfortunately that one was highly reworked and in relatively poor condition. This one was nearly pristine. Today my guitar would be worth at least $175,000. Back then $600 was a great deal, but I had not heard of any D-45 bringing over $1,500 in the mid 1960s. Times have changed.

> "George, it's Frank. I found an old Martin that is stamped inside D, Four, Five. Is that any good?"

A couple of months later it was time for the University of Chicago Folk Festival. They brought in traditional acoustic musicians performing primarily Southern string band and bluegrass music. My introduction to Bill Monroe, the Stanley Brothers, Maybell Carter, Jim and Jessie, The New Lost City Ramblers, and numerous other fantastic musicians was through this festival. Rather than keep my D-45 at my apartment near school, I had it at my parents' house in Morton Grove north of town for better security, but that weekend I decided to trek up to get it so I could show it off for the weekend. Mid-winter Chicago weather is typically cold, but normally it is no trouble to get around since the roads and public transportation are excellent. That weekend, however, turned out to be the occasion of one of the worst blizzards of the century. While I was in Morton Grove the snow started peacefully enough but soon turned into a virtual white-out. All roads soon became impassable. News stories showed pictures of Lakeshore Drive totally covered in snow with lumps indicating the abandoned cars buried underneath. On level ground the snow was over two and one-half feet deep and drifts were six feet and higher. I couldn't even get out of my parents' house without first taking the storm window off the outer door and shoveling enough snow away to permit me to open the door.

Needless to say, prospects for getting from Morton Grove at 9200 North to the University of Chicago at 5700 South didn't look too good, but I was determined to show off my D-45 that weekend and attend the festival. While there was no way to hike from my parents' home to the university or drive, the Illinois Central railroad track ran right by the house, and there was a passenger station about a mile and a half away. I bundled up, put on tall boots, and took off through the snow with my D-45 and made it to the station. The big Illinois Central trains could get through virtually any weather conditions, so I was able to make it downtown to the main station which was the end of the line. That left me still needing to get from the Illinois Central station to the elevated train in the loop downtown which was a goodly walk. It was an amazing scene. There were no cars or buses in motion and remarkably few people. Only total idiots and obsessive fanatics were downtown or outside at all. I am not sure which category I fit into—probably both—but I hiked to the elevated train and was able to go to the station at 63rd Street which was an easy walk from my off campus apartment at 61st and Ellis. From there it was not terribly difficult to make it to the festival, although attendance in general was way down since virtually nobody off campus was able to get in.

Most of the performers made it in somehow since in spite of how heavy the snow was, it didn't extend much south of Gary, Indiana. Quite a few of them, however, found that while they themselves were able to fly in, their luggage, including their instruments, didn't make it. My D-45 was one of the few good guitars available and ended up being used on stage by quite a few of the acts. That guitar continued to be my backstage pass for years afterward, and paved the way for me to meet and establish ongoing relationships with a wide variety of performers ranging from Bill Monroe and Red Smiley to Mike Seeger with The New Lost City Ramblers. While my playing skills were minimal, my D-45 was a great calling card and opened many doors for me. By 1976 I had amassed quite a collection and had six D-45s as well as quite a few OOO, OO, and O-45s, and numerous other instruments of merit. At about that time I sold off much of my collection and bought a building for my shop. While I made a very good profit, in retrospect I wish I had kept them. They certainly are worth astronomically more today than they were then. Plus, the emotional bond I had with my first D-45 has never been equaled by any instrument I have acquired since.

Visit George Gruhn at www.gruhn.com

Jack White

AIRLINE TRIP

When my sister Meg and I started The White Stripes in 1997, part of the aesthetic of the band was that all materials on stage or in our artwork would revolve around the number three. So everything would either be red, white, or black—Meg's drums, my amps, our clothes, and my guitars.

At the time, I was using a nameless 1960s red guitar from Japan, but I really wanted something more definitive, both musically and visually. I had been eyeing the plastic guitars called "Airlines." They were made by Valco and were sold in Montgomery Wards department stores. They were very cheap, and were a lot of players' first guitars as children.

About that time, I went to a show in Detroit by a band called The Oblivions. They were from Memphis and pretty popular on the garage rock scene. Before the show I wandered backstage, as I often do when I get bored (can't stand still for long) and I met up with Jack Yarber, also known as "Jack Oblivion." We talked for a minute and then he said he had something to show me. He opened up a guitar case, and there it was: a red, white, and black Airline Jetson. It was perfect. My eyes lit up. "Man, I would love to get one just like that," I said. "I've been looking for something just like that." Then Jack muttered, "Well, it's for sale." In my mind it was "sold," but I played a little dumb since I didn't have much money at the time. He told me he wanted to get the three-pickup version of the guitar, and so he needed to sell this one. So for $200 I bought it, but I had to wait until his tour was over to get it. And I didn't get the case because he was saving it for his new guitar. He later told *Mojo* magazine the story and ended his interview with, "Jack White stole my mojo!!!" Still, to this day, it was probably the best purchase I ever made, or probably will ever make—until Charlie Patton's guitar turns up.

Visit Jack White at www.whitestripes.com

Jerry Douglas

PASS THE BOTTLENECK, PLEASE!

I have long been drawn to the allure of vintage instruments. Their storied histories and checkered pasts seem to impart a depth of character that no new instrument can deliver. I had been playing a newer Dobro with my Washington-based band, The Country Gentlemen, when I really began to yearn for an older instrument—one like those played by my heroes, Josh Graves and Mike Auldridge.

In 1974, I learned of a Canadian collector who had decided to sell one of his prewar Dobros from his vast collection. We agreed to meet at a bluegrass festival in Ohio, where, accompanied by my father, we talked money and finally settled on the huge sum of $400. Having finished our business, my father asked the seller if he might be a drinking man. Well, being a good Canadian, of course he was, and he was proud of it. Dad had just finished a batch of home brew in his garage—just in time for the festival—and bottled it in 16-ounce Coca Cola bottles. Being a hot summer day, our new friend happily obliged, and upon downing the first bottle, and asked for another.

Now, this particular part of Ohio is home to a large Amish community. They're really big bluegrass fans there, and they were out in force. Out of the elder's sight, they were drinking and dancing, as well.

Our Canadian friend, now comfortably inebriated and feeling frolicsome, decided to dance with the Amish girls as the music played from the stage. Well, this didn't set too well with the boys they were with, so they took his hat and set it on fire. And lost in the festivities, he was also unaware that his ride had left him behind and was back on his way to Toronto. Somehow, though, he found his way home, because I received the old Dobro through customs about a week later.

It seems that alcohol and old Dobros keep regular company. Several years ago, a friend gave me an old Cyclops style Dobro, so-called because of the single sound-hole screen in the top, where the fretboard meets the body. A reasonably rare gui-

324

tar, I was flattered he thought of me when it needed a new home. It seems the guitar had some provenance, as well, as it came from the estate of Sonny Boy Williamson—the legendary Chigaco blues harmonica player. It then passed to Memphis producer, Chips Moman before being brokered to me through my friend. Needless to say, I was ecstatic.

My friend brought the guitar to my house, and when he opened the old case, we were hit with a powerful rush of whiskey fumes—a quality that my friend assured me was original to his purchase!

I've tried on numerous occasions to record with this great old guitar, but playing in a small, airlocked sound booth, I would be overcome by the fumes. I always ended up finishing the sessions with unscented guitars. As much as I would like for it to happen, it has yet to be successfully recorded—at least by me!

Visit Jerry Douglas, visit www.jerrydouglas.com

My playing is very pungent—like you can smell it—and
you can get that same smell in whatever idiom it's in.
That's my personality coming out.
—*David Bromberg*

Pete Yorn

FOR NANCY

The music of the Ventures really pulled me in; I was very much into their sound. And, of course, the Ventures played Mosrite guitars, which meant I had to have one, too. I found one I liked hanging on the wall at Black Market Music in West Hollywood, where they sell used and vintage gear. I didn't take much time to plug it in and test it out on different amps; it just felt pretty good and so I bought it. I hung with it for a few days at home, and realized that I didn't really like it after all. It sounded dull through my amp, and it was just so heavy—it felt like it was made out of teak.

So I took it back to the store to see what I could do. When I came in, I saw a guitar that I didn't notice the week before—a wine red Gibson SG. I thought, "Wow—I'd always wanted one of those guitars, too." I thought maybe I could trade up for it. Well, the salesman just swapped it out straight across, and that was it.

I took that guitar home, and almost immediately a song came pouring out of it. Now, sometimes you just get burned out with your writing, and a new or borrowed guitar can somehow snap you out of it—all of a sudden the same old chords sound fresh again. And that may have been the case with this SG. I don't know. But it really was an inspiring moment; songs don't often happen that fast.

> Then I flipped it over and I saw carved into the back of the guitar—actually it was scrawled with a knife—the name Nancy.

I started examining the guitar a little more closely then, much more so than I had when I was in the store. Well, right away, I realized two things I hadn't pick up on when I got it. The first was that the neck had been broken off where it meets the body. And I thought, damn! But then I learned that a lot of the early '70s SGs had that problem. Then I flipped it over and I saw carved into the back of the guitar—actually it was scrawled with a knife—the name Nancy.

I have no idea who this Nancy character is, but I dedicated the song to her. I don't even know if she's dead or alive. And I don't know when her name was scratched onto the guitar. It could have been back in the '70s, or it could have been done the week before I picked up. I just don't know. Nancy could be somebody's dog! But seeing her name there did conjure up a certain image in my mind. And that the previous owner scratched her name into the guitar says something about him—or her, as well. At that time I had recently watched the movie *The Red Violin*, which made me speculate all the more about its past.

When I wander into these used stores and pawn shops, I wonder about the stories behind the guitars, where they came from, who was on their last leg and finally had to give up their instrument. I can imagine someone who found himself in a desperate situation and was finally forced to hock his guitar. And perhaps his dream for his music died that day.

But still, there are songs in those guitars—good ones! And maybe the dream is reborn with the next owner. My song *For Nancy* became one of my more popular ones, and I believe it was lying there inside that SG, waiting for someone to come along and bring it out. So Nancy, whoever you are, wherever you are, this one's for you.

Visit Pete Yorn at www.peteyorn.com

Well, here I am. I'm trying to work. I'm trying
to bring people together. I'm trying to get people
to see that we *are* our brother's keeper.
—*B.B. King*

Bob Kilpatrick

THAT DEAR OLD GUITAR OF MINE

Redding, California in 1974 was a city of about 30,000 people. The population was sprinkled out over the rolling foothills that surrounded the city. The city sits at the point where the Sacramento Valley runs headlong into the formidable mountains of the Sierra Nevada range. Mount Shasta and Mount Lassen both stand majestically off in the distance. Lake Shasta chases through the mountains in a hundred different directions, and the inlets are constantly full of happy houseboaters and families on weekend outings. To even the most urbane person, Redding seems like a natural paradise.

We lived in a small house next to the freeway. Our church was down the road less than half a mile. It was our first home, and we were proud of it. Cindy and I had our own room, Joel had his own room, and we even had a guest bedroom. There was a fireplace in the living room, and a back yard for Joel to play in. The floors were made of hardwood, and the kitchen was spacious compared to any of our previous residences. For a young couple, it was a dream come true. But in the months after we settled there, I slipped into something of a depression—unusual for me. Furthermore, there was very little outward reason for such a mood. After all, I had found a job doing music, and even though the daily responsibilities of leading a choir crowded out ideas of performing my own songs for different churches in the area, I figured that I had gotten what I wanted: employment in a job that involved music. I told myself that I ought to be happy. "Isn't God providing for Cindy and me in the way that he sees fit?" I asked myself. But it didn't go away. In fact, it began to encompass every waking hour of my life.

It was rooted in the simple fact that my music had no outlet at all, and I wasn't performing for people. My primary position to the Sunday morning church congregation was with my back to them as I directed the church choir. I wanted to turn around, face the audience and sing! Cindy noticed the difference in my demeanor. There was very little zest for life in my embrace when I came home from work. More often than not she would catch me laying prostrate on the floor, deep in my troubled thoughts. I had been talking with her less and less as I tried to sort out what felt wrong in my life; whether what I was feeling was God's will or my own selfishness. I didn't want my own desires to perform to eclipse his desires for me. I knew what I wanted: To sing for people on my own. Somehow, the dream had been frustrated. I yearned to write songs and perform my own concerts, but there was no place for my music.

In an effort to move in that direction, Cindy and I decided to start a music group to play concerts on the side without my having to give up the choir job. With another couple and Cindy's brother we formed a band and began traveling to locations in Northern California. We played in many, many places: county fairs, festivals, youth groups, church services—anywhere we could set up and play. It was far from a money-making operation. And though Cindy and I were having ourselves a great time, we still didn't know if this was the Lord's will for us. We felt that it might, but it took more confirmation from the Lord to let us know, beyond any doubt, that I was meant to be a musician.

It was after a concert in Yreka, a small town on the Oregon border, that we were loading all of our equipment into the van that we used to travel. My guitar, the most fragile instrument in the group, always went in last, on top of the keyboards, microphones, and sound equipment. But this time, in the routine of loading, my guitar was left leaning against the back of the building. We drove happily southward to Redding, and it was only as I pulled the van into the driveway and put it into park that I suddenly realized, "Oh no, my guitar!" We immediately called our friends in Yreka who went to see if it was still there. It wasn't. The police put out an all-points bulletin for the guitar, but it was nowhere to be found. I was devastated.

The guitar, an Ovation, had been the center of my new career. We were too poor to buy another guitar of that quality, even collectively as a group. I went down to the local music shops and checked out some others, but none of them seemed right, and I couldn't justify spending hundreds of dollars on any one of them. I was reduced to borrowing guitars from people I knew whenever we had a concert. Of course, this was an uncomfortable and awkward arrangement, especially for someone who was trying to be a professional! What kind of musician had to call up friends and bum their instruments before each gig? The situation made me feel low, naive, unneeded. It also brought back the serious doubts I had. Was God speaking to me? Was he taking

> What kind of musician had to call up friends and bum their instruments before each gig? The situation made me feel low, naive, unneeded.

away distractions in order to prod me in a different direction? I didn't know. I went to the Lord in prayer and said, "Lord, if it is your will that I not play the guitar, I submit to that. I'll limit myself to singing; just guide me in the right direction."

I continued to borrow instruments and play with our band but the questions lingered in my mind. Then one day we got a call from our good friends, Jim and Carla Miller. Jim was a full-time musician, with albums and a full itinerary. He even flew his own small airplane around to his gigs. Cindy and I looked up to him for his accomplishments; his position was one I aspired to. I was very happy to hear him on the other end of the telephone line. "Bobby, do you mind if we come up and spend a few days with y'all?" he asked. "That would be great!" I said.

They drove up to our small house, and when they arrived I was in the back. As I came into the living room, Jim was opening up a sturdy black instrument case to reveal a beautiful six-string Martin D-28 guitar. Jim already owned a twelve-string Martin, and he had apparently gone ahead and bought the six-string, as well. "Look what the Lord did," he said. "Jim, it's beautiful," I said admiringly. "Go ahead and play it," he offered. I pulled it from the case and started strumming and noodling around. The neck was wonderful, the action was great, and it projected with fullness and power. "This is one of the nicest guitars I've ever played," I said. And it was. "It's yours," Jim said smiling. I could hardly believe my ears, so I stopped playing. "It's yours," he said again, relishing this moment. "The Lord told me to buy it for you, so I did. Carla and I flew down here so I could give it to you." It was the first time anyone had ever given me anything so nice as an act of kindness. I was touched deeply and extremely thankful, both to Jim and to God.

In that gift, God provided not only confirmation for my early ministry, but the actual means with which to carry out the work. From that point on Cindy and I knew that there was no turning back; our confirmation had come. I left my position at the church and started what has become a life-long music career. I still use the Martin guitar Jim Miller gave to me, both in concert and on recordings. It reminds me of how the Lord spoke to me at a crucial time in my life. It reminds me of his faithfulness to me. It is perhaps the most precious physical possession I have ever owned. And it is the guitar I was playing when I composed *In My Life Lord, Be Glorified.*

Visit Bob Kilpatrick at www.bobkilpatrick.com

John Renbourn

IN THE WONDERFULLY BEAUTIFUL MONTH OF MAY

Several years ago—it was in May—my old friend Duck Baker and I went over to Germany to play. Duck had persuaded me that it was a good idea on the grounds that he was well known and spoke the language like a native. In a way that was true. It turned out he was well known to an assortment of part-time barmen, and he did on occasion speak a bit like a native, but in a manner that appeared baffling to any of the natives of Germany. Despite that—or maybe because of that—we had some good times, and also found out what a big country it is. At some stage we wound up in a region that felt like one of the lost kingdoms. When we got to the old hall where we were due to play, waiting outside was a nervous-looking man clutching a guitar case. He wore a long coat that had seen better days and there was something of a manic air about him. As we were walking past he clutched my arm and said to me, "Guitar, guitar." I didn't know what to make of it, so we just invited him in. Duck and I had to go straight to sound check, so I asked him to wait in the back room. "I'll be with you soon," I told him. He just stood there repeating, "Guitar, guitar."

At the sound check German efficiency was well-matched by the combined Renbourn-Baker inefficiency, and it all took rather a long time. I think it was still going on as the audience was drifting in. By then the man in the long coat had disappeared, and other than the token, "Who was that weird guy?" he wasn't spared much thought. Anyway, we played, and afterwards a bunch of us were sitting around in the back room in the usual apres-concert sprawl. Eventually somebody said, "Come on, let's go." We got it together and were heading for the door when someone else asked, "Don't you want to take your guitar?"

Well, I had mine and Duck had his and that was the full quota. But sure enough, there was another case lying there. We looked at it. "Isn't that the case that crazy character was carrying?" Duck asked. It seemed probable. Nobody knew quite what to do. We didn't feel that we should take it, but we didn't want to just walk off and leave it, either. "Better open it," someone suggested. It fell to me, as I had been the clutched one. By then all attention was focused on the unopened case. I flipped the catches and raised the lid. Inside was an absolutely amazing guitar, glinting with abalone inlay. It was one of the very fancy Martins, the type that most working musicians only encounter at close quarters through humidified glass-fronted cases while trying to figure out all the numbers on the price tag. There was stunned silence and a general aura of "wow."

Tentatively I took it out and played it a little. It felt and sounded great, with a rich but well defined bass, and that beautiful sweet treble that only old Martins seem to have. Duck played it, too. "Well," he said, "that blows the myth that Dreadnoughts are no good for fingerstyle." We delved a little further. The case contained the usual bits and bobs, right down to a graded nail maintenance kit. But everything seemed strangely unused, and somehow a little too perfect. Right down at the bottom of the case was a scrap of torn paper, the last thing in there. There was writing on it. I picked it out and read it. "This is a beautiful instrument. But it was not meant for me. I have tried and I have failed. Please take it and make music with it. Share it with your friends and ask them to do the same. Goodbye."

> "This is a beautiful instrument. But it was not meant for me. I have tried and I have failed. Please take it and make music with it. Share it with your friends and ask them to do the same. Goodbye."

Nobody spoke for quite a while, then a quiet voice offered, "We'd better go past the bridge and look in the river. Sounds like he's gone and jumped in." That just about summed it up for all of us. It really did have that feel about it. Well, I don't think we got as far as searching the waterfront, but we did leave with the beautiful guitar, and we did pretty much what the note asked us to do. I have played it, Duck has played it, and plenty of our friends have, too. Right now it has a home in a little lock house on the river not far from Oxford. But of course, that isn't its real home. Everyone who has made music on it knows the story and understands. So, old Wildman, if you are out there and you happen to read this, please know that we all think of it as your guitar. You may feel like playing it again. We hope you do. Just give a shout and you'll have it back. Of course, some sort of verification ceremony will be in order. That will have to be conducted by Lord Baker, who speaks the language like a native.

And that's the story so far. I should add that before we left Germany, Duck and I went into Peter Finger's studio in Osnabruck to record a few things together. I played one solo arrangement on the beautiful guitar. The piece I chose was Schumann's *Im Wunderschonen Montat Mai*.

Visit John Renbourn at www.john-renbourn.com

Kathy Mattea

BUTTERFINGERS

While touring in southern California, we had a day off, so we took advantage of the break to visit the Taylor Guitar factory near San Diego. It happened that the day off was also my birthday, and when we finished the factory tour, we came back to the lunchroom where a birthday cake was waiting. It really was a nice surprise. But then Bob Taylor and T.J. Baden handed me another gift: a case—an empty guitar case—and said, "We'd like you to fill it with anything you like."

Someone had mentioned earlier that Bob had been working on a new guitar design, so the next thing you know, we were in Bob's office, looking at his computer drawings. And of course, that's the guitar I wanted.

Bob had a stash of Brazilian rosewood that he had gotten from the Martin factory; they had cut it too thin, but it met Bob's specifications perfectly. He took me through the stock, and I picked out the back and sides for my own guitar—a guitar that became the prototype for Taylor's 20th Anniversary model. And what a guitar it turned out to be. It has a beautiful Engelmann spruce top, and old, old Brazilian rosewood from trees that are older then me. When I played it, it occurred to me that it sounded young and old at the same time. I thought, "Oh, I can't wait to hear this guitar in twenty years!"

It sounds fantastic in the studio; it seems that everybody wants to borrow it now for recording. My engineer and others who have used it dubbed it the *Unobtanium*. It really is that special. But the guitar is also special to me for some very different reasons.

I woke up one day and I realized that I was on the road with some really great musicians. So I asked my guitar player, Bill Cooley, to teach me some things. I'm a pretty quick study, but I'm not good at finding things on my own. And Bill is my musical alter ego. He's been with me for thirteen years, and if I throw out a vague idea to him, he'll come up with the very arrangement I was trying to articulate. And so he started giving me little guitar lessons on the road, and we actually worked up some duets.

When Taylor started planning the first *Wood & Steel* CD project—a compilation of music by Taylor artists—we recorded one of the duets for it. A few years later, they were working on the third release in what has become a wonderful series, and asked us for another cut. And wanting to learn something new, I heard Bill playing an up-tempo bluely instrumental in open C he called *Butterfingers*. I knew it was going to be hard, but I said to Bill, "Teach me that one." So he started showing it to me, piece by piece, and I'd take it away and work on it.

In the meantime, my dad had been diagnosed with cancer. The first round of chemo was tough; the second round nearly killed him. The cancer was shrinking, but it wasn't clear if he would survive the aftereffects of the chemotherapy. If this weren't bad enough, my mother, just a month before, had been diagnosed with Alzheimers, and was already showing signs of disorientation.

I went home to be with them, and as things got worse, we had to make the difficult decisions about life support for Dad. It was a very, very intense time, to say the least. It was a pressure cooker at home and at the hospital, where we would spend endless hours just waiting. And in all the waiting was a tremendous amount of pent-up energy.

It was in those times that I would pull out the guitar and work on Bill's song. It gave me a place to focus all that energy. It was a way to transmute the negative energy and plow it into something useful, to transform it into something positive.

> It was a good feeling to be pushing myself and learning something new, even in the midst of all the chaos.

Dad pulled through, and though they had only given him three months, he hung on for another three years. I really came to associate that song with this journey, and all its struggles. When Bill began teaching it to me, I didn't know if I'd be up to it. I knew the plan behind all the sections; I just had to get my fingers to go there. *Butterfingers* was an appropriate title! And I don't think I would have had the time or the patience to sit down and really learn that song if these other things hadn't been going on in my life.

I learned a lot about practicing during that time, and how to do it. I really had to discipline myself. I would only allow myself sit for thirty minutes at a time, and when my concentration broke, I would stop. And I would only work on it when I felt I could make progress. That process really opened some things up for me. It was a good feeling to be pushing myself and learning something new, even in the midst of all the chaos.

I'm grateful that the guitar was there to receive that. My guitar became my companion through that time. I got to know it better, and I got to know myself better. I found that my limitations weren't what I thought they were after all.

Visit Kathy Mattea on the web at www.kathymattea.com

Margaret Becker

THE WISH

I was working as a bill collector in the early '80s for Sears. It was a hideous job—a horrible, horrible job. Every day I'd go to work and pray, "Dear Lord, *please*—I just want to travel from city to city and play my music." But despite years and years of trying, nothing was happening. I thought, Okay, if this isn't what I am supposed to be doing then I'll just apply for every job that I'm overqualified for, qualified for, or underqualified for—just start shooting for the moon. Anything but continue working at Sears. I had applied to thirteen missionary organizations, offering to do everything from dig ditches to wash dishes to type—whatever. Every single one of them turned me down—including the one I was already working for part-time! They wouldn't hire me because of ethnic quotas; I had to be an American Indian to be full time. Not one job came through, so I was stuck where I was, collecting bills.

At that time, I was also singing in a supper club at night, and sometimes on weekends I would play at coffee houses—if they would have me, if there was an opportunity. This went on for about five years—the longest five years of my life.

I came to GMA (Gospel Music Association) one year for the first time and met with some people who had heard some of my music, and I managed to get a demo into their hands. I was surprised to find out that they had actually taken the time to listen. They had written me a long letter about the demo, essentially telling me in five pages that I should probably think about doing something else. My work wasn't good, there were a million people like me, and basically I should just give up. So needless to say I was at a real point of despair. I had really been faithful with what I was given. I had gone everywhere for nothing. I traveled the tri-state area in the northeast in my red 1970 Nova that I bought from somebody for $200 because it had been in a wreck with a Mack truck. The front hood was bashed in and couldn't be kept down any other way than with a bicycle chain and lock.

> They had written me a long letter about the demo, essentially telling me in five pages that I should probably think about doing something else.

I had people run into me when I was in that car, and I wouldn't even give them my insurance card or ask for theirs because it was such a wreck. So I was driving around in this car with four bald tires going all the way to Brooklyn, all the way to Connecticut, driving to New Jersey. I remember showing up for one gig in Brooklyn. I sang and played for forty Chinese people who didn't understand a lick of English. This was my life.

It's not like I was prissy—I was really out there trying to hit it. But it was really discouraging. I just didn't know what to do. I told God, "I'm willing to put my music down. I'm trying very hard to put it down. I'm trying very hard to stretch out in other areas and to allow you to lead me, but every single door I find is closing."

After a long day at Sears, I came home and walked in the front door, and my mom greeted me saying that a guy had dropped something off for me. I said, "What guy?" She didn't remember his name. "He had blond hair and said that this is yours." She led me to the living room and there in front of the fireplace was a brand new guitar case. I knew that I had no brand new guitar; my guitar was really old and beat up. There had to be some mistake. Mom said, "I told him I hadn't seen it around the house, but he said it's yours."

So I opened the case and there was a brand new Takamine 12-string—something I couldn't afford but always wanted. The price tag was still on it! For the day, it was a very expensive guitar. And then I remembered. There was a fellow, about fifteen years older than me, who faithfully came to my shows. We had been talking one night about "wish" guitars. I told him the one thing that I thought would really break open my music was a 12-string that I could put in alternate tunings; I thought that would really release me. But I didn't have enough money for one, although I told him that one day I would.

I immediately went out and I found him, and thanked him profusely, as I still do whenever I see him. He wouldn't hear of it, though, let alone allow me to pay him back. He just said, "Look, I went to prayer and out of nowhere you came into my head. I knew I had to go out and buy that 12-string that you wanted."

> I sang and played for forty Chinese people who didn't understand a lick of English. This was my life.

Receiving that guitar really did open things up for me. And things finally did begin to happen with my music. Doors that seemed closed opened wide.

To this day I still have that guitar. One of the very first songs I ever cut—*For the Love of You*—was written on it. That guitar and all it brought was a beautiful result of fasting and praying, and of God moving people to move and encourage me. It was one of the kindest things that anyone has ever done for me.

Visit Margaret Becker at www.maggieb.com

Dan Tyminski

POSTER CHILD

W hen I first joined Alison Krauss and Union Station, I didn't have a guitar, so the hunt was on. After putting the word out and searching everywhere I could think of, I found myself leaving the Bass Mountain Bluegrass Festival in North Carolina, still not having found "the one." As I was leaving the festival, a man came running over and told me he had a guitar I could look at if I was interested. When I asked what it was, he sheepishly glanced over his shoulder and said, "I think it's a Martin." I thanked him for the information and continued on my way out of the festival grounds.

Another man stopped me in my van just as I was leaving, and asked if I was the man who was looking for a guitar. When I asked him what he had he said, "You just have to see it," which was what I really wanted to hear. I parked my van and went for a walk with the man. Just as the sun was beginning to set, he opened the case containing what he said was a 1946 Martin Herringbone. In the dim light I couldn't see the binding very clearly, and wasn't aware that it was, in fact, a pre-war Herringbone.

It wasn't until I played it and fallen in love with it that a glimmer of light hit the guitar and I realized from the binding what it was. I had to go to a friend and borrow the money to buy what is now, and always will be, my favorite guitar. I dubbed it the "Poster Child."

Visit Dan Tyminski at www.dantyminski.com

I've been electrocuted so many times now. It's quite a buzz actually!
—*Keith Richards*

Les Paul

with John Schroeter

ON THE RIGHT TRACK

Old-time piano rolls, telephone handsets, Victrola phonograph needles, the parlor radio, a discarded piece of railroad track. While such a collection might recall the forgotten trappings of a bygone era, they were the stuff of history to Lester W. Polsfuss, better known to the world as Les Paul. You see, this unlikely assemblage made up the primordial soup from which, in the hands of young Lester, evolved a veritable symbol of our age—the solidbody electric guitar. Such was the nature of this scrappy, yet ingenious boy who hailed from Waukesha, Wisconsin—whose lab was his family's living room.

It seems Paul inherited the ideal combination of genes from a loving, musically inclined mother, and a machinist father. Playing the harmonica at eight, building his own crystal radio sets at nine, and his first recording machine at twelve, young Les' leanings—both musical and mechanical—kicked in at a very early age. And while it is said that life is like a ten-speed bicycle—most have gears we never use—in the case of Les Paul, he has gone through gears many of us thought never existed!

An insatiable streak of curiosity honed his senses to the great subtleties of the ordinary, the over-looked, the obvious. He noticed the little things—a window vibrating in concert with a passing train, the player piano that took its orders from a perf-ridden roll, the grooves in a waxed side that yielded *music*. "How could these things be," he strained.

Born June 9, 1915, Les Paul entered an age of limitless possibility. Navigating his way through the 1920s, '30s, '40s, '50s, '60s, and now into the next century, he has not only witnessed logarithmic technological and cultural advances, he participated in bringing them about. He is certainly a seminal figure in the history of popular music—not only in the making of it, but in the very means of capturing it.

The sheer scope of Les Paul's accomplishments and influence is staggering. As a performing artist, he racked up twenty-two gold records, pioneered live radio, backed-

338

up and recorded with the legends. He's been inducted into the Rock and Roll Hall of Fame, has earned a Grammy, and has enjoyed virtually every honor his peers could bestow. As an innovator, he was the first to imagine a solidbody electric guitar, he invented multi-track recording, and he has inspired legions of fellow aspirants. In a letter from Frank Sinatra, written shortly before his death, Ol' Blue Eyes attests, "We would still be a million years back in the stone age, if not for Les Paul. I'd still be in the studio trying to get it right." Surely, no segment of the music industry has gone untouched by Les Paul's ingenuity—and all of it inspired by his unshakable love for the guitar.

He was known throughout the country at various times by a number of monikers: Red Hot Red, Rhubarb Red, The Wizard of Waukesha, Paul Leslie, "the nut with the broomstick with pickups on it" (more about that one later), but his identification as a controversial guitar revolutionary was always constant.

His early guitar interests were piqued as he listened by his homemade crystal radio, always tuned into the sounds of Nick Lucas, Eddie Lang, and the singing cowboy, Gene Autry. "I heard everybody on the radio that existed in that day," he fondly remembers. Interestingly, though, the first sound that really turned Paul's head was the harmonica. "I'll never forget the day that old sewer digger came by," he recalls. "He stopped to eat lunch, blew the crumbs off that harmonica, and started to play. I just stared him down till he gave it to me. And then he told me to beat it!"

Some time later, Les' mother approached him, commending him on his harmonica playing, singing—and even the tapping of his foot—but added that *something* was missing. Lester thought it might be the piano, but his mother quickly admonished him, explaining that playing the piano, he'd have his back turned to the audience. Furthermore, he wouldn't find a piano just anywhere. "If you're riding in your car," she said, "you've lost your act!" He then turned to the saxophone. Again came the counsel, "Well, now you've got something in your mouth, and you can't play harmonica. You can't even talk!" "Then I'll play the drums," he retorted. "Not in *this* house!" came the riposte. Says Paul, "She shot me down till there was nothing left but the guitar." And a guitar, a la Sears Roebuck, soon followed. In no time, he began playing for local clubs and meetings around town—but not before he learned that all-important third chord.

> My friend had a flashlight, and whenever Gene put his fingers down for that D7, my friend would shine the light and I'd put a dot down on my little graph.

"I went crazy till I found that third change," he says. "As far as I knew, there were only two on the guitar; I could only find a C and a G7. That was it. But I couldn't play *Stutter's Ball* without a D7. Well as luck would have it, Gene Autry was playing at a theater in town. I grabbed a friend of mine and we went down to see him. My friend had a flashlight, and whenever Gene put his fingers down for that D7, my friend would shine the light and I'd put a dot down on my little graph. We were there for two shows, and all I was looking for was that third change. Gene finally stopped the show, and said, 'There's something strange happening here. Every time I play this chord, a light goes on.' So he hit the chord, and the light went on. I wasn't listening to him talk, I was just trying to get that chord. My friend with the flashlight says, 'Hey, Gene Autry's talking about you.' Gene looked our way and said, 'What's going on down there?' I answered, 'Mr. Autry, I'm trying to get that chord that you're playing.' 'Well,' he responded, 'come on up here, and I'll give it to you.' So I went up onstage, and he unleashed his guitar and gave it to me. That's how I met Gene Autry, and that's how I learned my third chord!"

Well on his way now, and performing outdoors at Beekman's Barbecue Stand during the summer of '28, the young "Red" encountered his first critic. "I had rigged up my own microphone," he remembers, "by singing into the part of the telephone that you speak into. I wired this into my mother's radio, and I would sing into it and play the harmonica. Then a guy comes in riding in the rumble seat of an old Chevy. God knows his name. Well, he writes a note to the carhop saying, 'Hey Red, I can hear your voice and harmonica just fine, but the guitar's not loud enough.' And that's what sent me home determined to find a way of making the guitar louder. It was a critic in the back seat of that car!"

And so immediately, Les liberated the phonograph needle from the family Victrola, jabbed and taped it into the top of his guitar, and wired the signal to his father's radio. "I took that out on another Saturday night," he recalls, "put the second radio on the other side of the stage, and played. That was my first electric guitar—and first stereo performance! After a certain point, though, the guitar would feed back into my dad's radio speaker."

Stuffing the guitar's body with table cloths, napkins, socks—whatever he could find—he set out to conquer the nagging feedback problem. "I chucked all this stuff in there," he says, "but it was a lost weekend. I wasn't going to get anywhere with this."

What happened next was, well, a watershed. "I lived near a railroad track," he explains, "and I remembered a broken section of track that lay there down the road. I got five of my kid friends, and we borrowed a wagon, and we loaded up that piece of railroad track—a piece of steel that was almost a yard long. When we got it home, I strung a string on it. I then took another part of the telephone, the part that you speak into, and put it under the string. So Western Electric—old Bell Telephone—was already helping me out! Lo and behold, there was the sound of a railroad track with a string stretched on it. Then I attached a piece of wood, soft pine wood, and fixed a door hinge to it. This became my first vibrolo. So this contraption—and I still have it—had everything that you would want: vibrolo, adjustable bridge—you name it. But then I noticed that this piece of wood vibrated much more than the piece of steel railroad track. And in no time at all, I realized that the piece of railroad track walked all over the piece of wood. And my mother's comment, which blew me right down was, 'The day you see Gene Autry on a horse with a piece of railroad track...' And that was it. I knew my mother was right. I knew I had to go the way of the railroad track, but I had to remain with wood. And you know, when I open my eyes, the only thing I want to see, other than a pretty girl beside me, is a guitar. And I don't want to see a *steel* guitar; I want to see a beautiful piece of *wood*."

As for Les' knack for all things electronic, that's an aptitude that came the hard way. "You wouldn't believe it," he says. "I had gotten a bicycle. It was my first bike. Well, it's crazy what happened, but you know that bar that runs across the top? Let me put it this way: if I had a ladies' bike, I wouldn't have been in this fix. Because I had to get down to the pedals to pump, when I went down on one side, and then the other, I was beating myself up something awful. I didn't know it until that night, and I had put a lot of miles on that bike! When I got home, they got me in

> Let me put it this way: if I had a ladies' bike, I wouldn't have been in this fix.

tubs of water to bring the swelling down, and made a bed for me in a playpen. Well I lay there in that playpen, and remember, there was a railroad track across from my house. When that old steam engine began to chug and whine up to a certain pitch, my bedroom window would vibrate. I took my hand and I held it to the window; I could feel it. And I was aware that the window only vibrated when a certain pitch came about by the train. So as soon as I got well, I went to school and asked the teacher what that was all about. We went trucking over to the science teacher, and he explained that it was a resonant frequency caused by the train that coincided with the free resonance of the bay window. And when both of them reached the same pitch... and he goes through this whole thing. My brother, by this time, said, 'Well the nut's at it again.' But I was curious to find out what that resonance was. Now, that applies to your speaker, your cabinet, the guitar top—everything. So I started getting into all these things, but I wasn't getting all the answers I wanted. So I would pump my way all the way down to the broadcast station and go to the transmitter and knock on his door. It would be raining out, so he'd let me in, and I began asking questions. The next thing I know, I'm learning electronics from a fellow at the transmitter who knows resonance. He knows what a Piezo is. He knows what wire in a magnetic pickup is. He knows these things. And this is where I learned."

Paul's active curiosity, though, was in no way limited to the guitar. The same period of time found him experimenting with all manner of noise-producing and recording devices—not the least of which were his experiments that ultimately gave way to the world's first multi-track recorder. "But my first multiple," he says, "was not on a recording device at all; it was the player piano. I started poking holes in the rolls. Mom would come home, and all hell would break loose. I cooked up some hot intros on the long leader, though. That thing just fascinated me."

Again, Les sought out his science teacher to learn out how it worked. "I especially wanted to understand why, when I slowed the piano roll down, it didn't change pitch, but if I put my hand on a recording and slowed it down, the voice would get lower. So the science teacher said, 'Lester, come on with me.' He took me over to the library and he looks up *digital*. And that was the first time that I heard that word, and learned the difference between digital and analog—that if you take a phonograph record or tape machine and slow it down, the pitch changes—but not with a piano roll. So if you look up the word digital, you'll say, 'Well I'll be damned; they were doing it with a piano roll!' So it was a terrific challenge for me to take all these pieces and sort them out. And I've known for years that the piano roll was the way to go, but how was I gonna get my voice in one of those holes?! I was already banging my head up against the wall about that."

> So if you look up the word digital, you'll say, 'Well I'll be damned; they were doing it with a piano roll!

Still in his teens, and now sporting a Gibson L-5, Paul connected with Joe Wolverton, the "hillbilly" pair going by the name Sunny Joe and Rhubarb Red. Their summer-long gigging took them to Chicago, where Paul was introduced to the burgeoning, yet thriving jazz scene. His country roots soon gave way to the swinging sounds, and he and Wolverton, unable to reconcile their artistic preferences, parted ways.

Meanwhile, Paul's guitar experiments continued. In 1934 he retained the now legendary Chicago luthiers—the Larson Brothers—to build an instrument that would further flesh out his theories concerning the solidbody electric guitar. The result featured a half-inch thick maple top, no f-holes, and two pickups—"The first guitar, as far as I know," says Paul, "that had two pickups on it." That instrument would serve him well as he continued his radio performances under the persona of Rhubarb Red, and in late night—and sometimes all-night—jamming sessions with the likes of Louis Armstrong, Art Tatum, and other legends of the time.

His own trio would follow, featuring on vocals and rhythm guitar Jim Atkins—Chet's older half-brother. Ernie Newton held down the bass lines. In search of a break, the trio made their way to New York, but only because the other choice, Los Angeles, was lost in the coin toss. Once in Manhattan, they wrangled a gig with Fred Waring's large vocal ensemble, the Pennsylvanians. The association lasted until 1940, when Les returned to Chicago.

It was with Waring's outfit that Les Paul, on network radio, introduced the electric guitar sound to a doubtful public—and to the enamored likes of Tony Mattola, Charlie Byrd, and Johnny Smith. Paul remembers, "I was getting so much mail that Fred finally came to me and asked why. I told him a lot of it was from people who were complaining. You see, there was a big controversy going on at the time about my guitar. On the first show, performed for the east coast, I would play an acoustic hollow-body L5. The next show, for the west coast, I'd play my electric. And people would write in, asking me how I got that sound on the guitar. They liked it so much better than the acoustic. Those letters would be followed by a critical violin player, a legitimate musician, who would say just the opposite: 'For God's sake, get off of that toaster and go back to the L5!' And this whole thing was bigger than the argument going on at the time about *how* you played. In those old days, how you played a chord, or the style that you picked with, was a big deal. Whether you held your thumb in the middle of the neck in the classical approach; whether you put your guitar between your legs or over to one side—everything was a problem. And because I was a rebel, I said, 'I don't care how you get it, *just get it!*'

"So when it came down in 1937 to this controversy of the acoustic versus the electric, Fred, Ernie, Jimmy Atkins, and myself walked up to 53ʳᵈ and Broadway, where Letterman is now, and decided to settle it. We sat there on the 9ᵗʰ floor and played back the recordings of the first show and the second show. The first show was acoustic, the second electric. And after we listened, Fred had us put it to a vote. And the vote was unanimous; stay with the electric! We all felt the same way. And even though it didn't have the acoustic fidelity, we could do so much more with it, and really be heard. We could turn it up and not have to deal with feedback and all the acoustical problems you have with the acoustics. Fred himself said I could ride right over the top of these sixty-five Pennsylvanians with my little amplifier. I couldn't have done that any other way."

Having put the debate to rest, Paul etched another notch in the belt of his fledgling electric. Much more experimentation was to follow, and by 1941, Paul had reached another milestone—"The Log"—a section of 4x4 post fitted with pickups and a guitar neck. His workshop was the Epiphone factory, where they gave him run of the shop on Sundays. "They would come in and see what I was doing," he says, "and just shake their heads. The log was really an extension of the railroad track idea. But as my mother told me, that was out. Well, I took the log into a club and played it—and they all laughed at me. Hardly anyone applauded at all. So I went back down to Epiphone and put the two sides of a butchered acoustic archtop on it and went back and stopped the show. People hear with their eyes! Oh boy, did I learn. I learned something every night. Every day!" Leo Fender and Paul Bigsby learned, too, as Les recalls, "They were in my back yard all the time looking at that log."

1943 found him bound for Hollywood, California, where he began to work with the likes of Bing Crosby, Burns & Allen, and the Andrews Sisters. With the war underway, Les was drafted into Armed Forces Radio Services, where his commanding officer was none other than the legendary Meredith Willson, composer of *The Music Man*. "My job," Les recalls, "was to play for the Command Performances, Jubilee, all the major entertainment shows for the armed forces. I had a terrific position, in that not only did I get to pick the talent for the shows, but I played for them, as well."

> Well, I took the log into a club and played it—and they all laughed at me.

Paul's driving motivation throughout these years was his constant dissatisfaction with the current state of affairs. And certainly, he was dissatisfied with guitars. As to the limitations and shortcomings of the amplified archtops of the day, he says, "I saw a lot of them. One was the sustain. And the acoustical bodies, well you just couldn't make two alike. Not like you can make two solid ironing boards alike, either; they all have their little differences. But we found that there was much less a difference between true solidbody guitars from a sustain standpoint, and not having all kinds of unwanted and unpredictable elements, resonances, and characteristics of the sound that would contribute something we didn't particularly like. And that's why I finally approached Gibson in 1946—and they thought I was nuts! They labeled me 'the character with the broomstick with the pickups on it.' They ushered me right out the door! And for many years, I couldn't convince them that the electric guitar was here at all. I had nothing but problems all through my life convincing the other people in this business. I'd walk into Capitol Records with a hit, and there would always be someone to say, 'I don't think it will work. I don't think this is right. You ought to do this.' You'll always find there is someone who will shoot you down—and not because of anything personal, but because people just believe differently. And while one believes the solidbody guitar is the round wheel, another guy thinks it's lousy. If you talk to a jazz guy, many of them wouldn't go near a solidbody. They're still loyal to the idea that it's gotta have that body and have that sound before you turn it on."

Still, the critical and pragmatic need remained: an effective guitar amplification solution—and not only in the domain of the jazzers and rockers, but in the realm of classical players, as well—even among the most staunch of traditionalists. It's an interesting bit of trivia to note that both Andrés Segovia and Les Paul shared the same manager, Phil Braunstein. Segovia approached Braunstein with the desire to meet with Paul to discuss his needs for an amplified concert guitar. "Now dig this," says Paul. "Here is what Segovia wanted: He says, 'You don't see it. I don't want to hear it. I want it to amplify *exactly* what I hear, nothing better, nothing worse.' Now, what he hears is not what the guy in the 16th row is going to hear. And the size speakers and type of cabinets also come into play. And God didn't give us a good speaker! We haven't made one yet that will reproduce the sound of a guitar, or anything else that would represent that round pie. He wanted the amplifier and speaker to be on the seat that he sat on. That way, he could feel the vibrations; he would know that it was there, but no one could see it. And the pickup I'd build was not to be seen, or alter the tone in any way. And all of this was colored by the fact he hated to hear himself on a recording—it wasn't the way *he* heard it when he played. So you place the mic here, you get one thing; you place the mic there, and you get something else; you're two inches, you're five inches, you're twenty inches—you're a block away... they're all different. And the room enters into it—*everything* enters into it. I said to Andrés, 'I can't do it. I know what you want, but I can't do that. Someday, maybe.' But he never let up asking for it. He needed it, and he wanted it. So does every other classical player wish he had more power. Segovia had people working on these guitars for him in Spain, in Geneva, in Germany. I know. I saw them making a guitar for him in Spain like a Dobro, trying to reinforce that instrument to make it louder. It is a problem. And as you make the guitar louder acoustically, you're going to alter the sound—the *tone* of the guitar. So it's a multiple problem, and Segovia ran smack into it."

Familiar territory for Paul, but fortunately, he found more than a little success. Once he had what would become the Les Paul guitar in its first working prototype form, he found that it had an immediate effect on his musical thinking. "It changed my playing," he says, "as it did everybody's. It changed your playing, because you could now do things you could never do before. Not always do you want a full pie. And a full pie means a round wheel with everything in it. When you make an instrument that's got some slices out of the pie, it's difficult to get them in there. It's better to have

> **If Paul was unable to convince Gibson of his vision for a solidbody electric guitar, the success of Leo Fender did.**

everything in the pie, and take out what you don't want. If you don't have highs, you can't take highs out, because you don't have them to begin with! So what you try to do is make the instrument in a way that you have a *whole* pie, and you can take out what you don't want. And that's going with equalizers, the placing of pickups, the type of pickup—all these things contribute."

Meanwhile, if Paul was unable to convince Gibson of his vision for a solidbody electric guitar, the success of Leo Fender did. And in that same year, 1952, Gibson called Les Paul back in. It was a banner year, as the model bearing his name was released sporting a splendid gold top—a harbinger of Paul's Midas touch. That same year Ampex took to market the world's first eight-track recorder, designed, of course, by Les Paul.

Les was certainly hitting his stride. A few years earlier, he married a young vocalist working with Gene Autry, Colleen Summers, a.k.a. Mary Ford. A perfect complement to Paul's "New Sound," the pair became a fixture on the 1950's pop charts as they rose to national stardom. A TV show of their own followed, along with Les' reputation as the world's most famous guitarist.

Indeed, Paul had carved out a unique musical personality for himself, enabled in part through the guitar he created, the multi-track recording he pioneered, and the numerous effects he developed. "If you listen to electric guitar today," he says, "it's amazing how many different sounds you can get out of it. When I started out playing guitar in the '20s, I came running into my mother and said, 'Look! I can tap these things, I can pull these things, I can slide these things. Boy I don't think anybody knows what's going on with this guitar!' Those were the days when you're just finding those things out. There's nothing like starting out with nothing. Everything was magical."

Paul still gets a vicarious thrill from those that forge new sounds. "If you have a distinct sound, then that becomes *you*. You know Benny Goodman from anybody else in the world. Wes Montgomery had his own thing. And that thing is the *sound*. You can take this electric guitar, and you can maneuver it around the way you play, the way you attack the note, the way you mother it, to create something truly distinctive. And then the public votes on it, which is something that can cut two ways. Here's a story: If you look at the last video of Django Reinhardt, he was playing the same guitar as I was playing, an old Epiphone. He went out and got one exactly like the one I had, because he loved the sound. I tried to tell him it was a mistake, because his style of playing and his sound were inseparable. The public would not accept him playing an electric, and I told him he was a fool to go that way. We all get married to something, and I got married to that electric guitar. I remember Grappelli saying to me, 'You want to make an album with acoustical guitar?' 'No!' I said. 'I don't want to do that!' I think it would have been wrong. I think it was wrong when Django went to the electric. You take his personality away completely. He played the same thing, but it didn't come out the same."

> I knew that the electric guitar could walk all over an unamplified guitar. And the acoustic guitar, with all its feedback problems, made me quite confident that one day, the electric guitar had to be terribly important.

Django certainly wasn't the only other guitar player with an affinity for the electric. But did Paul ever imagine that some fifty years later, it would be so essential? "No!" he answers. "I knew it was going to be big, but I never knew it would be anything like it is. And for that, I'm grateful to a lot of people. I didn't do it alone. I knew that the electric guitar could walk all over an unamplified guitar. And the acoustic guitar, with all its feedback problems, made me quite confident that one day, the electric guitar had to be terribly important. It could almost be a deadly weapon compared to a saxophone or drums or anything else in the band. It just had so much authority. But did I ever dream that it would be this big? No."

While the guitar was enjoying tremendous commercial success, Gibson's production of the Les Paul was interrupted in 1964, owing to Les' complicated divorce from Mary Ford. Once settled in 1966, though, Paul was ready to return to Gibson's table, and get things back on-line. But to his amazement, the company had ceased all its electric guitar production, declaring the electric guitar "extinct." "This was 1966!" says an incredulous Les Paul. Of course, at that time the folk boom, whose epicenter was Greenwich Village, was indeed acoustically driven. Gibson saw the movement as the writing on the wall for

> **Furthermore, people were running up and down the street trying to find an old Les Paul guitar—and paying $10,000 for one! I said the electric guitar is not dead. It's anything but dead!"**

the electric. Paul, though, saw things quite differently. "A friend of mine and I got in a plane and flew back there to convince them otherwise. And the way I would convince them was to tell them what 48th Street was all about. I said to Gibson, 'Who is interested in the jazz player? He's out there starving to death, while the rocker is going crazy.' And the Jimi Hendrixes were out there doing things that were *impossible* to do on an acoustic box. I explained to the president, Mr. Berlin, just what I saw. Furthermore, people were running up and down the street trying to find an old Les Paul guitar—and paying $10,000 for one! I said the electric guitar is not dead. It's *anything* but dead!"

With the case made, Gibson not only agreed to reinstate production, but also to put Les Paul in charge of seeing that it was done right. "They gave me full reign of the place," he says, "to go in and see things were done to my specifications, which I did. And they went back into production, and the production was four. They made four guitars. The next month they made a hundred, and on up from there. And that was the way it went—and that was the second time around; '52 to '62 being the first run."

Interestingly, Paul's supervision of Gibson's production of the guitar should have been in place back in '52. "When the first guitars came out," he explains, "they had 'em backwards. The expensive version of the guitar had the mahogany top, and the inexpensive model had maple—just backwards!" Paul made the discovery while he and his brother-in-law were replacing the Gibson pickups with his own. "I called them up and told them to stop making those damn things. Then they ran the trapeze tailpiece backwards—upside down so the strings went *under* the bar instead of over. You couldn't muffle the strings with your wrist. What's more, they had to pitch the neck entirely differently to compensate for the change in intonation. There are a lot of them out there like that. I told Gibson they ought to go back and make them incorrectly again, because people loved them!"

Paul continues to this day to tinker in his home-based lab. "I'm in there all the time," he says. "There are a lot of things that I haven't done or thought of, or never finished doing. And there are always challenges that come up. I might want to improve something, so I'll make a change in the pickup, or the placing of the pickup, or something to do with the amplifier—whatever. I would be lost without it; there are just too many things to do. And let's say that it's a new guitar that we're putting out at Gibson. They'll send me one, and I'll debug it and tell them what I like, or don't like about it. When you're dealing with the mechanical aspects, people forget there are so many things that are barbaric about the guitar; so many things that we're working with day after day to improve."

> While there is no shortage of players who'd love to get their hands on an old Les Paul, people aren't exactly lining up to pay premium prices for the pleasure of recording on vintage recording gear.

With all its incremental improvements over the years, though, the Les Paul guitar, in form and function, has been relatively static, to which Paul says, "Well, I had to do something right the first time! It really hasn't changed a bit." When one considers our world of high tech/high touch and built-in obsolescence, that *any* product design has survived for fifty unmolested years is quite a remarkable achievement. Not quite the case with the result of Paul's other passion—recording technology. While there is no shortage of players who'd love to get their hands on an old Les Paul, people aren't exactly lining up to pay premium prices for the pleasure of recording on vintage recording gear. Yet this was—and still is—wide-open territory, ripe for trailblazing and exploitation. And Les Paul was, once again, point man.

Just as Salk's polio vaccination was first put to work in his own family, Les Paul's proprietary breakthroughs in recording were first heard in his own music. Previously, Les had experimented with multiple disc recordings, delay, reverb, echo, and other "secret" electronic techniques. Together, they contributed to what Les called, and Capitol Records promoted as, "The New Sound."

Bing Crosby took a particular shine to Les Paul's work, and offered to capitalize his efforts. Later, on the road with Mary Ford, it occurred to Les that if he could put in one additional recording head in the tape deck, he could perform multiple recordings anywhere, anytime. Using existing Ampex gear, he retrofitted the unit, and the multi-track recorder was born. On the heels of this new insight, Paul conceived the idea of recording on separate tracks, and then blending them together in a final mix. Working with Ampex, the result was the "Sel-Sync," the forerunner of the eight-track. Les immediately set up a studio in his garage, the capability and quality of which soon attracted many top artists of the day, among them W.C. Fields!

With all the advances in multi-track recording technology that stemmed from his work (we're in the digital age now), it is interesting to note that Paul still prefers to do things the old fashioned way. "Personally," he says, "I still like to do a live recording, but I know you can't do everything that way. Today they use eight tracks just on the drums! But I still think that the old way of recording is in some ways better. It demanded a lot more from the musician. Today you can go back in and fix mistakes and clean things up, whereas in the old days, when you had to get up there and do an hour drama on radio, if you blew a line, tough. And if you're with a symphony, when your part comes up, and you blow it, that's your fault. That situation doesn't exist anymore. Practically nothing is recorded live. It's only in live performance where it's really honest."

And speaking of live performance, true to form, Les has adapted to changing realities. While he plays regularly with his trio at New York's famous jazz haunt, The Iridium, his formerly flying fingers have been somewhat grounded in recent years by the onslaught of arthritis. But in place of the old flash is, perhaps, a little more cash. "I learned a long time ago," he says, "that one note can go a long way—*if it's the right one*. And it will probably whip the guy with twenty notes. With twenty notes, he's got a lot of problems." That's great consolation to a guitarist who has all but completely lost his chops. "I have no fingers on either hand," he says—and without a hint of lamentation. "The fingers are frozen. No movement. Just where they join the hand is the only place I can move them. So what I play is what I can get through. I can't make a chord, so I don't play chords; I play what I can reach. But as far as the public is concerned, they don't know it. And so I play everything that's possible, and it works out okay. We play a little of everything, but fingerstyle is out. I can't do any of that anymore."

> I learned a long time ago that one note can go a long way—*if it's the right one.* And it will probably whip the guy with twenty notes. With twenty notes, he's got a lot of problems.

Apparently unaffected by his current physical constraints, Paul claims that most players will be surprised at how simple things gets when economy is imposed. "You figure out the way to get there, and to your surprise, you should have been doing that all along! You'll say, 'Well shoot, I was doing this the hard way! All my life!' If you were to take your fingers now and freeze them, could you play? Sure you can—if you think about it. And if you really can't, then what's your alternative? How *can* you get it? It reminds me of the last time I saw Count Basie. His band was playing, and he was sitting up there in a wheelchair. I was talking with him just before it was time for him to go on, and he says, 'Watch this Les.' He took his right hand to lift his left hand and put it up on the keyboard. The band comes in, and they're blasting away. All of a sudden there was a little hole—a space of silence. And he comes down with one note. And it was the best damn note that you could play. It was perfect. He used to play ten notes there, now he has to play one or two. I learned so much from Count Basie. But always, he was so selective. He could do a lot of things, but he never did. He played the least amount to say what he had to say. And a lot of times, it's better to say less. Maybe if we have the ability, we play too much. I learned that playing with Art Tatum. He would play the intro and I'd say, 'Art, there's nothing left! Nothing!' Art had a terrible time playing with other people. He played too much. And there is nobody as great as Art Tatum; he wrote the book. But that's the difference between him and someone like Count Basie. Some are limited, and some just have the smarts to put a governor on themselves and not overplay."

And while the temptation to overplay no longer knocks at his door, Les Paul still can't get enough of playing at any speed. "My love is for the guitar," he says. "It has sure been good to me, and that's probably the thing I'm most pleased about. It's pretty hard to walk down the street and spit in the crack. And for someone to go out there and have a guitar be right the first time, that doesn't happen very often. If you're that lucky, you'll never get over that. I'll never get over any of it."

> It's pretty hard to walk down the street and spit in the crack. And for someone to go out there and have a guitar be right the first time, that doesn't happen very often.

Indeed, even a casual conversation with the man will reveal that none of his youthful enthusiasm has waned with his advancing years. "You don't fake that, do you?" he says. "We all have that same thing going for us. And a guy like Eddie Van Halen? You can bet on it! You can take his right hand, but he'd rather that than lose the guitar. We're all alike in that. A dentist? He goes home, and forget about it. His day's work is done. A butcher? He doesn't go home and jam! I can just see that S.O.B. calling up his friends and saying, 'Come on over.' Picture five guys splittin' up some pork chops. 'How'd you do that? Do that again! What a beautiful slice!' I don't think so!"

ABOUT THE AUTHOR

John August Schroeter is the founding publisher of *Fingerstyle Guitar Magazine*, and the creator of a line of solo guitar books published in cooperation with Mel Bay Publications. He is also an award-winning producer of audiophile-quality acoustic recordings (in whose studio he has banned the use of Piezo pickups of any kind).

Prior to his incursion into the music business, he did twelve years hard labor as a marketing manager in the semiconductor industry. His first book, *Surviving the ASIC Experience*, published by Prentice Hall in 1990, is about the design of custom integrated circuits, and still a favorite read among insomniacs.

When he's not writing, arranging, recording, or encouraging his dog to play in the street, he can be found serenading the dust mites in his den with a guitar in open tuning.

CALL FOR STORIES

Do you have a guitar story? Or do you perhaps know of one? If so, we'd like to consider it for possible inclusion in future editions of *Between the Strings*. Visit www.johnaugustmusic.com for details.